EXQUISITE CORPSE

£7.50

V

EXQUISITE CORPSE

Writing on Buildings

———◆———

MICHAEL SORKIN

VERSO
London · New York

First published by Verso 1991
Paperback edition first
published by Verso 1994
© Michael Sorkin 1991
All rights reserved

Verso
UK: 6 Meard Street, London W1V 3HR
USA: 29 West 35th Street, New York, NY 10001-2291

Verso is the imprint of New Left Books

British Library Cataloguing in Publication Data

Sorkin, Michael
Exquisite Corpse : writing on buildings.
1. Architecture
I. Title
724.6

ISBN 0-86091-687-1

US Library of Congress Cataloging-in-Publication Data

Sorkin, Michael. 1948–
Exquisite corpse : writing on buildings / Michael
Sorkin
p.   cm.
ISBN 0-86091-687-1
1. Architecture, Postmodern.   2. Architecture, Modern–20th
century.   I. Title.
NA682.P67S67   1991
724'.6–dc20

Typeset in Perpetua by Leaper & Gard Ltd, Bristol
Printed in USA by Courier Companies Inc.

To my readers
and, of course,
to Joan

CONTENTS

SOURCES

Sources of previously published chapters are as follows:

"Philip Johnson: The Master Builder as a Self-Made Man": *Village Voice*, October 20, 1978; "Let a Hundred Styles Blossom": *Village Voice*, March 19, 1979; "Aalto Et Al.": *Village Voice*, August 13, 1979; "The World of All Possible Bests": *Village Voice*, February 4, 1980; "Drawings For Sale": *Village Voice*, November 12-18, 1980; "Wolfe At The Door": *The Nation*, October 31, 1981; "Explaining Los Angeles": *California Counterpoint: New West Coast Architecture*, Catalogue 18, Institute For Architecture And Urban Studies and Rizzoli International Publishers, New York, 1982; "The Path Always Taken": *The Nation*, February 6, 1982; "Tower Hungry": *Skyline*, March 1983; "The Big Man On Campus": *Architectural Review*, April 1984; "The Official Style": *The Nation*, July 7-14, 1984; "SOM Story": *Design Book Review*, Fall 1984; "Scarpa, in the Details": *Village Voice*, December 11, 1984; "The White City": *Village Voice*, January 8, 1985; "Mr Wright": *Village Voice*, February 5, 1985; "Que Serra Sera": *Village Voice*, March 5, 1985; "Why Goldberger Is So Bad: The Case of Times Square": *Village Voice*, April 2, 1985; "Reforming The Institute": *Village Voice*, April 30, 1985; "Tipping the Circle: Will the World's Tallest Building Replace the Coliseum?": *Village Voice*, May 28, 1985; "Save the Whitney": *Village Voice*, June 25, 1985; "Two Primitives": *Village Voice*, July 30, 1985; "Another Low-Tech Spectacular": *Architectural Review*, September 1985; "Ferry Godfathers": *Village Voice*, October 1, 1985; "Dump the Trump": *Village Voice*, December 24, 1985; "Leaving Wright Enough Alone": *Architectural Record*, March 1986; "The Invisible Man": *Village Voice*, March 25, 1986; "Freed, at Last": *Village Voice*, April 22, 1986; "A Bunch of White Guys (and Three Japanese) Sitting Around Talking or The Three PPP": *Design Book Review*, Spring 1986; "The Real Thing": *Architectural Record*, September 1986; "Mask of Medusa": *Architectural Record*, November 1986; "The Name Game": *Spy*, December 1986; "Dwelling Machines": *Design Quarterly* 138, 1987; "Canticles For Mike": "Mega V": Temple Island: A Study By Mike Webb, Exhibition Catalogue, The Architectural Association, London, 1987; "Machine Dreams": *Village Voice*, February 17, 1987; "Silicon Implants in Brooklyn": *Village Voice*, March 31, 1987; "Alan Buchsbaum 1935-87": *Village Voice*, April 28, 1987; "Reconstructing the Holocaust": *Village Voice*, June 23, 1987; "Zaha Hadid": *Village Voice*, July 21, 1987; "True West": *Village Voice*, August 25, 1987; "The Garden in the Machine": *Design Book Review*, Fall 1987; "Minimums": *Village Voice*, October 13, 1987; "Corb in New York": *Village Voice*, October 27, 1987; "Canon Fodder": *Village Voice*, December 1, 1987; "Drawing Pleasure": *Village Voice*, January 12, 1988; "Brave New Worlds": *Architectural Record*, February 1988; "Skyscrapers From A To Z": introductory essay to Fulvio Irace, *La Citta Che Sale*, Milan Arcadia Edizioni, 1988; "Decon Job": *Village Voice*, July 5, 1988; "Where Was Philip?": *Spy*, October 1988; "Et In Arcadia Ego: Emilio Ambasz's States of Nature": introductory essay to *Emilio Ambasz*, New York, Rizzoli International Publishers, 1988; "Richard Rogers, Lloyd's and After": unpublished manuscript, 1988; "Auto Da Fe": "Paul Rudolph: Drawings for the Art and Architecture Building at Yale" (exhibition catalogue), Yale University School of Architecture, 1988; "George Ranalli: The Domestic Apparatus": introduction to *George Ranalli: Buildings and Projects*, New York, Princeton Architectural Press, 1988; "Post Rock Propter Rock: A Short History of the Himmelblau": introductory essay to Coop Himmelblau, *Blaubox*, Folio XIII, Architectural Association, London 1988; "Footnotes to Pesce": introduction to France Vanlaethem, *Gaetano Pesce*, New York, Rizzoli International Publishers, 1989; "Ciao Manhattan": introductory essay to Heinrich Klotz, *New York Architektur 1970–1990*, Munich, Prestel Verlag, 1989.

Permission given to reprint here is gratefully acknowledged.

Illustrations are courtesy of the following:

AT&T Building, John Burgee Architects; Fan Floor Plan, Artemis Verlag Zürich; Indeterminate Façade Showroom, SITE Projects Inc.; Hongkong & Shanghai Banking Corporation Headquarters, photograph by Ian Lambot, reproduced courtesy of Foster Associates; Stuttgart Staatsgallerie, photograph by Richard Bryant, reproduced courtesy of Stirling & Wilford; Brion Family Tomb, photograph by George Ranalli; The Destruction of Tilted Arc, Jennifer Kotter; Model of Whitney Museum Addition, photograph by William Taylor, reproduced courtesy of Michael Graves; PA Technology, photograph by Otto Baitz, reproduced courtesy of Richard Rogers Partnership; Javits Convention Center, photograph by Nathaniel Lieberman, reproduced courtesy of Pei Cobb Freed & Partners; Security, photograph by Helene Binet, reproduced courtesy of John Hejduk; Dymaxion House, courtesy of Columbia University Slide Library; Abstraction on Henley Regatta, photographed by Gary Gurria, reproduced courtesy of Mike Webb; The Peak, Zaha Hadid; Little Boy & Fat Man, AP/Wide World Photos; Ford Foundation, Roche, Dinkeloo & Associates; Armour for the Bride, photograph by Michael Moran, reproduced courtesy of Liz Diller & Ric Scofidio; United Nations Headquarters, United Nations; Plan of ICI Pavilion, Salter and Mcdonald; Geomechanical Tower, Lebbeus Woods; King Kong 1933 (Radio Pictures) and 1976 (Dino de Laurentiis), BFI; Vertebra Chair, Emilio Ambasz; Lloyd's of London, photograph by Richard Bryant, reproduced courtesy of Richard Rogers Partnership; Ranalli Studio, photograph by George Cserna, reproduced courtesy of George Ranalli; Rooftop Remodelling, Coop Himmelblau; Maison des Enfants, Gaetano Pesce; Battery Park City, Battery Park City Authority.

INTRODUCTION

When I was in architectural school in the early '70s, it seemed almost impossible to practice architecture. Building was so bound up with structures of power, the only responsible thing, I thought, was to resist; to be something other than the wagging tail of the Yankee dog. I turned to writing as the extension of architecture by other means, trying to make a space in which I could practice. I never saw myself as an architectural writer but as an architect for whom writing was an additional, necessary medium. If the work has tended to divide itself largely into panegyrics and polemics, it's because big issues were at stake.

A deep love of modern architecture has been the center for me: I grew up on modernism which always seemed to harbor both adventure and hope. When I started writing, however, modern architecture was beleaguered. By the '70s, conventional wisdom was that modernism was a burned-out monolith; that penal-style housing projects, antiseptic glass slabs and dead cities were its inevitable issue. This insistent reading had many sorry consequences. To begin, the link between modern architecture and failed social policy was used as a lever to discredit the idea of architecture's engagement with social activism, a modernist bedrock. The past two decades in the U.S. have produced an architectural culture preoccupied with empty style, acquiescent in trivializing the full constructive scope of architecture's possibility. It seems, sometimes, to have been non-stop lifestyles of the rich and famous, all beach houses and Disneyland.

An ironic corollary of this obsessive style-mongering (so in tune with the larger culture of yuppification and Reaganism) was to obscure the actual diversity of modernist expression. Modern architecture had been so thoroughly identified with anti-style, its geniuses — El Lissitsky, Niemeyer, de

1

Klerk, Scharoun, Candela, Lautner, Goff, even Wright — became virtual non-persons. Although post-modernism arrived riding the nag of history, its view was blinkered, its horizons hemmed by the Villa Giulia and Monticello. That architectural culture at the end of the twentieth century should be dominated by apostles of "classicism," however ersatz, can only be the symptom of an institution in deep distress, a vile zit on the schnozz of culture.

Not that modern architecture was blameless. In its own internal wars, functionalism — that moralizing discourse of effects — vanquished all comers. Like much of modern art and architecture, this asymptotic discourse tended to an impoverished, minimalist condition, hubristically muddled about chicken and egg. The bad message of functionalism was simply that every element in a building had to give an account of itself in terms of a limited range of uses, expunging pleasure, whimsy, joy or happy irrationality. Cloddish neo-con reaction to modernism's failures of argument has lead to the present crisis of authority and the dumb exultation of the historic, the last refuge of banality. This has yielded truly freakish results: an orgy of solipsism, narcissist architecture, absorbed with self-reference and façade.

A willingness to look outside of architecture for invigoration is one of modernism's happiest proclivities. Functionalism's historic affinity was for technology, and modern architecture has been deservedly bopped for a certain servility before the machine. It is, after all, a small stretch for the mechanical — a logical (and inevitable) terrain for architectural invention — to lapse into the mechanistic; for technology to seem oppressive and autonomous. While the logics of mass-production are still intermittently introduced as potentially redemptive (an old trope), the products are, with few exceptions, dreary, alienating and uneconomic: a Taylorized equality of deprivation; back to the USSR. But, whatever the successes and failures of factory production as a solution to the housing question, locating science only here has served to de-poeticize the architectural act. For me, always fascinated by big technology (my architectural formation was *inter alia* at the time of the moon shots) and its scintillating relation to architecture, tech's cooptation by the Pentagon and Detroit was another reason for dismay. The recuperation of dreamy science for architecture has been a high hope for me.

The biggest baby chucked out with the functionalist bathwater, however, was the prospect of an inventive urbanism. The very idea of city planning had been made disreputable by post-war experience and its two spectacularly failed models: urban renewal and the suburbs. Physical planning is still flinching from the disrepute of this love-enslavement to social engineering, and had been almost entirely abandoned as a municipal function in the United States; the public realm reduced to reacting to the shoves and slaps of the invisible hand. A clear result of this paranoid fear of innovation has been the elevation of nominally historic forms to the status of the only complicit possibilities for the new. In Manhattan — to cite only the example closest to hand — the route of Disneyfication, the projection of a muzzy and spurious past authenticated by putative links to local tradition is the dominant paradigm. From the phony carnivalesque of the South Street Seaport, to the veneered festivity of the new Times Square, to the anorexic vision of Battery Park City, we're awash in trumped- (often Trumped-)up history. Absent any other municipal imagination, the Landmarks Preservation Commission has symptomatically risen to the status of planning agency, empowered just to say no.

New York has been at the center of my writing activities and I'm beholden to the *Village Voice*, which has been my primary journalistic venue. However, this connection impelled a certain direction: as a leftish New Yorker writing for a leftish New York weekly I've felt obliged to write mainly about New York. And — aside from the scintillating world-large parochialisms of local architectural politics — New York had only one real story in the Reagan/Koch years: Who profits? In a deregulated climate in which planning had devolved into a series of give-away strategies for stimulating "development," writing about architectural expression often seemed not simply irrelevant but complicit with the occlusive needs of capital. Their own fascinations notwithstanding, questions of style are simply peripheral to these issues: for the woman staring at the CRT screen in the windowless back office, whether the doo-dads on the roof are Tuscan or De-Con will be of no great import. To paraphrase a dimly remembered line from somewhere in Marx, "never mind the fluctuations in the price of beef, the sacrifice remains constant for the ox."

As chronicler of the price of New York architectural beef, I found myself consistently confronted by two striking absences. The first is the almost complete lack of serious building. Although New York City holds a breathtaking concentration of architectural talent, the last twenty years have seen not one great new work of architecture in the city. Our mode of architectural production has become so rationalized, and architectural patronage so myopic, that the hopes of our best reside in Tokyo or Los Angeles — anywhere but here. Indeed, the dizzying rise of the gallery and exhibition scene, if mainly due to the supply-side spiral of the eighties art market, is surely also a signifier of no alternative for those who would experiment or dream.

The second void is that of criticism itself. Although there has surely been a sharp increase in the number of people writing about architecture and an increase in the sophistication of academic writing, the quality of architectural journalism remains dismal. In part, this is a product of the long wave in architectural construction. Unlike other journalistic criticism, the function of architectural writing in relation to the seismograph of the market is not so direct, making the brisk commerce of overnight valorization dodgier. Absent such visible consequences for advertising revenue, most papers and general interest publications have little use for architecture. Although New York produces more such writing than most towns, this work scores very low on the acuity meter; mainly the higher publicity, drumbeating for development or hawking this week's fashion.

As suggested earlier, my work has mainly tended to fall into diatribes and encomiums. I have always had, shall we say, a certain penchant for invective; always thought my aim truer from the hip. Certainly, writing about culture in the Reagan era offered endless inducements to reach for my revolver. For this I have no regrets. My critical purposes are polemical and the situation in New York has been mainly bleak. If I have often focused on architecture's institutional culture, on critics, cabals, and power trips, it is not simply because these tempests have gathered wind in a city which has forsaken a real building culture but because these debates are agenda setters of global ramification. My Phillippics (you know who I mean) have been frequent because a critic's torpedo must home on power and its symbols. More, as an architect looking for the space of a joyful practice, these were the roadhogs blocking the way for me and many I admire.

This book, then, is a kind of envoi, an adieu to the journalistic trenches as I return at last to a more full time architectural practice. I've chosen fifty-odd pieces (winnowing is a painful trial — the infelicities that jump from the page! — the zingers forsaken!) from the past ten years which are, I think, representative. They appear as they appeared, in chronological order, rather then in terms of some taxonomy of coherence that never was. If, however, I might single out a lone thread, it is the celebration and defense of the repressed discourses of modernism — the technical, the social, the fantastic, the tectonic, the sensual — which flower again in the wake of the tattered hegemony of functionalist and historicist speech. My hope for post-functionalist architecture is not that it will be decoupled from an abiding sense of social purpose but that its agendas — political and artistic — will be both progressive and free; that the fun will get put back into functionalism. If these essays have in any way advanced these goals, they've served their purpose.

The title of the book celebrates one of the mightiest repressed discourses of them all. It's drawn from the famous collaborative folded paper game beloved of the Surrealists, described by Breton as capable of "holding the critical intellect in abeyance and of fully liberating the mind's metaphorical activity." Never mind that it's the greatest portmanteau metaphor for modern culture ever, demanding that its maddening, slippery concatenation somehow be read, it's also a perfect image of the city: our greatest, most out-of-control collective artifact. And it also seems to describe the somewhat aleatory basis for this collection.

Finally, to all of those who were kind enough to write over the years and to whom I never replied: thanks and forgive me. I dedicate this collection to you and to those anonymous friends who kept these articles circulating through the xerox ether of the architectural samizdat.

January 1991

PHILIP JOHNSON: THE MASTER BUILDER AS A SELF-MADE MAN

Philip Johnson is the last representative of architecture's glory days. Born to wealth, product of the best schools, he remains our greatest practicing Avatar of Taste, a towering symbol of haute bourgeois decorum. Unlike the parvenu patricians of post-modernism, Johnson is the genuine article, from the seven separate buildings he maintains for his private use in New York and New Canaan right down to his letter-perfect upper-crust wardrobe. By way of confirmation of his almost iconic stature as America's Leading Architect, Johnson has recently appeared — playing himself — in a TV ad for Mobil Oil, the Masterpiece Theater folks, intended to illuminate the scintillating proposition that "Nothing is so easy to see as the imagination of a genius and nothing is as hard to see as the imagination of a company." And what does the corporate spokesman for the imagination have to say?

To me, imagination is just one of those words that people put on to things that they like. I'm a worker. I have to sit down and figure out why one shape is better than another and still get the bathroom in the right relationship to the bedroom. I don't draw very well, I struggle, and I use the pencil only for making notations of what's going on in my mind.

Worker? Struggle? Bathroom? Is he kidding?

If the dissemblingly folksy tone of this statement is somewhat at odds with the high-toned reality of the utterer, Johnson's sanguine estimation of his ability at drawing is amply corroborated in a current show of his work at the trendy Institute for Architecture and Urban Studies, an establishment for which Johnson is both prime benefactor and éminence grise. In addition, the Institute's journal, *Oppositions*, has devoted much of its current issue to a veritable Johnson *festschrift*, an unusual move on the part of a publication that generally devotes its time to searching out the more perfectly arcane. Could it be that the Institute hopes to flatter the old man into a bigger bequest? Or is it simply joining in the frenzied accolade fever that has lately yielded Johnson a gushing interview with Dick Cavett, the Gold Medal of the American Institute of Architects, the Bronze Medallion of the City of New York, and the continued yapping sycophancy of the *Times*'s architectural critic (whose recent magazine cover story plumbed new lows of unctuousness)? What is the reason for this Johnson-mania?

If Philip Johnson has a talent, it is a tastemaker's talent: He jumps on a trend with the best of them. But what really sets Johnson apart — the knack that doubtless made him Mobil's designated genius — is his aptitude for publicity. This is well illustrated by the two buildings included in the current exhibition, the famous 1949 "Glass House" in New Canaan, and this year's model, the American Telephone and Telegraph headquarters now under construction on Madison Avenue. While neither design broke any new ground, each clearly established Johnson as the titular leader of the style involved. If it was Mies van der Rohe who provided the real inspiration for the Glass House, for example, it was only Johnson who could have built the house and lived in it himself. Johnson's career began when he turned himself into the Man in the Glass House. In an instant, he became the austere apostle of modern architecture — or rather the modern apostle of austere architecture.

Sketches of the Glass House show the apparent whimsy of its evolution as Johnson hunted for the right formula. Early studies show a house dominated not by chaste black steel and glass but by a series of stone Syrian arches. Johnson was clearly searching for *the* style, with a debate being waged between the stripped neo-classicism of his middle years and the more powerful anality of the carefully developed Miesian vocabulary. Mies triumphed. Even the site-planning studies for the stone version are preoccupied with the central Miesian dilemma of how to position several rectangular buildings around another rectangle. The final version of the Glass House was more a masterstroke than a masterpiece — Johnson had finally got it just right. Photos showing the architect sitting in his pristine house, which contains nothing save a few meticulously placed Barcelona chairs, are as of a priest in his shrine. With the Glass House, Johnson became the self-annointed guru of the modern movement.

As the years went by, Johnson firmly established himself as the Morris

AT&T BUILDING
(*New York*) Philip Johnson

Lapidus of the better classes, designing stately structures for the monied around the globe. New York was not skimped upon when it came to this work. Johnson assisted Mies on the design of the Seagram Building, as well as turning out such Miesian knock-offs as Asia House and an expansion of the Museum of Modern Art. These early works are followed by a period that might be described as Middle Masonry. Major examples in this genre include the New York State Theater in travertine and the Bobst Library at NYU in red sandstone. Both boast klutzy, inarticulate exteriors — Johnson has never been good at the articulation of surfaces — and interiors that aim at the grand but yield only the vertiginous. Bobst is a particularly gross imposition on its site and contains a mammoth inner court that seems a pastiche of the cell block at Riker's Island. But if Johnson's intermediate period yielded no building that was truly distinguished, the clients and budgets invariably were.

Within recent years, though, there has been a reversion to certain earlier tendencies. The dark glass curtain wall has so long been considered the standard of dress for tall buildings that Johnson could not avoid its use in his two major mainstream skyscraper projects prior to AT&T: Penzoil in Houston and the IDS tower in Minneapolis. Penzoil is the better of the two, achieving a kind of minimalist intensity in the interplay of its two towers. IDS is an attempt to confound the single glass box by means of a series of faceted erosions at each corner. This whittling style is very much the current vogue as designers struggle to reinvigorate the modern canon by cutting off a corner here or adding a schmancy lobby there — anything short of actually rethinking the box. One of the earliest and crassest of such attempts is the Gropius-influenced Pan Am Building, which, like IDS, is vaguely octagonal in plan. Both buildings are also uncomfortably tied to major pedestrian spaces — Grand Central in the case of Pan Am and a rather tacked-on looking but dramatic enclosed courtyard in the case of IDS. More recent hometown examples of this carving operation are Citicorp, with its silly lopped-off top, the oddly beveled and chamfered UN Plaza Hotel; and the grotesque Midtown megabuilding planned by the Fisher Brothers, which promises to have no less than 15 sides as well as an especially vapid "galleria" that the city, in its wisdom, swaps in exchange for permission to erect a structure far larger than zoning would otherwise permit.

The only two things that are certain in art criticism are death and taxonomy. One would not expect Philip Johnson — who was a critic before he was an architect — to work long in such a taxonomically diffident manner. For some time, in point of fact, Johnson has been peppering the media with barbs directed at that now fashionable whipping-person, "Modern Architecture." Penzoil and IDS, however, are nothing if not modern architecture as it is currently understood. Indeed, for anyone of historicist leanings — and no one has a keener sense of history than Johnson — the deboxification of the office tower hearkens back to many of the projects of the very heyday of the modern movement. No, the glass tower, no matter how elegant or obscured, would never constitute the venue for the next great leap forward. Fortunately, something was brewing that would enable Johnson to reassert his reputation as (in the words of Number One Toady, the *Times'* Paul Goldberger) an "enfant terrible" and a "shocking iconoclast" and to indulge his predeliction for shallow neo-classicism and learned historical allusions. That something was "Post-Modernism."

Architects have always looked to history for inspiration. Post-modernism looks to history for justification. Isolated from social questions, the American branch of the post-modern family chases only the grand allusion, inviting judgment mainly on the strength of its literacy. The best post-modern works are those in which the most succinctly paraphrased clues are most artfully hidden, the architectural equivalent of proposing that Hirshfeld's best caricatures are the ones in which he has concealed the most "Nina"s. Within American post-modernisms, however, there are two distinct tendencies. The first is the school of the High Post-Modernists, its mantel (not to mention its andirons) of leadership worn by New York's own Robert Stern (and by Robert Venturi in his more academic moments). The second school, the Low Post-Modernists, is led by Charles Moore (and by Venturi in his lighter moments). The difference between them is simple. High P-M draws its allusions from the likes of Brunelleschi or (the big favorite) Lutyens, the basic criteria being that the source be both renowned and deceased; while Low P-M learns from Las Vegas, McDonald's, or what is fondly called the "vernacular" — which is to say anything designed by someone who is not a graduate of one of the better architectural schools. This can take in everything from the local gas station to an Iroquois wigwam. Philip Johnson has, in a span of only months, cornered the market for both, an achievement only he, blessed as he is by that fortunate con-catenation of ready clients and chameleon panache, could have pulled off.

The low end of the spectrum is co-opted by Johnson's design for the Dade County Cultural Center in Miami, a project executed in what

Johnson calls a "Mediterranean" style: coral-colored walls, tiled roofs, and a general air of the hacienda. The project has apparently tweaked the sensibilities of the locals, who were, it is reported, hoping for something along more modern lines. But with humility appropriate to their stations, they have swallowed their objections lest they appear boorish in the rejection of the work of their certifiably Famous Architect. More congenial, apparently, was Johnson's relationship with AT&T. The resulting High Post-Modern design has received wider notice than virtually any other in recent memory, rating front-page coverage in the *Times* and garnering predictably dripping accolades from Johnson's usual retinue. The building, trumpets America's newspaper of record, is to be "the most radical skyscraper design of the 70s," "the first major monument of post-modernism," and even "the most provocative and daring skyscraper design since the Chrysler Building." Aw c'mon.

The deluge of well-orchestrated publicity surrounding AT&T, the nattering insistence that the building represents a bold departure from previous thinking, and the intimation that it embodies a new style understood only by a few prescient apostles of progress has had the effect of deflecting serious attention from the design itself. Not to put too fine a point on it, the building sucks. The so-called "post-modern" styling in which AT&T has been tarted up is simply a graceless attempt to disguise what is really just the same old building by cloaking it in this week's drag and by trying to hide behind the reputations of the blameless dead. Cribbing the odd detail from Alberti, Boullée, McKim, Mead and White, or Raymond Hood is all well and good, but ultimately such historicism means little unless it abets some larger aim. Johnson's borrowings are entirely decorative, a thin veneer meant to hide rotten goods. Decoration is a key word in the credo of post-modernism, an understandable reaction to its anathematization by many of the purists of traditional modernism. Johnson, though, has totally substituted decor for design, yielding in AT&T no more than a decorated slab, little different than the despised modern buildings it purports to confound. AT&T is the Seagram Building with ears.

Philip Johnson has always talked a good building, and AT&T is no exception. He advertises that AT&T represents "a new use of eclectic choices to suit the place and program: the base an open colonnade [Brunelleschi?] for scale and human reference; the middle a shaft from the '20s [Raymond Hood?], and the top, a broken pediment complete with cornice [late Rome?]." This division into base, shaft, and capital (in imitation of a classical column) has been a staple of skyscraper architecture from the beginning. Not only is this division a handy way of conceiving a building's design, it relates directly to the different scales of its encounter with the city: a base that reflects the pedestrian and the street; a middle, "lifting portion" that relates to the street at a larger scale and gives the building its basic form and proportions; and finally, a "capital" that contributes to the composition of the skyline. Even the most modern towers observe this distinction in a vestigial way: at the very least, their designers add a few extra vertical stripes to indicate the top. Johnson's design makes a lot of sound and fury about this division, but ultimately signifies nothing with it. It looks as if he chose base, shaft, and capital at random and then pasted them together on a sheet of paper, snipping and trimming until they more or less lined up. It is the architecture of appliqué, a building of words with no syntax.

As with the Glass House, Johnson's design for AT&T is hermetic, answerable only to its own style. On his New Canaan estate, Johnson was able to manufacture the perfect environment for his exercises. But in New York, where the context is beyond his control, he simply ignores it. Madison is one of the city's narrower avenues. It is not the kind of street where a building can stand back behind a plaza like Seagram's, nor does it have the width to allow very tall buildings to rest comfortably hard by it. As a result, most of the buildings along Madison are not so massive as those along Sixth, Third, or Park. Into this situation Johnson has introduced a prodigious building that rises sheer from the street with nary a set-back, placing its entire bulk right on the street, casting the entire block into darkness. The monumental entry and colonnade, while large and mighty impressive, also seem ill-suited to this location. The perspective rendering that has been produced to sell the public on the scheme is drawn from an impossible vantage point (inside an elevator shaft a block and half away), so as to present a monumental vista that real life will never offer: AT&T is a monument in search of an axis. Normal street-related commercial functions have been stuck around the back of the building in yet another "galleria" so as not to interfere with the heroic train-station façade. The arcade itself seems to have been tacked on at the last minute, yielding truly dreadful elevations on the side streets in which the huge building appears to be joined to a Louis Kahn-esque hut by spindly Victorian cast-iron half arches. The front elevation, while it may conjure up visions of the Pozzi Chapel for some, looks too delicate to hold up the millions of tons of stone mass it appears to support. The effect is much the same as might have been achieved had the Supreme Court permitted the construction of an office tower atop Grand Central. Of course, that scheme did have its devotees. Philip Johnson was not among them.

Moving on up, the eye rests on the middle "shaft" portion of the building, consisting of an unrelieved series of vertical stone stripes. Claims to the contrary notwithstanding, they have nothing to do with the work of the late great Raymond Hood, architect of such genuine pearls as the Old Daily News and McGraw-Hill buildings. Finally, there is that devilish rooftop that seems to remind many people who write about such things of nothing more than Aunt Beulah's old grandfather clock. The allusion is apt in some ways — Aunt B.'s clock, you will recall, was always left standing against the wall, because it was intended to be seen from only one side. The same is true of the AT&T building. Unfortunately, since there was no 650-foot-high wall available, Johnson has made his building into one. The wall faces east and west, with the result that a view from the north or south is totally senseless. The building only "works" from two directions. "Where is that whimsical profile?" strollers on Madison Avenue will ask themselves as they gaze on the looming pink rockpile. "Up against the wall," will come the reply.

In the recent show, several office blueprints seem to have been included only because of the presence on them of a small pencil hieroglyph or two by the master. Rumor has it that so infrequent are Johnson's sallies with the pencil that those working in his office scurry to squirrel away any scribble that falls from his desk against the day when they may become valuable. And they will become valuable, because they are Johnson's. The unremarkable, inept drawings symbolize the work as a whole, as well as the genius behind it: Johnson, with his demon flair for public relations, has always managed to cadge observers into confounding the work with the man. Johnson doesn't so much *design*, he *signs*, a Louis Vuitton among architects. With a building like AT&T, though, we're the ones who get stuck with the baggage.

October 1978

LET A HUNDRED
STYLES BLOSSOM

Reports of the death of modern architecture appear to have been greatly exaggerated. This, at any rate, seems to be the drift of the Museum of Modern Art's newly hung "Transformations in Modern Architecture." The show has been breathlessly awaited by the architecture set for years. When, everyone wondered, would Architecture and Design Director Arthur Drexler make his move? While fierce controversy roiled over the fate of the modern movement, the museum remained strangely quiescent, almost aloof. The factions raged furiously, each hoping to win the museum to its cause. After all, MOMA virtually made "modern architecture" in America with its famous show of 1932, and a likewise definitive stand could conceivably have a similar impact today. For Drexler, the opportunity was enormous.

But so was the pressure. Anybody with any sense knew that old-fashioned modern architecture, with all its imputed evils, had to go, but what would replace it? The megastructural maniacs seemed to have been suppressed but did that mean that we were to have the quaint eclecticists or the nouveau neo-classicists? All that was certain was that everyone, except the most unreconstructed Miesians, was yapping for a change. Robert Venturi's *Complexity and Contradiction in Architecture*, the little Red Book of the so-called "post-modernist" insurgents, was over 10 years old. Every callow architecture student was mumbling the famous aphorisms ("Less is a bore"; "Learn from Las Vegas!") coined by Venturi to flay the moribund corpus of canon-modernism. Clearly, the modernist empire was crumbling and the troops in the field were in open rebellion.

Still MOMA temporized, hedging its bets, keeping up but never summing up. A big Italian show acknowledged the shift in furniture and industrial design from the austerity and discipline of North Europe to the more exuberant fecundity of the south. Then came the beaux-arts shocker, a straight-faced presentation of florid 19th-century architectural drawings done in the robustly decorated style of the Parisian École des Beaux-Arts. What did this mean, pondered the crowd at Pearl's? Surely not that Drexler had been won into the camp of the *historicists*, for heaven's sake! The Modern couldn't just drop *modern* without a fight. Subsequent exhibitions did little to clarify things. A show of the work of post-modernist father-figure Ed Lutyens suggested one thing, but the choice of Cesar Pelli, the current Picasso of the curtain wall, to design the museum's huge addition and condo suggested another. All hope for clarification was pinned on "Transformations." Designers trembled over drafting tables, pens nervously poised, waiting to be told what to do next. Expectation was apoplectic; fortunes hung in the balance. Seventh Avenue shows a collection every season and the air is electric every time. The Architecture Department makes a major statement only a few times in a lifespan. What was the word to be?

Alas, MOMA copped out. The show is like Hamlet on matte-board: Arthur Drexler couldn't make up his mind. Instead of a Cultural Revolution we get "Let a Hundred Flowers Blossom." Instead of leadership, vacillation. Drexler exhibits almost every tendency of the past 20 years. The show is aggressively low-keyed, defensively casual. As exhibition design, it's minimal: 400 photographs, grouped. No plans, sketches, models, or materials, just a shot of each building (though naughty Bob Stern got in two of the Lang House) and a caption. The only pizzazz comes from what appears to be the most groveling curatorial act of the decade. One room contains a striking series of glowing color transparencies of buildings clad in the currently fashionable reflective glass. This cannot but have pleased one of the show's major benefactors, the Pittsburgh Plate Glass Company. But why not? The whole thing might have been culled from the news section of one of the middle-brow architectural journals read by the rank and file in Omaha, Kansas City, and Jeddah, the traditional venues for such architectural product advertising. Like the magazines, the show plays it safe, seeking its excesses at the Mantovani rather than the Sid Vicious end of the architectural spectrum.

Of course, what's really interesting about compilations, Drexler's Four Hundred Buildings as much as the Newport Four Hundred, the Social Register, or the Whitney Biennial, is who gets left out. Here, the choices get wiggy. Virtually Philip Johnson's entire oeuvre is included but not a single Alvar Aalto! Anybody could become Philip Johnson given the right historical circumstances but only Aalto could have been Aalto. Vulgarians like Harrison and Abromowitz of Albany Mall fame survive the last cut but Pier Luigi Nervi doesn't even get on the court. Is this sensible? Where are those splendid Dutchmen Herman Herzberger and Aldo van Eyck? Where are Steve Baer's Zomes and Bucky's geodesics? Where is SITE? Wasn't the Guggenheim finished in 1959? Some of this seems just plain bitchy. The whole town is asking why John Hejduk's fine work is not to be found with that of the other members of the New York Five, inexplicably reduced for the occasion to Peter Eisenman, Charles Gwathmey, Richard Meier, and Michael Graves. The four have even written a letter protesting the absence of the fifth, threatening to withdraw from the show (as of this writing they remain.) Ultimately, though, what do Drexler's peccadilloes matter: Group shows always entail a certain amount of grievance. Let them form a *salon des refusés* if they want.

Actually, a salon has already been organized. Such are the politics of these things, Drexler himself was browbeaten into turning over a room in the upstairs Goodwin Gallery to one of the leading *refusés*, the delightful Gaetano Pesce. It seems Drexler had invited three representative "visionary" designers (Pesce among them) to submit proposals for what he lyrically called a "free architecture," unfettered by the "reductionist" chains of functionalism. These projects were to be the core of the show, occupying, one would imagine, the space currently taken up with the Magic of Mirrors exhibition. However, for reasons still obscure, Drexler got cold feet and decided that free architecture was out, as he put it with unintended irony, "for reasons of space."

The trouble was that he forgot to tell Pesce. Imagine, then, Pesce's surprise when, after months of work, supported by $10,000 of his own money, he arrived with his project, his wife, five assistants, and a travel bill for another five grand, and nobody at MOMA knew him. "Didn't you get my wire?" asked Drexler. He had, after all, sent it two days ago and there was simply no longer any way to include Pesce in the show. Needless to say, Pesce was piqued. MOMA commissions carry real prestige among architects and, having told journals and friends about the project, his personal and professional reputation was on the line. After days of frantic negotiation and only after considerable pressure from Philip Johnson, the department's alter ego (for once on the side of the angels), Drexler offered Pesce a one-project show. This was hastily and inadequately installed and opened last week, accompanied by great lack of fanfare. The two other spurned visionaries, Allan Greenberg and Roger Ferri, are also to have their own show in June. Of the whole affair, Drexler will say only that Pesce has "a legitimate gripe."

Pesce's work offers much that the show lacks — most notably a point of view. It is a self-contained polemic on modern architecture, executed in rubber bas-relief. One large and three small panels depict a "skyscraper" intended to stand at the current site of the Seagram Building. This substitution is "not difficult to argue," writes Pesce in an exhibition brochure he was forced to have printed at his own expense. Its form is of a vast hive of polyurethane foam carved from within by its users. But what is actually carved into Pesce's spudlike building mountain are not such everyday things as bedrooms and executive suites, but rather a series of fairly funny jokes on modern architecture. From behind the gridded modernist façades of neighboring Park Avenue towers, a face screams as from behind bars. Here and there are bits of famous projects by Le Corbusier, Adolf Loos, and other modernist lions. In these, Pesce explains, are to live the order-obsessed likes of politicians and labor union functionaries. Such politics! No wonder the mad dog couldn't be let in the show.

Downstairs in art historians' heaven, things are calmer; everything is classified, placed in context. Scholarship obscures indecision. Three major styles are propounded: the "structural," the "sculptural," and the "vernacular" or regionalist. The sculptural, it is said, derives from Cubism and Expressionism, filters through the later work of Le Corbusier, batters its way through '60s brutalism, finally resolving itself into the twin streams of organicism and the architecture of "interlocking volumes, transparency, and thin planes" characteristic of the young Corb. As with renewed interest in the young Marx, this is clearly revisionism. The second of the three categories, the structural (as if that word retained a shred of meaning) derives principally from Mies and is said to regard architecture as the "systematic solution of technical problems," the old "form follows function" gambit. This, of course, is the major myth of "modern architecture" and Drexler drubs it soundly in the show's text for its priggish disdain for architectural "fiction." The final grouping, the vernacular, is the one in which "modern forms are subordinated to traditional modes." That is to say, anything with a pitched roof, as long as it's not too funky. Perhaps Aalto was left out because it would have been too embarrassing to stick him in this category, which includes the architecture of California singles' marinas and the like.

Within each of these major categories, Drexler subclassifies manfully, putting such upstart taxonomists as Charles Jencks, the Anglo-American Boswell of post-modernism, in the shade. Drexler's divisions, unlike Jencks's more *engagé* schemas, are entirely based on motif, and include the likes of "Blank Boxes," "Flat Roof," and "Clustered Vertical Shafts." The distinctions are entirely pictorial. Seldom does the show exhibit any interest in space, only in mass and composition, and any broader meanings are emphatically ignored. Like "Let a Hundred Flowers Blossom," this panoply of styles is the officially sanctioned liberalization that follows protracted reactionary stagnation. But, as in any autocratic system, such liberal periods never last. Eclecticism is only the contest for the next great idea. The MOMA show signals that the race is still on, the new paradigm prize still unbestowed, and most of the major contenders still largely unbloodied.

But, is the smart money already placed on a new favorite? There are certain signs. Perhaps the mirror-glass room was more than simple fawning. Maybe it was really meant to be seen as it seems, a shining jewel in a monochrome setting. After all, since America discovered China a few years ago, we have all become great masters of diplomatic subtlety, burying our true meanings. Could it possibly be that mirror buildings are being groomed to emerge as the designated architecture of the '80s? To be sure, the competition is less than stiff. Most of the crazies, zanies, and craftspersons of the '60s have fallen away. Content has been thoroughly vanquished by "meaning." The formal output of such neo-rationalists as Aldo Rossi is dull to the point of being soporific. The major remaining theoretical opposition comes from the neo-eclecticists, commanded by Venturi. While clearly possessed of the largest propaganda apparatus and the toniest polemic, the complexity and contradiction cult has been a little short on charismatic images. Relative hacks have been throwing up 60-story reflective rhomboids while the best the post-modernists have come up with are mouldings and painted wainscot. It is to the Hyatt-Regency that the tourists get taken, not to the brilliant cubist beach house. The eclecticists and historicists are dwarfed, little more than a pleasant eddy, too timid in their convictions to make much difference. Irony is a crippling trait in a form-giver.

No, what really seems most interesting in recent architecture is a kind of back-to-basics trend, a renewed fascination with the eternal verities of geometry, pure form and heroic space, with volumes, and with the iconographic possibilities of "high-tech." This mood is well embodied in the work of architects like Arata Isozaki in Japan, by Foster Associates, the English mavens of the slick, and even by the much abused John Portman of Atlanta, who makes up in chutzpah what he lacks in taste.

Reflective glass is the perfect material for this neo-futuroid pre-occupation. The stuff is compelling. Even Ada Louise Huxtable, erstwhile Hedda Hopper of post-modernism, came out of the closet about her love of mirror in her review of "Transformations." The material, however, is much misunderstood. Drexler, for example, describes mirror as producing buildings in which "substance dematerializes and objective technique culminates in the subjective contemplation of clouds and sunlight." Most critics seem to think that mirror makes a building invisible, somehow turning it into the sky. But this is not the preoccupation that has made every architect alive mad to try one of these buildings. What mirror glass really does is to provide a material that, like a real "skin" can be applied contin-uously, uniformly. This leads not to a dematerialized architecture but to an architecture of pure volume, the doodler's wonderland. Elevations need no longer be sullied by the alternation of solid spandrel and transparent window. Mirror buildings are unscaled, their proportions entirely abstracted by their uniform surface. One hardly wants this to become the universal mode — two or three such buildings in each municipality are quite sufficient. Universality is the kiss of death for any style. I offer the following lines from the Bard to architects gripped by the desire to do the next branch bank or medical office building in mirror: *Look in thy glass, and tell the face thou viewest/Now is the time that face should form another.*

Arthur Drexler and Ada Louise also take note.

March 1979

AALTO ET AL.

Putting on a show of architecture in a museum can be tricky: a building is not easily displayed in a gallery. The problem is not simply one of scale, but of communicating something about the physicality, the complexity, and the content of buildings. The minimum solution to the architectural curator's dilemma is to present photographs, as in the recent "Transformations in Modern Architecture" at the Museum of Modern Art, a show organized on the one building, one photo principle. More photographs are better but the reliance on a single medium inevitably distorts. This is particularly true of architectural photographs. For a start, there are almost never any people in them; the scale and composition of these shots are not so much derived from a sense of the way in which a visitor or user might perceive the building, but from the aesthetics of photographic composition. The best photograph generally triumphs over the best view, diverting attention from the architecture to the means by which it is reproduced. Indeed, architecture and architectural photography have come to have a kind of mutually parasitical relationship in which buildings come to be designed to yield that one striking snap.

Even when plans and sections are added to photographs it is still an attempt to approximate by two-dimensional means an object that draws its life from its three-dimensionality. One could never imagine a show of sculpture that consisted entirely of shop drawings and photographs of distant installations. "Transformations," then, was a show not so much about architecture as about its image. Since the argument the show presented was flaccid, the viewer was left simply with the photographs — not enough.

A wonderful contrast is offered by a show of the work of the great

Finnish architect Alvar Aalto at the Cooper-Hewitt. Organized by the Museum of Finnish Architecture in Helsinki, it is a model of its kind, going well beyond the plans and photos necessarily at its core.

To begin, there are a large number of models, including site-planning and interior models. In addition, a number of presentation drawings — rendered perspectives — done in Aalto's office for competitions and unbuilt projects are displayed. These are literally pictorial and represent the imposition of a point of view on the unbuilt project *by the architect*, much like the one the photographer imposes on the built project with his or her feeling for photographic composition. Especially interesting are Aalto's sketches, mainly fragile-looking early drawings in pencil on tracing paper, fluid and beautiful crystallizations of his incredible feeling for line, for the kind of sensuousness that permeates all his work.

Throughout the exhibition one sees the mixture of Aalto's work, displayed straight, without a surfeit of curatorial gobbledygook. The only text consists of a number of apposite quotations from the architect's small but succinct body of writings. There are also a series of his paintings and his experimental constructions in bent wood, formal explorations, many of which are quite beautiful. These show the character of Aalto's visual sensibility at its most abstract, and as one wanders the show it is fascinating to see the transformation of his basic visual ideas into increasingly complex and practical objects. From the curve of a collage in wood, one proceeds naturally to the curve of a chaise or a chair leg, to the curving plan of an auditorium, to the siting of a group of buildings on the contours of a hill. To my eye, the continuity, the almost casual-seeming way he makes beautiful forms useful, is unbelievable. The loveliest plans in 20th-century architecture are those of Aalto and Frank Lloyd Wright; plans which do not simply organize spatial relations brilliantly but which are always striking compositions in themselves: sensual, varied, full of surprises, of broken regularities, of new forms. In particular, Aalto has come to be known for the limpid, accelerating curves that appear in many of his projects, from vases to building plans, and for a gorgeous fan shape, to me the most beautiful single *form* in recent architecture. Whether Aalto uses it to make an auditorium or an apartment house, it never seems forced, always integral, organic to that project's particularities.

This ability at integration, the choreographer's sense rather than the packager's, is to be found at all levels in Aalto's work. Meticulous to the last detail, his feeling for material and the textures of surfaces is supple,

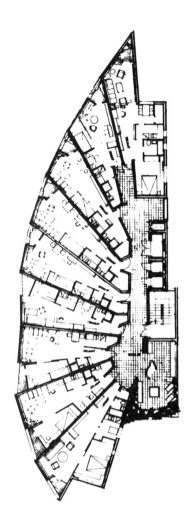

FAN FLOOR PLAN
(*Neue Vahr Apartments, Bremen*) Alvar Aalto

humane, and careful. The show contains striking examples: photos of the great undulating ceiling at the Viipuri Library (a casualty of the Russo-Finnish War), actual panels of the semicylindrical glazed tiles Aalto used both inside and outside, a lovely door handle of metal and leather and a large selection of his fresh, graceful, comfortable furniture. This includes a scattering of his famous little three-legged stacking stools for the use of visitors. Aalto's interiors are almost Matisse-like in their supple combination of form, pattern, and color, blending elements that are very different into a whole that seems completely unforced. The entrance foyers of the Jgvaskyla Teachers' College and at the cultural center in Wolfsburg, West Germany, use different patterns in floor, ceiling, column, stair, lighting, wall, and fenestration treatments, yet in each case the whole vibrates together, one lovely ensemble.

A striking, if unpopulated, photograph of the Jgvaskyla College emphasizes another special quality of Aalto's genius, the wizard integration of his buildings into the natural landscape. The photograph is of a large lobby that ends in a wall of plate glass, opening onto a grove of birch trees. Rather than framing the landscape like a picture, the opening acts more as a plane of transformation, the line at which inside becomes outside, the one flowing into the other as effortlessly as one room might flow into the next. This harmonious relation to nature is everywhere in Aalto, from his impeccable sense of orientation — exemplified in an apartment tower in Bremen in which he uses his fan shape to orient all the apartments to the end of the work-day afternoon sun — to his direct suggestion of natural forms in a project for a town hall in the Swedish mining town of Kiiruna that takes the surrounding hills as inspiration for its profile and pulls it off without a hint of kitsch. This natural sensibility is equally evident in his site-planning, perhaps, as has been suggested by some, the result of long tramps in the woods at an impressionable age with his forester grandfather and his surveyor father.

Aalto developed an intensely personal, comprehensive, and essentially inimitable style: total design. This sense of design did not spring from the cannibalization of historical or functional motifs but from the more fundamental pleasures of sense, from a love of nature and materials. Aalto always valued integration over ostentation. He was interested in an architecture that worked at every level, and this shaped his concern with landscape, human scale, his elaborate attention to acoustics and lighting, his understanding of the full range of sensory involvements in architecture and design. Above all, his work is friendly to people, gracious, never authoritarian. One of my favorite details in Aalto's work, a device he uses repeatedly, is a grouping of round skylights, each of which is lit by a small lamp suspended on the outside. I remember sitting in a room that had a ceiling punctured by such lights one rainy day. The rain beat on the thin domes of the skylights, and at the apex of each was a yellow twinkling and a zig-zaggy pattern of light diffused by the water on the outside surface.

Lately, one hears Aalto pooh-poohed a good deal by architects who seem to regard him as not much more than a kind of eccentric regionalist, much the way that Wright's work is belittled by architects full of secret terror of his genius. I think the reason is that their work is so tactile and unashamed, so ... *sexy*. Today's architect is so often the anal retentive or the prig, this kind of sensualism can be embarrassing. Both Wright and Aalto were fond of striking the biological analogy, of speaking of architecture in terms of natural phenomona. Nowadays the fashionable analogies are historical or technological, or with language or mathematics. No self-respecting architect would even consider comparing a building to a fish these days, something Aalto did repeatedly. Salmon and trout were on his mind, not transformational grammar or British architecture under the Raj. As far as I'm concerned, I'll take the trout.

I was interested to find in the June/July issue of *Portfolio* magazine an article by Paul Goldberger entitled "Ten Buildings with a Style of Their Own." These the eminent critic has personally chosen as "some of the best buildings in American history, buildings that have refused to be bound [sic] by the narrow limits [sic] of style." As he explains, "It is not necessarily an aesthetic unity that ties [sic] together the places listed here: If they have anything in common it is a quality of pleasure [sic]." Surely the most stimulating choice among these seats of pleasure is that of the slave quarters at the Evergreen mansion down in Louisiana. To Goldberger, "The main house ... is of good design quality, but it cannot compare with the slave quarters as an architectural experience." One can easily imagine what an uplifting experience it must have been to return, after an invigorating day in the cottonfields, to "a simple wood box with a tin roof and a small front porch," to an ensemble that was "so carefully conceived a work that even the outhouses behind the central shacks echo the symmetrical pattern of the shacks themselves." Ah, the Old South.

Several weeks ago I wrote in these pages of the abysmal tower that the Trumps are planning as their contribution to the destruction of Fifth Avenue. I argued that there was no argument, save greed, which could be raised in defense of the misbegotten structure. It seems I was mistaken. The *Times* of July 1 carried a piece by Ada Louise Huxtable in which the doyenne of development develops a number of interesting apologies for the upcoming erection, viz:

1. "It's only following orders." Huxtable dismisses naysayers on the project as "objectors ... whistling in the wind, or up the wrong skyscraper." This because such hideous buildings are not only permitted but encouraged by current zoning laws. A bad building is not made good by the fact that you can get away with it.

2. "It isn't really there." This is getting to be an Ada Louise favorite, the ethereal mirrored building drawing its meaning from its context, melting in sky or cityscape, evaporating blah, blah, blah. She forgets that if anything is going to be seen in this particular mirror, it will be the AT&T Building, of which one, I am sure, will be enough.

3. "More is More." Huxtable's defense of Trump's "shimmering facets" ("if four sides are good, 28 sides are better") is apparently a rebuttal to the old "less is more" school of thought. There are, however, other readings of the word "more" than "more of the same."

4. "I don't care if we are in Managua, the way to build igloos is with ice." This argument is especially dismaying. It was this kind of hyped-up concern over the "integrity" of single buildings that led to the sterility of the modernist conception of the city, yielding the Sixth Avenue pattern, a suburban layout of single towers, each sitting on its own stupid little plot.

Great urban streets like Fifth Avenue do things differently: single buildings defer to a larger ensemble, informed by a sense of the street as a whole, not simply as a collection of "parcels." Unfortunately, the parcelization of Fifth Avenue is accelerating dramatically. Just announced is the dreaded "Son of Saks," a 50-story tower intended to loom over that venerable landmark, and rumours fly about Korvettes' and Bergdorf's towers. These schemes threaten the murder of the greatest and best-known street in the world. The Planning Commission has decided to "study" the matter, but this, of course, simply translates into at least a year of jerking off. Only an outraged citizenry stands between sanity and the designs of the developers as even our senior architectural critic continues to pander to the pillagers.

Finally, a note for Piranesi freaks. Under construction on 63rd Street between Park and Second is a station for the new crosstown subway. Under the false street — concrete panels supported on enormous steel beams — is a gigantic cavern crisscrossed with mammoth cylindrical braces. Dimly lit at night, it appears as some fantastic grotto, scary and mysterious. This is enhanced by the fact that to see the space you must peer through a small grating in the street, and the partial view makes it look even larger than it is. Best gratings are at 63rd and Third, and during the day, when large sections of the roadway are often removed for the delivery of materials, allowing a better view. Definitely the full four stars.

August 1979

THE WORLD OF ALL

POSSIBLE BESTS

One of the problems with "post-modernism" in architecture is that its moral center is a joke. Wit, or a painfully constructed facsimile, has come to be a major preoccupation of many designers, an understandable, if too easy, reaction to modernism's glum sincerity. The result is a scene as strewn with bad jokes as modernism's was with mediocre truths.

Irony is the main mode of this architecture of the defensive critique, and post-modernism's major monuments tend to abound in sardonic allusions and literary cracks. While genuine wit is always in season, the typical post-modernist joke (generally a double entendre about a building being other than what it seems to be, or a throw-away historicist fragment meant to legitimize some larger banality) has ceased to be funny. Johnny Carson has long since given up on Richard Nixon and Gerry Ford, and architecture's current funsters might come up with some new material as well. The doric order never really was that funny, anyway.

The recently opened "Buildings for Best Products" show at the Museum of Modern Art is a nice object lesson, as it were, in the potential of architectural wit as a means to serious innovation. The Best Products Company, the largest catalog-showroom merchandiser in the country, has, under the enlightened guidance of Sydney Frances and Andrew Lewis, become a leading and thoughtful patron of architecture. The MOMA show includes both a group of buildings the company has built for itself and a group of proposals commissioned specifically for the exhibit from six well-known architects. The problem addressed is the same: how can the façade of the basic Best building, in essence a big square brick box, the interior formula fixed, be transformed in such a way that it will yield some special visual distinction to the whole?

INDETERMINATE FAÇADE SHOWROOM
(*Houston*) SITE Projects Inc.

29

The simplest solution is to muralize, the strategy taken by Robert Venturi, who adorned a recently opened Best showroom in Pennsylvania with a pattern of abstract flowers, a lot like the kind of contact paper with which we all decorated our undergraduate shelves.

More inventive are the buildings that first put Best on the architectural map: the marvelous and genuinely witty structures by James Wines and SITE Architects. Rather than appliquéing a visual order that comes ready-made from some specialized sensibility, SITE starts with the basic Best building itself, investigating the possibilities it suggests. SITE's wit is genuinely visual, like a Chaplinesque pratfall, because it does not depend on standards or information that are not immediately accessible, and because the order of the transformation is so fundamental, embracing — like Chaplin — such basic issues as standing up straight, being held together properly, conforming to some comprehensible standard of wholeness, and obedience to the laws of gravity.

SITE's first project for Best, built in 1972, added a veneer of brick to an existing showroom, making it look like the façade was peeling away at the corners — as if it had simply been glued on, which, of course, it had. Another building has its entry at a corner from which a huge chunk seems to have been bitten. The improbably missing piece is itself mounted on tracks, and at the end of the day is rolled back into place to recreate the "deconstructed" box. Still another building has a façade that appears to have been attached askew, raised up at one end and tilted out, like a hiked skirt, revealing the contents behind. A Best showroom in a Houston suburb seems to crumble into ruins, a great cascade of bricks pouring down onto an entry canopy. A stunning photograph shoots this building through a hazy, almost murky atmosphere, suggesting smog, heat, and suburban torpor. In the foreground of the picture is a freeway with lines of traffic and in the middle distance a flat suburb, grimly festooned with phone and electric wires. In the background looms the dark and jagged silhouette of the Best showroom, strikingly forceful and appropriate, an apparently natural part of a totally artificial landscape.

If SITE's buildings are based on a kind of merry but direct commentary on the four-square brick box, the wit displayed in the newly commissioned proposals in MOMA's show has larger ambitions. Robert Stern, post-modernism's current point-man, has suggested a vulgar pastiche of a classical porch, replete with lurid scale and coloration and a silly icono-graphic program that lambasts the life of the meso-American consumer, presumably Best's best customer. The image of the transformed Greek temple intends to reveal the showroom as consumption's shrine, although such sacred allusion would surely be more appropriate to a more genuinely holy spot, like Bloomingdale's or Bendel's. Stern has subtitled his project "The Earth, The Temple, and the Goods," a joke on a famous book on classical architecture, *The Earth, The Temple, and the Gods* by a Yale mentor.

This classicizing mode is embodied in two new projects, one with painful literalism and the other with greater abstraction. The first is a curiosity by Allan Greenberg who has been arguing for several years, dead straight to all appearances, that architecture should immediately revert to the classical idiom. His inclusion in the show is a striking testament to the power of an idea operating in a vacuum. Not that it's such a new idea: After all, half the filling stations in America are at least vaguely Attic. Conceptually speaking, I find myself unable to see any difference between the standard Georgian A&P and Greenberg's Tuscan colonnade for Best, although Greenberg surely does handle the orders with greater suavity, and learning. Still, everytime I see his work, I find myself wondering if he's really serious.

Micheal Graves's project also proceeds from a classical model, the Greek *stoa*, but then transforms what is basically a simple idea — a covered colonnade at the edge of an open square — into a design both individual and compelling. Graves' "pergola" is composed of fat, drum-like columns, joined by plant-covered trellis work, which support a glass roof. There is a kind of joke here — giant columns holding up a spindly and transparent structure — yet the forms have such weight, and are so removed from simple trabeation, that the joke disappears and a serious, intelligent, and poetic work remains.

The proposal of Stanley Tigerman is pure drollery, a funny one-liner that doesn't overdo the joke. Indeed, the project is not overdone to the point of having been submitted on yellow tracing paper — a material antithetical to the art mode which has lately galvanized so many architects into looking upon their drawings not simply as scores for architecture's frozen music but as frozen assets just waiting to be thawed out on the walls of some warm gallery or other. Tigerman's joke is simply this: His proposed façade is a giant-scale version of a cruddy suburban ranch house, complete down to mammoth TV aerial and basketball hoop, and displayed in appropriate seasonal decoration, viz, Santa and sled for Xmas, bunting and giant picnic table for the Fourth of July, etc. Tigerman's major drawing is a cartoon that would have been perfect for a late '50s number of the *New Yorker*, showing an aerial perspective of the huge Best ranchero surrounded by a sea of identical domestic-sized versions of the same.

A gentler wit is evident in Charles Moore's scheme, in some ways the most directly historicist of the lot. Moore's source, however, is not Lutyens or Sir John Soane but the so-called "elephant towers" that flanked the main gate of the 1939 Golden Gate International Exposition in San Francisco. For the uninitiated (and here I have only five minutes jump on the rest of you), these were a pair of 12-story stepped affairs by the architects Bakewell and Weihe, surmounted by three enormous elephants each, planar modernist pachyderms complete with howdahs, by the sculptor Donald Macky. Moore has taken these elephants, covered them in a reflective enamel skin, and arrayed them as as a façade. The effect is jolly and fine, as is Moore's attractive drawing.

Of the six proposals, my favorite is the unabashedly sculptural scheme by Anthony Lumsden. The work is presented in two particularly beautiful models, the first an elegant one in polished wood, which treats the object as a unified surface, obscuring its constructed nature, and the second a more literally descriptive representation of a smaller portion of the project. The first of two parallel walls of masonry is pierced by an undulating glass canopy, which passes through it at an angle just a few degrees off parallel and reemerges on the other side, contained there by the second wall behind. A cluster of tubes runs beneath the glass, which, as it emerges from the wall, becomes a garden court and entry. The work is almost spare of literary overlay; that the profile of the glass canopy is a "cyma reversa" or "cyma recta" is irrelevant since the terms here are simply descriptive, not the center of content. The form is handsome and sensual.

The show also contains drawings and photographs of a partially completed building for Best's corporate headquarters in Richmond, Virginia, designed by the firm of Hardy, Holzman, and Pfeiffer. Although it seems that this may be a very fine piece of work, it is almost impossible to tell from the poorly chosen photographs and sketchy drawings.

Meanwhile, down on 40th Street, the Institute for Architecture and Urban Studies has mounted a show of the work of Wallace K. Harrison — architect of such masterpieces as the Metropolitan Opera House, the Albany Mall, and the new buildings of Rockefeller Center — part of a continuing series of exhibits devoted to the work of mediocre older architects who are also men of substantial means. This interesting exercise in connoisseurship began with a Philip Johnson tribute and will allegedly continue with an appreciation of Gordon Bunshaft, the man who made Skidmore, Owings, and Merrill three household words. I suspect an even larger pattern. The Institute's house organ *Oppositions* — the *Commentary* of the architecture set — just ran an interview with Albert Speer. And director Peter Eisenman — the Milton Friedman of the architecture set — recently jetted off to Chile and is allegedly planning to open an architectural practice with Jacquelin Robertson, the Haussman of Teheran. I have been keeping an eye on flights to Panama City, adoptive home of the greatest patron of architecture since Hitler. Can a substantial bequest be far away?

The text accompanying the Harrison show describes it as "based on the assumption that 'good' and 'bad' are the least interesting judgements that can be passed on [sic] about architecture." This is either the most artfully tendentious sentence on record or else the most banal. A glance at the remaining text confirms it as the former, especially a description of Harrison's oeuvre as "a secret — and perhaps even agonized — dialectic between the rectangle and the free form, between the grid and the kidney shape."

This notion was so intriguing to me that I rushed at once to Avery Library, where I discovered a fragment of a work by the famous neo-platonist theorist Modulus of Rupture, in which the following dialogue between the grid and kidney appears:

Grid: How then can a citizen be commanded to stand in a corner when there is no corner?
Kidney: But the invention of corners perforce precedes our own concept of them. Nature is herself without corners. She is all curves, like this bean.
Grid: Curves to be sure, but you insult nature with this comparison to a lowly legume.
Kidney: Much as you offend nature after eating of such beans.
Grid: Ha. Ha.
Kidney: Ha. Ha.

Apparently the framers of the Harrison show, not content with slavering after the old man's money, are sending him up as well. What other interpretation could explain a caption under the photos of Nelson's Valhalla on the Hudson that describes Harrison's professional swansong as "the finish of a marathon that was too long." This is just cruelty. This show does nothing to illuminate the real enigma of Harrison's career: how a man of conspicuous talent and taste — designer of the Trylon and Perisphere — could have done so many dreadful buildings.

Both critics at the *Times* worked up their great enthusiasm over the recently revealed plans for the convention center. Such adulation inevitably flows from the twins whenever the sounds of their common mantra (I.M. Pei, I.M. Pei) are chanted. Unfortunately, the 22-acre building has only about six good moves. Yes, the space frame appears impeccable. Yes, the lofty arcade should be nice. Yes, the crystal palace schtick is a good idea (if a klutsy execution). But what else? Westway notwithstanding, why no serious address to the riverfront? Is mirror glass the only solution to anything? What will happen around those endless edges? Does the setting make that little difference?

Someone said to me the other day that, given the constraints of time and budget, virtually any architect would have come up with this same building, differing only as to doodads and decor. Perhaps my faith in the profession is naive, but for half-a-billion big bucks, the least you should expect is great architecture.

February 1980

DRAWINGS FOR SALE

Located somewhere between *Popular Mechanics* and *Modern Bride* on the racks of every suburban drugstore are publications with titles like *100 Architect-Designed Homes You Can Build Without Tools*. These riveting compendia feature hokily rendered illustrations and juicy descriptions ("Ye Olde Colonialoid combines the traditional charm of the Loire Châteaux with a knotty pine rec-room and an eleven car garage …") of houses in an astonishing array of styles, plans available by return mail. A more upscale version of this idea currently hangs on the walls of the Leo Castelli Gallery in a show entitled "Houses for Sale", which, according to the press release, "for the first time will make buildings available to the public through an art gallery." This ingratiatingly transparent ruse is, needless to say, simply another excuse for a drawing show by the usual architects. At these prices, who needs to build anything?

The economics are straightforward. The eight houses are proposed to cost $250,000 each (a hopelessly optimistic estimate in several cases) and, assuming an architect were to build a house of that cost, he (is there another artistic discipline in which an all male group show is possible?) would expect to retain fees equal to about 7 per cent or so of costs, say 20,000 to 25,000 bucks. The drawings at Castelli run in the $2,000 to $50,000 range, and the models go for up to $13,500. What this means is that the return on four or five drawings can be greater than on actual construction, with its elaborate technical and supervision requirements. The drawings themselves are often not even produced by the "name" architects themselves (although the argument is made that design is divorced from the production of any artifacts) but by their offices or by the subculture of freelance airbrushers and prismacolor masters, often working for 10 dollars an hour or less. Cost to the architect? Maybe a couple of hundred bucks tops.

Because of this obvious return, and because the usefulness of art galleries as an instrument of both polemic and auto-publicity is great, presentations often play, as it were, to the gallery. What one sees on gallery walls is transformed to conform to a new set of expectations: what architecture is likely to find its most succinct expression not as a building but as a representation of certain ideas about an unbuilt building? As the emphasis shifts, the qualities of the drawing take on greater consequence (one of the disturbing things about the un- or underacknowledged joint authorship on many drawings), and the importance of representation recedes in favor of values more indigenous to the page: composition, technique, texture, and so on; values which move things in the direction of the imaginative. This, of course, departs from the "working" drawing at the core of practical architecture, in which the entire purpose is to exclude the imagination, to make every reference, as it were, completely concrete.

Of course, there is more than one way to be representational. The working drawing is representational largely in the way written words represent sounds, abstractly. But there is also an ancient tradition of directly representational drawing, in the pictorial sense. Like 20th-century art generally, architectural drawing has occupied many positions along the line stretched between the poles of abstraction and pictorialism. But architectural drawings, rightly, are called architectural for reasons beyond the subject matter: their magic and force comes from their implicit relationship to the unbuilt. Thus one looks at these drawings at both levels: the drawing as artifact and the drawing as the representation of certain ideas about some architecture. Naturally, one can be powerfully affected by the interaction of these two levels. Architectural drawing almost inevitably contains a rhetorical element, the essay to produce conviction about the building's rightness.

At the simplest level, a beautiful drawing can produce the impression of a beautiful building, the technique of drawing masking dull architectural goods. Then, since all drawing is abstract, even that which seeks to simulate like a photograph, the method of abstraction can distort. An attenuated perspective can make a clumsy building look graceful, a boxy one lofty. Axonometric projection confers a kind of instant rigor and discipline. Freehand drawing can convey romance and informality. The use of certain techniques can transfer the implied karma of their progenitors. Virtual cults have sprung up around Michael Graves, for one, and Aldo Rossi, for another, as countless drawings in imitation of their distinct styles attest. The irony — especially in the case of Graves — is that these drawings are the architect's principal representations to the public, built work being sparse. This is in line with a great tradition of visionary architectural drawing, stretching from Piranesi to Sant'Elia, but differing from these two in that it generally constitutes a description of a project in which there is the intent to build, something lacking in the purely polemical tradition.

Some drawings are made great, others have greatness thrust upon them. In this century, the great natural hands have included Frank Lloyd Wright, Hugh Ferriss, and Eliel Saarinen, all of whom — to a degree — can be said to have emerged from the powerful 19th-century drawing tradition of the École des Beaux Arts, a tradition based on perspective and compositional and pictorial conventions dating back to the early Renaissance. But there is another tradition in architectural drawing that is of more recent character, embodied most originally in the work of the Russian constructivists, drawings that are informed by the concerns of modernism generally. Here, the values of collage, non-orthogonal composition, and the passion for geometry and science became touchtones — and a powerful graphic aesthetic emerged which today constitutes the main legacy of the period.

The work in the Castelli show — if one were to try to characterize its relationship to architectural production — is generally of a class with what architects refer to as "presentation drawings." There are, in essence, drawings produced to convince a client or the public of the validity of a given scheme, drawing at its most rhetorical. At Castelli — whatever one makes of the pretense of realism — the rhetorical program for the work attempts to induce the feeling that the projects are not simply valid solutions to the problem of the $250,000 house, but also that there is some significant address to the larger worlds of art and ideas. The resultant fetishizing of the drawings themselves thus sometimes comes into direct conflict with the presentation of the could-be content of the houses they are meant to represent. The position of this work as a separate category of production — encouraged by invention of a market for these drawings — raises fundamental questions about exactly what they are and what they represent. But let us get down to cases.

Going clockwise around the gallery, the first work one comes to is by Arata Isozaki, a Japanese architect who has the most stimulating practice of any of those represented in the show. His house is based on the configuration of the nine squares, an order that has informed architecture from the traditional Japanese house to the villas of Palladio to the houses of John Hejduk (whose influence hovers over a number of the projects in the show). Isozaki's version is a compact and elegant villa on three levels surmounted by a U-shaped barrel vault, completely convincing as habitable architecture. In the show's catalogue (edited with a graceful introduction by Barbara Jakobson, the organizer of the show), it is clearly presented in a set of simple ink drawings; at the show, however, Isozaki exhibits a series of shallow reliefs in cast lead. These are exquisitely crafted but a smidge curious in intent. Like works in the same medium by Jasper Johns which iconographize familiar objects, the medium lends a spurious dignity to the object depicted. For Isozaki, the casts are most striking where they are more abstract: most beautiful is one which depicts a diagram of the nine square formal principle. Those which literally represent the house, lacking the irony of Johns' pop product, seem ponderous, if compelling. These casts are clearly the bargain of the show at $2,000 a pop.

Next on the wall is Peter Eisenman's overblown rumination on axonometric projection, a subject that has arrested his attention for some years. The enormous and beautifully made models (which, like Isozaki's casts, spring from the art of the '60s, geometric branch in this case) are easily the most striking objects in the show and easily the farthest from any reasonable standard of legibility as habitable architecture. Dissemblingly cognizant of this failure to reify, the project cites the collaboration of structural and mechanical engineers as a sort of sop to saleability. For many years, Eisenman has been a hero to the more thoughtful elements of the architectural profession for his persistent pursuit of research into the possibilities of architecture as an art of pure cerebration. His major output has been a series of houses, numbered rather than named in order to preserve them from any coercive association, based on a set of semi-mathematical transformations in the relationships between architectural elements at their most abstracted and dematerialized: lines and planes of no specific substance, "cardboard" architecture as Eisenman has it. Eisenman was one of the early purveyors of the once intensely fashionable analogy between linguistics and architecture, perhaps more than anyone else making Noam Chomsky into a set of household phonemes at the schools of architecture. For my money, this analogy has always seemed less productive than it has been cracked up to be, notwithstanding the obvious appeal of glomming onto a theoretical apparatus that already contains terms like "deep structure" and "surface structure" and which constructs and deconstructs just like any other job site. The point at which the analogy staggers is where it aims to become a working method for the design of buildings, the point at which cardboard (a Platonic substance) must become sheetrock and stucco. Even in the cave, there must be walls upon which the shadows can play! Eisenman's several built projects, while sculpturally provocative, beg too many tedious questions about use which simply don't come up in the drawings and models. While they are too abstracted from everyday reality for comfort, they come too close to retain the validity of the abstracted. Not only are they built of modernism's most familiar materials, they show disturbing signs of a fairly particular taste. In color, composition, and concern, the Eisenman style yields a kind of serendipitous de Stijl, Reitveld redux. One wonders, thus, why the fuss. Why the rigamarole if the forms are going to come out so familiar? What are the advantages of programming a computer to simulate Mozart?

The piece in the Castelli show, fortunately, despite feints, remains at several removes from built reality. In previous projects, Eisenman has presented buildings in which most relationships were orthogonal by means of austere axonometric drawings. Axonometric projection is a technique for representing architecture in three dimensions. This has several advantages. For one it is easier than perspective drawing. For another, all dimensions in the drawing are to scale, unlike perspective in which dimensions are corrected to conform to perceptual distortions. On the page, an axonometric drawing is rotated 45 degrees, thus implicitly introducing that geometry into a project in which such relationships may not exist, yielding a characteristically modern, rakish aspect to the composition. The Eisenman house (called "House El Even Odd") (El even equals eleven, get it?) is described by Eisenman as "an axonometric object" which "explores the conditions of representation and reading in architecture." What this means is that Eisenman has embarked on an operation to convert a technique of representation which has a characteristic mode of distorting into an object which makes those "distorted" relationships real. In practical terms, this means that the house contains both 90 and 45 degree relationships in both plan and section, yielding a series of potentially unusual and stimulating spaces. However, it also means that a perceptual "dislocation" occurs in viewing the object in the gallery. Since both "axonometric object" and the "house object," if we can separate them for a moment, are based on the same rotated system of projection, they tend to cancel each other out in the viewer's eye, making it hard to figure out what is what, yielding integrity without clarity.

While this may be clear as a formal exercise, its scrupulous isolation from certain larger realities tends to diminish its ken. Who, after all, *really* wants to live with or in a Sol Lewitt? Clearly conscious of the atmosphere of unreality that pervades and desiccates his work, Eisenman has provided a second text to elaborate more quotidian realities. In this he describes House El Even Odd as an "earth-mass object," which is to say, the house is supposed to be built underground. This enables one of the 45 degree objects to become a solar collector, another a murderously steep staircase, and generally bestows the energy-efficient cachet on the whole enterprise, which is fine, I guess. Still, that 45 degree dirt looks a lot like cardboard to me.

Moving right along (I feel like Mussorgsky), we come to another underground house, this one by Emilio Ambasz, which turns out to be accompanied by an elegant, if gushing, text by myself. The house is a compendium of a number of motifs familiar to Ambasz lovers: sunken courtyard, monumental stair, strong symmetries, bermed earth, solar collectors, somewhat underdeveloped plan ("It is the architect's intention to adapt the house's interior layout to suit the client's family needs" reads a faked newspaper ad Ambasz has written to accompany the project). While breaking no new ground (you should forgive the expression), the project is elegant and clear if not up to the standard of the same architect's Cordoba House, recently shown at the Max Protetch Gallery. Likewise, the drawings at Castelli hold no special charm (Protetch had a number of winners) although Louis Checkman's photographs of the two models are quite spiffy.

Cesar Pelli's "Long Gallery House" explores territory familiar both in his own work and in that of John Hejdk. The plan is simple, even schematic: a long glass-roofed gallery sprouts a series of pavilions along its length which contain the various activities of the house. Pelli's Castelli version is less interesting than his own Biennale House of a few years ago, a more poetic application of the same notions of both organization and growth. The Long Gallery House is at its most handsome in plan where its dead straight geometry is appealing. Elevations are less interesting, lacking any particularly original moves. Additionally, the choice of materials — massive and thuddy masonry gallery, flimsy clapboard pavilions — is uninspired, providing contrasts that are not especially illuminating or purposeful. The drawings are up to the Pelli organization's usual high standard, the nicest being a delicately rendered plan. The prices are $2,000 to $5,000, $12,000 for the model.

The Hexastyle Texas Style house by Charles Moore not unsurprisingly turns out to be a typical Charles Moore house. It is outwardly the most conventional in the show, a "choreography of the familiar and surprising" as Moore describes it. Thus, pitched roofs, French doors, chimneys, and carport. But, Moore being Moore, it is also awash in allusions, including, in this case, the Villa Giulia, the Farnese Gardens, Schinkel's Charlottenberg Palace, and the American ranch house tradition. Thoroughly sensible and well behaved, the most dramatic gestures are a sort of grotto and pool and a sweeping plant-lined gallery. Descriptive drawings are straightforward, although there are a number of watercolor sketches in the architect's own hand, priced to move.

Vittorio Gregotti was clearly taken in by the houses-for-sale ruse and sent along drawings with almost enough detail for construction to start tomorrow. Having accepted the premise of useful drawings, he also largely accepted their convention, and the drawings on display are the most literally descriptive and the least private. Gregotti, to his credit, has not even sent his originals, simply a set of reduced reproductions which are therefore rendered relatively valueless as collectables. The house, unfortunately, is a bit of a bore. It is organized around two long sets of paired brick walls, vaguely reminiscent of an Aldo van Eyck scheme for a sculpture garden. The walls themselves are not particularly nice, and Gregotti piddles away what potency they have by trimming and filling in, reversing the directionality implied by the walls, and creating a rather ordinary, if *luxe*, courtyard scheme. Primarily of interest to those curious about the way Italian offices do brick details.

Back in the front room is the charming English architect Cedric Price's "Platforms, Pavilions, Pylons, and Plants." Like so much British architecture of the '60s (and this is an eminently '60s scheme), the written description, with its resonances of democracy and fun, is far superior to the thing itself. How can you argue with: "As householders become increasingly prepared for and capable of changing their houses for personal reasons such as affluence or old age, the role of the house as a long-term adaptable living box becomes less important than its performance as a *twenty-four-hour living toy*" (Price's italics). Or: "The conscious incompleteness of the overall layout is combined with the particular quality and content of the components in order to enable the users to knock it about or care for it before passing it on or laying it to rest." Or: "Once occupied it should look as particularly occupied and well used as your favorite shoes." Love it. The architect as

Faber Ludens. *La vie en* shoe. But the house is so dull and dated it cannot begin to fulfill its text. The '60s idea of the well-serviced packing crate, in both its arcadian and urban variants, has been so thoroughly replaced by the designer architecture of the current moment that Price's *4 P's* looks as ancient as *Ralph Roister Doister.*

Finally, the "House Within A House" by the German architect O.M. Ungers. Alas, this is also a disappointment, the more so because it is organized around a strikingly beautiful and poetic idea: a house that changes with the seasons, expanding and contracting, "breathing out in warm weather, drawing inward in cold." What Ungers proposes is essentially three houses nestled inside each other like a Russian doll. Innermost is a masonry "winter house," a cube form with a wedge shaped studio on top. This is surrounded by a glass house enclosing a continuous veranda and meant to be dismantled in winter. Finally, just beyond the glass skin is a framework on which some sort of foliage would grow, providing shade in the summer, turning the whole house into a growing green mass.

The reasons for the house's ultimately unwinning character are several. First, the plan of the inner house is extremely rigid and tightly dimensioned, to the point of claustrophobia. The claustrophobic condition, it strikes me, is exacerbated rather than relieved by the three layers: the winter contraction is simply too severe for a non-hibernating species, while the summer expansion seems too circumscribed. There is an overweening formality to the project which contradicts the poetry of its conception: the site plan is almost military, and the house's elevations — with plants stripped away — have the look of a typical northern European tract house. In fairness, however, I must mention that my sources (Page Six, just like your sources) inform me that Jackie Onassis, whose taste is beyond reproach, has bought this project. The clear and well-executed drawings cost $4,000 to $5,000 apiece.

Wandering through the Castelli show I was reminded of that scene from the end of *Casablanca.* Bogie has just blown away the Nazi who is trying halt the flight of Paul Henreid and Ingrid Bergman. Everybody's fate lies in the hands of Claude Rains, the vacillating Vichy. "Colonel Strasser has been shot," he tells his adjutant. "Round up the usual suspects." So it is with shows of architectural drawings: the same well-hung cabal ever dominates.

It is time to introduce some criteria beyond membership of the Century Club or the reservations list at Pearl's for inclusion in these shows, as well as more rigorous standards for the drawings themselves and for their attribution. This latter particularly concerns me. Having at last gained broad recognition for their artistic qualities, it is critical that their collaborative nature be suitably recognized and compensated. After all, it is the drawing that is being sold, not the idea. Therefore let the draftsperson profit.

November 1980

WOLFE AT THE DOOR*

What Tom Wolfe doesn't know about modern architecture could fill a book. And so, indeed, it has, albeit a slim one. *From Bauhaus To Our House* is an unoriginal, if vicious, account of what Wolfe finds wanting in modern architecture and modern architects, particularly what's wanting in their clothes and complexions. Here, for example, is Le Corbusier: "a thin, sallow, nearsighted man who went about on a white bicycle, wearing a close fitting black suit, round black owl-eye glasses, and a black bowler hat." And here is Louis Kahn:

a gray little man ... not much to look at ... He was short. He had wispy reddish-white hair that stuck out this way and that. His face was badly scarred as the result of a childhood accident. He wore wrinkled shirts and black suits. The backs of his sleeves were shiny. He always had a little cigar of unfortunate hue in his mouth. His tie was always loose. He was nearsighted, and in the classrooms where he served as visiting critic, you could see Kahn holding some student's yard-long blueprint three inches from his face and moving his head over it like a scanner.

Wolfe's argument, such as it is, is that a cadre of badly dressed émigrés conned an innocent America into accepting an architecture of diabolical ugliness and discomfort. This was accomplished through the takeover of such key institutions as the architectural schools at Harvard and Yale, where the hypocritically antibourgeois ideas of the Bauhaus were foisted on several generations of students who have only lately discovered what hit them. Of these ideas, the most insidious and unAmerican was the notion that everyone should live in simple, undecorated buildings, "worker's

*Review of Tom Wolfe, *From Bauhaus To Our House*, New York 1981.

housing," the very apogee of all that is unattractive. In Wolfe's account, such architecture was the product of the pseudoprogressivism of early European modernism, which he seems to feel was no more than a kind of inverted snobbery. In a studied series of set pieces, Wolfe presents various dissembling modernists in the act of sneering at all we presumably hold dear (colors, decoration, a decent chair), dismissing it with the phrase "how very bourgeois," which, in line with the book's dominant and energetically applied religious metaphor, is repeated with catechistic regularity.

A curious thing about this account is that it essentially accepts the modern movement's view of itself. Hate it or not, modernism seduces Wolfe at the first premise, leaving him entirely convinced that architects really were behind all those troubling changes in the environment. Architects have historically suffered the delusion that building is the major factor in shaping society. Only logical. Architecture provides a physical description of social relations, ergo it invents them. Wolfe buys this hermetic view, arrogating to architects the power of which they have always dreamed; he seems incapable of reading in buildings any messages other than those explicitly imprinted by the designers themselves. But are the endless, dreary glass office buildings and penitential public-housing projects simply the irresistible realization of Walter Gropius's pathetic polemic? Are no other forces at work?

Modern architecture triumphed not because a few émigrés managed to dupe a class of clients gone totally supine or because of the abiding credulity of Americans hopelessly drawn to any idea presented with an accent. Modern architecture triumphed because it fit both the expressive and the functional requirements of those who built it. It may have been invented in Europe, but we sure were ready. Those buildings were the cheapest you could build and as replicable as the Model T. They were as anonymous as the bureaucracies they housed. And they fit anywhere. Modern architecture didn't conquer America; it was the other way around. With a particularly American genius, modernism was stripped of its naive and hopeful ideological apparel and reattired in a business-as-usual suit. A vision of housing that, for all its tedious simplicity and blind hostility to cities, was intended, however arrogantly, to liberate the poor from their dark, tubercular slums was transmuted into an instrument of subjugation and discipline, a more hygienic ghetto. Was Gropius responsible for this? I think not.

Wolfe does have an unerring eye for the easy mark. Zapping Gropius for his politics is a little like attacking Brooke Shields for her conversation. The point is that it's *easy*. For Wolfe, though, the worst invariably becomes emblematic of all. If you can point out Gropius's feebleness as an ideologue, why mention Hannes Meyer or El Lissitsky? The same standard can be applied to buildings. Why look at Alvar Aalto or the Amsterdam school when you can trash everything with Gerrit Rietveld's Schroeder House? Why mention Ronchamp when you can bop Corbu with Pessac? Why talk about Kahn's Kimball Museum when you can dismiss him with the Yale University Art Gallery? Indeed, why describe Kahn's inspiring teaching when you can get him for shiny sleeves, a childhood scar, or reading plans like a scanner? Following his preconclusion that architecture is merely the built word, Wolfe feels relieved of the burden to look, his eyes following merely where his Selectric leads them.

Wolfe's own values spring from a position slightly to the right of Diana Vreeland. For him, politics is fashion, and Wolfe knows what he likes and which side he's on, never mind that his idea of class struggle is a freshman-varsity scrimmage. But Wolfe's position as the apostle of bourgeois taste becomes more tricky when he gets around to the current architectural scene. Consider this description of Robert Venturi, an architect he lumps with the mass of modernist pariahs:

Venturi's academic credentials were excellent. He had studied architecture at Princeton and was on the faculty at Yale. Like his friend Louis Kahn, he had also studied for a year in Rome as a fellow of the American Academy. In fact, Venturi was the classic architect-intellectual for the new age: young, slender, soft-spoken, ironic, urbane, highly educated, charming with just the right amount of reticence, sophisticated in the lore and strategies of modern architecture, able to mix plain words with scholarly ones, historical references of the more esoteric sort — to Lutyens, Soane, Vanbrugh, Borromini — with references of the more banal sort — to billboards, electric signs, shopping centers, front-yard mailboxes.

Irony, sophistication, Yale? Why, how very bourgeois! Indeed, how very Tom Wolfe.

The apparent muddle here — the bourgeoisie as its own worst enemy — is resolved on two levels. First, objectively speaking, the idea of a fashion-able, well-published, nonbourgeois American post-modern architect is as ridiculous on its face as the idea of a working-class orthopedic surgeon. One can scarcely suggest such a thing without goring someone's oxymoron. Second, however, one must remember that Wolfe has built his reputation by being a little naughty. If he is not exactly prepared to betray his class, he is at least ready to tattle on it. Thus, when it comes time actually to defend something, it turns out to be Morris Lapidus, John Portman, and Ed Stone, those architectural Liberaces. Likewise, Wolfe affirms his affection for Thai silk pillows, zebra-striped upholstery, gold leaf and a few *chotchkies* around the house. Such is the slippery apostasy of the bourgeoisie that it betrays, but only a little. The haut bourgeois affects the tastes of the petit. We go to Morey's but we drink our beer from the bottle. How very petit bourgeois!

Finally, Wolfe's book falls flat for the banality of its conclusions and its open contempt for its subject. Of course, any polemic hectors the facts into line. Wolfe bludgeons them and then asphyxiates what's left under an ooze of prose. Maybe because the material is so far from his sympathies, Wolfe's familiar flash turns into a whine. To be sure, he delivers just about every-thing from his old catalogue of devices: the demon appositives, the peppy repetitions, the surfeit of particulars, the hyperbolic comparisons, the vaguely taboo lingo, the exclamation points, the frisson of near-brushes with serious subjects. But the cleverness is only intermittent, the point hackneyed. Tom Wolfe is a great one at the snobbery of being less of a snob than thou, at playing nobody's fool. Nobody's fooled.

October 1981

EXPLAINING LOS ANGELES

It never rains in Southern California. Seems I've often
heard that kind of talk before.
ALBERT HAMMOND

In an era when so much of our architecture seems to stagger under an
explanatory — even exculpatory — burden, the architecture of Los Angeles
is especially encumbered. If it has come to be a near norm that buildings
explicate themselves, the coastal kin must, in addition, provide some decent
account of their setting. As with no place else, we demand that this architecture produce some sort of regional ID, that it pull over to the curb and
demonstrate a little license. Whereas talking about "New York-ness" would
be cringingly retardataire, nobody erects a stick in LA without seeking to
understand and justify Southland to man.

The East is a career.
BENJAMIN DISRAELI, *Tancred*, 1847

Go West young man.
HORACE GREELEY

Let me try to help. The whole culture buys the myth that California is
adjacent to the US, not exactly contiguous with it. Beyond that, the prejudice loses its unanimity, the arena of interpretation appears. It's a hoary
business developed to the point of industry. More, its collective impact
models visions which cohere and grow, occluding large, shadowing
successor efforts. LA is probably the most mediated town in America,

nearly unviewable save through the fictive scrim of its mythologizers.

Like the "Orient" of the 18th and 19th centuries, the common image of LA is the invention of outsiders, a traveler's version, chained to the hyperbole of discovery. In the abiding atmosphere of otherness at the core of such views there is always an implicit superiority. Edward Said calls Orientalism a form of paranoia and so it is with the Occidentalism of the Los Angelists, who persistently remain unsure of whether they have journeyed to Eden or to the Brave New World. Let's not labor the point too much — Reyner Banham is no Richard Burton nor Charles Jencks a T.E. Lawrence. But the analogy has appeal. Banham's exultant celebration of learning to drive a car in order to attain one of the pillars of wisdom as a prerequisite to writing about the city might a hundred years earlier have involved a camel. Jencks's efforts to organize the natives — like the two concurrent shows of their work (mea culpa) orchestrated from back East — conjures up General Gordon or the Revolt in the Desert.

It is striking that so many Los Angelists are English, outcome of whatever mimetic gene that has made them such a race of colonizers and impersonators. Banham is salient. Jencks (an American impersonating an Englishman impersonating an American) is a more recent case. The city of angels is a crucial destination on the Archigram/*Architectural Digest* pilgrimage route. Nor should one forget the assimilation in varying degrees of Huxley, Isherwood, Waugh, Hockney, and the myriad lesser lights in their wake and thrall. Nonetheless, theirs is a relatively recent intervention. The pattern of expatriation has a considerable tradition. Like any colonially conceived clime, Los Angeles embraces both exile and expectation. The most emblematic embodiment of this bind is surely the literary pilgrim to Hollywood, struggling to vitiate guilty greed by the act of understanding. The writer erects a bulwark of irony, confesses in order to expunge.

Because, like the "Orient," LA is by definition, exotic, the forms giving account of it have special perquisites. Richard Burton called the chronicle of his great disguised journey a *Personal Narrative of a Pilgrimage to al-Madinah and Mecca*, and it is just such a personal narrative that has become LA's most characteristic form. Such personalization embraces novels, movie-star autobiographies, license plates, putative works of scholarship, "custom" surf-boards, architecture. This is part of the larger Los Angelist myth. Since there is no "there" around, only individual versions are supportable. A long view is simply what you see from the hills.

Which suggests another Los Angeles mode. A recent special double issue of *AD* devoted to Los Angeles is sparse in text but illustrated with an enormous number of photographs arrayed as in an album: collection becomes interpretation. Carrying a Nikon may be more wieldy than transporting the Elgin marbles but there is a kinship of impulse. New arrivals in LA covet a special kitschy house they have "discovered" and eagerly explore unfamiliar terrain in the hopes they will stumble upon something hitherto undocumented. Perhaps they will publish a little photo book of Krazy Kottages or dog-shaped drive-ins. While the situation is changing fast, much of LA is still regarded as terra incognita, wanting the civilizing gaze of a 35mm lens. And, as it is unfamiliar, any framing or comment must be considered fresh.

LA's architecture has been obliged to uphold ideas about its particularity at least since the beginning of the century. In 1908, Montgomery Schuyler reported in *Architectural Record* on a western swing made three years earlier. Like most early observers, he extolled Los Angeles' natural beauties and frontier dynamism. He also expanded on the great formal and civilizing impact of the architecture of the area's original colonizers. "Going about Southern California," he wrote, "one always finds reasons for being thankful that the 'Greaser' preceded the 'Gringo' in those parts." He describes his hopes that the city will produce a truly democratic kind of architecture, one which would "avoid the vulgarity of crudity on the one hand and the vulgarity of ostentation on the other." This pretty much sums up the turn of the century line, expectantly affirmative though often mingled with some alarm over the disorder and mess of the cheap and hasty hovels of the hopeful newly arrived poor. "The West," Irving Gill wrote in 1916, "has been and is building too hastily, carelessly, and thoughtlessly."

But this was a quibble: Gill was far more concerned with setting the region's heroic agenda. "The West has an opportunity unparalleled in the history of the world, for it is the newest white page turned for registration." With the other, largely émigré, American architects of California's great first wave (the Greenes, Maybeck, Coxhead, Polk), Gill wanted to invent an architecture that was quintessentially indigenous yet a great departure (a difficult irony at the core of everything Californian). This was to be done, to quote a familiar phrase, by quaffing at the "source of all architectural strength — the straight line, the arch, the cube, and the circle." As it turned out, of course, there were quite a few fonts at which to quaff in California and this first wave of architects set out in as many different directions. Yet any of these could be marshalled to support the hegemonic descriptive ideology. A 1912 article on the Greene brothers in *The Craftsman* proclaims, "The main virtue of those Western homes lies in their essential fitness for democratic American life."

The great Los Angeles-centered second wave, which effloresced in the '30s, was also largely émigré, although from a more considerable distance. Ain, Schindler, Neutra, Harris, Soriano, et al. also assumed a sense of mission (challenging the dominance of Mission), if one more clearly tempered by the going architectural missions of the times. Yet as this wave was reaching its crest, signs of a break were washing in from all sides. Democracy and the innocently progressive longings of arcadia were sinking fast and in their place came a slightly more temperate nexus of aspiration, centering on a nature-proximate lifestyle and on an idea of California as creatively liberating. "I realized," exclaimed R.W. Sexton in a piece entitled "A New Yorker's Impressions of Californian Architecture," "as any other New Yorker would realize when visiting California for the first time, that the San Diegans live entirely different lives than we do in the East."

While this registration of difference was typical of many observers, the quaintly unabashed enthusiasm of this author was less so. By the end of the thirties, a number of negative readings had attached themselves to the Eastern view of LA. The sources were diverse, ranging from the sinister account of Nathanael West to the more flippant view of Dorothy Parker. Los Angeles, by depression's end, was no longer seen as peopled by the raw material of Jeffersonian democracy but by citizens who were, charitably, yokels or, in the worst suspicions, pathological. What civilization there was was either patently false – Hollywood – or hopelessly in exile – Faulkner, Fitzgerald, and those Germans desperately huddled on the cliffs, looking out to sea. And there was a new idea to accompany all of this, the gathering notion of a place that was incomprehensible; understandable, in Fitzgerald's phrase, "only dimly and in flashes."

Architectural observers, though predictably less articulate, were similarly swayed. While enthusiasm continued for the work of the state's architects, there was often concern about the health of its culture. Talbot Hamlin includes, in a 1939 round-up, a photo of a mild-looking strip, captioning it "A Los Angeles Highway. Traffic debauching the countryside. The real estate speculator's delight. Suburbanites uncontrolled, a disease not limited to Los Angeles!" Something of a contrasting view was also expressed, informed by modernist messianism and containing the seeds of an idea not fully developed until after the war. This posited the hope of salvation through the automobile, the national symbol of democratic mobility, then nearing the apex of its charisma. Its effects on architecture might also be salubrious. Henry Russell Hitchcock waxed enthusiastic, in a 1940 essay entitled "An Eastern Critic looks at Western Architecture," over the "anonymous" drive-ins along Sunset Boulevard which he declared the most interesting things in Los Angeles outside of the work of Neutra and "his group." He hoped that they might be models for "a new widely popular architectural expression" to be based on "the development of new functional types," something at which he found Los Angeles "peculiarly adept."

More recent history is too familiar to need much recapitulation. In the post-war years, LA boomed into the city we know today. These were years of partisanship, a celebration of the manifest destiny that had anointed Los Angeles as the galaxy's premier motor city and which was flinging the great grid of model homes toward all available horizons. Architecturally, it was the time of the case-study houses, those stunning refinements of technical enthusiasm, outdoor living, and optimism for the Future. It was also the period of America's most effulgent consumerism, when cars were cars and roadside architecture of pure attraction hit kismet. Then, of course, the shit hit the fan.

By the sixties a new set of "progressive" ideas had become architectural writ and by their light Los Angeles became monstrous. Now LA was the great spawning tank of anomie, a centerless matrix of nothingness, enslaved by the cars that were to have set it free. It was a monument to banality and to the awful haphazard tawdriness of consumer culture. It was the town that apotheosized ugliness. Before long, though, an alternative discourse arrived. Using an ironic wedge to pry forms loose from meanings, what had been hideous became beautiful. New, legitimate sounding cultural aspirations were affixed, historically corroborated relevances were adduced. The freeways again began to look like they worked and those little houses — whether they managed to aggregate into a walkable community or not — were a damned sight more comfortable than that dingy, overpriced studio apartment on West End Avenue, recently left behind. And it was *fun*. It was about driving around looking for amusing craziness, about the beach, hot-tubs, parties, exercise, health, sunshine, the movies. Los Angeles had a renaissance on its hands.

Inevitably a new architecture had to be discovered and the old redefined in terms of this adulatory resignification. But something was very different here. Unlike its predecessors, the new wave of Los Angeles architecture was widely interpreted before it was created. Instead of seeing the viewpoint of their work elucidated and described, today's group must struggle to produce work which embodies descriptions already made. This can be tough. Los Angeles is America's city of ideas, known predominantly by description rather than by substance. As the currency of the former is vastly more ephemeral than that of the latter, an architect, trying to get a grip on just what LA is all about anyway, runs into a welter of possibilities, too densely packed for their private cogencies really to sparkle. But the rules of the game demand a choice. One from Column A, one from Column B...

The central dilemma of the Los Angelist is that his or her faith dictates the city's ultimate mysteriousness, yet his or her duty is to explain. As successive efforts skirt piecemeal around mist-shrouded essences, faith in the possibility of a (probably unknowable) unified field theory spurs the effort. The catalogue expands, the taxonomy branches. Los Angeles is hermeneutist's heaven: everybody expects an answer. The deity here is Quincy (Jack Klugman's, that is, not Quatremère). All this activity tends to produce inconclusive ways of speaking rather than ways of knowing. Los Angeles has a rhetoric but no epistemology.

Like any rhetorical system, the Los Angelist product organizes itself into a series of tropes. The list of these topics outlines the range of strategies for argumentation as well as the parameters of a sufficient description of "Los Angelesness." What sets the system apart is its heavy reliance on irony and unrestrained enthusiasm in argumentation. The brilliance in this is that it permits current Los Angelists to subsume the entire inventory of their predecessors into their own canon. If the results sound foolish or inconsistent, never mind. Foolishness and inconsistency are what LA is all about. The following list is by no means comprehensive, aiming mainly to show high-points and something about range and the problems of working on an architecture that carries an inescapable rhetorical charge.

1. APOCALYPSE

We reached California in time for an earthquake.
F. SCOTT AND ZELDA FITZGERALD

Apocalypse poeticizes the entire discourse, gives it tragic stature. The "big one" could strike at any moment. Potential apocalypse gives nature an edge. Things are so beautiful and yet ... Floods, quakes, or fire can carry it all away in an instant. Architecture is similarly charged since buildings are likely to be the main agents of megadeath. The architect responds by rigorously adhering to the building code (knowing full well that no code in the world will save a building from the "big one"), by a complete pretense of normalcy, by an abandoned celebration of flimsiness, or by the kind of anticipatory skewing so brilliantly embodied by Frank Gehry.

2. THE WEATHER

Boosterishly salubrious except as embodied in the preceding or the following.

3. MADNESS

There was a desert wind blowing that night. It was one of those hot dry
Santa Anas that come down through the mountain passes and
curl your hair and make your nerves jump and your skin itch. On nights
like that every booze party ends in a fight. Meek little wives
feel the edge of the carving knife and study their husbands' necks.
Anything can happen. You can even get a full glass of beer at
a cocktail lounge.
RAYMOND CHANDLER, "Red Wind," 1946

This trope has an animist core. Perhaps more than any other place in the world, Los Angeles is seen as a city which irresistibly induces behavior, mainly demented. The craziness celebrated is by no means benign, not the New Yorker's Woody-Allen-charming neurosis. LA breeds Mansons,

Freeway Killers, random violence. Latent violence gives the city power and stature, adds another dimension to the heroism implicit in its tragic reach. In architecture, it encourages gesture, sometimes cynical, sometimes sensitive, always irrefutable. Pelli's Blue Whale edges up to this sensibility — not for any madness of form but because of the apparent arbitrariness of the placement of its mass in the city.

4. DISNEY

The future always looks good in the golden land, because no one
remembers the past.
JOAN DIDION

Disney is perhaps the transcendent Los Angelist concept, the probable site for the resolution of the city's enigma. For mainstream Los Angelists, Disneyland itself represents an ideal of benign manipulation, the crypto-vindication of the planner's fantasy no architect is ever truly without. Charles Moore's *Perspecta* article "You Have to Pay for the Public Life" — a seminal Los Angelist text — offers an early formulation of the position, arguing that Disneyland provides a highly successful solution to the problem of public placemaking, comparable, in some way, to Versailles. The article is a benchmark in the emergence of the current argument that Los Angeles truly has found alternative answers to conventional city problems.

But Disney is more than an argument about urbanism, it is also an argument about style. Its legitimation — and by extension the legitimation of all one-dimensionally iconic commercial architecture — frees the present, licensing a limitless profligacy in rummaging the past. But this is relatively unimportant. The Los Angelist view of Disney critically institutionalizes a kind of quicksilver taste by introducing a standard based on amusement which is here purged of most — but not all — traces of patronization. It permits the architect to appropriate virtually anything he or she wants from among the forbidden fruits of commercial imagery and yet still hedge the bet.

5. DEATH

Watching them, Hook realized that beyond his grief as Chris's father and
beyond his rage at the suicide lie, was another, smaller hell, and
it was simply that his son had died here, in this land of sunshine and
desperation. For it struck him that to die in California was to
fall not on foreign soil so much as in a foreign time, an alien and brutal
and loveless future that he despised as well as feared.
NEWTON THORNBURG, *To Die in California*, 1973

This is a concept more ambiant than central, except as it figures in other categories. Los Angeles as Necropolis was certainly an abiding motif in local fiction, from *Day of the Locust* to *The Loved One*. To Los Angelists, Forest Lawn is less a shrine than a Disneyland for stiffs. For them, death is simply a lesser attribute of the region. Frederick Fisher's solar crematory is interesting in this sense, for its regionalism rather than its architecture.

6. THE MOVIES

My first evening in Hollywood. It was so typical that I almost thought it
had been arranged for me. It was by sheer chance, however, that
I found myself rolling up to the home of a millionaire in a handsome
black Packard. I had been invited to dinner by a perfect stranger.
I didn't even know my host's name. Nor do I know it now.
HENRY MILLER, *The Air-conditioned Nightmare*, 1945

Like death, movies are peripheral to the Los Angelist. What they crucially represent for writers — simultaneous artistic degradation and a lottery for very high stakes with deceptively good-looking odds — they do not suggest to architects, for whom success is somewhat differently calibrated. Like death, the movies are a regional attribute that is important in setting tone. To a limited degree. They do represent an alternative practice, but a truly discontinuous one. The role the studios play for writers in symbolizing and propagating a culture of fantasy and shadows is, for the architectural Los Angelist, played by Disneyland and related effluvia.

7. BANALITY

He dropped off his work clothes, hung them in a closet, and stepped
naked into the bathroom, where he turned on the water for
a bath. Here again was reflected the civilization in which he lived, but
with a sharp difference. For whereas it was, and still is, a
civilization somewhat naive as to lawns, living rooms, pictures and other
things of an esthetic nature, it is genius itself, and has forgotten
more than all other civilizations ever knew, in the realm of practicality.
The bathroom that he now whistles in was a utile jewel; it was
clean as an operating room; everything was in its proper place and
everything worked.
JAMES M. CAIN, *Mildred Pierce*, 1941

Again we near the heart of the matter. The cheerful inclusivism of the Los
Angelist must embrace this tradition as well. Thus must banality be stripped
of its evil and so confer the pluralist benison. If to any enterprise, it is to this
one that the emerging wave devotes itself. Gehry, of course, is the titan, the
single-handed redeemer of a whole home supply mart of taboo possibilities.
He is joined in this by the swelling *Gehryschule*. The problem is that they —
unlike James M. Cain's character — are not naive at all as to lawns, living
rooms, pictures, and other things of an aesthetic nature, which leads to a
troubling hierarchical confusion: there is yet no cogent view of the actual
relationship between aestheticized banality and its predecessor sensibility
which relies for its art on a gaze. Equality is clearly not on the cards, nor, I
think, is an evolutionary model; certainly not a thuggish Pevsnerian dividing
line which forces architects involved with this trope to wink at their own
work.

8. AMERICA

Los Angeles is the Middle West raised to the flash-point ...
REYNER BANHAM

Such is the common view: Los Angeles as America in extremis. The position differs from that of the Los Angelists at the turn of the century who
saw the West as the tabula rasa on which a perfected version of America

might be written. Both then and now, though, the issue is the same: the relation of California to the rest of the country, the problem of isolating its singularity within the American context. The new view springs from a much modified take on the US, full of destiny still but drained of charm. Indeed, the pejorative vision of the Los Angelist shapes up right at this locus. Los Angeles is a place where nothing is done by halves, a culture which exaggerates by nature, a town that gives full throat to others' latency. For LA this represents integrity. For the rest of the country it conjures a hulking, evil unconscious, waiting to vent its rage. If anything, it is this sense of virtuous difference that cements a bond between architects of the region and exonerates them from misunderstanding.

9. CARS

And now, as he drives, it is as if some kind of auto-hypnosis exerts itself.
We see the face relax, the shoulders unhunch themselves, the
body ease itself back into the seat. The reflexes are taking over; the left
foot comes down with firm, even pressure on the clutch pedal,
while the right prudently feeds in gas. The left hand is light on the
wheel; the right slips the gearshift with precision into high. The
eyes, moving unhurriedly from road to mirror, mirror to road, calmly
measure the distances ahead, behind, to the nearest car.... After
all, this is no mad chariot race — that's only how it seems to onlookers
or nervous novices — it is a river, sweeping in full flood toward
its outlet with a soothing power. There is nothing to fear, as long as you
let yourself go with it; indeed, you discover, in the midst of its
stream-speed, a sense of indolence and ease.
CHRISTOPHER ISHERWOOD, *A Single Man*, 1964

The Zen view is definitive Los Angelist. How could any real embrace avoid the main symbol of the culture? Architectural consequences are fuzzier, more to be grasped by tourists than practitioners. Banham's paean to freeway landscaping and auto-liberation, with its invocations of Sixtus and Haussman, is most representative. The opposing view has been made eloquently by Peter Plagens in his article "The Ecology of Evil."

10. THE ARTIST

Ars Gratia Artis
MGM Motto

The figure of the artist enjoys particular pride of place in the Los Angelist pantheon. For it is the artist who embodies the major element of the Los Angelist method: the organizing gaze. Los Angelism is more of a gift than a theory, a faculty for seeing things the right way, the power of the comprehending eye. Tod Hackett, Nathanael West's hero, is the archetype. Hired out of Yale to work in a studio, he watches fascinatedly from somewhere on the sidelines as the city's madness unfolds in front of him, storing and transforming it and finally putting it down in a painting called "The Burning of Los Angeles," which, West writes, would definitively prove that he "had talent." Has there ever been a book about LA that doesn't have a David Hockney or Ed Ruscha illustration? With Los Angelism, the artist is king because, like Plato's philosopher, his understanding is deepest.

How many architects in LA think of themselves as artists, how many chroniclers think of their slide collections as works of art? The answer is, of course, very many: the cooptation of view is the most important Los Angelist act. Alteration of some known reality, whether the surfboard decorated, the stick-style bungalow Hispanicized, or the Oldsmobile customized, affirms that you've got the basic operation in your grasp, that you understand at least something. Architecture likewise operates under an imperative to find the unfamiliar which, in its strangeness, will attest clearly to what it is not. Just look at it.

11. BACK EAST

Wish they all could be California girls.
The Beachboys

This good-natured anthem of local imperialism actually takes in the whole country of which the East is also not precisely a part. If Los Angeles is distinct from America in general, it is seen as the opposite of the East which therefore represents the alternative. It is the place to go to shun the heightened Americanness which lies somewhere near LA's ambivalent core. It is also the place to tap into jettisoned history, the only place where the affirming balm of continuity corroborated is dispensed. By now, bicoastalism is a contemptibly familiar concept; but rugged in practice. The greatest threat to the Los Angelist is to lose grip of the balance and let his or her work get stained by the goo of sameness that comes from the Easterner's reverence for an architecture of convention. You could lose your bolds. This is what happens to mental or literal peripatetics. It is what happened to Hodgetts, possibly the most brilliant of the group, whose built work pales into tameness beside the vivid imaginings that flow from his pen. The East is, above all, the civilization that created the Los Angelist, symbiotically locked into the system of falsification they invent.

12. THE FUTURE

Why is our work missing here? What are we passing by, what aren't we
doing? What aren't we listening to?
FRANK GEHRY

Los Angeles has ceased to be America's most current version of the city of the future, a role taken over by Houston or perhaps by EPCOT. This may explain the current surge of interest by Los Angelists, for whom the place has taken on a comforting stasis, destined to be historically unique, like London. The less it seems a prototype, the more its special place is affirmed. Without the hounding impetus to progress, the system can close in on itself and shake off the troubles that come with being exemplary. Let the chroniclers move in as we internalize our system of references so that what we do becomes comprehensible. The future is over, we have arrived, so let us present ourselves to the public.

I have great nostalgia for the future. But the Los Angelist cannot abide these continual interruptions and upsets. Clarity overwhelms speculation, the parts — as in those exploded drawings Morphosis specializes in — obliterate the whole. It may be that the end of Los Angeles's prospects for unexpected transformation will prove congenial to the nurturing of new architecture, to the growth of some climax form. Who knows? At least it won't go unrecorded.

1982

THE PATH ALWAYS TAKEN*

It's not that banality is evil. Just that seriousness recedes before it. Criticism locates, or at least tries to locate, seriousness. Its first task of interpretation is the job of siting. The banality of the times is nowhere starker than in what passes for a critical tradition in the mass media. Here, by and large, critics tend to stand in the same relation to their subjects as advertisers do to their products. This has to do not simply with puffery but with the use of a limited lexicon of valuation, of a cluster of categories that by their very incantation assure legitimation of a subject.

Architecture, as an object of media consumption, has lately received a tremendous amount of attention. And the *New York Times* has played a leading role in inventing a standard for journalistic criticism of this subject. With the recent retirement of Ada Louise Huxtable, Paul Goldberger has become that paper's single architecture critic, and thus wields great influence. The symbiosis of *Times* and talent could not be greater. Goldberger's work is exemplary of the criticism of the age, of a kind of writing that seeks to code rather than to analyze, of the idea that taxonomy constitutes judgment. His new book, *The Skyscraper*, treats its fascinating subject as a typical *Times* piece might, but at greater length.

The Skyscraper is, to be sure, a "popularization," a general work, and thus relieved of a certain duty to apparatus: mere recitation acquires a certain methodological force, implying predetermination, as if history were its own author. A well-known building is shown, a reaction to it is quoted (more often than not from a hoary issue of the *Times*), and so we proceed to the next newsworthy event. By presenting history as intact, it seems inevit-

*Review of Paul Goldberger, *The Skyscraper*, New York 1981.

able — not something to be invented, merely something to be looked up. The canon of buildings presented in *The Skyscraper* is completely standard, if somewhat skewed in favor of New York City projects. Nothing is discovered, nothing unfamiliar intrudes on the corroborative act. The enshrined myth of origins, the Chicago-genesis, is recalled, and established problematics of skyscraper "development" are rehearsed. The picture that emerges grants virtually sole authorship to architects, and complete powers of interpretation to journalists, critics, and a small number of artists and writers who represent skyscrapers in their works, thereby affirming (like the inevitable *King Kong* shot) the potency of the skyscraper's image over the contemporary imagination. And so we set off, issues firmly in mind (the expression of "newness," the representation of "verticality," the errors of modernism) and ends clearly in view. What is left to do but annex, a chapter a decade?

If Goldberger has made no contribution to the invention of architectural history, he has surely added to the refinement of its rhetoric. As in most newspaper writing, in the absence of argument conviction is solicited by formal means. Goldberger's stature as a sophist is indisputable. His writing is smooth and ingratiating, his manner all reason and politesse, with a teeny bit of wit. Judgments have the appearance of balance, filled with Jesuitical unities; the casuistry is not of indecision but of transcendence, of the certainty of never saying anything disagreeable. Of course the Monadnock Building is rather great; of course Raymond Hood and John Mead Howells "were perhaps the most gifted molders of skyscraper form"; of course Louis Sullivan "prefigures" the International Style. One can scarcely rebuke Goldberger for shunning controversy and keeping to the path always taken: The critic of the *Times* does not dispute; he affirms. What rankles, though, is not the utter conventionality of selection, but the nearly total eradication of seriousness, the substitution of a code so simplified as to be nearly untrammeled by meaning. Here, then, is the rhetoric of the accepted categories in action.

The construction of these categories depends on only a few actual operations: grouping, juxtaposition and association. Grouping makes a category by establishing a threshold (here are a large number of buildings that look alike); juxtaposition promotes an opposition in order to embrace apparent disparateness (architecture today is in the midst of a conflict between "computer" and "historicist" aesthetics); association gives a more general kind of validation by introducing certain key terms and concepts that confer legitimacy and substance via the force of their status. While "abstract," "sculptural," "intellectual," "pure," and "panache" are not exactly words without qualities, they are words whose main quality, as Goldberger uses them, is their ability to suggest quality, to raise the aura of meaningfulness in the absence of meaning. And Goldberger, with his gift for pithy, summary statements, the kind of simplified discourse whose proper home is the movie marquee, uses these phrases well.

In a chapter called "The Triumph of Modernism," Goldberger presents Frank Lloyd Wright's Price Tower, built in 1955 in Bartlesville, Oklahoma. In his brief discussion there is a nice bit of Goldbergerese: "The tower is full of Wright's tense, energetic desire to break out of the box — it is a study in angles and cantilevers, tensile and tart, a building with far more ideas than its modest size seems to justify." A vigorous sentence, to be sure, but what does it actually mean? What is this box inside which Wright finds himself? Certainly not one of his own designing — if anyone was unfriendly to boxes, it was Wright. Then is it the modernist box, those Miesian buildings mentioned elsewhere in the chapter? Wright was never in this box, either, although he was arguably "boxed in" by the "modernist" (as if that meant anything) fashion of the time. Just a sentence or two back, however, we've been told that the Price Tower is based largely on an unbuilt scheme from 1928, a time when nobody was building boxes, the time of Deco's "flamboyant theatricality." Is Goldberger suggesting that the 1955 building has different desires than the 1928 project? How can he tell? And what is "tense" and "energetic"? Wright's desire to break out of the box? Yes. *And* the building, one assumes. But *how* is it tense and energetic? Expression seemingly devolves on "tensile and tart" angles and cantilevers, and on a seemingly unjustified number of ideas.

Goldberger apparently uses the hieratic word "tensile" more or less as a synonym for "tense." Here meaning is totally confounded. In a technical sense, "tension" is a simple, but crucial, concept of statics, a particular kind of physical stress. Of course, Wright's tension might also be stressful. Neither angles nor cantilevers, however, can be accurately described as tensile, nor, by extension, can the building. And what of "tart"? Beyond its obvious alliterative appeal, is it meant to suggest that the building is sour, piquant or saucy? And this notion of a relation between size and ideas? How many ideas are too many? And what about those buildings Goldberger admires for their powerful "minimalism" (quite a concept at fifty stories)? Do buildings ever have too few ideas? But there is a hedge here: there are "far more ideas than its modest size *seems* to justify." But are they justified? Is desire fulfilled? Is tension relieved?

This passage, like many others that typify the book's style and argument, if bankrupt at the immediate level, finds significance at a more profound one. It serves to add to the legitimacy of such discourse in the "criticism" of architecture, and, by so doing, helps preclude other ways of seeing and understanding. Buildings are to be viewed not as complex, condensed products of cultural aspirations, as instruments of social forces or as texts susceptible to and demanding readings of rigor and discipline, but as discrete incidents, as individual acts, as just another consumer product. There is no real harm in this book. Its mediocrity is too transparent and its photographs are too appealing. The harm is in the attitude that this is enough, in a spreading belief in the substance of banality. In any event, we await a real history of the skyscraper.

February 1982

TOWER HUNGRY

The point of the current MOMA skyscraper show is definitely at odds with its pleasures. Indeed, the curatorial rationale behind it entails such a heart-rending declaration of angst that one wonders whether the show is meant as the death-knell of civilization itself. Drexler writes: "Skyscrapers are machines for making money. They exploit land values to the point of rendering cities uninhabitable, but that is no reason to stop building them: in a free society [sic] capitalism gives us what we want, including our own demise." Never mind the interesting test of repressive tolerance at a Rockefeller institution currently involved in purveying condos in the clouds at a million a pop; this statement raises truly frightening prospects. Are we to expect Drexler's high-rise defenestration? Is this an allusion to the dangers of getting conked by debris tumbling from an upper story? The towering inferno? The apocalypse?

Fortunately, paranoia has not interfered with business as usual or deformed familiar rationales. The show presents three projects, all of which are designed for what might politely be called "financial institutions," although this programmatic commonality has no serious impact on questions of design. The buildings are by Norman Foster, Gordon Bunshaft, and Philip Johnson, the latter two of whom are museum trustees, a point actually observed in print by Paul Goldberger in an unprecedented nibble at the feeding hand (*New York Times*, January 30, 1983).

In fact, the three buildings fit nicely into the Chinese restaurant approach to exhibitions, representing three familiar, if languid, taxonomic streams in the critical approach to current building: "high-tech," "abstract-modernist," and "eclectic-historicist." Like all typological inventions, these categories have the useful side effect of falsification. The show's text claims that the three were selected for their contributions to the transformation of the nature of skyscrapers, but the buildings themselves seem to raise arguments largely about appearance, an argument reinforced by the familiar categorical lie of the objects in question.

Of these, Philip Johnson and John Burgee's is the clear loser. The main design schtick of this group of towers for a site in Boston is the attempt to mingle three unusually dreary skin types throughout the project. The catalogue refers to this as the "deployment of contradictory façades" entailing the "synoptic inclusion of most varieties of modernism, including the 'Palladian'." Such hooey notwithstanding, the project betrays the usual Johnson problem. Having cloaked himself in erudition he beggars seriousness for the most banal and random tactic. (A Palladian window! You don't say!) As with so much of Johnson's work, one sees only the outline of architecture, building more described than designed. The problem — skins, clusters of towers — gets stated but remains unsolved. Philip's tragedy is that the polish and politesse that has permitted his free movement among the older monied has deflected the delicious Robertson Boulevard sensibility that might otherwise have emerged. I'm not saying that a skyscraper with Palladian windows is entirely unamusing: merely that it represents the tip of a mighty iceberg likely never to be exposed.

Bunshaft's contribution is his well-published bank tower in Jeddah, the current architectural capital of the free world (sic). This is the triangular building with aerial oases that Drexler proclaims the first "Muslim skyscraper." What this means I am not sure: the orientation is not to Mecca. On the other hand, there *is* something Saudi about its feudal elevations, easily defensible should the local lumpen grow restive and decide to try to liberate some of the petrojillions from the burnoused oligarchs within. And the helipad might be useful for falconing. Mainly, though, it is a building without a context and as such must be seen as the source of its own problems. These are fairly straightforward and can be considered "resolved" on only two of three sides. On the third are glommed the elevator towers. Then again, two out of three ain't bad. Goldberger lamented the fact that the show fails to include any of the architect's study drawings and presents the Jeddah project as if it sprang full panoplied from Bunshaft's head. What can Paul be thinking? I can see Gordo crumbling yards of yellow trace as he struggles to arrange two identical squares on a rectangle.

Foster's building, on the other hand, is absolutely sensational. Perhaps Drexler's secret agenda was to humiliate Johnson and Bunshaft with the

HONGKONG & SHANGHAI BANK
(*Hong Kong*) Norman Foster

contrast. The tower — for a bank in Hong Kong — is strikingly original in concept and carried out with a meticulousness and dedication that is well embodied in the stunning models and drawings included in the show, themselves well worth the trip. To categorize this building in terms of its imagery is to slight its subtlety, sophistication, and effects, many of which promise to be dazzling. Foster has designed a fully resolved technical and aesthetic system which is so suave and convincing as to be virtually unprecedented, whatever its declared affinities with the Gothic cathedrals or the iron works of the nineteenth century. Still, for all its pizzazz, the building doesn't really depart from familiar *parti*: its typological triumph is in the slipped slab redeemed. The brilliance of the solution lies in the familiarity of the problem.

If Foster's tower is a mighty work of art, it cannot — as the show's premise somehow means to suggest — be regarded as a modification of the skyscraper's characteristic mode of production, either of space or of profit. Indeed, it is the perfect paradigm of that mode, occupying and abetting as it does one of the most artificially inflated pieces of real estate in the free (sic) world. The building's vaunted space-saving structural innovations will presumably be of interest to its owners principally for their ability to increase rentable space. Drexler nonetheless argues that the three buildings on exhibit represent a "rethinking of what constitutes a humane environment." How this differs from his lament over skyscrapers that merely embody "features" memorable enough for advertising value is not clear: the three buildings in no way alter the bureaucratic production relations that have always lain at the heart of the skyscraper's real inhumanity.

March 1983

THE BIG MAN ON CAMPUS

The Academy holds a long and hospitable history for James Stirling. The wondrous creative burst that flung him to prominence comprised a collegiate quartet: Leicester, Oxford, Cambridge, St. Andrews. One remembers these projects as more than merely magnificent but as sumps for controversy, sending greybeards from their smug ruminations around the commons' tables into the zones of apoplexy. Here was boldness and shock, an architecture whose native beauties thrived, it seemed, in opposition. Now a quadrivium from America's inner circle of learning has commissioned Stirling & Wilford to build their first projects in the new world, and naturally one looks for an intensity to rival the first famous four. But something has happened! The master has been somehow seduced: the new projects carry the uniform taint of complacency and the current (American) thing. It's all so well-mannered and genial it doesn't even seem to be there. The standard anecdote among architects making their first pilgrimages to Rice University is the one about not being able to find the building. Sympathetic critics scramble to uncover Stirlingesque tokens in describing the work, like art authenticators judging an attribution that was in some doubt. Underneath lurks a Delilah-like satisfaction at seeing the mighty tamed. His Pritzker Prize gets referred to in substantiation as if it were a good-conduct medal.

What can be the reason for this American dilemma? Perhaps it's another story of the English abroad, trekking out in pith helmets and returning in burnouses, the pith taken out of them by the natives. Perhaps it's just nerves at a debut performance, the intimidations of competing with the first American efforts of the likes of Corb or Aalto. Perhaps there's the playing-it-safe of a man whose native commissions are so sporadic that his tread must be sensibly cat-like in the promised land of the fatted client and the big building. Perhaps it's the further unfolding of the unspoken Krier-neurosis that seems to underlie such a chunky problematic area in the current oeuvre. Whatever it is, though, the American production is a dis-appointment, reflecting both profound change and profound ambivalence.

Notwithstanding Stirling's own arguments to the contrary, the new work is different. I'm not arguing here that the neo-classical mode is neces-sarily unbecoming, simply that it's a departure. Moreover, it's a departure that seems thoroughly consonant with the times, with the current hegemony of the stolid and the fuss over copy-book forms. Yet what strikes me most about Stirling's situation is the Janus-like divide that cracks across so many of his projects, the literal twoness of expression that's now become endemic. It's a tricky line to toe: there's a point at which collage becomes schiz, a point that becomes more visible every time it's made. Judging only from photographs, the Stuttgart museum looks to be a satisfying building, a vindication of the new manner. Much attention has already been called to those spindly, brightly-coloured industrial bits, grafted on or inserted as a decorative strategy. It's an amusing and ironic conceit, ribbing the current appliqué fetish by *applying* the tech instead of obscuring it with dumb festoons of classical doodads. But if the gesture has wit, it also has pathos: there's an element of Stirling's resistence to the surrender of a language he loves, a fight against the tides of assimilation. Stirling wants to make sure we know he still remembers the old (new) language, that his roots are still intact, however much he decks himself out in fashionable garb.

The building at Rice — the first of the four to be completed — derives its strategy through the contrast between in and out. The elevations of the building are all "contextual" (which in the current reading seems to mean imitative) responses to the surrounding campus, a Ralph Adams Cram confection of red brick, limestone, and a certain wacky Moorish abandon. Stirling & Wilford's wing is itself an addition to a lesser addition to this larger ensemble, the boringly detailed and clumsy School of Architecture building, not the work of the campus's distinguished progenitor but of some forgotten successor hack. With a reverence vacillating between archae-ologism and silliness, Stirling's wing shows the original a respect that would never be its due outside the larger context of good behavior. It's a work caught in the bind of emulating mediocrity and the result is what one might expect from such an enterprise.

Part of the reason is that the process takes Stirling into a region where

STAATSGALLERIE
(*Stuttgart*) James Stirling

he's never been especially adept. He has always had stronger skill at the composition of masses, textures, and volumes than at the delicate and lithe array of the fragments of an elevation. Rice shows a compendium of failed details, unconvincing rhythms, and kitsch wit. I'm not sure why, but Stirling — master of the use of circular forms in plan — cannot use them in elevation to save his life. That round window on the wing's end wall, for example, is an indisputable lapse. The interior of the addition is a different matter. Here the idiom is the old (new) Stirling, the marvelous maven of the modern. It's a bit white (another American obsession) but at least the forms have some oomph, especially the weenie-shaped lateral insertion that serves as the conceptual and literal joint between the new and old wings. The new even pops strainingly through the old in the form of two winsome shuttlecock-shaped skylights.

Still, taken as a whole, it's a wimpy and undistinguished work. And what a contrast with the school of architecture which Philip Johnson proposes to erect for his supine clients at the University of Houston across town. No timid reverence for the grand borrower but a dead-on and deadly copy of an unbuilt Ledoux. In America, nice buildings finish last.

The Fogg Museum — presently nearing completion — is also an essay in the campus-context trope. Here, though, the context is more convoluted, for not only are there the predictable particulars of site and adjacencies, complicated by the eclectic range of neighboring structures, there is also the larger context of Cambridge, Massachusetts, a town which is some-body's version of Parnassus. As John Coolidge suggested in his article in *Architectural Review* (March 1983), Stirling's Fogg is to be his certification and welcome into the Cambridge (and hence cosmic) pantheon, so brilliantly described by the earlier efforts of Aalto and Corb. The masterpiece is pre-certified.

This is a lot of pressure for a relatively modest building to sustain and, as far as I can tell by a look at the incomplete structure, the work isn't really up to the event. The building is actually an annex — located across a fairly busy street — to the dull neo-Georgian Fogg Museum, repository of the Harvard University Art Collection and department of art history. The new piece also combines gallery and office space, if on a smaller scale. What the Stirling building has uniquely, though, is a monumentally sized grand stair and entrance foyer. Indeed, the building is otherwise essentially a shed to house this dramatic section.

The gesture is an interesting and curious one. At one level, it's a response to the great Cambridge tradition of the straight-run stair. This is most notably exemplified in the gorgeous, luminous staircase of Aalto's Baker House at MIT. The big circulation gesture equally animates Corb's Carpenter Center, just up the street, with its soaring ramp, as diagrammatically straight a run as one could find. Likewise, John Andrews' adjacent Gund Hall (a signal failure to gain entry to the "sanctum sanctorum" with the resultant exile of the architect to the Australian outback) is organized around a stepping section, a straight run on a jumbo scale. The weird thing about the Fogg, though, is that the thundering heroics of entry and ascent lead nowhere, all that axiality just gets you to the top. It's as if the building were a piece dislodged from a much larger structure or waiting for a big building to grow up around it. It's the Asplund library entry without the library. By siting the entrance to the building opposite the present Fogg, one crosses from new to old by climbing the stair and then doubling back through a little corridor to a big and awful bridge spanning the street. This issue, however, may prove moot given spirited citizen opposition to the link.

Outside, the strategy is stripes. The envelope is a comparatively dumb one, filling out the site lines, holding the street in all the right places. The façades are got up in alternating floor-deep bands of glazed brick of unusually putrid color. Into these bands apertures are punched and glazed with standard-issue-good-taste bronze-colored sash. Much has been made of Stirling's having eschewed the opportunity to position these windows in a regular pattern, instead locating them according to the position of maximum utility for illuminating the rooms behind. Here's the site of the building's bifurcate irony: the windows get spotted as per the old functionalist formula, appliquéd to decorate a façade that's busy sending the contrary signal. The post-mod theme is affirmed by the building's main outward move, its massive quoined portal, columned "ex antis" and penetrated by a little Mycenaean-shaped glass entry shed.

Perhaps the final irony in the building's weighty recantation of modish mod lies in the fact that the previous occupant of the site was an utterly canonical white brick International Style lecture theatre, demolished in the name of progress. "Sic transit gloria modi."

Of the four projects, the Columbia chemistry lab is the only one likely to be left unbuilt. This is through no fault of Stirling's but the result of budgetary and bureaucratic retrenchment. The project itself, however, remains perhaps the strongest example among the four of the directly double manner. The building was to have filled in the last vacant corner of

McKim, Mead & White's great palazzoid beaux-arts campus. Stirling does the right thing by his responsibilities to the envelope, proposing a street side volume that lines nicely up with its neighbors and grooves on their fenestration rhythms. The only real florishes are a Stuttgart-style Egyptian cornice and an unconvincing pattern of three-sided window framers like those more consistently applied in the swell Berlin science center project.

Round the back, though, things are mighty different. Here a great trussed wing protrudes at an angle from the main volume of the building, dramatically supported at its far end by a single column. The rationale offered for this is the fact that the wing is obliged to span over an existing gymnasium, itself built to provide bearing opportunities for new construction above at specific points. The rationale for the span is extended to the rationale for its trussed-up and technical language; the form, to coin a phrase, following the function. Of course, this was the same ostensible reason for the McKim style dress-up back on Broadway except that the authority for the two rationales answers to very different sources, the one technical (the old functionalism) and the other contextual (the new historicism).

This is fine, I suppose. What's troubling is that the line of transformation seems so totally whimsical. After all, the context (the backsides of the same buildings that formed the context on the street) hasn't changed, and neither has the generative functional situation (it all sits on top of the gym). One naturally expects to find a clue to the answer at the joint but here the expression is most ineffable. There is an incised knuckle at the intersection of the two wings but it's filled with a curvy and insubstantial glass shape, mod-arch at its most amorphously pretty. The little lounge (for this is what it is programmed to be) mediates by throwing its hands in the air. The building — like the manner behind it — finally just can't make sense of itself.

Like the Berlin science center, the Cornell arts complex is a study of forms in conjunction. It draws its coherence from a long linking gallery (with detail similar to a gallery in the Berlin project) which overlooks the gorge along which the project is dramatically sited; on some interesting sectional moves; and on a general expressive consistency. While the strategy of aggregation is legible volumetrically, it largely disappears at the level of plan to the project's detriment. Where the Berlin scheme had the tension of rotation, collision, and dissimilarity of shape, the Cornell center is everywhere arrayed orthogonally, strung along at right angles to the organizing arcade/loggia. The bulk of the items along the axial link is such that one does not read the project as a "long" building (like the master's great long work such as the Olivetti headquarters or the Dorman Long scheme) but as an aggregation of fattish volumes.

This said, however, it's also clear that the Cornell building is the best, most sophisticated, most cogent of the American projects. Stirling & Wilford have been stimulated by the programmatic complexity of the center into producing a building of relatively complex expression. More, the scheme's main event, that gorge-skimming loggia, is a lovely thing, handsome in conception and clearly destined to be handsome in use. The central body space and the sequence of arrival to it is also measured and fine. Indeed, the core of the building is its most coherent and graceful interlude, a fact emblematized by the perspective views put out by the Stirling office by which the project is now essentially known. I refer in particular to the one which depicts two Krier-esque Homo Faber types hoisting a wooden beam (presumably hewn from the tree whose stump occupies the foreground) into place to finish off the job.

The import of this charming William Morrisoid view strikes me as somewhat larger in scope than simple publicity, limning the heart of Stirling's current concerns as stylist. The Cornell project is decked out in a style that's a sort of stripped Italianate collegiate, a classicized neutrality meant to at once evoke solidity and the picturesque. It invokes the good feelings that attend the image of hill towns and the moral cachet that is currently associated with explicitly primitive trabeation. It's a style that identifies making good with making nice and it fills itself with iconic courtesies. To its credit, it avoids the fraudulent learning of current American historicist concerns: Stirling knows, at least, that his problem is not the concealment of incompetence. Still, he seems to have been taken in by an ethic that has, in large measure, grown up for precisely that purpose. Perhaps it's just personal pique, but I hate watching the progress of this seduction. The great man's temperament seems too tempered by the times. I want the old Jim back.

April 1984

THE OFFICIAL STYLE

There is no mistaking Washington for anything but a capital city. Every intersection seems to be obstructed by some bronze Cincinnatus on his pigeon-streaked nag. The whole town is in uniform, whether the baroque military version or the more austere Brooks Brothers regulation mufti. And looming at the end of every Federal vista is the backdrop of monumental officialdom, "classical" architecture.

From the earliest days of the Republic, classical architecture has been the designated idiom for national construction. To the founding persons — especially Thomas Jefferson — classical architecture evoked the Athenian polis and the Roman republic, the very cradles of democracy. But whatever meanings the 18th century hitched to it, classical architecture has come to be less a symbol of liberty and citizenship than the pre-eminent icon for architecture itself. Heavy with the import of permanence and continuity, it fairly reeks of dignity and authority. From Moscow to Manila, the most marginal despot, if he has any pretensions at all, longs to be remembered in Corinthian perpetuity.

Today, however, the vocabulary of architectural classicism has dwindled to a mere repertoire of institutional gestures. The problem is no longer how to achieve architectural authenticity, but simply how to get the most bang for the buck, that is, how to retain maximum authority with minimum form. In its most common guise — so-called stripped neo-classicism — today's official style reduces classical tropes to a handful while adding emphasis via multiplications of scale. In the new Madison Building — a mammoth addition to the Library of Congress — classicism is recalled abstractly by an endless entry colonnade. The ideas "steps," "columns," and "enormous" are efficiently blended to signal truly great official weight.

Many observers have noted the building's uncanny resemblance to Ludwig Troost's *Haus der Kunst* in Munich, the most enduring building of the Third Reich.

The recently completed Philip Hart Senate Office Building makes even more subtle use of classical authority. The building manages to look undeniably official without recalling any of the standard classical images: no pediments, no pilasters, no perspectival devices. The logic of its closet classicism — in which allusion is substituted for quotation — emerges from the building's juxtaposition with its two older neighbors. The three Senate Office Buildings together form a striking museum of architectural devolution.

The earliest, the 1906 Richard Russell Building, exemplifies neoclassicism in full beaux-arts bloom. Designed by Carrère and Hastings, architects of the New York Public Library, the building is encrusted with the entire repertoire of ancient forms. It also happens to be grand architecture with a richness and complexity of space and expression that at once acknowledges and is enabled by the rich and complex tradition from which it so consciously springs.

By contrast, its neighbor, built by Eggers and Higgins in 1958, is just hack work. The Everett Dirksen Building is the sort of edifice one might expect to find housing the speech or hygiene department at an excessively prosperous state university. The style here is less a stripped than what might be called a relic classicism: a mainly mute mass spruced up with a few token cartouches, carved doorways and decorative incisings — buzz forms to jog the architectural memory.

The Hart Building lacks even these gestures, bearing no direct relation to the style of its predecessors other than its carefully adjusted stone coursing lines. But the renunciation of classical drag has not sapped the building's power to express official authority. In its devolved form the building has a studied inventory of persuasive rhetorical devices.

The first tactic is the invocation of the official material. Hart is covered with a layer of marble so dazzlingly white, so conspicuously lavish, that the specifics of architectural detail are rendered irrelevant. Rhetorically, the gleaming marble serves two purposes. The first is to suggest a continuity that was previously evoked by classical forms. Here, though, the legitimizing thread has been pared down to the simplicity of an advertisement, a paragon of semiotic efficiency.

If the expressive means are lean, their second message is fatted. Those planar expanses of marble are unadorned so that nothing will interfere with the perception of their extent. Profligacy is the current theme of official expression — the articulation of power through waste. During the seven years of its construction (Rome wasn't built in a day), the Hart Building was a constant source of controversy as costs spiraled and overran and as the luxuries the one hundred Senators were providing themselves with were revealed, debated and disavowed. The construction process thus became paradigmatic of the process of government, the architectural equivalent of the B–1 or the MX. Excessive in itself, the building asserts a willingness to incur tremendous, pointless expense as an affirmation of mutual resolve and a symbol of official consequence.

Perhaps the most admired recent example of the new official style is I.M. Pei's addition to the National Gallery of Art. The East Wing is widely held to be an exemplar of successful devolutionary neo-classicism, a modern building that manages to evoke and complement the spirit of its more literal predecessor. The means employed are similar to those used in the Hart. Here, too, are profligate planes of stone, overwhelming in their continuous extent. The great achievement of this building, though, is the way Pei supplants the classicist expectation of elaboration and ornament with a simple rhapsody to mechanical stonecutting, replacing craft with precision. Instead of elaborately carved capitals and decorations, there are angles and joints that are giddily smooth. Instead of texture, the building offers an orgy of the uniform. Truly, this is the triumph of bureaucracy and expense over art and tradition.

The East Wing and the Hart Building share another important feature: each is centered on an enormous atrium. The official grandeur of machined marble is made emphatic by a profligacy of enclosure. At the National Gallery, the functional display areas are arrayed in stultifyingly inefficient subservience to the admittedly impressive central gesture, which at least retains some rationale as an exhibition space.

At Hart, the extravagance is purer, more unabashedly functionless. This literal waste, however, is transcended by a resonant symbolic agenda. In proportion, and substantially in detail as well, the atrium of the Hart Building closely resembles that of a typical Hyatt Regency Hotel, lacking only the essential cocktail bar. Like the enclosed spaces in suburban shopping malls, atria have come to represent the late-20th-century American ideal of a civic place: enclosed, hermetic, regulated, and grand, but without any reference to cities, city dwellers, or citizenship.

If there is a general threat to architecture in this country (and there is), it is that meaning is being reduced to a restricted set of codes yielding a Pavlovian architecture of instant, superficial recognition. Seen this way, these latest official buildings are the civic equivalent of a roadside McDonald's: the primary function of a colonnade, a marble façade or the golden arches is simply to provide a recognizable icon. Style becomes defined not in terms of any independent "artistic" consequences but simply in terms of how efficiently it serves the purpose of manufacturing recognition. You need only a few architectural signifiers to get over the message "classical" and thereby invoke whatever additional meanings have attached themselves to it.

Many people — especially post-modernists — argue that the solution to this impoverishment is to revert to ancient models. This misses the point: the loss is not of a particular exhausted style but of something much larger. Official Washington offers no resistance to rampant historicism of any kind. Neither can the capital's architectural bankruptcy be blamed on modernism. In fact, modernism has had almost no influence here. However simple their forms, the Hart and Madison Buildings aren't remotely modernist; they are rather examples of neo-classicism at its most anorexic, self-starved of serious meaning. These buildings are the architectural analogue of neo-conservatism; they attempt to replace architectural laws with a kind of aesthetic law and order. Intended or not, their message is precisely in their failure, and in their lawlessness, which is the real meaning of Washington's official style. We may have exactly the official architecture we deserve.

July 1984

SOM STORY*

Some years ago, I had a job which put me in the position to dispense a certain amount of minor league architectural largesse. As a result I often found myself at lunch with architects looking to do the small projects under my control. On one of these occasions, my luncheon partner was a man who, in his previous life, had worked at Skidmore, Owings and Merrill in New York, where, among other things, he had been job captain on the Beineke Rare Book Library at Yale.

If you recall, Beineke is the one designed by Gordon Bunshaft, where the translucent marble panels of the exterior walls produce a fairly astonishing lighting effect. Well, according to the story related by my supplicant of the day, it was not originally intended to be thus: Gordo wanted onyx. The problem was, very few onyx quarries existed rich enough to yield sufficient material in the dimensions required. So, as the tale went, my friend the job captain was dispatched to scour the globe for a suitable source of the precious mineral. After a long and frustrating journey, met with many disappointments, he heard about an Algerian quarry that sounded unusually promising. Only trouble was, the civil war was in full heat and battles were raging in the vicinity. What to do? SOM's emissary cabled New York for instructions. I put my coffee cup down in anticipation of the denouement of this tale, and it was well that I did. Gordo's cabled reply had been terse: "Arrange truce."

Apocryphal or not, this anecdote has always meant Skids to me. The point isn't the architecture, it's the power. My sense of the historic amplitude and potency of the organization was recently affirmed by the delivery

---

*Review of *SOM: Sidmore, Owings and Merrill, Architecture and Urbanism 1973–1983*, introduction and regional prefaces by Albert Bush-Brown, translated by Oswald W. Grube, New York 1984.

into my hands of a publication of the syndicate's work for the years 1973–1983. For starters, the tome weighs a ton, and reproduces an aggregate square footage of built projects comparable to the land area of Sierra Leone, never mind a collective budget greater than the GNPs of the entire Third World. The text, written by Albert Bush-Brown with the astute emptiness befitting a corporate brochure, treats the firm less as an architectural practice than as a national entity (multinational, in fact) which responds not to artistic developments but to shifts in the social and political milieu. In tone, it aspires to *Foreign Affairs* rather than *Artforum*. This is appropriate: SOM is one of the first architectural operations to have its own foreign policy. Reinforcing this global reading is the presence of a parallel text in German, the other pre-eminent language of fully rationalized Western corporatism.

The book is divided by region, a format apparently dictated by marketing rather than aesthetic concerns: the work itself is completely indistinguishable. Each of these sections is heralded by a two-page cityscape (San Francisco, New York, Jeddah), bearing a somewhat overweening if not entirely unjustified implication of proprietorship. About the work there is little to say that you don't already know. Perhaps the real secret of Skids' success is in entirely insulating their clients from the unexpected. In detail and in part, the same projects appear over and over again. The most successful of these, as ever, impress by either simplicity (the woodsy Weyerhauser in Tacoma) or magnitude (the Haj Terminal in Saudi). The only newish development revealed by the catalogue is a certain ad agency facility at mild variations of image, yielding a vague if distinguishable Arabism, Classicism, Baragànism, as required, as well as a somewhat faster uptake on appropriating and recombining elements gleaned from the work of other firms – although it may finally be pointless to try to assign authorship to the chamfer, echelon plan, or greenhouse lobby.

Obviously, this is not a book that's really meant to be bought, not at fifty bucks a pop. But at one copy to each of the firm's clients, there should be many printings. The book about Skidmore, Owings and Merrill that I'd actually like to buy is the one without any photographs (except maybe that of the partner caught *in flagrante*), the one that tells how they did it and how they keep it up, the one with purloined memos and unbelievable gossip. God may be in a mullion but the real story of SOM's power lies in another kind of detail.

1984

SCARPA, IN THE DETAILS

When the Italian architect Carlo Scarpa died in 1978 at the age of 72, the body of work he left behind was small and virtually unknown in this country. His position in Italy, if somewhat less obscure, was strongly enigmatic. Both Scarpa's production and his persona entailed difficulty. As a designer, his output was intensely singular, not easily classified within any familiar tendency or taxonomy. Passionate for the artisanal practice of architecture, he was dismissed by some for pursuing too small a territory, for the parochialism of his poetic preoccupations. During the rabid sectarianism of the '60s and '70s, his failure at alliance with any of the contesting factions resulted in his being embarrassed out of his academic post. At the same time, he was the object of a lengthy lawsuit by the professional organization of Venetian architects for practicing without the sanctions of an academic degree. Ironically, his accidental death came on the eve of some redress of this abuse: he was about to be presented with a doctorate, *ad honoris causa*.

Happily, Scarpa has begun to receive the recognition and influence long his due. His work is being published, his drawings displayed, and his projects are now firmly established on the architectural pilgrimage route. This is a bracing development, especially in the United States where Scarpa's work is a strong antidote to the vapid posturing and superficial appliqué that is the leading element in current practice. An object lesson in the seriousness, the profundity, of Scarpa's concerns is to be found in a small exhibition of his drawings, recently mounted at the School of Architecture at Yale under the curatorship of my colleague George Ranalli, one of a series of shows that has made the school's gallery a center for serious architecture.

The Yale show is devoted entirely to drawings from a single project, the

BRION FAMILY TOMB
(*Treviso*) Carlo Scarpa

Brion family cemetery in Treviso, arguably Scarpa's masterpiece. Built in the years 1970–72 to house the tombs of a design-loving industrialist and his family, it was to become, in addition, Scarpa's own burial place, a fact that vividly materializes its central position in his oeuvre. The cemetery itself is an extension of a small-town graveyard and takes the form of a contemplative garden, providing its precincts — comprising tombs, chapel, cloister, meditation pavilion, pool, and lawns — for use by the public. In spirit, the tomb defies familiar strategies of monumentalization, substituting memorial by the intensification of private experience. It offers — in lieu of some schematically synthetic gesture — a collection of incidents that proposes to absorb rather than to awe, to animate all the individual acts (remembering, mourning, praying) entailed in graveside visits instead of subsuming them in some unitary symbol of the ineffable: this is no pyramid.

If the Brion Cemetery represents a scrupulous and dense architectural expression of human ritual, it is also a veritable Rosetta Stone for Scarpa's formal predilections. Architects nowadays love to arrogate to themselves the title of poet. But, for the most part, these are poets without prosody, lacking the meticulous crafts of language (save in their self-serving verbal polemics) that distinguish poetic endeavor. Scarpa is the genuine article. Possessed of one of the greatest aptitudes for architectural detail of any modern practitioner, he's in a league with Otto Wagner and Frank Lloyd Wright, two of his recurring sources of inspiration. It was Mies van der Rohe who first mouthed the seminal modernist aphorism, "God is in the details." The investigation to which he referred, however, was somewhat different from the one Scarpa's output embodies. The classic Miesian detail, while particular to its problem (say, how to turn a corner with a curtain wall), was generally the resolution of some difficulty in a system. That is to say, the solution was replicable. With Scarpa, moving always in the spirit of craft, every detail remains particular, the investigation of some unique condition. This is the power of his work. One cannot represent it with a diagram or describe it with a sentence: it unfolds bit by bit, gathering intensity.

As the drawings reveal, Scarpa's working method was completely isomorphic with his architectural intent, his drawing effectively continuous with the construction of his buildings. For those whose experience of architectural drawing is confined to the current gallery scene, these may prove unexpected: they are not precisely pretty, nor is precious pictorialism their purpose. Looking at them, one sees Scarpa at work, manipulating forms and images, investigating, solving problems: designing. The sheets themselves, generally starting out as measured studies of some particular aspect of the project, are covered in sketches, dense with alternatives and inventive refinements. In his office, according to accounts, Scarpa worked by over-laying drawing after drawing until the build-up became so dense that he resorted to painting over it with white tempera and starting again, thickening further a page straining at the limits of its two-dimensionality.

Taken together, the drawings present studies — at various levels of resolution — of most of the elements of the cemetery ensemble. In their slow accretion of the specific, Scarpa's methods and rhythms emerge, above all his patience and private inventory of imagery. This includes, among other things, an almost obsessively repeated ziggurat form, a fascination with circular openings, an amazing sense of the use of materials in juxtaposition (the project arrays concrete, metal, stone, glass, tile, wood, water, and planting with complete calm), a wonderful discourse of the mechanical (including a glass door which the user must force down into the earth to pass, an action expressed and enabled by a beautiful mechanism of pulleys and polished brass counterweights) and a marvelous affinity for water, a sensitivity perhaps too often attributed to Scarpa's close relationship to the Veneto.

In many of the drawings one notices that Scarpa has sketched a woman, often nude — either as a scale figure within a drawing or as a doodle in the margins. At first balance, this seems like late-blossoming adolescent prurience, a slightly lascivious addition to the page, never mind the graphic balance that the more organic form counterposes to the Euclidean order of the architectural investigation. One notices other amendments to the page as well. On several sheets, for example, there are considerable blotchy red marks, unmistakable wine stains. And it's in this context that the women really figure. In his work and in his interviews (Scarpa scrupulously never wrote) there is a fascination for fecundity, for metaphors of birth and renewal, for the corporealization of architecture. And this is the message he leaves: that the sensualization of architecture is a craft revealed only through the most patient investigation and only by dedication to architecture at its most primary locations. Scarpa was a man who spent his life contemplating the relationship of a wall to its openings, and if architecture has anything approximating a metaphysic, this is certainly where it's at.

Anyone who's read Emma Goldman's autobiography is sure to have vivid impressions of her apartment on East Thirteenth Street, the one described by her as a "home of lost dogs." Thanks to the vigilance of the War Resisters' League, a plot to expunge this landmark has been exposed. When the property was sold several years ago, the landlord quietly changed its street number from 210 to 208 for reasons which, if undisclosed, are obviously sinister. As the League has pointed out in a recent leaflet, this sly mystification has born ironic fruit: even the *New York Red Pages*, a radical guide book, identifies the house as 212! Let us not stand still at this denumeration of our history!

December 1984

THE WHITE CITY

There's an interesting, even poignant, show at the Jewish Museum devoted to International Style architecture in Israel, most of it from the 1930s. What distinguishes the work exhibited is not so much the quality of any individual buildings — though there are a number of real winners — as the fit between architecture and ethos. At its wellspring, the architecture that was known in Palestine as "Bauhaus" was linked to a reformist social polemic. Values indigenous to Labor Zionism and the kind of utopian socialism espoused by activist European modernists are radically joined, not simply via shared 19th-century sources, but in terms of a common vision of social therapy: the fetishization of sunshine, hygiene, labor, and the out-of-door. Workers' housing cooperatives, kibbutz dining halls, and hospitals represent the kind of programs modern architecture always wanted for itself.

The connections are direct. A significant number of the Jewish architects working in Palestine during this period were trained by modernist lights. According to the show's catalogue, no fewer than 10 former Bauhaus students were active in Palestine, most prominent among them Arieh Sharon, whose autobiography *Kibbutz and Bauhaus* explores the affinity alluded to above. Also involved were students or former employees of Le Corbusier, Auguste Perret, Hans Poelzig, Mies van der Rohe, Bruno Taut, Hannes Meyer, and Erich Mendelsohn, a virtual modernist who's who. The great Mendelsohn himself arrived in 1934 and maintained an office into the 1940s, producing a large number of works — several major — and settling in as the éminence grise of the local architectural scene.

This efflorescence in Palestine is also apt in another light. The catalogue speaks astutely of the "repatriation" of modern architecture to its sources.

For Le Corbusier in particular, the experience of Mediterranean architecture was seminal. The whitewashed and angular vernacular of Greek hill towns and North African villages swam perpetually in Corb's imagination, and the source was popularly associated with the modernist vision from the first. Indeed, at the opening of the famous 1927 Weissenhofseidlung in Stuttgart, an exposition for which a number of major architects designed buildings, the Nazis distributed postcards of the project captioned "Arabendorf" (Arab village) onto which images of camels, Arabs, and palm trees had been collaged.

The presence of this cadre of European-trained Jewish architects in Palestine was, in growing measure, the result of flight from Nazi dominion in Europe. This must surely have heightened the sense of an architectural practice in opposition to oppressive convention. Further, the "Bauhaus" style in Palestine clearly counterposed itself to the official architecture of the British Mandate, whose construction tended to a heavy, devoluted colonial classicism. A minor irony in all of this is that the label "International Style" is the coinage of Henry Russell Hitchcock and Philip Johnson. Their book of the same name contributed to the reduction of the heroic attempt to link architecture and social practice to nothing more than a set of stylistic preferences: a trap the Jewish Museum show, in accepting the label, abets. It is perhaps no coincidence that the period during which most of the buildings in the exhibition were actually constructed was the same in which Johnson was most deeply involved with promoting fascism in the United States, a pursuit that culminated in his outright anti-Semitism.

However, if this architecture can be considered a response to various colonizations of land and spirit, it is also distinctly colonial. Looking at aerial photos of Tel Aviv from the period one sees the only city in history built almost exclusively in the "Bauhaus" manner. Whatever the arguments from "repatriation" of the Mediterranean or from Socialist Internationalism, it is clear that, in the Palestinian context, this architecture is a Western importation. Here is Mendelsohn's own description of his architectural project:

the Orient resists the order of civilization, being itself bound to the order of nature. This is why I am so strongly attached to it, trying to achieve a union between Prussianism and the life-cycle of the Muzzein. Between anti-nature and harmony with nature.

Orientalism's stamp is unmistakable here as it is in examples — mostly from the 1920s — of efforts to superficially "orientalize" architectural projects. This same lurid juxtaposition — Prussianism and the Muzzein — is visible in today's photos of modernist new towns on the West Bank, little white cities, hard by yet completely estranged from the Arab villages they overlook.

Mendelsohn's work, his rhetoric notwithstanding, shows a wonderful sensitivity to landscape. His Hadassah Hospital on Mount Scopus, constructed in 1936–39, is a spare, modern work built of the golden stone native to Jerusalem. Its minimalist expression and the terracing of its wings leave it sitting comfortably yet evocatively on a barren, dramatic Judean hillside. Other first-rate works on show include two apartment houses by Theodor Menkes, both with exceptionally fine stair treatments; Zeev Rechter's Engle House (apartments), a genuine masterpiece; two fabulous de Stijlian villas by Sam Barkai; Leopold Krakauer's Bendori Rest Home, a suave juxtaposing of unusually strong shapes; the same architect's dining hall for Kibbutz tel Yosef, a simple but powerful essay in rotated squares, unusually forward looking; the beautifully massed Hamaalot House (apartments) by Meir Rubin and Alexander Friedman; and Tel Aviv's own Seidlung, a group of cooperative workers' residences designed by a group of architects.

The show itself is on the parsimonious side: captioned photos, a little slide show, and two models, all ready to travel. Accompanying it is a separate exhibit of photographs by Judith Turner which records a variety of details from buildings of the period as they exist today. These are well observed, if somewhat annoyingly decontextualized. Particularly beautiful is the documentation of a sinuous staircase by Alexander Friedman. But the resonances in this show are not in the details. Rather, they lie in an introduction to an architecture — whatever the ultimate complexities and contradictions of its objective situation — impregnated with optimism, an architecture at work trying to realize a profoundly beautiful dream.

Not too long ago I was schmoozing with Lebbeus Woods when he produced a current copy of the *Encyclopaedia Britannica Book of the Year*. In the entry under "Physics" he pointed to a variety of advances in understanding the nature of matter, to new theorizing, as to the cosmological imperatives of the universe. Then he turned to the entry marked "Architecture." Here, there was a photograph of the AT&T Building.

For the past decade or so, in a vast opus of visionary drawings, Leb Woods has been working to redress this imbalance. He has set himself the task of reinfusing architectural poetics with the expression of cultural evolution, and rescuing the use of Big Science from the ever more quaint ruminations of traditional modernism on one hand and the banalities of *Star Trek* on the other. Woods is one of the heroes of this struggle to redeem the future as a central trope in architectural speculation. Clearly, though, he finds himself poised at some sort of a crossroads, the visionary's eternal conundrum, the moment of doubting whether drawing is enough.

In Woods's recent work, notably the series of drawings produced under the rubrics "Aeon" and "Region," the sci-fi problematic is inescapable. For this he's hardly culpable: the architectural community has ceded proprietorship of images of things to come to those operatives in the culture who have an abiding interest in using them — which is to say, Hollywood. Yet Hollywood's hegemony shouldn't divert attention from genuine differences in Wood's production. For, despite the somewhat occluding metaphysical and narrative apparatus he attaches to it, his is a formal investigation of genuinely architectural character. In all of it, issues of space making, geometry, combination, elision, and other basics are close at hand. Social implications are less consequential: this is not utopian work, it is fantastic — images of buildings, presented enthusiastically, like the travel sketchbook of the first architect on Mars.

Three of Woods's most current projects were recently shown at the Storefront for Art and Architecture, a shoestring venture virtually alone among New York venues in promoting a polemical, activist view of architecture. The theme that purports to unite the three — for Paris, Times Square, and an undesignated site in the Midwest — is that of "centers." A few meanings are intended. First, Woods is preoccupied with the idea of buildings as nodal, with marking points. The Times Square building (on the Times Tower Site) is an axis mundi (beloved of neo-Platonists), a literal crossroads of the world. A gorgeous rendering depicts Times Square on the eve of the millennium, as a mysterious golden sphere descends from God knows where to alight on the landing platform of the tower: a truly evocative synthesis of *Close Encounters*, dirigible moorings at the Empire State, and the old New Year's falling ball. The midwestern project — for what Woods calls an "Epicyclarium" — is even more overtly nodal, rendered in another gorgeous drawing as what looks to be a point on some galactic grid. These are images both naive and profound, a distinction largely swept away by the power of Woods's technique.

The fixation with centers is also evoked in a persistent fascination with spheres, the centroid's centroid. The Paris project and the Epicyclarium are literally spherical, the former proposing a giant orb as the termination of the great axis of the Champs Élysées. The Epicyclarium is at once more concrete and more diffuse. It is meant to house devices that create — on a 30-foot disc suspended above a viewing floor — a two-dimensional "global image," kind of a kaleidoscopic representation of the state of knowledge as we know it. Now, this is an ingratiating, if somewhat overweening, metaphor for artistic enterprise but one that must be taken in the proper light. It serves to identify the work in front of us — a pretty, domestically scaled, rather antique and picturesque little building — with a larger enterprise; it purifies. It also offers rebuke to current species of historicizing by choosing a 19th-century, Jules Vernean, vision of fantastical architecture to house a late-20th-century fantasy. It's a blow in favor of the history of leaps forward into the unknown instead of backwards into archival certitudes. It neatly evades the present by viewing the future from the past.

January 1985

MR. WRIGHT

Frank Lloyd Wright — "Mr. Wright" to the lingering Taliesin Fellowship, few of whom seem yet able to bear leaving the party — was a giant. Wright's talent was so prodigious, so blinding, that some resentment and a certain amount of sightless thrall seem inevitable. For decades, Wright both generated and took American architecture's heat. Not simply a great architect, Wright was the personification of a great architect, the real Howard Roark. And Wright loved it all, canny enough to know that nothing so becomes a demiurge as a healthy dose of public- and auto-fealty.

Max Protetch is currently conducting a second sale of drawings from the Taliesin archive, the major portion of whose profits will endow that operation. The show surpasses its predecessor — which was terrific — in both scope and quality. Wright (and those who assisted him) drew magnificently. The strength and singularity of Wright's hand is continuous with the power of his building: formally dynamic, precisely composed, exquisitely theatric. And the show includes several of the master's greatest projects. A lovely set of drawings of the Unity Temple of 1904 is included, designed at the height of Wright's first and most pristinely Eastern exploration of an architecture conceived in planes. Companioning it is a perspective triptych of Fallingwater (1935), another incident from the same long recherche, its imagery now radically transformed to produce probably the greatest of all modern houses, certainly the greatest of any kind built in the United States. Minor irony: rumor has it that the purchase of at least two of the three will remove them beyond the US border.

As was the case with Protetch/Taliesin's prior outing, there's a certain amount of grumbling about the venality of it all and how dare they sell off so much as a hair from the old man's head. Let's run through the arguments here, beginning with greed. It seems clear that the sale will genuinely benefit the most useful work of the foundation, preserving and restoring Wright's archive and remaining property. Indeed, the foundation seems to be going out of its way to send out the right sorts of signals about its intentions, including the hiring of a professional fundraiser.

The second set of arguments, related, are those from the higher scholarship, the "it's a pity to break up the set" school. Some grouse that vital architectural research will be jeopardized if each and every emanation from the Wright hand is not available at the same time in the same place and no facsimiles please! This line leaves me unmoved. The loss of two dissertations per annum on the subject of the exact moment of Wright's transition from watercolor rendering to the use of colored pencil will not be widely mourned. Indeed, the foundation is selling less than 1 per cent of its holdings, although these include real winners. The dispersal of a few dozen presentation drawings (if a halt is called to the culling after this sale) isn't likely to force the *Journal of the Society of Architectural Historians* to close up shop.

More to the point, though, is the question of who gets the drawings. Given the foundation's lack of zeal in making them accessible to either a scholarly or general public, any institutional acquisition of these drawings will result in wider viewing. Moreover, the drawings up for grabs are very rhetorical, very seductive, obviously done for an audience. Wright loved to draw and he drew both to investigate and to persuade. The renderings produced for client presentation and publication are made to be seen, not merely maintained or inspected. However, even if some percentage of the work goes to the wretched rich or to covetous architectural hacks eager to molest greatness with their daily glances, *tant pis*. At least someone gets to drool over all that gorgeousness. And, without the rich, how do we valorize art? Having undertaken to sell, I only wish the foundation an immense return.

Of course, the underlying objection to this deaccessioning is the *profanity* of it all. Taliesan invites this. If a priesthood guards a legacy, any shifts in its position are going to look like apostasy to somebody. There's sadness here. To anyone who really reveres Wright (count me in!), there's no escaping the sheer dimensions of his genius, the astonishing beauty of the work: a talent like Michelangelo or Mozart. And avidity always sinks into cupidity. To know a Wright drawing is to want one. So go look while you can.

*

To continue with the divinity and corruption theme, St. Bart's is back in the news. By the time you read this, the Landmarks Commission will have taken its first public meeting about the subject of the second proposal put forward by the Reverend Thomas Bowers and his architect Peter Capone, now the main man in Edward Durell Stone's old firm. As you will recall, when we left this saga last June, the commission had just offed Bowers's and Capone's first proposal, a hulking troglodyte tower, all facets and mirror, that actually cantilevered itself over the dome of the church. Opposition to the scheme was vigorous from the preservation crowd, many of whom are daily obliged to frequent Park Avenue. The *Times* thundered. I recall one editorial in its inimitable Classic Comics' version of Old Testament dudgeon, which inveighed against the Reverend Bowers — man of God! — for getting too cozy with Mammon. For its side, the church argued that it needs the money to maintain the property and intends to use the considerable additional profits to feed the poor and perform other good works.

The lurking guns-versus-butter question was largely ignored in the last round because the building itself was such a plump target: bad architecture, bad urbanism, bad politics. Or was it? There is a school that argues — after the style of such things — that the first submission was mere stalking-horse: a scheme so dumb and ugly that anything else must seem a relief, especially anything smaller. And this is what Capone and Co. have now proposed, a smaller building.

But there's more as well as less. The new scheme is as ornamented with good intentions as its ancestor was bereft of them. It employs orangey brick and limestone to match the church; picks up existing motifs, continuing, for instance, the line and rhythm of the church's entry; bares from certain angles the previously obscured rose window; matches heights with, even flirts with, the tops of the adjacent Waldorf-Astoria and G.E. Building; piles on setbacks with such dervish fervor, makes so many moves all at once, that no one can miss it calling out with every frantic zig and zag, "I'm architecture, dammit, I'm architecture!"

Will Landmarks heed the cry? We'll know in a few months. More interesting are the issues. The fact is this: the new building is bad, but surely less bad than the first one. At one level, the process of redesign brings to mind that old operatic anecdote about the young tenor making his debut in the notoriously tough Parma house and having his first big aria greeted by wild acclaim and repeated shouts of "encore!" He sings again. The crowd is in a uproar again. He sings again. Uproar again. "The show must go on," he reluctantly explains through tears of joy, "I just can't sing it another time." From a nether balcony an elderly gent shouts, "Young man, we're going to make you keep singing it until you get it right!" Alas, poor Ed. D. Stone and Associates. No matter how you skin it, it's only a pork purse that comes from a sow's ear. Added pathos: Stone Associates apparently got the job only after a raft of more marketable, name-brand designers turned the tainted commission down, an act of courage in the architectural community that's the rough equivalent of having fought in the Lincoln Brigade.

But whether or not Capone has made a better building than Philip Johnson (the man Frank Lloyd Wright once called "educated beyond his capacity") would have is beside the point. The project won't really sink or swim on the basis of its architectural quality. When I visited the Landmarks Commission to check out the scheme, I was given two different press releases describing their rejection of two different projects: the St. Bart's Tower and a tower proposed at about the same time for the top of the New York Historical Society. The strategy behind the pairing seemed to be first to forestall any appearance of discrimination (in the pejorative sense), and second to show that the standards by which the commission discriminated were above reproach. The key passage is one in which the commission describes the Historical Society tower as both "an extraordinarily good building" and completely inappropriate. By thus disengaging architectural quality from its context, the commmission re-establishes the traditional limitation on its regulatory territory. To wit, it doesn't matter if it be ugly or beautiful, it's only a question of whether or not it plays the game by the rules.

There is a little room for maneuver. If the argument against the Historical Society tower was that *no* building could possibly be built here, then an opening is left for the argument that the *only* building that will do next to St. Bart's is a beautiful one. But such an insistence would be clearly discriminatory. As a glance at every other recent building in the neighbor-hood reveals, the common weal does not yet seem to have called for the abridgement of every developer's right to put up the most vacant piece of garbage his architect can conjure. One empathizes with the Reverend Bowers' outrage at the obstacles in front of him. There he sits, at the epicenter of a real estate market where value is assigned by inches, and he wants to capitalize on this gift, not for private gain but to help the helpless. There's a part of me that would be happy to see him build 100 stories for such a purpose and to hell with the view from the Waldorf.

One last observation. Citicorp was a classic "what to do about the church on the site" situation, which the architects solved by raising the whole building up to provide an unobstructed view under. The only problem was, they also tore down the church, giving the exercise a certain hollowness. St. Bart's is a genuinely precious object — perhaps such an extravagant strategy might be apt.

Called upon to offer an assessment of the work of his longtime acolyte (for an article in the January 13 *New York Times Magazine*), Johnson gave unstintingly, comparing Sterno to those twin titans of American architecture, Charles Platt and Mott Schmidt. With friends like these....

February 1985

QUE SERRA SERA

On March 6 and 7, the US General Services Administration (GSA) will hold hearings to consider the fate of Richard Serra's "Tilted Arc," the big steel wall which has, since 1981, inclined in the plaza beside the Federal Building in lower Manhattan. The work was commissioned (and subjected to extensive review) as part of that agency's "Art-in-Architecture" program, which allots one half of 1 per cent of the budgets for government buildings to art. The impetus for the current hearing comes from a group of people who want the thing out of there, most prominent among whom is Edward D. Re, chief judge of the United States Court of International Trade, whose chambers adjoin the plaza in which the Serra sits. Re has been tilting at "Tilted Arc" since it went up, attributing to it, along with sundry artistic offenses, a vast increase in the number of rats presently scurrying along the halls of justice. The man who called the hearing and is likely to decide the future of the work is William J. Diamond, GSA regional administrator.

This opposition is an easy mark: troglodyte Reaganoids, everyday paranoiacs, boors. But couching the question in easy Us v. Philistines terms evades the real trickiness of the issue. There are, after all, plenty of circumstances envisionable where one wouldn't have the least remorse at the removal, even the destruction, of a work of art. In any case, the feds apparently intend to relocate the "Arc" (Storm King Art Center has offered to take it, as has the Parks Department), not to melt it down to make B—1s. But here is the crux of the matter. Serra and supporters argue that to relocate the work is precisely to destroy it, that the piece is so site specific, it would be totally evaporated of its present, intended meanings if moved.

Although I admire much of Serra's work, "Tilted Arc" strikes me as a superficial, schematic response, another dull sibling from a generation of too easy art. Its specificity is of a low order, Minimal sculpture mocking minimal architecture. Sure, it's about the plaza, about, in Serra's words, "a volumetric space that defines the otherwise undifferentiated plaza in sculptural terms." But does it really do so much more than those cloned Calders and Noguchis, sitting like suburban flamingos on other plazas in front of other office slabs, work Serra himself dismisses as mere "baubles"? Not for me. I've seen other Serra arcs (at Castelli, by the Holland Tunnel, in Paris) and they're a little too ripe with signature: so much more Big Art. That the Dubuffet bauble is used to certify the consequence of its setting while the Serra intends elucidation does not, ultimately, make a helluva difference. Moreover, the lack of complexity, the failures of particularity, the obvious aggression, force judgment back on the artist's intentions, never a happy place.

I do not, however, deny the basic facts. There is a range of very specific readings for "Tilted Arc" that depends completely on its presence in the current setting. While it may be true, as the director of the Storm King Center maintains, that "Tilted Arc" would "fit beautifully" in a rural environment, the transformation would be absolute. One reads a Givenchy differently on Mr. T than on Christie Brinkley.

Serra's larger project is the investigation of boundary conditions, the edges at which categories — architecture, sculpture, landscape — blur. Thus, to the degree that it distinguishes itself from those Calders and Noguchis, Serra's work also manages to separate itself from "sculpture" and the judgments conventionally applied to it. Sculpture which exceeds itself, however, must be ready to bear the consequences of its fresh impingements. Too often, the slippage in category merely abets the evasion of judgment. The way it looks from here is that this expansion obliges one to judge the work according to not fewer, but extra, criteria. If "sculpture" behaves like architecture, then it gets judged that way. If "sculpture" makes space in the city, then it takes the rap for its cock-ups as urban design. Just calling it art won't do.

To critics of the piece, this means that "Tilted Arc'"s alteration of its space is legitimately judgeable by the usual standards for public space (addles circulation, collects garbage, casts a shadow, makes it tough for the Marine Band to play, whatever). But — the giant but — singling out "Tilted Arc" requires amazing myopia: the total exclusion of the rest of the environment. Richard Serra and his measly one half of 1 per cent are taking the heat for the vastly greater failures of the other 99 ½. If anything, this is what the

THE DESTRUCTION OF TILTED ARC
(*New York*) Richard Serra

specificity of the work reveals. Let's face it, the status quo ante down at Federal Plaza was pretty grim: horrible plaza, horrible buildings, horrible bureaucratic interiors, the worst. The hearing about the Serra points up exactly the degree to which citizens have no control over their environment. It's sham democracy offered as a cover-up for the real crimes, a show trial after which the miserable "Arc" will be taken out and shot and the Federal Building declared once again to be humane. Gimme a break! The Serra's being threatened because that's what can be threatened. And that's why it needs to be defended.

The issue finally comes down to just what the government's contractual obligations to Serra and his work are. At one level, it's easy to whip up a big head of ambivalence over the travails of Art Stars and their clients. Don Judd's present contretemps with the Dia Freaks over the precise number of millions to be placed at his disposal is not one of my top candidates for the annals of Crimes Against Art. More, too much indignation at Uncle Sam's failures of enlightened patronage is just a tad naive. Nevertheless, though the Serra flap may not be in the same league with Diego Rivera getting canned for painting Lenin's picture in the lobby of the RCA Building, some part of this whole matter does have to do with the censorship of art that affronts. I may not much like "Tilted Arc", but the man did have a deal. What did the GSA think it was buying in the first place? Serra hadn't exactly been carving scrimshaw before he got the commission.

Serra's lawyer has written a letter to the feds, outlining the basis for a potential suit to prevent the removal, based on the original contract with Serra to maintain the work. The language of that contract stipulates that the government may "convey" the work to the safekeeping of the Smithsonian. The letter argues that any such conveyance would amount to the destruction of the work since it's site specific, etc., etc. One almost longs to see the matter go to trial, if only for the spectacle of the opposing experts lambasting and defending the rusting item. But while this might be fun, the issues adjudicated would be beside the real point, made elsewhere in Serra's lawyer's letter. What's worth some amount of alarm is the likelihood that one of a declining number of government arts programs will belly-up, becoming the creature of the retrospective vagaries of any bureaucrat's opinion. I wouldn't really shed tears over the Serra — the troubling question is who gets trashed next.

March 1985

WHY GOLDBERGER IS SO BAD:

THE CASE OF TIMES SQUARE

Reading the *Times* magazine one Sunday not long ago, I came across a full page ad for some gigaluxe new condo on Park Avenue. The spread simulated a blueprint: a measured floor plan in the center (replete with upscale nomenclature like "library," "breakfast room," and "gallery," and dimensions in metric for the transatlantic crowd), gushing text at the base, and a laudatory quotation in large letters at the top, imputing to the uninteresting goods "a sense of flowing space that recalls the best apartments of the 1920s." The source of this quotation was Paul Goldberger, architecture critic of the *New York Times* who had penned it while reviewing the building in a previous issue of the paper, the same Goldberger who more recently opined that "in architecture, the relationship of criticism to the marketplace is probably the least clear and direct of any field."

Of course, the condo ad wasn't the first instance of the Goldberger imprimatur in such a context. For many months Paul's encomium ornamented the lobby of the Trump Tower, doubtless the source of great pride for the young master builder responsible who, coincidentally, also turns out to be the selling agent for the apartments mentioned above. Paul's paragraph originally shared wall space with a passage by Ada Louise Huxtable (his predecessor at the *Times*), although she — on discovering the incriminating locale of work she'd come to regret — demanded publicly that it be removed. No such plaint was heard from Paul, who seems to have a radar-like instinct for the buttered side of the bread. Indeed, if one seeks to characterize Goldberger's critical practice, it's just this aspect of publicity that leaps to prominence.

Goldberger's main loyalties are directed to the architectural clique that invented him in the first place (plucked from undergraduate obscurity to serve) and to his employers at the *Times*, for whom he doubtless represents the embodiment of the aesthetics of Yuppification now ascendant at the newspaper of record. His fealty to these patrons has a statistical regularity. Philip Johnson, Robert Stern, and Robert Venturi are, by actual count, his most frequently recurring subjects; never mind the one's a monstrosity, the next's a mediocrity, and the third, for all his merits, has built almost nothing in the city (though he does threaten Westway Park, a subject on which Paul has been notably quiescent). Goldberger also apes the social behavior of this cabal: a sometimes adornment at Philip's table at the Four Seasons, member of the Century Club, and frequent participant in the boys-only back-room architectural affairs there.

The same fealty is extended to his employer. John Hess's recent *Grand Street* article reports what surely is one of the high points in the history of the grovel, Goldberger's description (quoted in *Newsweek*) of Arthur Gelb as "one of those extraordinary forces, like Harold Ross must have been at the *New Yorker*." This, according to Hess, was identified by a *Times* colleague as a "Pulitzer quote" and, in fact, Goldberger got the glittering prize not long after, a choice perpetrated over the recommendation of the Pulitzer jury.

Goldberger's devotion must surely have been put to a severe test by recent events in Times Square. As you will recall, there's a plan for the area — strongly backed by the *Times* — to impose a Bernie Goetz-style urban renewal scheme intended, by means of massive construction, to blow away those persons whose troubling body-language has come to typify the Times Square experience for many. The centerpiece of this initiative is a group of four extravagantly ugly and mercenarily large office towers designed by Johnson in flagrant disregard for the design guidelines proposed for the area. While they're so gross as to guarantee a permanent pall for blocks, they're just large enough to ensure huge fees for the firm and colossal profits for the developer, all at our direct expense, thanks to mammoth tax giveaways.

As architecture, it has not been oversubscribed with defenders. Even the normally wimpy Carter Wiseman at *New York* magazine wrote a strong and effective piece denouncing the scam (although, having written it, he seems to have vanished from the scene like that creature — is it the dragonfly? — who, having shot his single wad, withers and dies). Clearly, this was a project that could give Goldberger problems, his marching orders so clear, his objective so indefensible. What would he do? Even he must have had an inkling it was truly a stinker.

Paul's strategy was to rely on well-honed fundamentals. Typically, a Goldberger argument centers on a spine of Jesuitical vacillation, occluded by a thick appliqué of qualifying rhetoric. As literary style, it's characterized by the incantational repetition of certain key words and phrases like "rather" (the unqualified qualifier!), "a kind of," "not altogether," and "on the other hand." The effect conveys the impression of measured consideration while at the same time camouflaging a lack of independent insight and avoiding the risk of expressing a point of view which fails to accord with the constituency for which he is a mouthpiece. At his best, Goldberger leaves the reader with the impression of an opinion but with no recall as to what it might actually be. Goldberger fanciers will recall a fine recent example of the young critic's labors in these fields, a piece about St. Bart's called "What has Architecture to Do With the Quality of Life," in which a compendious number of platitudes was arrayed according to that hoary canard: "Two recent letters to me, one from a liberal, the other from a conservative ..." Where a difficult position must be taken, Goldberger artfully presents the existence of conflicting opinions as means of showing the superiority of having none.

Paul's first go at Times Square came in December 1983, the day after the scheme was publicly revealed. His "Appraisal" was accompanied by a photograph of the top part of a large model of the buildings behind which were seen the grinning heads of Johnson and his partner John Burgee along with Mayor Koch and Matilda Cuomo. It's an effective photo, simultaneously lilliputianizing the scale of the thing, focusing on the goofy mansard roofs praised in the article, and conveying the aura of a happy, unblemished, civic event. Accordingly, Goldberger leads with praise for towers "likely to be among the most striking additions to a skyline that has had its share of striking things." He rehearses Johnson's ample credentials and places the project firmly within the larger oeuvre, describing it as "the latest chapter in the return to historical architectural form encouraged in recent years by Mr. Johnson and Mr. Burgee." Sources for the imagery are adduced, in this case with a comparison to the old Claridge and Astor hotels, an artful allusion as these buildings signify not only a certain fecundity of historical expression but the kind of upscale good times that would be oh, so right for Times Square.

Goldberger then turns to the contrary argument, presenting it with immediate internal qualification. "Though they would not be unusually tall," he writes of the towers, "they would be quite bulky and thus would dramatically change the present conditions of open space and sunlight in Times Square." Goldberger here approaches the nub. The issue is to be Nice Buildings versus Light and Air. Setting aside for a moment that the dichotomy is false (they're not nice buildings and, even if they were, calling them so depends on fairly skewed values, allowing something to be judged handsome when its every effect is hideous, the equivalent of defending the gulag because you think Stalin had a cute mustache), this does look like the point at which a position must be taken, one way or the other.

But no. The Goldberger strategy is to take all the positions. Thus, while the towers may be bulky, it could be no other way. First, because the developer needs such big buildings to make money. Second, because if the Floor Area Ratio (FAR) of the towers is taken as a percentage of the *entire* redevelopment scheme, the average FAR is not really so great (a fine piece of sophistry, this). And finally, because if we're going to really clean up Times Square, what's needed is a project with a big impact. Hence the big project.

Now, the twist de résistance. Having established both that it's too bulky and that it *must* be too bulky, Goldberger argues that some of the open space about to be obliterated by the project can be recovered by the simple expedient of obliterating something else, in this case the original Times Tower that currently stands, in dreadfully altered form, in the middle of Times Square. It's a tricky thing, this reverence for history. Goldberger reports that there could be "no better use for this site than as open space to pull together new towers that are to surround it." Defending the indefensible often calls for imaginative thinking.

By the middle of the following year, as objections mounted and the *Times* began to pull out the stops in support of the development ("Get Out of the Way of Times Square," one editorial thundered at detractors), Paul felt or was caused to feel the need to write again. He begins his column of July 5 by acknowledging that there had been a "mixed reaction" on the part of the public to whom "the sheer size and bulk of the towers must have come as something of a surprise." Immediately, he rediscovers his former difficulties. What gives him fresh impetus, however, is the fact that Johnson and Burgee have now made a few changes, most significantly pasting on some neon gimcracks at street level by way of addressing the general feeling that their work had totally missed the boat, context-wise. From this emendation, Goldberger derives a concept that will sustain him through the piece: small changes at the last minute.

After acknowledging that the bulk of the towers is unaltered, he writes:

The basic shape of the four towers remains as well. Mr. Johnson and Mr. Burgee's design is alright *in itself* [my emphasis], rather better, in fact, than many of their recent efforts at integrating historical architectural elements into modern skyscraper form. If the buildings were smaller, less overwhelming in bulk they would not be bad at all. They contain a mixture of formality and playfulness that could be just right for Times Squares, if only there were less of it.

And finally, an actual thrust: "From ground level, a pedestrian will never see the sloping mansard roof tops; he will only see huge masses, and they will all look exactly the same."

Of course, there's no way out of this dilemma. By seeing styling as the central matter in architectural expression, the schizy position is inevitable. Everything else – including the real core of architectural experience – gets viewed as so much impedimenta, hampering the real business of the archi-tect: decoration. The narrowness of his understanding leads Paul lockstep toward the deep end. In this case, Goldberger's apparent desperation to do right by his subjects must be acute. He surely also realizes that he's toe to toe with the bottom line: developer, architect, and municipal authority haven't the slightest inclination to shrink the behemoths by so much as a square inch, no matter what the *Times* critic has to say. The issue, in every sense, becomes one of face. And this is exactly where Paul winds up, pleading for cosmetic alterations.

While [he writes] we would all be better off if the buildings also managed to shrink by one third, there are ways in which these other problems can be solved without changing the overall size. Why, for example, couldn't the high arch be a rectangle on one building, perhaps a gable on another and low vault in another. Similarly, the detailing of the shops and cafes at the ground level could be varied, yet still remain consistent with the overall themes set by Mr. Johnson and Mr. Burgee's design.

Oy gevalt! Is this guy for real? Does he really think that this project can be redeemed by changing an arch to a "low vault"? How low must it go? Paul's been seduced and abandoned. Philip and Sterno have filled his head with so much whimsy about decor that when he's confronted with a truly rotten piece of goods, decor is all he can think of.

If any further evidence of desperation were needed, it's provided by the second half of his July 5 piece (too difficult to sustain the grotesque argument at normal length), which is devoted to a proposal solicited by the developer from Robert Venturi to place a giant apple on the site of the old Times Tower. Clearly, Goldberger is so relieved at not having to discuss the buildings any longer, he totally loses his grip and delivers the following classic paragraph:

The Venturi plan is shocking: difficult to accept at first — and brilliant. Like the best sculpture of Claes Oldenberg, the apple has meaning as a symbol and as an abstraction, and the genius of this work lies in its ability to manipulate proportion and the element of surprise in such a way as to make us think of the apple as a monumental object, not as a common piece of fruit.

Brillant, genius, piece of fruit, symbol *and* abstraction: the mind, as they say, boggles.

Goldberger's final word on Times Square came in September of last year, in a review of a competition run by the Municipal Art Society to attract proposals for the Times Tower site (the one that Goldberger had argued in his first go be left for open space to redeem the overbuilding he was supporting). Hostility to the official plans of both the jury and the majority of the hundreds of submissions (one of which pictured a wrecking ball in the act of demolishing Johnson's towers) was evident. Goldberger himself quotes jury chairman Harry Cobb (as conservative as they come, partner of I.M. Pei and at that time chairman of the architecture department at Harvard) urging that "Times Square be occupied by a building... it is not an appropriate site for an open plaza or a monument." Here's trouble: an undisputed authority, strongly identified with the core of the national architectural establishment, has gainsayed Paul's two opinions to date, his support of an open plaza and a monument. Goldberger gets busy, immediately going after the waffle with an ingenious two-stage argument.

He begins by setting up a straw building, choosing to discuss an entry that proposes to restore the Times Tower to its status quo ante. Like Venturi's Big Apple or Philip's current proposal to strip the tower to its skeleton and bedeck it with fairy lights, this represents an obvious solution, the sort that 95 per cent of the participating designers probably thought of and dismissed in their first five minutes on the job. Goldberger praises the solution extravagantly, positioning it as the kind of absolute alternative it is. Having done this (at the expense of ignoring the substantial positions taken by the hundreds of more inventive proposals) he proceeds to knock it flat. "But does it make sense," he wonders, "to recreate the Times Tower as it was? It would be an act of architectural bravado, a way of taking issue not only with the destruction of the building but with the very idea that Times Square should be transformed."

Well, naturally. But Paul has torqued a schematic argument for saving a particular artifact into a species of architectural Ludditism, an assault on the very idea of progress. The twisting continues. Goldberger now changes gears to treat the suggestion, previously labeled critique, as a practical proposal for intervention in an *already reconstructed* Times Square, accepting Johnson's project, instead of the structure actually standing, as the given. "But it would not, in the end, make much sense, at least if the proposed Johnson and Burgee buildings do get built." Paul is once again left exposed with no values to inform his thinking beyond the value of supporting that which he knows he must.

The final resolution of the question of the Times Tower site is a scosh enigmatic. "While it is true," he writes with a casual conviction that suggests this as his view of the subject from the first,

that this is not the place for an open plaza, some sort of smaller structure with equal symbolic power to the original Times Tower is needed as a centerpiece. And for all the passion that this competition revealed regarding Times Square's future, the ideal design for that centerpiece still remains to be found.

Curious. At last writing, we'd found a work of symbolic and abstract genius. Perhaps Paul simply means that this *competition* has not yielded that smaller structure with equal symbolic power, Venturi's scheme being the result of direct commission from the developer. Or could it be that there's been a change of heart about the monumental piece of fruit. Either way the effect is to dismiss the work and conclusions generated by the competition (an open one as opposed to the biz-as-usual approach that got Johnson and Burgee the real job) while further helping to secure the inevitability of the plan most competitors spurned.

The disdain and disappointment I feel whenever I pick up a piece by Goldberger is only in small part the animosity of a writer with opposing views. I abhor these buildings. Goldberger, with over a year to think and with ample opportunity to write, is unable to do anything but equivocate. Does he or doesn't he believe — as it is proposed and will likely be built – that this project serves the best interests of the public? Following the lead of his patrons, he refuses to see a colossal social engineering exercise as anything other than a question of low arches and gables. To Paul, the Times Square project is just another Broadway show.

Of course, I'm annoyed that such a toady should be in a position to set a tone and standard for critical discourse about a subject I love. Bad newspaper writing is, however, a survivable offense. The real anger comes when I contemplate Goldberger from my position as an architect. By expending his partisanship on behalf of the superficial stylings of the worst kinds of corporate production, Goldberger is complicit in the restriction of the territory of architecture to its most banal possibilities. That Goldberger is an acolyte is neither here nor there; that the objects of his veneration are so awful is. The main problem with architecture in this country is the stranglehold that people like Johnson and Stern have on its institutional culture, the way in which schools, museums, patrons, and the press call their tunes, excluding so many others. American architecture is too important to be held prisoner by a bunch of boys that meets in secret to anoint members of the club, reactionaries to whom a social practice means an invitation to lunch, bad designers whose notions of form are the worst kind of parroting. It is for being the unquestioning servant of these that I accuse Paul Goldberger.

April 1985

REFORMING THE INSTITUTE

Developments at the Institute for Architecture and Urban Studies. A little over two weeks ago, the institute's director, Steve Peterson, resigned. Almost immediately, John Burgee, president and chairman of the institute's board of trustees, ordered the cancellation of all public programs with no explanation offered. Questions of demise loomed. The reasons for Peterson's abrupt departure remain obscure.

Writing about the institute, it's hard to avoid gagging on the vulgar sociological analysis its history invites, but a dehydrated account is useful. This history describes the classic trajectory of an organization forged in personal vision as it undergoes the problems of succession and institutionalization. The *moi* the present *déluge* is *après* is Peter Eisenman who, for 15 years, ran the institute with a combination of brilliance, fancy footwork, charm, canniness, and enterprise. The greatness of the institute in its glory days was secured, in large measure, by its familial character, its members picked by pater Peter. As the place grew up, though, the crisis of its own adolescence was inevitable. Growing large, the family was taxed, conflicts flared, disgruntlement among disenfranchised younger members impatient with Eisenman's authority and predilections arose. Growing older, Eisenman's own interests and those of the original cadre began to shift. The charms of the theoretical receded in the face of a series of architectural mid-life crises as the lure of building loomed larger, assuming increasing now-or-neverness. And, as in the life of all innovation, fatigue set in. The cementing energies of earlier days began to wane.

When Eisenman stepped down two years ago, there was a new set of facts in place. Salient among them was the prominence of the board of trustees and a newly pervading spirit of the bottom line. Eisenman had kept the institute going via a series of breathtaking escapes from financial disaster, purchased, in many instances, with withheld salaries, last-minute grantsmanship, and other feats of financial legerdemain. At the end, Eisenman was sharing power with an administrator, Edward Saxe, hero of the Museum of Modern Art condo deal and a former CBS executive (where he enjoyed the sobriquet Saxe the Ax). More, there seemed a detectable shift in Eisenman's own loyalties, away from the family of "Fellows" (finally disbanded) and toward the professional prominences on the board of trustees (yet another all-male list). And it should come as no surprise that the dominant force on the board was Philip Johnson, whose financial support of the institute (both direct and indirect) had become crucial. The Eisenman/Johnson relationship was a long-standing one. Johnson's personal and financial generosity to Eisenman had been considerable: at one point he'd made a large and unsolicited gift when Eisenman was hard-pressed to finish a project. For his part, Eisenman had positioned himself to become the official Johnson hagiographer.

The roiling intrigue that befell the institute in the wake of Eisenman's departure ultimately culminated in a face-off between Eisenman and Burgee (Johnson's partner and designated gauleiter for institute affairs) over the subject of succession. Eisenman's candidate was Danny Liebeskind, then head of the architecture department at the Cranbrook School of Art, a man known for the tenacity and magnetism of his theoretical position and for the intensely mystifying character of his graphic output. Peterson, a man of far more conventional proclivities, became the candidate of the Johnson/ Burgee faction which ultimately prevailed, resulting in Eisenman's angry departure from the scene.

A prominent architect on the board of trustees recently explained Peterson's selection in terms of a feeling that what the institute needed was a calm and competent hand on the helm, someone who would run the place not by being its greatest prominence but by gathering consequence about him: a curator of talent. This faction was joined by a group of former Fellows who saw Peterson as malleable, unlikely to rock the boat, a safer bet than the more dynamic and presumably unpredictable Liebeskind. Everyone must have been a bit surprised: Peterson and the former Fellows faced off almost immediately, resulting in a total rout of the Fellows. Peterson, it seemed, was serving notice that he really intended to run the place. But, when the year's programs were finally set, their main distinction was their lack of it. Peterson seemed to be turning the institute into no more than a watered-down school of architecture, an instrument for the replication of the status quo.

In this, the trustees may have concurred. When I spoke to Burgee last week about his intentions, he avowed a desire to keep the place open, citing as its most crucial accomplishment the number of its students admitted to Harvard last year. This, it seems to me, is exactly the kind of accounting that ought not be applied. The institute's importance has always been as an alternative. In its heyday, the institute was responsible for a dramatic transformation in the character of architectural discourse in this country, a retheorization of architectural speech. This is now in danger of being totally lost.

What, then, is to be done? Burgee, in our recent chat, may have suggested the answer. Although offered with the tediously fey irony learned from his master, his suggestion that "young people" take over and throw the older generation out seems apposite. New York badly needs some version of the Institute for Architecture and Urban Studies, a place of research, controversy, provocation, and seriousness. But it's clear the powers presently in charge haven't the slightest interest in such a venture. Things will wind up in the old death versus dishonor conundrum if a way isn't found to purge the hacks. Coup d'état, anyone?

This year's Pritzker Prize went to Hans Hollein, a fair choice. Hollein, a 51-year-old Viennese, is both talented and productive and had been a presence on the world scene since his lapidary little Retti Candle Shop was published in 1965. His work, if uneven, is concise, witty, sensuous, intelligent, and reasonably engaged. While most of his executed projects to date have been on a small scale, he seems poised for a breakout into the big time. One large project has already been completed: a museum in Mönchengladbach, near Düsseldorf. This project – which I know only through photographs – seems a mite precious (a lingering danger for Hollein) but trusted informants tell me it's quite nice, and very good as a gallery.

By giving the award to Hollein, the Pritzker jury has, as its seventh choice, selected its first really contemporary sensibility, finally recognizing an architect conversant with the kinds of formal and intellectual issues that engage the best architects of the younger generation, although it has again ignored a number of more appropriate, mature talents, designating a winner of promise rather than influence. When the jury pats itself on the back for choosing in Hollein an architect who is also an "artist," I infer an indirect commentary on earlier choices. These have been, to put it mildly, a mixed bag. Awards to Philip Johnson, I.M. Pei, and Kevin Roche seem basically cronyism. To Richard Meier (as perhaps with Hollein), let us say that the recognition was premature. Luis Barragan and James Stirling were absolutely deserving. If the bag is mixed, however, the signals are even more so.

For all the prestige the prize arrogates, three winners out of seven picks ain't exactly a great record. The jury seems unable to decide whether it wishes to recognize persons who are credits to American architectural big business or credits to some higher notion of Architecture. The ambivalence may be a direct result of the nature of the jury, which changes a bit from year to year but retains its basic configuration. Three of the members are architects, currently Roche, Ricardo Legoretta, and Fumihiko Maki. Their predecessors include Philip Johnson (he's everywhere! he's everywhere!), Cesar Pelli and Arata Isozaki. A small parenthesis: rules were altered recently to reduce the time between a juror's service and his (everyone's male — is there a more sexist profession?) eligibility for the prize to three years. Jimmy the Greek take note.

Another three members are high-class plutocrats, the suave Giovanni Agnelli, chairman of FIAT; J. Irwin Miller, former chairman of the Cummins Diesel Company and a big architectural patron; and Thomas Watson, chairman "emeritus" of IBM. The seventh, the swing-seat (the Lord Clark of *Civilisation* chair), is the reserve of an upscale connoisseur, the present occupant being J. Carter Brown, director of the National Gallery of Art. Doubtless as influential as any of the voting jurors is their nonvoting "advisor," Arthur Drexler, the eternal architectural curator at the Museum of Modern Art and a Philipoid of historic standing. Drexler's role is to "present" the candidates for the award, the gatekeeper and agenda-setter.

Interestingly, at least three of the four nonarchitects on the jury have been involved in the relationship of client (which is to say, employer) with at least one of the prizewinners they've decided upon. Pei has worked for the National Gallery and in Columbus, Indiana, under Cummins patronage. Roche has built several projects for Cummins Diesel. Meier has worked at Columbus and for FIAT. With Watson, the link is less clear. He probably had some connection with Roche from his days at the Saarinen firm which built for IBM.

The Pritzker people are at pains to compare their prize to the Nobel. Well, I take no issue with the idea of fat prizes: if my practice ever picks up, I'd love to get a hundred grand myself some day. Where the Pritzker differs from the Nobel is not in the idea of recognition but in the question of who recognizes. As I understand it, the Nobel is awarded by peer juries, physicists recognizing physicists, chemists chemists, and so forth. Having big businesses decide an architectural prize seems a little like letting the president of B. Dalton choose the Nobel for literature. If I were inclined to an uncharitable reading of what's going on with the Pritzker (for every Barragan a Pei), I'd say that the alternation of "artistic" with corporate recipients is simply a strategy for conferring a higher legitimacy on you-know-which half of that particular equation. It's a lousy, igNobel shuck.

Anybody who had even the remotest architectural consciousness during the '60s and early '70s knows about Archigram. That group of irrepressible English visionaries created an amazing wealth of images, perfectly embodying the galactic optimism of the times. Archigram was to architecture what the Beatles were to rock and roll. No less.

Michael Webb was one of the group's leading lights, a wonderful man with amazing gifts. He still is, though he now lives in New York. And he's still drawing: since Archigram's breakup his pursuit has been a solitary, even monkish, research into architectural essences, months of study devoted to analyzing the quality of light as it falls on a difficult compoundly curved surface. Webb gets by on a teaching salary earned at the New Jersey Institute of Technology (NJIT). And he's a terrific teacher, sensitive and fresh-visioned.

It will therefore come as a shock to know that his tenure has been turned down — despite the unanimous recommendation of his department — by NJIT. Whatever one thinks of academic tenure, it's clear that people like Mike Webb — those dedicated to research in its purest realms — are its best recipients. He has one slim chance remaining to secure it. The president of the university has yet to pass on the conflicting recommendations. It is quite probable that his decision can be influenced by support for Webb from the architectural community. I urge all who know Webb and his work to write to his dean, who will forward all letters to the university president.

April 1985

TIPPING THE CIRCLE: WILL THE WORLD'S TALLEST BUILDING REPLACE THE COLISEUM?

One of the code concepts of recent urban practice was the "tipping point." What this purported to describe was the moment in the life of a community when the racial and economic balance shifted that unquantifiable fraction, causing the area to "tip," turning stable environments into festering Beiruts. The most crucial consequence of the tipping point was its companion concept, "white flight." No mistaking the direction of the tip: this was always racism at its most anemically concealed.

Nobody talks much about the tipping point in Manhattan nowadays. The reason is scarcely obscure: everything's tipping the other way. From Times Square to Cathedral Parkway, "development" is unrestrained as various threatening populations are ruthlessly displaced by surging good times. In this context, it can be difficult to write about "architecture" since the consequences of so much building are ultimately so dire for the imperfectly privileged among us. If architecture — which reproduces social relations almost schematically — has an ethic, this terrain is one that measures collusion by degrees. While the professionally preferred agenda is formalist, the real issues tend to lie elsewhere. Of Manhattan architecture, the pre-eminent question is always a simple one: whose interest does it serve?

On the first of May, 13 developers submitted schemes for the re-development of the site currently occupied by the Coliseum at Columbus Circle. This property, owned by the Metropolitan Transportation Authority, is about to become redundant, due to the impending opening of the new Convention Center. It is, to put it mildly, a choice parcel, the largest to hit the midtown market in 50 years, expected to fetch a minimum of $300 million. In Manhattan, value is extruded directly from property: size is everything. The site is so big that its new owner will be able, if he so

114

chooses, to build as of right (that is, with no zoning variances) the tallest building in the world. The height of the submissions thus corresponds directly to the degree of developer greed. Not surprisingly, Donald Trump has submitted (in collaboration with Peter Kalikow, of whom more later) two proposals, each for a building which would be world's tallest.

The Columbus Circle project is exemplary in linking architecture with its ends. The decision among the competing projects is likely to depend not on any fine point of archiectural fashion but exactly on the MTA's self-evaluation of its motives vis-à-vis the public interest. Present indications are that the MTA's priorities are drastically skewed. In its Request for Proposals, the MTA set out its criteria for selection which, like those of any other developer, identify the commonweal totally with the bottom line. "The Sponsor," reads the document, "intends to sell the Site to the applicant whose proposal most successfully meets the Sponsor's goals, particularly the goal of realizing the highest financial return from the sale."

Of course, one could make the argument that this profit is to be extracted for good ends, that the money will go for transit improvements that will ultimately benefit the public. But such reasoning is specious, hardly grounds to justify the kind of disasters most of the proposals represent. It is true that the Request does invoke the totemic criteria of sound urbanistic practice: subway improvements, mixed use, masonry street-wall preservation, transition between mid-town and the Upper West Side, respect for the park, respect for pedestrians, yak, yak, yak. But the problem with criteria like these is that their practical substance depends on interpretation, interpretation that can respond to an array of values.

In this case, the burden falls on an eight-bureaucrat panel, four each from the city and the MTA. To my eye, this appears an amalgam uniquely unqualified to decide in the public interest, if that interest is to be judged by any test other than profit. As anyone who has descended into the subway any time during the last 30 or so years can attest, quality of design does not seem to have been one of the MTA's abiding priorities. Equally, the city's current attitude toward development unmistakably benefits only three classes of people: the rich, the very rich, and the extremely rich.

Let's look at some possible interpretations of the MTA's proposed urban design standards. The most crucial of these is "mixed use." The history of this concept grew in reaction to cities rigidly zoned by function, residence isolated from workplace, workplace from shopping, etc. The opposing notion of an integrated urban environment became a standard urban beau-ideal. However, the concept only genuinely makes sense when one considers specifics. Clearly, a Benetton, a David's Cookies, and a Pottery Barn constitute a different order of mix than a day-care center, an SRO, and an artist's co-op. The idea of mixed use — as represented by many of the submissions for Columbus Circle — has come to be a surrogate for the real integration that was originally one of its inspirations. Instead of facilities intended for use by the mix of people that composes the city, the planners now offer facilities preferred by a single group. Convenience replaces social purpose as the informing ideal.

But that's not exactly right. The project for Columbus Circle can hardly be said to be devoid of social purpose. Which brings us back to the tipping point. There's no mistaking that the Municipal Imagination sees Manhattan's manifest destiny as a purified preserve of privilege, the moated domain of the eminent. A key strategy for achieving this result has been the placement of giant, officially sponsored projects at tactical intervals up the length of the island, projects of sufficient magnitude to tip the terrain between. Battery Park City, the Convention Center, Westway, Times Square, Columbus Circle, are all intended colonially, to secure territories for development. Columbus Circle puts in place the last element in the siege of Clinton, a staggering display of urbanoid firepower: Times Square to the south, the West Side Plan to the east, and Columbus Circle to the north. Against this, poor neighborhoods are defenseless.

Whatever its role in larger agendas, though, Columbus Circle is a major incident in the life of Manhattan's form, a place of civic magnitude. Columbus Circle marks the intersection of the great slashing diagonal of Broadway, Central Park, and the grid. It mediates this great formal conjunction by providing a crucial and complex corner that must act as both edge and gateway: the Upper West Side begins at the Circle. The solution to the dilemma of Columbus Circle is finding a suitably comprehending formal envelope to resolve this array of vectors. One doesn't have to look too far for the right choice: a circle is perfect.

At the moment, the circularity of Columbus Circle is almost entirely inferential. The only real clues are the curb line, the demarcating central shaft topped by the local eponym, and the slight inflection in the façade of the much maligned Edward Durrell Stone shrinette for Huntington Hartford, now housing the City Department of Cultural Affairs. To its credit, the MTA has insisted on — and all competitors have provided — bases for the projects which continue and reinforce the circle. But this is scarcely enough. Witness only the most inanely cosmetic of these mandatory bases straining under Sam Lefrak's 135-story exoskeletal *escisse* in naked structure, authored by the Chicago office of Skidmore, Owings, and Merrill. The designers have actually gone so far as to tart up the street wall in retro-classical drag, complete with statuary (Koch, Kiley, and Sam in togas?).

Don't get me wrong. I'm all in favor of the world's tallest building. It just doesn't belong in Columbus Circle. There are a number of reasons. First, the shadow from such a building would sweep along an arc from the Hudson River, over Lincoln Center and the outdoor cafés in that fabled fun zone, to wind up darkening the south end of Central Park, just in time for the close of the working day. Such an intrusion on our premier public amenity is indefensible. A giant building would also be completely misplaced in the skyline, an artistic resource that demands conservation. Despite intrusions, the basic figure of the Manhattan skyline depends on the legibility of the double crescendoes of midtown and downtown. To locate its tallest structure outside this rhythm of peaking would be to assault its most central qualities, a terrible vandalism. This seems to have been sensed even by the editors of the *New York Post*, who juxtaposed a photo spread of the 13 proposals with several shots of "mild mannered architect-turned-avenger" Charles Bronson blasting away at three "punks" in a scene from *Death Wish III*.

All the schemes presented are flawed in some serious way. For the majority, it's simply a case of hack architects begetting hack work. Nearly all are too tall. Excepting the three world's-tallests, the median height seems to be about 80 stories. Columbus Circle must take its cues from the layer of buildings which directly border the park — it owes primary urbanistic responsibility to its role in making up that edge. Ideally, one looks for heights comparable to those of buildings like the Sherry-Netherland and the Pierre, facing the site across the park.

Only three of the schemes struck me as even remote possibilities. Michael Graves's proposal for Zeckendorf is the lowest of the 13 but is otherwise so ineptly expressed as to suggest a student knockoff. The New York Skidmore, Owings, and Merrill proposal for Larry Silverstein is also one of the lower projects and has the potential to be fairly suavely expressed, although it would work much better massed as four buildings rather than three. Finally, Cesar Pelli's scheme, designed for Rich-Eisner, if too tall by perhaps a third, has the best, most Gothamesque spirit of any. All three of these projects are mixed office, residence, and commercial facilities, which seem the best combo that can be hoped for. Rich-Eisner has apparently also offered 1 per cent of profits to the homeless, a tiny tithe to be sure but a promising act of conscience.

Developer Peter Kalikow's lust to blight has recently found another arena. As the new owner of the square block bounded by York, East End, 78th, and 79th streets, he is currently proposing the largest mass eviction in New York history, aiming to chuck out over 2,000 tenants currently occupying 1,300 apartments, many of them fixed-income elderly clinging to rent-controlled oases. Irony is added to outrage by the fact that this block was developed early in the century as model workers-housing by the City and Suburban Homes Company, a limited-profit, civic-minded operation. The buildings themselves have been attributed to Ernest Flagg, architect of the (vanished) Singer Building, but this is a matter of some uncertainty.

Kalikow's architect for the intended ensuing condos is Eli Attia, the author of the 137-story Kalikow/Trump Columbus Circle scheme. Attia's other New York work includes a tower at 40th and Park and the Republic Bank Headquarters, that rhapsody to the fluorescent tube at 40th and Fifth. I noted several columns ago the frenzy among "responsible" architects to decline the job of designing the St. Bart's Tower, lest they be associated with the evil of effacing that hoary monument. An architect's conscience is a curious thing: courageous on behalf of building but supine when it's merely a matter of human lives being destroyed, the Albert Speer syndrome in excelsis. Kalikow's villainy in attempting to perpetrate this horror is so clear, no architect should touch it, no matter how promising the fees. Let's hear a little something from the profession about this (perhaps from the recently organized Architects for Social Responsibility, who so far have prudently limited their protests to the arms race). New York City is under far greater threat from Peter Kalikow and his servile masterbuilder than from the A-bomb.

A last irony. Kalikow might be blocked via the designation of the New York and Suburban Project as a landmark. Landmarking has become virtually the last remaining urban planning instrument available for constructive ends, the one social value (other than greed) invested with the authority to intervene in the process of development. It's a pity that they only way we can conserve the way of life of those dwelling athwart Kalikow's designs is by protecting the shells of the buildings they inhabit. Courage to the Landmarks Commission.

May 1985

SAVE THE WHITNEY

History seems poised to take its revenge on poor Marcel Breuer. The late architect, you may recall, was justly lambasted some years ago for designing a scheme to place an office tower on the roof of Grand Central Station. Opposition to that venture was the Agincourt of local preservationism, a victory after which the climate changed decisively. Now, the Whitney Museum, in apparent tit for Breuer's historic tat, proposes to expand itself by building on top of his great gray granite original an architectural affront of such magnitude that the only conceivable explanation is whimsical redress of the dead man's nearly forgotten gaffe. Poetic justice, however, will be symmetrically served only if the current scheme meets the fate of the former.

The Breuer Whitney is a masterpiece. With Edward Durrell Stone's original Museum of Modern Art and Frank Lloyd Wright's Guggenheim Museum, it completes a trinity of marvelous museums, a virtual recapitulation of the modern movement. All three of these institutions have lately felt the need to expand and all have been imperiled. At MOMA, the damage is already done: the original building has been reduced to its façade, its elevation hanging like a modernist painting on a gallery wall. Plans for the Guggenheim have not been revealed in detailed form. Perhaps the threatened instrusion will be held at bay by the totemic power of Wright's original, the master of hubris hexing attempts at effacement from beyond the grave.

At the Whitney, there's no doubt. The violence offered by Michael Graves's proposed expansion is almost unbelievable. Adding to a masterpiece is always difficult, calling for discipline, sensitivity, restraint. Above all, though, it calls for respect. The Graves addition isn't simply disrespectful, it's hostile, an assault on virtually everything that makes the Breuer original particular. It's a petulant, Oedipal piece of work, an attack on a modernist father by an upstart, intolerant child, blind or callow perhaps, but murderous. Yet for this the blame is not entirely the architect's. *Society* asked him to do it. Graves, after all, is a designer with an idiom and could scarcely be expected to throttle his own voice at a moment of tremendous expansion in his career. Graves was simply a wrong choice. The degree of the error is what startles — somebody with influence must really have hated the Breuer building.

The strength of the Whitney's architecture is not simply its singularity but its refined embodiment of the modernist spirit. Breuer may be presently out of vogue, but he's indisputably one of the tops. A member of the core cadre at the Bauhaus, Breuer wound up in the US after the school was shut down by the Nazis. Like the furniture for which he's so universally renowned, his architecture is shapely, strong, and frank. It shows the crafts-person's love of construction and materials, attentive always to an idea of integrity that modernism elevated to an ethic. For Breuer, pouring concrete and bending tubular steel were kindred, essential operations, the center of his art. His work was always, in some primary way, about its own materiality, an address to the solidification of concrete rather than the concretization of fashion.

The Whitney — like the Guggenheim — is an investigation of a boldly sculptural form, part of an architecture conceived as mass — not, as with Graves, as surface. Breuer's take here extended well beyond the primary form of the object to the specific gravity of its constituents. The Whitney is an essay in architectural density, an extremely subtle and revelatory exploration of shades of gray, of texture, weight, and variation in stone and concrete. Breuer was scarcely alone in his fascination with this research. Le Corbusier's post-war production was formally centered on heroic sculpting in concrete. Likewise, Paul Rudolph was — at the time Breuer did the Whitney — pouring out his own fabulous concrete period. Indeed, a worldwide fascination with the stuff had come to bear the soubriquet Brutalism, a somewhat unfortunate play on the French for raw concrete, *béton brut*, a term reflecting the traditionally worshipful Gallic mystification of the natural (*eau sauvage*).

The Whitney is miles from brutality, light years from those rough-cast shrines to abrasion that gave Brutalism its bad name. This is a building about sequence, conceived modernistically — according to a "free plan." Virtually every moment is spatially imagined and dramatic. First comes the building's

WHITNEY ADDITION (SECOND SCHEME)
Michael Graves

startling presence on the street. Breuer recognized both the scale and the jumble of that reach of Madison Avenue and made a building at once distinct and deferential. The flip side of its ingenious in-stepping excavation of the below-grade sculpture court and inflection (the current word) toward its entrance, is the out-stepping of the mass as it rises until its upper-most part presses against the street-wall, like Marcel Marceau limning a window. In a time before cornice heights became a matter of legislation (the Whitney lies in the present Madison Avenue Special Zoning District), Breuer made a building whose top almost precisely accords with current wisdom as to where that line should be.

Recognizing the party-wall character of the row, Breuer divided his Madison Avenue elevation into three parts: a thin concrete wall butted up against its neighbors; a narrow zigzagging band containing, among other things, the great stair; and the main stepping mass, housing the galleries, to which are affixed the winning "eyebrow" windows, apt symbols of museum-going. This division into three has the additional effect (in concert with the lovely bridge and the splatter of windows) of pulling one's reading of the building off the symmetrical, reinforcing the strength of its corner.

Breuer's covered bridge makes one of New York's finest entries. Its angular form and cast concrete construction are reflected in the zigzag band containing the stair, a nice unity between the building's two primary icons of movement. Bridging the sculpture-filled moat, one glimpses behind it the social life of the café, a lovely introduction, and arrives in the slate-floored lobby space, both day-lit and illuminated by a beautiful array of silvered bulbs in saucer-shaped reflectors. From the lobby, one is offered three swell circulation experiences, a happy dilemma of potential progression. The options are: to go down a monumentalized open stair to the café and court-yard visible beyond; to go up in the gigantic elevator, that wonderful ascending room; or to enter the staircase.

As the stairway is one of the great architectural problems, Breuer's is one of the great solutions. On each floor the sequence begins with an orienting curved wall that sets up the experience in terms of direction, materials, and lighting. Then comes the stair itself, both complexly con-figured and perfectly, restfully modulated. Let me recall some fragments. The initial overlook to the street. The fine rail of metal and wood. The rhythm of compression and expansion of the space. The stone treads canti-levering out from the concrete armature, visible only from beneath. The investigation of adjacent values in materials, rough, smooth, dense, and less.

The mysterious diffusion of light. The benches like altars. A helluva place.

Finally the galleries. Their high rooms use strong textures of floor and ceiling as datums against which to register shifts in wall. The periodic surprise of the variously sized eccentric windows offers counterpoint to overall orthogonality. This is the building of a designer working at the height of his powers, a complete work of art, not alterable. Too young to be an official landmark, it's one in every other sense, an historic structure.

The Graves scheme leaves no aspect of the Whitney unvandalized. The overall strategy is to obliterate the building by rendering it subsidiary, turning it into no more than a subordinate part of a larger whole. At the level of massing, this is accomplished by adding a volume of similar size and height at the other end of the block, where it acts — along with the supressed original — like one of the bottom members of a human pyramid. On the backs of these two structures, Graves loads level after klutzy level of building, now a tier with little setbacks, now a tier with a cyclopean lunette, now a gross pergola, now a rustic cornice. It's a strategy meant to dazzle us out of so much as noticing the buried Breuer, a relentless assault of mass, materials, shapes, and phony style. Between the two bottom volumes is perhaps Graves's most inane and subversive invention, a stepped cylinder which has assumed one of those faux-naif monikers so beloved of architects: the hinge.

The hinge is pivotal. It centralizes the composition, erasing both the Breuer's own asymmetry and its asymmetrical relationship to the rest of the block. It further rationalizes the spurious balance between the original and its hulking doppelgänger by picking up the Breuer's coursing and set-in lines and conveying them to its apish kith. To do this, it literally obliterates the two narrow vertical bands mentioned earlier and attaches itself to what remains, causing both sides of the composition to step down symmetrically from the middle of the block, a complete transformation of Breuer's intent. Affixed to the old Whitney like a goiter, the device obscures and intrudes on the stair and irrevocably blemishes the front façade.

In plan, the hinge provides the opportunity for a circular form which Graves uses to achieve several juvenile rotations off the grid and to create a number of cylindrical spaces. Breuer's original free plan has been overwhelmed by axial relations, banal symmetries, and facile scale tricks. The eyebrow windows no longer float in space, they're at the ends of corridors or trapped in little rooms like pigs in pokes. There are major axes and minor axes, chambers and antechambers, portals and vestibules, the whole shitty beaux-arts apparatus against which modernism rebelled. No doubt there will be the usual fey pastels and precious neo-conservative details as well. Absolutely nothing is left untouched. The curved stair-entries will go, as will the window. The big elevator will no longer serve. The café will be yanked up to the roof. Graves even proposes to dump steps into the sculpture court. The man's a kamikaze.

Whatever else he is, though, Michael Graves is surely a creature of the current climate, an architect for the age of Reagan. I imperfectly understand the institutional imperatives that make the Whitney want to tart itself up in the moth-eaten retro drag of Capitalist Realism, to make a museum that looks like a *museum*, but here's the proof that it does. The question now is, how can it be stopped, how can a magnificent building be saved?

I think this scheme may be vulnerable. Not because it's unbearably, stupidly ugly (no crime here and besides, Goldberger thinks it's a work of genius), but because it's bad of its kind and because it so clearly affronts everything that we hold dear, preservationwise. Looking at the drawings, it struck me that Graves's heart wasn't really in this: the plans and elevations were so dull, so filled with hackneyed figures and arrangements, the whole thing so autoplagiaristic, no better than a bad rip-off, looking like it was done in two weeks. Properly apprised of this, perhaps the Whitney will demur, call for a redo, not want to add a third-rate piece to its collection.

More promising may be the preservation route. While the Breuer enjoys only weak protection, the adjoining brownstones cannot be destroyed without permission from the Landmarks Commission. Their demolition is defended by Graves on the grounds that the new building will "enhance the urban characteristics of the surrounding neighborhood." This, of course, is the old "we had to destroy it to save it" argument, of a class with the idea that we might as well tear down Paris since we've got a perfectly good facsimile down at Disney World.

Graves himself identifies the key physical characteristics of the nabe as being small-scale and "figurative." This may or may not be true, but I can't see how this analysis jibes with banging in the equivalent of 20 stories and wiping out a fine group of traditionally figured remnants. I'm no knee-jerk preservationist, but if the only way to get this awful addition subtracted is to save those brownstones, let's save the hell out of them. Hands off the Whitney, Graves!

June 1985

TWO PRIMITIVES*

Last year's big "Primitivism" show at the Museum of Modern Art told an origin tale of modernism. The juxtaposed objects were intended to convey via the visible appropriation of motif the confirmation of authenticity, the identification of modern art with a soulful and spontaneous source. Ah, it's a familiar mode, this hunt for a validating state of nature, our major social myth. From the Bible to Rousseau (Jean-Jacques and le Douanier, tous les deux!), falls — fortunate, paradoxical, and otherwise — figure. Ronald Reagan's rhetoric is also filled with such nostalgia, with the presentation of the social dilemma as one of "recovery" and a return to the more "genuine" values of some misty antecedent.

Architecture — that oscillating tale of the social dog — has a long investment in this particular myth. Again and again, theories of building have problematized the moment of architecture's emergence from the natural. The body of literature (most feverishly produced in the 18th and 19th centuries) that wrestles with the actual description of the "primitive hut" or "Adam's House in Paradise" is almost unbelievable. Even now, though architectural "theory" rarely does more than conflate the polemical and the practical, it's still crippled by an inability to absorb and manipulate its own metaphors. Whatever the conceptual charms of the primitive hut, they are precisely that: its physicalization is an architectural project not unlike the construction of the Tower of Babel.

Today's discourse is heavily into this folly. One understands the origins. As the West invented itself over the course of the last 500 years, it needed a serviceably evocative birthplace. For architects in Europe, this process of

---

*Review of an exhibition by Leon Krier and Ricardo Bofill at the Museum of Modern Art.

auto-Westernization must have been especially gripping. As the cultures of Greece and Rome were transmuted into the golden age of Civilization Itself, their physical remains — neglected and pillaged for centuries — emerged from the background haze to dominate architectural consciousness. Confronted with these decaying monuments, architects had a direct route to the recovery of the classical: the restoration, the *reconstruction* of literal antiquity. The actual presence of these classical structures physicalized architectural inquiry, even as it focused that inquiry on the idea of a single authentic: classicism.

Whenever I hear the word classicism I reach for my Dramamine. Even discussing its validity seems beyond absurd. Imagine abjuring Charlie Mingus for not composing after the manner of a Haydn symphony, cajoling Adrienne Rich for not writing in Latin, or denouncing Robert Morris for not producing sculptures that look like Michelangelo's. In no other realm would such antiquarianism be other than preposterous. Although the long view will surely expose the irrelevance of the current historicist belch in architecture, this movement backwards has gained a shabby if widespread currency in its self-presentation as critique of that great disreputable bugbear, Modern Architecture.

Leon Krier — paired at MOMA with the Spanish architect Ricardo Bofill — has cagily emerged as the leading theoretical point-person of the fashion for retro. Over the last decade, Krier has taken a vow of self-primitivization, styling himself the new Adam of the neo-neo-classical risorgimento. His means have been canny. Krier does not build, insists he does not want to build, for fear of compromising his position. Instead, Krier draws and writes banal — if schematic — aphorisms. Krier's drawings are architectural in a limited sense. They're ideological illustrations, Classical Comix, resistant to detail, interested mainly in mood ... thin. I find them lifeless. His position as classicism's absolute apostle number one is further complicated by his point of entry into the debate. Even the most progressive among us will not dispute Krier's finding that modern times are fraught with alienation and anomie, that much that is precious and human perishes in our cities.

Krier — in tandem with his brother Rob — first emerged as a nostalgic modernist, vaguely allied with the Italian so-called Rationalists whose parsimonious, degree-zeroid attitude surely helped to initiate Krier's own. Like the Rats, he was visibly fascinated with the integrity and the mood of early — especially Italian — modernism. The focal moment was the point of transition from the technical innocence of early industrial construction to a simple modern architecture. Krier's drawings from the period are characteristically ornamented with ancient cars and biplanes, corroborating the innocence of the architectural discovery. The work also shows a certain passion for symmetry, manifested in a recurrent penile and aeronautical bilateralism. And Krier's current preoccupation with the town early emerged in a group of projects within historic cities, including Paris, Rome, and Krier's native Luxembourg.

I have no line on why Krier let his modernism lapse, the motives for his angry turn against its progenitors. However, it's clear that by the later '70s he'd become totally, resolutely identified with archaeologism. It seems there's a missing term in the Krierian syllogism. One understands the assault on modernist urbanism, the movement's most signal failure, but a reversion to classicism? Certainly, in some context, one might be charmed by Krier's imaginary reconstruction of Pliny's Villa or his sweet little odes to rural trabeation. However, the firmness of his position, insisting on the indispensability of classicism for the completion of a historic and shared human project — what he calls "global ecological reconstruction" — is just wacky. "Global Ecology," naturally, is simply the modernized nomenclature for the State of Nature that Krier seeks to reconstruct, based on his ideas about a natural — which is to say, classical — architecture.

States of nature have politics. This is the reason they exist. Depending on whose state of nature you're in, these politics can be brutal or benign. In Krier's case, the politics are fascist. The stench of the evidence is everywhere. First comes the rhetoric, the calls for the "concord and leadership of a handful of individuals," the exultation of the "homeland," and the nostalgia for the social life of the Germanic Middle Ages. Astonishingly, Krier has even elected a role as apologist for the architecture of the Third Reich, befriending its leading figure, the unlamented Albert Speer, and attempting his rehabilitation. Krier's dodge here is a sophistic and dangerous attempt to celebrate Nazi neo-classicism while separating it from Nazi politics, a disingenuous maneuver that points only to the location of architecture's power to oppress. This is precisely in the effort to universalize style: Ein Volk, Ein Führer, Ein Reich, Eine Architektur. Krier tries to portray Nazi neo-classicism as an anomalously astute choice on the part of the Reich, something on the order of giving the people bread, an indisputable social necessity. But this is simply another instance of the oppressor's version of history. To those unwillingly colonized with it, classical architecture seems neither exalted nor inevitable.

The centerpiece of Krier's section of the show is a plan for the reconstruction of Washington, DC. While the classicizing lens produces the same vision everywhere (much like the lens of modernism Krier so abhors), that's not to say it inevitably distorts. If anyplace, dulled classicism is apt to DC, which has a long history of it. As official style, it's tenacious as Rodan or the Blob: just when you think it's snuffed, it's born again.

What's notable about Krier's proposal is not all the phony-baloney palaver about neighborhoods and citizenship, invoked but undrawable, rather that it's yet another proposal to solve urban problems by adding monuments. There's a spray of new ziggurats, pyramids, temples, and cenotaphs, including, one presumes, a nice big one for Reagan who so perfectly shares this pharaonic vision of culture. The core of Krier's scheme is the evaporation of the grassy, strollable center of the city by its aquafication; to better Halicarnassize Washington, Krier floods the mall. Krier forever invokes democracy. The kind he intends, however, is the ultimate one, the democracy of death, a city of tombs.

The adjacent presence of Bofill in this show is curatorially accounted for by his co-membership in the rejectionist front of former modernists. In a previous incarnation, Bofill's office did some lovely work, full of a bracing Catalan flamboyance. This is not on display. Instead, the focus is on a group of projects — all for housing, all built in France — constructed since Bofill's shift in sensibility. In addition, there are some dreary drawings for a hypothetical skyscraper, commissioned for the show. Here's some fairly serious irony. Classical costume notwithstanding, these are modernist programs par excellence, the most Foucauldianly oppressive products of mass culture, what one would have otherwise expected to bear the heat of the Krierian critique.

How, then, is Bofill to be judged? No theorist himself, his elective affinity to Krier is visible only formally. Bofill's recent work is encrusted by a C.B. De Mille-style scenographic classicism in the form of monster orders and gargantuanly baroqued-out site planning. As photo opportunity, the projects are certainly arresting. As critique of the sick modernist stylings of most French new-town architecture, Bofill's work does differentiate itself. I find the so-called classical component of this architecture silly and peripheral at best, sinister and colonialist at worst. The question it begs, however, when read in the context of its implied polemic, is, do people prefer it? A statistical answer won't do. There's a prior question: prefer it to what? Obviously, more generously designed buildings will be preferred to mean ones. Tourists will also likely prefer the Universal Studio Tour to a bus ride through Watts. But perhaps the residents of these ex-urban dormitories would really rather have a nice big place in the center of Paris. Perhaps they'd have liked some actual self-determination in the matter of their homes. The presentation of classicism as the issue here is only another example of architecture's power to obscure.

The Krier/Bofill show is the first of five promised by the Modern under the sponsorship of the Gerald D. Hines Interests. The institutionalization of this link between a real estate developer and the museum's Architecture Department is only the latest episode in its breakneck backslide into the most miasmatic regions of the architectural production. The only remotely charitable interpretation for offering the show as premier in the series (not to mention first in the new space and first in years) is that Arthur Drexler, that Lysenko of curators, has conceived it phylogenetically, a positivistic ascent from this primally slimy primitivism to … what? Mirror glass? Johnson? I'm not holding my breath.

July 1985

ANOTHER LOW-TECH

SPECTACULAR

The latest from Richard Rogers — Patscenter, a new building for PA Technology — lies in the Americanoid technological latifundia, an islet in the prestige think-belt around Princeton, New Jersey. The telephone-pole-lined road down which it's approached is flanked by numbers of scientific and manufacturing installations, all garbed in the dumb functionalist mufti Banham so deplores in the circuit ranches of Silicon Valley. Patscenter's neighbors are buff black boxes, unspecific about pursuits within, as noncommittal about their secrets as the forms of domestic suburbia which surround them, straightforward fairings for God knows what.

The new building is an exception, and the locals predictably love it or hate it, say it looks like a ship, grasping for a referent and coming up, dependably, with the right one, modernism's own. "Looks like a ship," rings pleasingly to me: I'd personally sooner contemplate a rusty tramp steamer than a dozen templettes by Michael Graves, the local alternative, and a ship steaming through the suburbs, like Hollein's carrier ploughing over waves of grain, seems doubly delicious. Not that it really looks like a ship, more reminiscent of an aircraft hangar or — to delve into the more debased reaches of the image bank — of a California drive-in restaurant, broad canopy hung over open cars filled with milkshake-swilling teens. Anyway, though, it's a not quite but nearly native presence.

What it is, of course, is laboratory and office space for a "high-tech" consulting firm. What it isn't is a factory. The image of the ship, therefore, serves as a surrogate for an end product, conceived on the premises, but executed elsewhere. The building's like one of its neighbors turned inside out. Across the street, a huge bland structure is consecrated to the assembly of things; here, the manufacture is mental, cowled in something which

PA TECHNOLOGY
(*New Jersey*) Richard Rogers

strives to make the idea of technology visible — "advertising," as the head of the operation explains. It's more than a lab, it is a zone of seduction where clients are entertained and briefed, a formal testament to the operation's ship shape.

As signifier, the building is effectively imprecise, not quite arbitrary but surely laggard, filled with imputation but ultimately lazy in the meanings department. As technology goes, it's of a low order, but then most buildings are. Rogers does represent the apogee of some kind of Victorian optimism, the happy Brunelian satisfactions of spanning long and visibly. This surely is the appeal of the building to the very contented client, its technological enthusiasm. But the real expression of this modernist joy comes not from a walk along science's (or even science fiction's) leading edge but from a canny decorative strategy and old-fashioned, classicizing architectural virtues.

The building works via two memorably iconic instruments. First, the visible, heroicized apparatus of suspension, those A-frame towers and the wonderful wacky order of giant washers used as joints. And second, the visible, heroicized apparatus of piped and ducted servicing, a long-standing Rogers signature. These devices are used as totems of reasons, manifestations of method, stand-ins for science. The services are elaborately color-coded. This parsing (silver for the movement of air, green for sprinklers, orange for electrical, etc., etc.) is Patscenter's central authoritative act, its moral. And what a fine moral for the modern age it is! Useless information marshalled with bone-headed rigor signifying nothing beyond the act of signification. Image-wise the message is right for a company which wants us to know it's on top of things, even the things on top of it. It's also a broadside at the peaches and mauves of the current palette, a proud coating of the lurid certainties of the '60s.

Of course, at the level of *parti*, Princeton is a doppelgänger of the chip works at Gwent. The suspended roof, the high towers holding air-handling equipment, the central spine, the undifferentiated interior space, the bilateral symmetry, the repetitive section, the tech-y decoration. Gwent is larger and genuinely a factory, its game of suspension more robust, wrought via great trusses rather than with Princeton's shorter, shallower, roof-integral beams. And Princeton, in its present, first-phase, incarnation is visibly too short, the impact of its regular rhythms vitiated by premature truncation: the building clearly wants to be long.

But the A-frame is terrific, much more dynamic than Gwent's rather stodgily substantial and rectilinear towers. Princeton is so ineluctably tensile, it nearly sings, its triangulations evoking the sinuousness of tents as much as the puritanism of machinery. Here, indeed, is an appropriately American reference; the evangelical big top, pitched in a field, for the conduct of ecstatic revivals. The image, then, the view from afar, is satisfactorily compelling. As a landscape piece it both distinguishes itself and provides enough accessible identifications to avoid irrelevance or whimsy. Given current parlance it announces its technologism and, given current practice, it equally announces its refinement and distinction.

Entering the place, though, things do get blurrier. Here, one is obliged to approach the building as functioning rather than functionalist and here the suspending thunder, becoming imperceptible in the lowish space, doesn't count for so much. Naturally, there's the use-rationale of flexibility, those partitions filled with incipient mobility, the prospect of another configuration one day. Quotidianly, though, the structure barely registers. The absence of columns, the justification for the acrobatics above, is not noticeable within. The scale of the space, the columnar spine, the substantial presence of partitions, all dissipate the reading of span. Indeed, to participate from within in the primary activity without, one looks through special apertures provided for the purpose, the bubble skylights surmounting the spine. It's a fine view, well composed, but it does seem a bit of a contrivance, engineered to underlook another contrivance.

One is therefore forced back to the level of detail. Rogers is a classicizer, building the same kind of building over and over, working on refinements of his orders, his kits of parts. The question begged in all such operations, from Parthenon to Patscenter, is perfection. Princeton is caught — almost unavoidably — in the middle ground between doing too much and doing too little. The line between the comprehension of its kit of parts and the inclusions and modifications that take place outside of it is blurry. Princeton is poised between paradigms, between the idea of a system that takes account of everything, down to the pencils, and the idea of the well-serviced shed, the rigid envelope absolutely distinct from its contents.

When I visited the building, there was some concern lest I mention a bare light bulb hanging from a string attached to one of the pipes, an anomaly that had already figured in one reporter's account. It was a revealing anxiety. Clearly the pressure's for totality rather than for the sort of circumscribed funkiness of a place like Herzberger's Centraal Beheer. Patscenter does not send an altogether clear signal vis-à-vis the potted plant and family photos of those toiling within. There's pressure for meticulousness and efficiency but also certain circumscribed countervailing tolerances for the ad hoc. Thus, the dangling light bulb can be seen either as a failure of the system to get things perfectly right or as evidence of the friendly malleable informality of the place. At a more architectural level, the same split is visible at the entry indentation at one end of the central spine. Like the scene at the back of the Seagram Building, this provides the setting for the little drama of a system that cannot turn an inside corner. The junction of clear entry glazing, "Kalwall" exterior cladding, and visible interior partitioning is — adopting the classicizing reading — a bungle. But, if one sees instead a biopsy, a benign slice of life, then the conjunction offers an incitement to the helpfully random, an aesthetic rationale for bare bulbs and browning geraniums.

The palaver at places like Patscenter nowadays is heavily invested in the idea of "corporate culture," a concept that smacks of oxymoron to me. The stiff, if amiable, Brits in pinstripes who run the place were eager to impress me with their feeling that this building was somehow an artifact-isomorph with the larger anthropology of their institutional aims. These have to do with the quantification and organization of thinking, with research that doesn't simply yield results but which is also billable on a hourly basis. To them, Rogers' work was important because it yielded an environment which was the "antithesis of the ivory tower," an environment which symbolized the displacement of the cloister, the antique, individualist model of the university environment, by the higher rationalizations of the shop floor, the Taylorization of knowledge. The incident that best emblematized this attitude to me was a series of little elbow-height ledges located on the tops of the dwarf partitions that carve up the space of the central spine. These were designed (by Rogers? by the Invisible Hand?) as social zones, spots where — in the absence of so much as a comfortable chair — harried engineers might pause to interact "informally," effecting the free, if reimbursable, exchange of ideas so devoutly sought by management.

The degree to which architecture is directly culpable in any of this is surely arguable. One would not, for example, implicate Rogers for the virtually all-male work-force visible at Princeton, its females tending mainly to "traditional" roles. On the other hand, the ensemble does participate deliberately in an historical machine culture, overwhelmingly masculinist. One has read in the pages of *Architectural Review* theories of "British high-tech" which pin its prominence on the early childhood training of its progenitors, their pre-pubescent bedrooms glutted with Meccano toys and scale replicas of Sopwith Camels. More directly relevant may be the sartorial history of men managing machines, from the resplendently haber-dashered admiral on the bridge of his gigantic dreadnought (never mind the coal-choked navvies in the engine room below) to the nattily turned out Marlboro man on the flight deck of the 747. The point is simply this: it's a history of the machine that stands outside of the history of architecture and which brings with it special prejudices about the social environment. Whether they be sailors or package holiday makers, the organizational rigidities intrinsic to the working of the great devices they inhabit exceed the happiest norms of everyday life. The Savile-Rowed captains of industry at Princeton are certainly conscious of this.

As *envoi*, no more, I must take note of Rogers' truly daffy site plan for the development of the surrounding 50 acres into an industrial park (talk about oxymorons!). It's a typically picturesque suburban tract array of presumably identical structures, perfunctorily landscaped and hemmed by parking, another go at the machines in the garden. The scheme's banal, too soft an order for the right angle congruences demanded by the crisp repetitive integrity of the handsome and habitable first go.

September 1985

FERRY GODFATHERS

Within the next several months, the city will designate a developer for what is probably the most spectacular building site New York has to offer: South Ferry. If this sounds a familiar scenario, it is. Although the sponsoring agency is different (in this case it's the Department of Ports and Terminals) the setup is the same as that used by the MTA in selling off the Coliseum earlier this year. The results of that sale left the public with a classic good news/bad news conundrum. The good news is that the city cleaned up price-wise, almost half a billion into the MTA's coffers. One's satisfaction at this outcome is, of course, tempered by the knowledge that the MTA's maw has proven itself capable of scarfing limitless cash with zero visible results as far as transport is concerned. But the germane bad news is that the superior financial deal ultimately chosen came with a 75-story reflective glass, faceted, atrium-bedecked millstone in the form of one of the plug-ugliest buildings ever prismacolored on bumwad.

This troubling outcome was not exactly unpredictable. The Coliseum competition was — like the South Ferry Stakes — a *developer* competition. In my ideal universe, such a strategy is not the one I'd pick to guarantee the quality of architectural results. First of all, the choice of architect is left to the judgment of the developers. The designs in competition are prefiltered through the sensibilities of individuals and corporations who have been credentialed into the running on the basis of financial statements. I don't know about you, but I'm not quite ready to mortgage the architectural ranch on the strength of an IOU for good intentions from Donald Trump, Tishman Speyer, or the Catco Group, whoever they are. In setups like this, the adjudicating body is confronted by a group of schemes executed, for the most part, by the usual palsied hands in the usual palsied style. But, even in the case when superior designs actually emerge, the decision is still structured as a Hobson's choice. Which would be most responsible on the part of a city agency: to choose the best design or to choose the best deal? Both arguably serve the interests of the people.

In order to forestall such dilemmas, guidelines are promulgated, criteria proposed. In the South Ferry competition, the Request for Proposals is convincing in its call for buildings of quality and articulate in laying out its concerns for the important urbanistic, public space, and preservation issues raised by the development of the site. Jay Feiertag, project manager at Ports and Terminals, the man responsible for the elaboration of the guidelines, is exemplary in his dedication and personally involved in the site and its destiny. But the system is fatally flawed. Of course, 1 per cent of the budget can be mandated for art, and a "view corridor" in line with Whitehall Street cannot be faulted. But calls for "respect," recognition of "uniqueness," a "sense of place," modulation of size, enhancing the skyline, and "reflecting upon the best tower development in Lower Manhattan" add up to a pretty ineffable set of instructions, never mind the intent. Without a mechanism with the capacity both to judge and to insist, such insistences don't amount to squat.

The fact is — and the importance of this site throws the situation into profound relief — that too many things are being decided together. Compromise is intrinsic to the process. It recapitulates the broader mode of production of urban space in a capitalist environment: government mediates the trade-off between the rights of profit and the people's right to amenity in the public realm. In such a system, good architecture is not a requirement, merely one of the possible byproducts: nobody's necessity.

There is, however, a solution to this dilemma and a simple one. The architectural aspect of these competitions should be separated from the sale of the property. Let the city develop an architectural and functional program in the public interest and let it sponsor an architectural competition to find the best solution. Then, invite the developers to bid on the project. Such competitions may not inevitably lead to world-historical results but they have a long and honorable history and do represent an opportunity for new ideas. In any event, I'd much sooner take my chances with a competition among several hundred architects than with one among half a dozen or so developers. Just look at the record.

It's too late for a great work at South Ferry. Most of the solutions submitted are no more than business as usual, the glories of the site inspiring no particularly glorious responses. Most of the projects are dressed in current neo-con suits, tailored with varying degrees of confidence, finished with enough haberdashery detail to give the decision-makers an illusion of choice. The nostalgic theme that so predominates in the entries is doubtless meant to evoke those immortally totemic views that still signify Lower Manhattan for most of us: a black-and-white photo from the 1920s or '30s, the *Normandie* or similar in the foreground, a gorgeous clump of spindly skyscrapers behind.

But things have changed. Most of those great older buildings are still there (pace Singer) but new context has erased their predominance. Downtown is flanked by a phalanx of Sun Belt slabs that have left it forever transformed. The island's tip — which has layered itself farther and farther into the harbour since its earliest European days — demands to be composed in a new way, and South Ferry represents the crucial spot for doing it.

While most of the proposals make some tithe to scenographic demands of the area (the majority with various lighthouse evocations, glowing orbs surmounting), only two have attempted the whole hog, prominence-wise. Helmut Jahn's go for Olympia and York looks a lot like a spaceship from a '50s sci-fi movie, a gigantic V-2 resting on its three great fins and tapering to a rocket nose. In surer hands than Jahn's such a daffy extravagance might be supportable, but Jahn's recent work (cover photo on *GQ* notwithstanding) has been so dismally inept, so finesse-free, that risking him in the full flush of his megalomaniac success seems too risky. Besides, he's got far too much work in Manhattan already.

This leaves Arquetectonica, the Florida firm whose graphic condos weekly flash by in the credit sequence of *Miami Vice*. It's damned photogenic work although (and I've seen none of it in the skin) its preoccupations are, alas, mainly decorative. Nevertheless, theirs is easily the shrewdist submission (for the Jack Parker Corp.) in the Ferry race. In image, the project is sheathed in a jolly constructivoid suit, bristling with Tchernikovian doodads and early '60s funk, okay by me. In shape, the building — which gets a bit wider at the top — shares proportions with the Trade Center. It's the only submission that seems to have recognized the importance of that particular trialogue. Siting is also apt and smart. The building sits a little ways offshore, on its own tiny island, a nice evocation of accretion and a recognition that making land is Manhattan's way of making money. It doesn't say much about the candidates, but I guess this one gets my vote.

*

I paid my first visit to the Portman Hotel (Marriott Marquis, to cite its phone book moniker) the other day and urge you to do the same if you can get past the Edwardian dicks at the front door. Indeed, if you can find the front door. This is a perennial problem in Portman's work, ambivalence about arrival and departure. In the Times Square instance, the way in is a kind of drive-through in the middle of the block, all asphalt and Fugazys and — wait a minute — isn't that a revolving door over there, Marge?!

Portman's psychosis isn't exactly that he hates cities, it's that he hates the fact that they're different from each other. Maybe he was a severe preemie but the only thing Portman can deal with is being *inside*. And in the fullest sense of the word: the interior of the Marquis (currently lined with floor after floor of metal grille-work, awaiting the installation of dangly green things) looks like the Big House itself, endless, vertiginous, penitential tiers rising from the exercise, er, cocktail floor.

Little needs to be said about the placement of this huge building in the city: Portman designs as if the city weren't there. The thuggish presence of this hotel in Times Square is an easy shot. We know the architect didn't care, never cares, whether in Los Angeles, Detroit, or New York, about local particulars. He simply builds to type, getting ready for the first franchise on Mars or Uranus where the outside atmosphere will be genuinely hostile. One only notes that this is another big dong in the death knell of Times Square. With this pivotal block gone over to the millennial Anyville style, the total transformation of the place simply becomes more imaginable. The neighborhood now holds too many vantage points from which nothing is visible but the hulking new order. The Marquis, paired with its neighbor to the south, is simply an advert for the future, a preview of coming attractions.

Where one does expect Portman to deliver is in the glitzerama of his atriumed-out insides. Unfortunately the Marquis is bad Portman, big but energyless, lacking the usual level of zoot. The Marquis was lovely under construction, largely because of a slip-formed, cylindrical elevator tower that shot up first, independent of the rest of the structure. This tower is now the main interior event, standing at one end of the vast atrium (give the man credit — plenty vast), with twee glass elevators shooting up and down its perimeter. What we have here is, in effect, a skyscraper indoors, in captivity, like King Kong!

But Portman blows it, doesn't play up to the tower-ness of the tower. By stepping back the section of his atrium as it rises, he obscures his soaring shaft at its culmination, its most seminal point, its moment of entry into the disc of the as-yet-unopened surmounting revolving restaurant. Just goes to prove, though: size isn't everything.

October 1985

DUMP THE TRUMP

Great cities find their forms through compact. New York entrusts its destiny to deals. Donald Trump will direct the future of 77 acres of our most vital territory not because he's in any way earned the privilege but because he's paid for it. This is the urbanism of the shooting gallery: put your money down and take your shot.

I refer to the young master builder's recently announced plans to build a "Television City" on the old Penn Central rail yards stretching from 59th to 72nd Street along the Hudson. In case you missed the hype, Trump intends to put up the following: one 150-story ("world's tallest") building, six 76-story buildings, one 65-story building, and one 15-story building. These are to be filled with condos and offices and would sit on a titanic "podium" that would contain the eponymous TV production facilities as well as department stores, shops, parking, and other mall-style amenities, all topped by 40 acres of what the press release describes as "parks." The architect for this scheme is Helmut Jahn of Chicago, a designer of particularly primitive sensibilities whose shallow insights and unfettered esprit de glitz must have struck Trump as especially congenial. I can almost hear the conversation between them. "Helmut, I like your style," says Trump. "And Donald, I like *your* style," says Jahn.

The scheme is so stupid, my initial reaction is to think it's a phony, a stalking horse for some marginally less barbaric proposal Trump is willing to trade down to. Even in shrunken form, though, we haven't been treated to a towers-in-the-park proposal for quite some time. There's a reason for this. The architectural profession has — over the past 20 or so years — woken up and smelled the urban bacon, come to the realization that most of what we prize in our climax metropoli, like Manhattan, comes from formal strategies in which the urban ground is favored over the architectural figure. This privileging is the compact of character that makes such cities singular. Over time, certain means have emerged as central to the particularity of these great cities. In Manhattan, for example, the skyscraper, the brownstone row, the hard-lined, even-topped avenue, are among the keys to our urban specific.

One of the great powers of cities conceived in terms of convention is that they can be forgiving of mediocre architecture. Helmut Jahn's several midtown skyscrapers (now going up) will be absorbed in that forest, a few more trees (however twisted) among the multitude. The West Side project, however, is apparently unaffected by so much as a whiff of the genius loci. Looking at the boneheaded proposal, one wonders whether the architect even visited the site. Indeed, there's evidence that he did not. The rank of glyphs bespeaks lakeside Chicago, and the centerpiece of the scheme, the 150-story erection, Trump's third go at the "world's tallest building," looks to be the same world's tallest building proposed earlier this season for the Columbus Circle site. Was ever a man more preoccupied with getting it up in public?

If one were actually to approach the Penn yards site in terms of its particulars, one sees first an edge, the meeting of land and water, the moment at which the island asserts itself. Manhattan offers plenty of precedents for this. Our characteristic edges include the hard ones (Central Park West or Fifth Avenue along the park), the soft ones (Riverside Park, which depends on the wall of the drive for its special reading), and the fingered ones (the vanishing system of piers, their economic rationale fading but their physical possibilities very much alive). After a million years of struggle over Westway, these issues should not be strange to even a vaguely conscious designer.

There's also the instructive recent case of Battery Park City. Naturally, conditions down there are somewhat special: this is newly created land not yet entirely of the main. Two strategies are being used to invent the connection. First, there's the World Financial Center gambit, a complex centered on a fresh-carved harbor, an attenuation of the shoreline. This idea of making a big civic space directly at waterside is A-OK. It recalls the first schemes proposed for Battery Park City, now abandoned, which were filled with '60s-style megastructural grandeur and marvelously monumental waterfront spaces. The residential zones under construction in Battery Park City take a different tack, largely in reaction to this earlier vision. The big shtick here (propagated in an atmosphere of endless self-congratulation) is laying out the landfill in "traditional" streets and blocks, culminating in a waterfront promenade. In addition, a set of architectural codes have been imposed on the site, intended to establish a homogeneously Po-Mo decorative strategy for all new construction.

The Battery Park City "idea" is an attempt to ape a "natural" process of city extension, to describe and replicate an indigenous way of building. Ironically, this residential gridding and platting has no real history nearby. The choice to build according to some idealized vision of a New York City residential neighborhood (whatever the conservative appeal of the defense via precedent) is — at this specific place — really just whimsical. In terms of the economics of parcelization, it does have its vulgar logic, facilitating the handing out of pieces to the usual developers. But the real visionary genius of New York lies in the tension between precedent and innovation. There's no better example than the area of lower Manhattan that Battery Park City adjoins, where 20th-century skyscrapers rise from the medieval-style street pattern laid out by the Dutch.

Alas, the visionaries of the Reagan Era are all Edward Tellers and Donald Trumps, arrogant apostles of the indefensible. Television City is exactly that, an urban vision apt for the TV era. Like television, Television City is all about unnatural juxtaposition. Just as the TV system validates any adjacency, not blinking an eye at those quick cuts from commercials to carnage, so too Television City simply inserts itself in prime time. There's no point in building the world's tallest building or a row of 76-story apartments, beyond the logic of anything goes if it sells.

Trump owns a couple of casinos in Atlantic City, one of them called "Trump's Castle," which advertises on TV continuously. In the ad, a little Henry the Eighth arrives in a coach as the chanteuse belts "You're the King of the Castle" (king at least until you've lost all your money to Don). A message flashes on the screen: FREE INDOOR PARKING. This is important. Atlantic City is a fine example of the way people like Trump see cities, hostile places to be secured by means of strategic enclaves filled with glittery fun. Television City is likely to have the longest expanse of indoor parking in Manhattan and its first full-blown suburban shopping mall, safely tucked into the podium to protect it from the rest of town. Atop this (at an elevation of 85 feet) will be the "public" space. It would take an oxymoron to embrace this notion. I've no doubt that this park will (like the pathetic little upstairs amenity in the Trump Tower, supposedly public) never be anything of the kind, just an inaccessible, shadow-darkened nowhere.

At least one distinguished architect turned this commission down. And, although the man adamantly refused to go on record about any part of the circumstances, it's reported that he was loath to undertake a job so predicated on haste. As far as great cities are concerned, haste makes wasteland. Whatever your specific stylistic predilections, it's clear that cities thrive on a certain density of elaboration. The Trump scheme may have fewer architectural ideas per unit volume than any project since Robert Moses's most malnourished housing schemes. It's the kind of work that would get a D— at a second-rate school of architecture. The only reason for the passing grade would be that the student had at least finished the presentation.

I can imagine the final review. Somebody would ask what the *idea* behind the scheme was. Since making a fortune is an answer that is disallowed before graduation, the kid would be forced to come up with an explanation of a more architectural or social character. The first effort would be to pin up various spurious diagrams of circulation, covered with red magic marker arrows pointing to the river and the city, phony signifiers of accessibility. "You mean that to get to the river you'd have to walk several hundred feet down that ridiculous spiral ramp?" someone would ask, "I put it all on a *podium* so you could look out over the highway," might be the next gambit. The ass-backwardness of this approach could be entertained. The kid would then revert to some stock palaver about composition. "I put the big building in the middle and balanced it by putting three 76-story buildings at either end of the site." The klaxon of asininity would sound and our student would scramble once again. "It's got the tallest building in the world!" he'd finally blurt out. And then the jury would go on to the next project.

Unfortunately, *we* cannot go on to the next project.

"I wanted to be an architect, I was an architect. I consider myself as a sort of witness." So aphorized Oscar Nitzchke during an interview a few years ago. Born in 1900, Nitzchke — recently the subject of a lovingly organized show at Cooper Union — was certainly present at the scenes of many of mod arch's most memorable creations. He's a man who clearly loved — and still loves — being there: helping Van Doesberg and Arp on the Café L'Aubette; at the Salle Pleyel for Duke Ellington's Paris debut; sitting with Picasso and Joyce during their first meeting at the Café de Flore; hanging out at the

Cedar Tavern with Pollock, de Kooning, Kline, and Gorky; schmoozing at Black Mountain with Cage, Cunningham, and Bucky Fuller; holidays with the Braques; a stint in Le Corbusier's office; work on the UN project; student in Auguste Perret's Atelier du Palais de Bois along with Nelson, Goldfinger, Lubetkin. How could 85 years of such ubiquitousness have left Nitzchke so little known today?

Certainly, as teacher, collaborator, and colleague Nitzchke has many friends and admirers. The depth of this respect is corroborated by the fact that Nitzchke's small renown is the result of efforts by the sons of two of his associates. The Cooper show, for instance, was the work of Gus Dudley, whose father, George, was Nitzchke's student at Yale. But the influence of personality and comradeship is an anxious and ephemeral one, always begging the question of works. And for Nitzchke, there's a complication. The project that is the prime guarantor of his architectural reputation – the 1934 Maison de la Publicité – is unbuilt, commissioned by a man whose enthusiasm for Nitzchke's preliminary designs was soon mitigated by his taking a mysterious powder. Bad history's intervention also aborted the 1937 Palais de la Découverte, a vast and forward-looking science museum, victim of the war. Nitzchke's corpus, while exquisite, is more drawn than built.

Placing Nitzchke demands some sort of attention to categories. He doesn't slot into the visionary niche with those delineators of the not-quite-possible – Sant'Elia or Chernikov, say. Nor is he one of those great solidifiers of paradigm, source of coherence for some currency of fragments: there's no Maison de Verre here. Nitzchke's an exemplar rather than an avatar, a man with modernism in his veins, in love with a vision of the life of his times. And because his cognizance was sharp, his work has always been to the point, not derivative but original, continuous with a founding generation.

Nitzchke's gifts as a draftsperson were considerable. The Cooper Union show held many fine drawings, appealing for their combination of discipline and informality, for a relaxed technique that never confuses itself with primary architectural ideas. Their pleasures, though, are tinged with the retrospective sadness of latency, the work filled with the possibility of construction. It's a testament to Nitzchke that the enthusiasm that suffuses these drawings never dissipates into irony, empty technique, or the easily current.

The summary artifact is the Maison de la Publicité, a paper masterpiece that might have become one of modern architecture's monuments. The building was designed for a site on the Champs Élysées and meant to house both offices for an array of adpersons and a variety of spaces addressed to the public. In its programmatic complexity, the Maison was an ideologically deformed version of a "social condenser," the modernist ideal of an architectural pressure cooker meant to form the new socialist citizen. While the truth the Maison was meant to propagate wasn't exactly *Pravda's*, its means were familiar, sibling in spirit with the Vesnins' 1923 tower for the above-mentioned daily. Both were transparently graphic, literally communicative, kinetic and mutable as the "news."

The Maison fronts the Champs with an ever-changing façade of "information," projected in luminous electric signage. Nitzchke's vision concentrates a phenomenon that was transforming European cities: the enlightenment of neon times. This was the heyday of the movie palace which, with an array of vast illuminated façades, helped re-form urban nightlife. But Nitzchke's signage is not simply veneered, it's consistent and continuous with a fully configured overall vision. At street level, the building presents an exhibition area meant for a changing show of products, a space anchored by four squarely composed cylindrical columns that broaden to dramatic mushroom capitals. Up a level is a café, overlooking. Down a level, an egg-shaped newsreel theater, cranked winningly into a corner of the volume. The upper-story offices are organized into two buildings, flanking a central café court and linked along one side of it by an undulating circulation spine of glass block. It's beautifully done and beautifully drawn, so strong and so assured as to, at least partially, dissipate the sad question of "what if."

Oscar Nitzchke's triumph is not merely one of talent but one of keeping the faith. In project after project he sustains modernism's enthusiasm for its version of the new. In 1929, Nitzchke and two collaborators won a competition for the design of a "Maison Métallique." It's a swell solution to the confrontation of architecture with new, industrially produced materials, one of modernism's favorite intersections. The project is thoroughly realized and unsentimental, a machine for living. Reconfronting the question of the metal building in the late 1940s, while working on the design of the Alcoa Tower in Pittsburgh for the office of Wally Harrison (his long-time employer), Nitchke's enthusiasm for the problem is undiminished. While my feelings about the final project are mixed (intervention of committee design?), there's no mistaking the vigor of Nitzchke's investigation. Later projects reveal the same drive: a church in Tanganyika echoing Ronchamp, a cathedral in San Salvador under the Perret sway, neither built, yet still tributes to modern architecture's possibility. And this does seem like Nitzchke's legacy, this enthusiasm for prospect, this optimism for architecture.

It's always nice to have the winds taken out of your journalistic sails by the arrival of an event you were just preparing to argue for. On November 19, the City Council passed an extremely important piece of environmental legislation, requiring strict regulation of the way in which buildings are demolished in order to prevent the poisoning of both workers and the public by asbestos. It should be an object of great pride that New York has become a national leader in this crucial issue. Although use of asbestos by the construction industry has been widely curbed, vast quantities of the stuff remain in many buildings, ready for release into the air during fires, demolitions, and other decompositions. If well-enforced, the new legislation will offer crucial protection to many of those most directly at risk from this terrible pathogen.

December 1985

LEAVING WRIGHT

ENOUGH ALONE

A consequence of the profession's present preoccupation with "context" is a kind of collective confidence about the possibility of adding on. There's an implicit argument that architects, duly skilled and sensitized, should be able to intervene anywhere. We're absorbed with the architectural equivalent of method acting, with thinking we can inhabit the skull of any sensibility. Even when "contextualism" stops short of replication, it encourages action in difficult situations.

The result inevitably, is to eviscerate the idea of the architecturally sacred. If adjacency is always a possibility, history becomes irrelevant. As all of architecture is ransacked alike, its field becomes continuous and the logic of its monuments ever more indistinct. Today's vaunted pluralism is really just an excuse to be weak-willed about principles. It confronts architecture opportunistically, as a developer confronts the city. Large proprieties recede before the ethics of occasion. Finally, there's never any need to draw limits.

These matters have been thrown into special relief in New York City over the past several years by the expansion schemes of Manhattan's major art museums. The role of these institutions in the proprietorship of artistic culture, if incidental in terms of real fundamentals, has still focused things. Commonly, we see these places as zones of cultural privilege, susceptible to higher tests than the more quotidian matrix. And the role of MOMA, the Whitney, and the Guggenheim as guarantors of the memory of modernism itself has put a fairly fine edge on architectural questions. Each, after all, is housed in a seminal modernist building.

Without question, the Guggenheim raises the issues most schematic-ally. Not simply is this a work of undisputed genius, perhaps the greatest building in the city; it's one of the pre-eminent icons of American architecture. On the postage stamp that celebrates Wright, the Guggenheim is visible over his shoulder, standing in for the most important body of work ever produced by an American artist. This is not to slight the difficulty in adding to a marvelous building like the Whitney or to detract from the egregiousness of the current proposal. But the circumstances on Madison Avenue are, at least theoretically, more generous than those on Fifth. There is both literal and conceptual space around the Breuer building: the Whitney is an end piece, it asks to be built beside. The Guggenheim's aura occupies a wider territory.

Wright built the Guggenheim to be exceptional. Its form draws power from its inscription in an environment where it represents almost complete otherness. The great broadening spiral looks like a cliff dwelling, carved from the Dover of dignified orthogonality which extends the length of the east side of Central Park. Although it's been argued that the Guggenheim is the product of urban antipathy, there's no mistaking the affection of the results, striking for both their originality and their clarity. The amazing elegance of the primary composition is only enhanced by Wright's simplicity of means and elaboration: like its avenue, the Guggenheim has great gravity. Here is Wright's answer to detractors who can't see beyond the decoration of his late work.

As an architectural statement, the Guggenheim is complete. The scheme to expand prepared by Gwathmey Siegel & Associates — whatever its local merits — is thus forced to contend with the fact that it may be impossible. This has obliged the architects to position the project in terms of one of the justifying rhetorics that invariably arise around such seemingly doomed enterprises. This is nothing new. In the old days, one heard talk of "background" buildings receding into invisibility, of "jewels in anonymous settings." More recently, though, the rhetoric of contextualism has provided a far more elaborated means for describing this kind of relationship. Today's pluralism offers the idea of the "translation" of one architectural language into another. Such "contextual" thinking promises the Rosetta Stone of transmogrification. One might *be* like Wright, instead of simply aping him à la Taliesin, or just fading into the woodwork. With the rhetoric of pluralism, it becomes possible to propose an *equivalent* architecture.

The problem with genius, though, is that it doesn't compute. There can never be real equivalence. Of course, some kind of parity might be achieved by another work of equal (but not comparable) brilliance. But what brilliance it would take to reconfigure our sense of the Guggenheim's life in relationship to its informing constraints! In any event, such a barely conceivable work is not at issue. The Gwathmey Siegel proposal presents itself defensively: we're confronted with a rhetoric of giving no offense, the rhetoric of preservation, with plans described as "referential, contextual, and interpretively sympathetic." Indeed, the real justification for the expansion is not architectural but curatorial. There's a need for more space for offices, storage, additional exhibition areas. This necessity is apparently beyond questioning; it is museological manifest destiny.

There's one argument here, though, that clouds matters. Wright himself prepared a scheme for the expansion of the museum, published in 1952. Associating the new scheme with Wright's own initiative obviously has great potential benefit rhetorically. After all, if it can be argued that the new addition is actually a *completion*, the carrying out of the master's original intent, then the inevitable claim of the violation of a landmark is strictly circumscribed. The primary issue of whether to build is displaced by the question of how. And the existence of the Wright scheme opens the door to an appeal to precedent, the main mode of understanding in current thinking about the authority of any existing architectural condition.

Citing the 1952 sketches is a red herring. To begin, the fallacy of privileging a particular moment in the evolution of an artistic intention is clear. We know of a variety of studies for the building — some dramatically different from the built version — which, if interesting in showing the evolution of Wright's thinking, are scarcely to be regarded as more authoritative than what actually went up. The Guggenheim has simply never been seen, in the community's eye, as incomplete. Whether or not there are those who might have preferred another version (say, the one in which the spiral narrows instead of broadens at the top) is beside the point. The question — at this moment in history — is moot. One would not add a mustache to the Mona Lisa, even if one found a sketch in Leonardo's notebooks in which he had studied the possibility.

Still, the argument from the 1952 scheme is not quite so easily dismissed. The '52 proposal and Wright's mention of an "orthogonal curtain backdrop," as well as his shifting of the big spiral from the northern end of the site to the south, all give evidence of a desire somehow to neutralize and discipline the Guggenheim's setting. However, the actual proposal, sketchy in the extreme, gives one the sense of a highly ancillary gesture, one that would be read — in its strict orthogonality, dumb repetitiveness, and fenestrated transparency — not so much as part of the Guggenheim but as a more satisfactory version of the end condition on the block behind. Poised between the Wrightian slab and Central Park, the Guggenheim would become a bioptic summary of the Wrightian monument in a Wrightian city, a lateral strip of Broadacre City, embracing greenery, roadway, and the organic style.

This is, naturally, a kind of precedent and a vaguely invocable one. It is, however, not a precedent for adding on so much as it is a precedent for sealing off. The 1952 scheme, among its other attributes, is almost dysfunctionally skinny, a mere 25 feet wide, slab in extremis, an architecture of pure backdrop. With such a manifestly scenographic device, the issue becomes not one of its existence but one of its location. And there's no question that the concept undergirding the grid was precisely that it be behind. To me, this is the absolute limit of the argument, the possibility that a simple piece, exquisitely slim, be inserted twixt the Guggenheim and its built context, a drapery to obscure the urban stage machinery and foreground the starring performance of the spiral museum.

Although it presents itself by means of this argument from precedent, the Gwathmey Siegel proposal substantially exceeds it. Their scheme is not about a recessive addition but about a co-equal one. The net effect, according to the architects, is to make the "bipartite" composition of the present building "tripartite." The value of this reconfiguration is allegedly corroborated by the "precedent" of the 1952 slab, which is presumed to justify a reading of a building that wants to be three. This apparent longing for trinity allows Gwathmey Siegel to impute legitimacy to what can only be seen as a drastic and destructive alteration.

Distilled, what's proposed starts with the construction of a skinny core wall, 15 stories high, against the side of the adjoining apartment house on East 89th Street. From this wall is to be cantilevered a green gridded porcelain enamel box containing office and storage space, its top edge slightly lower than the core wall behind, and its bottom somewhat less than halfway down the fat upper band of Wright's rotunda. The base of the box rests on a lower element which utilizes the structure of the present addition, itself designed in anticipation of ultimately supporting some sort of tower above it. A tripartite rationale buttresses this box: to establish its own objectness, to provide wider floor dimensions and, finally, to fragment the overall composition and thereby avoid bashing a single disproportionately great lump down the Guggenheim's backside.

This box is a bummer. The rationale of the "third element" seems spurious, premised retrospectively on the architects' decision to create another piece. The need for wide floors to accommodate offices and storage space (form follows function … anywhere) is also a backwards piece of thinking, built to the dimensions of a premise that was faulty at the first go. Arguing for the efficiency of the internal arrangements of the piece can in no way justify its intrusion into airspace that incontestably wants to remain clear. More, the effrontery – that's the word for it – of using this precious volume to house *storage* is almost too much to believe. We all know space is tight in Manhattan but this is ridiculous, exactly the sort of shoe-boxing that Wright was so vociferously appalled by.

Finally, there's the strategy of assemblage. By its own declaration, the Gwathmey Siegel scheme is – at some presumably meaningful level of abstraction – "derived" from the Wrightian original. This notion lies at the conceptual nub of their proposal, this argument from translation. To buttress the conceit of implicit continuity, Gwathmey Siegel has produced a series of formal analyses of the Guggenheim. These take the form of conventionally simplistic art-historical geometric studies, aiming to demonstrate, in essence, that the Guggenheim is conceptionally orthogonal. But, like any technique of analysis, this one tends to prove what it sets out to prove. It's scarcely a coincidence that an architectural firm whose work has been religiously square would discover that a four-foot grid was the "key" to the Guggenheim.

This isn't to say that Gwathmey Siegel's analysis is exactly "false," rather that its filter is too coarse: real essences slip through the mesh. The prejudice of the grid leads to a view of architecture in stasis. In an assembled architecture, the grid has the effect of stabilizing relationships among forms, quieting their latent kinesis with the security blanket of an implicit ordering datum. This is precisely what the proposed scheme does. It seeks to create an essentially homogeneous reading by assembling an array of forms nominally subservient to a privileged formal ideal. The architects' obvious aspiration is to create an ensemble in which one will not perceive the Guggenheim and its addition or even the Guggenheim against its backdrop but *the Guggenheim*. This may be a responsible urbanist strategy, this favoring of the whole, but it is altogether wrong vis-à-vis a holy monument.

The loading on of Gwathmey Siegel's "asymmetrical assemblage" is, in fact, a drastic attack on the Wrightian spirit. The Guggenheim is one of history's most signal examples of an architecture of fluidity and motion. However one parses its geometry, this building celebrates movement, the stability of the spin. Wright's is an architecture of spiral and collision. Gwathmey Siegel's is one of right angles and reveals. It's the opposition of an architecture conceived in three dimensions with one conceived in two. Unlike the stable surface of a circle or a square, the spiral shifts constantly, propelling relationships rather than ossifying them. The Guggenheim, like the abstract expressionism with which its design was contemporary, is action art. The new addition tries to compose it.

Looking at the plan of the Guggenheim, I'm always impressed by the funkiness of Wrightian shapes, the interest in the coincidence of forms as a way of elaborating their purity. Those ellipsoids, partial circles, and weird angles demanded by the moment are what animate the building, give it its propulsive counterpoint. It's a really musical work, intricately elusive compositionally. To call the Guggenheim "bipartite" is to miss its most central aspect. Two rotundas, for sure, but what about the deep linking band of its second story? Is this a third element (is there a clue in the three bubbles off-centered over the entry or the three portholes above them?) or a part of one of the other two? A bipartite reading resonates only from vantage points that Wright intended to reveal two-ness. One of the building's most satisfying aspects is its unendingly subtle resistance to such simplifications.

While I don't question the conscientiousness of intent behind the Gwathmey Siegel proposal (unlike the artistic demolition derby over at the Whitney), this in no way modifies its disastrous potential. It simply intrudes too much: the looming cantilevered box violates a plane of respect that should be absolute. The color strategy (in spite of silly relational palaver about making the box green to respond to the park) is also terribly destructive. That glossy green box will hover like a billboard, calling attention to itself at Wright's expense. The architects seem to believe that skinning the box in a grid somehow makes it the moral equivalent of Wright's "orthogonal back-drop." This is reasoning on the order of thinking that an elephant can be turned to a zebra by applying stripes.

I find, though, that it's the puritanism of the proposal that rankles most. By puritanism I do not mean simplicity; rather, an architecture more controlled by inhibition than passion. Wright is a romantic, an architect of intersection and joinery. In the Gwathmey Siegel proposal, the forms seem too upright to touch. Every volume demands to be distinct, the whole simply the sum of its parts. Looking at the scheme, my eye focuses and refocuses on a little glass cylinder which sits under the cantilever, covering a stair that leads to a new rooftop sculpture garden. Its angled top is sliced off for no apparent reason other than to contrive some interest and rationalize the fact that it just sort of stands there, nervous about not engaging the horizontal plane above it. From across Fifth Avenue the tube will appear to sit on Wright's roof, a form nominally compounded of the same components as Wrightian ones (the glass of his skylights, the circle of his geometry, the ellipticizing rake of his spiral), but assembled with a sensibility that comprehends, it would seem, nothing of the spirit of the original. This little stub stands in for the whole, a lexicon of wasted intentions.

The real tragedy of this proposal is in the Guggenheim's willingness to trash a treasure for so little benefit. To be sure, the existing building is "inadequate" to a set of "reasonable" museological ambitions: to show more of the collection, to have nicer offices, to serve the public tea. The fact remains, however, that the inclusion of these possibilities on site is in direct conflict with the conservation of the greatest item in the Guggenheim's collection — the Guggenheim. Acknowledging the preciousness of this building is to render all questions of whether the addition "improves" it irrelevant. It's sufficient that it makes it very different. This isn't to say that a modest expansion is impossible: who would lament seeing the 1968 wing blown away and replaced? Second-guessing genius, though, is the purest folly. To build this new addition would be ruinous.

March 1986

THE INVISIBLE MAN

In 1963, Paul Rudolph bestrode American architecture, a brush-cut colossus. The school of architecture at Yale, where he was in the sixth year of his chairmanship, had just moved into a new building of his own design which was festooned *partout* with extravagant praise. Commissions of substance and prestige abounded and his office was a mecca for would-be disciples, training ground for a covey of architects who themselves went on to eminence. Rudolph had clearly emerged as the leading light of the group of designers — including Philip Johnson, Ed Barnes, and Ulrich Franzen — who had studied at Harvard during the Gropius glory days in the late 1940s. Rudolph was flying.

By the early '70s, it was over. Rudolph was still building, but it wasn't like before, and it hasn't been that way since. Today, Rudolph's office has shrunk drastically and his major commissions are mainly in the Far East, out of local sight. He's no longer prominent on the academic scene, the architectural magazines have forgotten him, and his name seldom figures in the discourse of architectural precedent. Even those whom he trained seem no longer to regard him as a vital presence, relegating him to some anachronistic margin. But one thing has not changed: Rudolph is still the most brilliant designer of his generation, an architect who continues to produce magnificent work, richer and more complex than virtually any other American makes. That Rudolph is insufficiently esteemed only symbolizes today's atmosphere of easy architectural virtue. The Pritzker Prize is handed to Johnson, Pei, and Roche — designers Rudolph can draw circles around — while the greater man isn't even mentioned as a contender.

Why is this? A line not infrequently offered is that Rudolph has designed the "same building" too many times. Even if this were true, it's a

155

strange criticism, one nobody would think of applying to Mies or, more relevantly, to Kahn — architects whose work is no less powerful for being focused. The real import of this remark is that fashion has neither dissuaded Rudolph from his primary investigations, nor led him to embrace the fatuous discourse that currently passes for architectural speech. Like Wright, Rudolph pulls no punches: his frank manner and great architectural intelligence have doubtless alienated lesser peers.

Rudolph first hit the scene in the late '40s as the architect of a number of houses in Florida, initially in collaboration with Ralph Twitchell. They're wonderful, airy projects, post-war American modernism at its very best — the Florida version of what the "second generation" of California modernists (Ain, Ellwood, Soriano, et al.) were investigating so successfully on the opposite coast. In both instances, the benign climate — both architectural and meteorological — was tremendously liberating. The result, for Rudolph, was an architecture of wall-lessness and flow, a manner of building that valued suspension over compression and continuity over barrier. As with all of Rudolph's work, these houses are most astute in the invention of space via the modulation of light, engaging the whole array of tropical apparatus — louvers, shutters, porches, and breezeways — with style and discipline.

As Rudolph's work developed, he retained and elaborated the central aspects of the Floridian idyll. The sensibility of space and light — surely the primary architectural virtues — burgeoned. Rudolph's uncanny command of spatiality, his knack of conceiving volumes as aggregations of photons cannot be overstressed. This is the power of architectural genius — it goes straight for the gut. Rudolph makes little sketches of the movement of space through the volumes he's designing in which "space" is represented by a series of tiny arrows, little atomist surrogates. Like no others, Rudolph responds to the tactility of the void at every scale, from the domestic to the civic. Congruent with this concern for the movement of space, Rudolph has long focused on the expression of assembled volumes. His approach to mass is absorbed with combination and repetition. This is visible in works as diverse as the de Stijlian Bass House of 1970, the Mondrianesquely screened Milam House of 1960, the great Burroughs Wellcome Labs of 1969 (which appear as establishing shots in film after film with "high-tech" settings), and a series of projects which investigate the possibilities of modular construction, culminating in the fantastic, unbuilt 1967 Graphics Art Center for the Lower West Side. At a time when, for better or for worse, the theme of factory-built housing dominated the discourse of architectural responsibility, Rudolph attempted to make a real architecture out of this problematic technology with unrivaled commitment.

However, for all the supple diversity of this work, Rudolph has come to be linked with a much narrower range of output. Mention Paul Rudolph to an architect and the immediate association is with his poured concrete buildings, most dramatically represented by the Yale Art and Architecture Building: projects which — in their sensuousness, weight, and occasional Roman gloom — are out of step with our ephemeral and veneered moment. It's not just that we're nervous about the avoirdupois, about the unabashed permanence of this work, it's that we cannot countenance the aspiration to grandeur untinged with irony. A post-modern monument like the AT&T Building draws its consequence from jaded appropriation, not from the soul-baring ambitions of a Rudolph, an architect who seeks to ennoble every project he touches. Indeed, one of my favorite Rudolph works is a parking garage in New Haven, a bleak program turned out with unbelievable plasticity, elegance, and even urbanity.

If Rudolph can be said to lack a quality, it's irony. At a time when anti-heroics were obviously the preferred stance, Rudolph's position was simply too unmediated. Rudolph is, in many ways, another victim of the '60s. He arrived at an architecture of unabashed grandeur and thickness at precisely the moment when history was busily sweeping the very idea of such master-building away. Rudolph's stately vessels were simply left becalmed. An investigation that had incorporated increasingly sophisticated visions of space, volume, mass, and now (massive) materials simply had no place to go.

Three events in New Haven clearly iced this particular cake. Rudolph was succeeded at Yale by his virtual opposite, the drolly learned Charles Moore with his proclivities for pop and funky lightweight construction. If any single event is a harbinger, Moore's deanship was the starting gun for the eclectic field of architectural post-modernism. Then, almost by way of a rebuff to the A&A Building, the 1970 competition for a new mathematics building at Yale was won by Robert Venturi with a polemically comprehensible, two-dimensional scheme that swung 180 degrees from the highwater mark of flamboyant Rudolphian expressionism. The victory of this project (won under something of a cloud since Venturi was teaching at Yale at the time) also represented the triumph of an academic clique at Yale (led by Vincent Scully) long disquieted by Rudolph. But the biggest blow was the incineration of much of the interior of the A&A Building by a fire of undetermined but suspicious origin, resulting in the temporary relocation of the school. Its return was preceded by drastic alterations, an unmistakable rebuke to Rudolph's intentions and an act of some hypocrisy from putative preservationists.

But why write about Rudolph now? First, because he's alive and well, because he's the pre-eminent designer in town, and because it's a pleasure to know that such a talent is still getting exercise. One also writes as antidote to the scandal of Rudolph's invisibility throughout virtually every stratum of American architecture's institutional life. But, most centrally, one writes because of the bracing inspirational nature of Rudolph's practice, and its uncompromised devotion to the arts of architecture. A recent show of Rudolph's drawings at Max Protetch was fabulous. They're among the most analytic, individual, and refined in American architecture's history. They also exemplify the character of Rudolph's production. Rudolph doesn't preside over a committee or help himself to the ideas of talented underlings, he designs.

One of the curiosities of the current scene is the fixation of a great body of sculpture on the "architectural," even as architecture relinquishes the sculptor's prerogatives of space-making in favor of easier, more fashionable representations. In the new Equitable Building, for instance, architecture unburdens itself of its artistic aspect through a system of surrogacy. Stupid, dimensionless design is redeemed by the appropriation of some totem of taste: we'll put the Whitney Museum in the lobby, get Andrée Putnam to do the model apartment, ape classicism. At a time when the artistic may be the only viable domain left for architecture, its only visible point of resistance, there's a stampede to sell out. Paul Rudolph is not for sale.

The point of intersection between architecture and the situation of the homeless is a difficult one. At one level, even proposing a coincidence is dubious. As Friedrich Engels pointed out some years back, the problem doesn't exactly devolve on design but proprietorship. That Manhattan has been turned into a manufactory of homelessness isn't a question of buildings, it's a question of justice. There's plenty of space for the rich.

Still, it's encouraging that designing for the homeless has become somewhat faddish in the schools lately. At least consciousness of the problem is an advance over the usual preoccupation with large country houses in the manner of Hadrian's Villa and gentlemen's clubs on constrained urban sites. The crunch comes in the character of the confrontation. If designing for the homeless is simply an occasion for the further reduction of architectural minima, for the unselfconscious design of tiny pods or pneumatic suits, then it's no more than slavishness as usual. If, on the other hand, design becomes the medium of challenge, right on!

The Storefront for Art and Architecture (recently installed in a swell new space down at 97 Kenmare Street) has an exhibition called "Homeless at Home" which raises plenty of issues. The Storefront, creature of Glen Weiss and Kyong Park, has stepped into the nearly total vacuum of responsibility created by mainline architectural culture and asserted itself in the vanguard of the local architectural conscience. The current show is the fourth in a series devoted to the question of homelessness, a concern Park and Weiss have extended through a fine and visible campaign of leafleting and stenciled graffiti.

If nothing else, this show reveals the expressive dimensions of current architectural concern, conceptually hemmed on either side by irony and the repressions of liberalism. There are examples from municipal authorities of a variety of decently intended, clean, well-lighted places, ranging from rehabbed old buildings to an extremely sinister proposal by the housing bureaucracy in LA to make trailer parks for the (mobile) homeless. The most jaded proposal in the show is architect Christopher Egan's design for an elegant sort of pushcart-cum-hut, a proposition which lies along the same axis as the LA park, save for having passed (if just) over the present boundaries of cynicism.

The most "beautiful" artifact is a shelter constructed by architects Pfau and Jones out of the detritus of industrial civ (old cars, planes, trains, etc.) in which to house the human detritus of industrial civ. Gregor Kwashiokor supplies a decorated sleeping bag. J. Bacon, P. Shinoda, and S. Ozalp offer poignant metal cocoons nestled under an elevated highway. Let us not forget that irony can also be a revolutionary virtue — the ironist must be judged by his or her subject matter. Finally, I note in passing the large number of projects involving little Rossian pitched roofs. The Jungian emergence lately of this particular archetype of domesticity represents a troublingly unexplicated longing. Home is where the roof is, I guess.

"Homeless at Home" — if somewhat underfocused in its eclecticism — is an important act of consciousness-raising and another brave secession from architecture's vapid, reactionary scene. Its organisers have my sincere admiration.

March 1986

FREED, AT LAST

Thucydides begins his history of the Peloponnesian Wars with a rationale for writing. If dim undergrad Mnemosyne serves, the reason was that the wars were pretty much the biggest damn thing to have happened around the isles for ages. The new Javits Convention Center demands attention in the same way: much of its qual is tied up in its quant. Javits is enormous, enough room — according to its PR — to provide playing space for all of the NFL simultaneously (football fields being the unit of measure standard to these enterprises), a maw into which flocks of jumbo jets could easily vanish.

We do tend to associate the architecture of a given age with certain totems of extent. After all, one of building's constants is the old struggle with gravity. The Coliseum stands in for Rome, soaring, vaulted cathedral naves summarize the Middle Ages, the 19th century is repped by railway sheds and crystal palaces (in Flaubert's *Dictionary of Received Ideas*, the following appears under "Railway Station": "Always go into ecstasies about them: cite them as models of architecture.") As for us, we have skyscrapers, the Vertical Assembly Building at Canaveral, Portman atria, and convention centers. Size may not be everything; but it is a big thing.

As a building type, convention centers are heavily constrained. What's needed is basically a vast and uniform interior space, well serviced by bathrooms, air-conditioning, cafeterias, loading docks, etc. The nondifferentiation of the building's major element suggests two basic architectural routes in trying to redeem what is, in fact, a gigantic warehouse. The first of these is to elevate the tectonics of spanning to a major expressive role — the way the vault and its supports animate the Gothic, or the mechanism of suspension informs the appearance of the Brooklyn Bridge. The second possibility is to

JAVITS CONVENTION CENTER
(*New York*) James Freed

focus on the parts which serve the core spaces, to let more malleable and particularized places take up the expressive slack.

James Freed (of I.M. Pei and Partners), the architect of the Javits Center, has pursued both of these strategies. The business of spanning (and to a large extent, walling) is accomplished with a space frame. This is a structure which gains its strength via a lattice of many light members, a uniform network of pieces rather than the heavy hierarchy of beams and joists. Space frames are both strong and light, able to span very large distances at a uniform height (unlike an arch) without becoming impossibly heavy and thick (like beams and trusses). However, the measure of a space-framed convention center is not simply sui generis. There's a powerful image that any architect working within the medium must confront: Mies van der Rohe's seminal convention center project for Chicago, a beautiful model of which is currently on display in the Mies MOMA show.

Although Mies's project is not technically a space frame, the image idealized by its structure is identical. What Mies's building proposed was a single great room, completely free of columns, its enormous roof supported only around the building's perimeter. The walls of the building — containing the roof-bearing compression elements — were themselves beautifully articulated to express the transfer of the forces in the lateral span into the vertical dimension. The unbuilt project is a highpoint in functionalist expressionism and remains (along with Pier Luigi Nervi's amazing spans in concrete) one of the beaux-ideals of modernist enclosure. While I certainly don't mean to argue that a space-framed convention center can be solved only with a structure like Mies's, it nevertheless locates the designer's agenda with tremendous clarity.

For the Javits — squarely informed by the Miesian tradition — the comparison is somewhat disappointing. Though its structure is elegant, it pursues the big space without the added pleasure of the really big span: the space frame is supported on columns arranged only about 90 feet apart. Moreover, in the movement from the horizontal structure to the vertical there's (for me, at any rate) a certain lack of hierarchical refinement, a missing zone of expression between column and roof. Along the same lines, the decision to fold the space frame over 90 degrees to provide wind-bracing on the window walls points to a certain ambiguity: should the frame be read as roof or as shell (as in Richard Foster's Sainsbury Center)? The composite system obscures somewhat the clear reading one seeks in such functionalistic architecture.

However, the architects' expressive eggs seem to be mainly in the basket of the nominally public spaces which surround and serve the exhibition areas. These comprise a long gallery along the length of the building's front on Eleventh Avenue from which one either ascends or descends to the two exhibition levels; a "great hall" or "crystal palace" located toward the southern end of the front façade; another gallery, intended to house shops and restaurants, which bridges over the exhibition space; and a glass pavillion on the river. The really big deal is the crystal palace, at once the building's greatest achievement and source of considerable ambiguity. The space itself is spectacular, 15 stories high, glazed on all sides. It really does evoke the greenhousey vibes of 19th-century crystal palaces, soaring and light, and commanding a super view of the city. No question that this is one of New York's great rooms, an exhilarating place, an achievement to be celebrated.

But the relationship of this lofty enclosure to the larger character of the center is problematic. Circulation from space to space lacks the energy and proportion of the spaces themselves and the sequence of spatial events is unconvincingly arranged. Entering the great hall, one is set up for axial movement towards the river. But the actual activities of the center are a 90 degree turn to the right and downstairs, off the long entrance gallery. The sequence from this gallery to the exhibition halls is also graceless, requiring passage through a concrete barrier meant to read as pavilion but actually more evocative of bunker. The movement toward the river itself is frustrated by fussy, symmetrically off-axis circulation; by an ill-conceived round hole in the floor, intended to add sectional interest; by the gloom of the unglazed linking galleria; and by the underscaled and poorly located river pavilion one finally reaches. Indeed, the worst aspect of the center is its relationship to the river. The architects have devoted this edge to loading docks, storage, and mechanical rooms, erecting a vast and brutal concrete wall along the West Side Highway, unequivocally declaring this the building's backside. I don't want to be too pious about missed opportunities, but this is a real affront.

The relationship of the crystal palace to the rest of the center also raises more conceptual questions. Looking at Javits, listening to its celebratory rhetoric, one thinks that this is a glass building, gloriously transparent. After all, it's covered with a glass skin, however over-dark and uniform. But, as it turns out, only a fraction of this skin is actually window; the major portion is spandrel glass, decorative facing over solid walls. Most of the center is simply decorated with the idea of transparency, obscuring opacity with the image of the crystalline. Now I don't want to get caught up with questions of honesty versus mendacity in the use of materials, but I do find this ambivalence unproductive. Indeed, reliance on this illusory glassiness has impeded the search for a richer treatment of the center's enormous perimeter, for a more specific response to the particulars of the center's context. That kind of attention to the edges might have made the project great.

There certainly are some memorable images in *Pride of Place*, Robert Stern's unbelievably boring eight-part series on American architecture currently airing out on PBS. My personal fave is a slow pan up Plymouth Rock in episode one which comes to rest on Stern's firmly planted Gucci loafers. Almost as good is a sequence in which Stern and the appalling Leon Krier are driven about colonial Williamsburg in a horse-drawn carriage. They're deposited at some old colonialoid saloon where a periwigged-out waiter serves them pewter mugs of Meisterbrau with which they toast "the truth."

This is real William Dean Howells stuff, a memoir of attempted assimilation. Whatever its nominal subject matter, it's actually about how a Jewish boy from the Bronx can make it among the goyim, conquer Plymouth Rock, design ersatz classical architecture as if to the mannerism born. Only in America, fer sure! Our pilgrim's progress begins at Yale (strolling down Chapel Street with Vincent Scully) and never strays too far from the bowers of power. Down to the University of Virginia to chat about Mister Jefferson, a stroll in New Canaan with Philip Johnson (whose work appears more often than Frank Lloyd Wright's, which should give you an idea how fucked up somebody's values are), a visit to Princeton, a virtual compendium of formerly restricted environments, a Cook's tour of Episcopal nirvana.

Of course, the series does have its villains. Poor old John Portman's Renaissance Center in Detroit gets trashed in two separate episodes, and Stern just can't let go of the benighted Walter Netsch, two of whose projects are excoriated in succession. This compulsion to repeat (Jesu, not the U. Va. Rotunda again!) pervades the series. The filmmaker with whom I watched used the word "padded," and gratuitous attenuation does seem to lie behind the ennui that overwhelmed us as we sat through four straight episodes of this show. Not that Stern doesn't do his best to liven things up, squinting at the cue cards and karate-chopping the air like Crazy Eddie. He even wears costumes. His best such moment comes in Grand Central Station, where we find him in foul weather commuter drag, all buttoned up in his Burberry and fedora. Behind him, citizens are entering the building in T-shirts, perspiring from an obvious scorcher of a day. Where's Robin Leach when we really need him?

April 1986

A BUNCH OF WHITE GUYS

(AND THREE JAPANESE)

SITTING AROUND TALKING

or

The Three PPP*

Prologue:

P. EISENMAN:
I've an idea to make an impression
I'll get all the boys to come to a session
The Whites and the Greys (but no women or blacks)
Just the usual stars (and the usual hacks)
But how shall I name it? Of course! After me!
Let's have a conference and call it P. 3!
You'll note I've deployed deft conceptual notation
A 3's just an E awaiting rotation.
Plus P connotes mystery, fascist, Masonic
What a marvelous joke, never mind it's moronic.

The Charlottesville Tapes (New York, 1985) is a transcript of a conference held at the University of Virginia in November 1982. Invitations — in which the invitees were enjoined not to discuss the event — were sent to a group of (male) architects under the imprimatur "P. 3." This was the coin of Peter Eisenman, the organizer of the conference, itself an extension of the all-male architectural gatherings organized by Philip Johnson at the (all-male) Century Club in Manhattan. Twenty-five architects plus a representative from Rizzoli (publishers of the transcript) attended. Each architect presented a project to the group, led by Johnson who declared in defense of a much-maligned skyscraper "I am a whore and am paid very well for building high-rise buildings." The conference closed with a vote on a petition formulated by Carlo Aymonino and Leon Krier urging the reconstruction of the Roman Forum. This parody is drawn from positions taken by participants in the much-gossiped-about event.

First (and only) scene: Twenty-six men are seated around a table. Twenty-five of them are architects. They show slides. The twenty-sixth holds a tape recorder. From time to time there is a knock at the door. The twenty-six pay no attention to this. As the scene begins, an old man rises to speak.

PHILIP:
Bonjour, I'm a whore.

THE OTHERS:
Bonjour! Bonjour!

PHILIP:
Here's a new building that should make a buck.

THE OTHERS:
It's ugly as sin!

PHILIP:
I don't give a fuck!

REM K. *(from the side)*:
This work is pathetic
Creatively bare
And all you can say
Is that you don't care?

PHILIP:
I yam what I yam
I build what must be
I don't give a damn
Don't you all envy me!

LEON:
At least this guy's honest,
For the rest, go to hell!
You've totally missed
What we Kriers know so well.
Build like the ancients

Divvy towns into quarters!
Or I'll have you lot shot
For not following orders
And to teach you a lesson
I'm not going to smile
Nor will I build (at least for a while)
And now I'll sit down.

ROB:
Sieg Heil! Sieg Heil!

STERN:
What this man says
Has a lot of attraction
Death to the modern!
Death to abstraction!
We need columns and lintels
I always employ 'em
I copy the past
Just the same as these goyim!

ISOZAKI:
Well done little Bob
You make a nice palace
But I prefer buildings
That look like a phallus.

TIGERMAN:
Very droll Iso
I love it to pieces
Look what I've done for Knoll —
It's just like one of Mies's!

UNGERS:
And here's one of mine
That's totally gridded
It's also enormous
No missing I did it.

LEON:
Better you'd hid it
It's nothing but kitsch.

UNGERS:
Shut up you puerile son of a bitch!

ROBERTSON (*moderating, as usual*):
Calm yourselves, boys,
No need for alarm
Look at this building
I built on a farm!

ROCHE:
Rot! Humbug and Bah!
Why didn't you say
Na, Na, Na to the Shah?

AYMONINO:
The imperial mode!
That's one I feel at home in
What say we vote
To rebuild all that is Roman.

HALF THE GATHERING:
What a splendid idea!

THE OTHER HALF:
Completely hare-brained!

HARRY COBB (*sotto voce*):
Would anyone know if I quietly abstained?

THE 26TH MAN:
It will not escape note
I've taped everything wholly:
Do you mind if I vote?
I'm the man from Rizzoli.

ALL:
The man from Rizzoli has got it all down!
Who here was pithy and who was a clown.
Vote with us please (history won't blame us)
If this man weren't here, we wouldn't be famous!
Let's give three cheers for all we hold holy
The first for ourselves, number two for Rizzoli
And a third for the thing that unites all our nations
Our outstanding sense of public relations
So let's meet anon (excluding the rest)
To prove once again that we are the best
And no one will care how many buildings we flub
They'll know we're important 'cause we belong to the club.

1986

THE REAL THING

This week's favorite post-modern artifact is a McDonald's commercial. It's for their breakfast product and features the usual contingent of cheerily scarfing model citizens, hygienic and helpful just-post-pubescent personnel, and zany animated foodstuffs, in this case serried eggs marching toward McMuffin heaven. What distinguishes the ad, though, is the soundtrack, done after the manner of the Andrews Sisters. McDonald's soundtracks are always cagily market-segmented ("soul" music plays as a black dad buys his kids a burger at the all-black McDonald's), and this one is designed to appeal broadly, going after the ethic rather than ethnics. And the ethic is this year's favorite — Americans pulling together in the country's good (war) times. The "historic" music is an instantly recognized allusion, shrouding the same-old-thing in the mantle of some absent genuine.

"You cannot not know history" is one of Philip Johnson's more endearing quips. History, however, can be known in many ways. Johnson knows it, like the McDonald's commercial, not as a means of inquiry but as a medium of concealment. This is history with tunnel vision, seeing only forms, blind to context, the actual circumstances of production. In the historically vexed climate of today's architecture, such a version has found easy acceptance. No need to undergird formal enthusiasms with theory or relevance, to struggle for elaboration: the historic grab bag yields images for any occasion, an endless series of snapshots, history without memory. Remembering nothing, this history can explain anything. History becomes the extension of show-biz by other means.

Philip Johnson has been a seminal influence on the disengagement of architecture from its real sources of meaning. He is the architectural analogue to Ronald Reagan, another seamless producer of a seemingly endless series of contradictory statements. Both men resolve the manifest conflict by forcing attention away from their acts and onto themselves. And, for both Johnson and Reagan, old age occludes the extreme currency of this position. The two are true epigones of the age of television, apostles of a consciousness that transcends traditional structures of logic, ethics, and — for that matter — time and space. Television invents via juxtaposition and re-juxtaposition. On TV, no sequence is precluded, anything can follow — or go with — anything else. Indeed we're perfectly habituated to the segue from starving babies in Ethiopia to Morris the Finicky Cat, from Mr. T. to Mother Theresa. Judgment is always circumvented by rearrangement. This is the world which Ronald Reagan inhabits (our side freedom fighters, their side terrorists) and which Philip Johnson designs. Mies today, Mizner tomorrow — what's the difference, it's only images.

Hollywood practitioners of the recombinant arts are always looking for what's called "high concept." To go forward, a project must prove itself reducible to mnemonic pith, advertisable in a phrase. The best such "concepts" are those that enfold previous certifiable hits — "Romeo and Juliet on Drugs" or "Rocky 25" being model distillations. No film is produced that doesn't discernibly ape a bankable predecessor. Johnson's working method is comparable. Weekending at New Canaan, he rummages through his library until an image presents itself. The page is duly marked. Monday morning at the office, a designer is given the designated images and a doodle or two (Johnson is no Walt Disney — he never could draw) and told to proceed. Thus equipped with the "concept" (Bramante on the bottom, Raymond Hood on the top), the office synthesizes the project. It's a typical art director's approach.

What makes the project Johnsonian, then, is nothing about it, strictly speaking. An attribution-minded architectural historian from Mars, spared the literature of this production, would find it impossible to assemble the oeuvre on the basis of internal evidence. Its "meaning" lies in the whimsicality of its aggregation, not its consistency; distinction isn't in consequence but in origins. The ersatz C-note may be indistinguishable from the genuine article, but only one producer goes to jail. Sorting out such acts of appropriation has become one of the central conundrums of our culture.

Andy Warhol is, of course, the seminal genius of strategic borrowing. By signing Campbell's Soup cans, he located precisely the single consequential act in a system without real boundaries. When content goes out of control, we're all obliged to look at labels. Johnson's art — like Gloria

Vanderbilt's or Betty Crocker's — is in forming his signature. He recognizes that the first rule in this kind of practice is to broaden the product line to the maximum, to place the valorizing imprimatur on everything. The source of the goods is immaterial. It is a particularly Augustan mode, an enterprise where all fixes upon "taste."

Writing this, I feel caught up in several of the central contradictions of this system. You will have noticed that accompanying this text is a series of handsome, advertising-quality color photographs of three of Johnson's recent projects, all of which I visited this past summer. As you may have further discerned, I'm not exactly sympathetic to the progenitor of this work. This dissonance, though, is precisely what is enabled by the recombinant cultural system that produces the lurid juxtaposibility of television. The point is not merely that this system is more than a little crazy. The point is that this craziness is enabled by the fact that something vital is missing here.

There is an artist called Cindy Sherman who has produced a series of photographs which she calls "Film Stills." The conceit behind this work is of isolated frames from a movie. Each shot is an evocative, costumed self-portrait in which Sherman dresses as some resonant female image in order to show the primacy of that image in inventing — not merely representing — women. Sherman appropriates a familiar cinematic context by placing herself in its midst. Importantly, in most of these "stills" her eyes are fixed on someone or something out of frame, imposing the idea of a missing narrative.

To complete a reading of one of Johnson's costumed buildings, one is also directed to an absence. Here, though, what's missing is the architecture. Johnson's major contribution has been in aiding the entry of "real" architecture into the realm of what Jean Beaudrillard has called "hyperreality," a terrain in which "signs of the real are everywhere substituted for the real itself," in which all ideas of authenticity or originality are eviscerated. What Johnson has done is to help move architecture out of the arena of artistic production and into the system of consumer objects. His special genius (after all, there are plenty of hacks) has been the simultaneous preservation of the cultural rhetoric of traditional practice. Johnson is the first great "architect" of the age of Ray Kroc: his mansards and those on the local McDonald's are indistinguishable, save for the magazines in which they are likely to appear.

If it's moved into this zone, it seems a sputtering cavil to complain that this really isn't architecture. I myself watch television; I eat fast food. And indeed, my recent tour of Johnson's latest projects found me weirdly sans spleen, indifferent. Take The Crescent, Johnson's new mixed-use project in Dallas, succinctly called the "croissant" by the locals. The project consists of hotel, office towers, shopping center, and garage — no more than the standard ingredients of upscale mall mix. Arriving, I was immediately reminded of another TV commercial I often take note of. It's an ad for chocolate, and the actor who announces it delivers the tag line, "The chocolate Europeans love most." The appeal from the putative sophistication of the continental palate is clear. But there is a strange twist. The actor pronounces the word "Euro*peen*," an unmistakable reading that's surely the result of calculation. (Nobody makes an error in commercials.) He addresses this source of authority not as the sophisticate we initially take him to be, but as the slightly underassimilated consumer to whom he's presumably trying to sell the cheap candies.

The Crescent is about making a similar kind of pitch. It's an armature filled with totems of vulgar gentility, from the high-class shops, to the vaguely tacky metal grille work, to the totally tacky ersatz gold toilet-paper holders, to the athletic valet parkers in their Izod shirts presiding over a forecourt swimming with enough Mercedes to stock a dealership. It's the sort of place that makes a statement of adequate consistency to warn off people who don't belong there. The brigade of lunching ladies are designer-clad, strictly from Neiman's, discerning money. This isn't a joint to drive to in a Caddy or to enter in boots, Levi's, or a cowboy hat. It's a little essay in the iconography of the no-longer-nouveau-rich, a decorator milieu, as consistent as the one at home.

Not surprisingly, the neighborhood in which The Crescent sits is filled with decorating establishments and antique shops. Thus, there is a contextual isomorphism that's unmistakable. Johnson's project merely extends the local mansardic sea, the atmosphere of surrounding shops crammed with their high-status bibelots. God is in the details and, god knows, you can buy them here. The Crescent is perfect to a culture which dines at restaurants called L'Ambiance (down the block) and which inhabits — in the continuous suburban carpet — an environment where every coffee table holds *Texas Homes* and *Architectural Digest*. Philip Johnson has always dreamt of being *l'architecte du roi* and in a setting where every person's home looks like a castle (be it Norman, Tudor, Loirish, or just plain Tara), he truly is. He's Mario Buatta with a Harvard degree.

Johnson has a hoary history in Houston. In many ways, he is the leading architectural personality of the town, progenitor of a large number of its monuments, the man who put Houston on the architectural map. Thus, he was — at some level — a logical choice for the commission to design the new building for the architecture school at the University of Houston. And Johnson delivers what he always does: a serviceable, if schematic, *parti*, clad in an image. Like his corporate projects, the school is a three-dimensional logo, a building that takes as its single investigation the question of "identity."

In this instance, as always, the identity is lifted, here from Ledoux's House of Education intended for Chaux. This is architecture as a high-class ad agency might conceive of it — Lite Architecture — in which the goal appears to be delivering the message with the minimum signifier. On the dreary campus, the architecture school distinguishes itself. And, in the pages of architectural journals, its two strokes — the learned appropriation and the central court — reproduce nicely, even indelibly. There's no question that the strategy shows a certain élan on Johnson's part. Where a Rudolph or a John Andrews might struggle actually to make architecture, Johnson seems content merely to signal it. And, when all is recorded in the (four-color) pages of history, there is no doubt that the tactic will have gained a kind of equivalence.

Again, to focus on any specific seems inappropriate. Johnson has moved his architecture out of the realm of detail and invention and into the arena of *l'ambiance*. These are projects most fully incarnate in the Ektachrome realm, souvenirs of architecture. The work reminds me of the 19th-century practice — in the days before sound could be mechanically reproduced — of publishing piano "reductions" of the scores of symphonic and operatic works to be played in parlors across America. Johnson, too, reduces, stripping away any element — formal or ideological — that will interfere with a clear reading of the signature. To reproduce Ledoux once is to make it possible to reproduce him endlessly. Like any other product-packaging, architecture devolves entirely on styling.

The new office building at Third Avenue and East 53rd Street in Manhattan responds to similar imperatives. In a forest of towers, each clamoring for recognition, what strategies remain for assuring distinction? The typological parameters are heavily constrained. Ironically, an architect is obliged to provide acres of undifferentiated space in an envelope that differentiates itself from the decorated extrusions that surround it. Available resources come, in the main, from three areas: skin, shape, and, for want of a better word, urbanity. Johnson manipulates all three of these possibilities with varying degrees of success.

The Third Avenue site lies on a New York street that — with the addition of palm trees — could easily pass for the Sunbelt. This is a part of town dominated by recent construction, a place in which the idea of a continuous urban convention — never mind an indigenous one — has almost completely disappeared. As in Houston or Dallas, the plot is privileged over the aggregate, the suburban model, a perfect parable of capitalist initiative. Johnson apparently does not choose to question this pattern of isolation but to reinforce it, to go it one better — a logical choice in Houston and, alas, a logical one in this quarter of Manhattan.

When I first saw the published design, I had reasonably high hopes for this building. I was braced by the oval: curvilinearity at last in a town whose relentless rectilinearity seems needless. And, at the level of form, the building is just fine, a good shape and distinct. But the project loses it in the details. The streamline of the strip windows is suffocated by a surfeit of materials and poor proportions. Moreover, the building doesn't know how to land, resting on awkwardly capped, woefully striped, and badly spaced columns. As with so many Johnson projects, the idea — a banded oval building — is insufficient to solve the problem of making the architecture; the slick slather of stone too inarticulate to substitute for real detail.

There is a last project I'd like to glide by that seems particularly revealing. It's called PortAmerica (sic) and is to be built on 223 acres edged by the Capital Beltway and the Potomac River in the Maryland suburbs of Washington, DC. In many ways it is the prototypical site for urban development in New America — by the highway, out of town, its connections global and electronic rather than local and physical. It's the kind of urbanism that Johnson's discontinuous architecture implies, a place where the genius loci is pretty much irrelevant. It's also Johnson's first project of this magnitude, the traditional arena for the architect's musings on the Big Picture, on how it all comes together to support a vision of a social, as well as architectural, order.

What Johnson has produced ("designed" always seems the wrong word) is some version of Busch Gardens. In its current ad campaign, the popular theme park bills itself as just like Europe, "only closer." The image is an attractive one, especially at a time when terrorized Americans are staying away from the genuine article in droves. How comforting to be able to walk from Old Heidelberg to Pall Mall without worrying about a surprise appearance from Abu Nidal. Johnsonville-on-the-Potomac shares this television of free juxtaposition, deploying bow-fronted row houses, mansardic hotel, neo-classic waterside promenade — the whole apparatus of Euro*peen*ness to create his Erewhon of creative geography, as they call it in the cinema.

One image does stand out from this thicket of dim appropriation. Sitting waterside in front of the gold-domed hotel is a pavilion, its low pyramidal roof supported at the corners by four little towers. Wait a minute, though, haven't seen this somewhere before? Of course we have. It's one of Leon Krier's images, meant to organize social space in his "reconstruction" of the European city. Never mind the joke on Krier's "I'm an architect, therefore I don't build" position; this does look like the line over which appropriation becomes rip-off. I think what's being taken here is not just a form — something Johnson has shamelessly done from his earliest days — but an idea. Absent a vision of urban life, Johnson simply appends one.

In 1783 an inventor called Jacques de Vaucanson exhibited in Paris a mechanical duck that could waddle, quack, beat its finely detailed wings, eat grain, and, eventually, excrete the digested residue. This is a classic Enlightenment exercise, this essay in scientific simulation. Indeed, the proto-robot does contain a startling degree of duck-ness. Yet it is not a duck. Philip Johnson's work has much in common with this mechanical bird. It scrupulously appropriates images from certified architectural sources — Ledoux's quack, Nash's waddle, Krier's excreta — and assembles them to produce a figure that is like architecture in many ways. And yet it is not. I do not wish to place too great a metaphysical burden on ducks — never mind their recent architectural history — but de Vaucanson's fowl and Johnson's projects, like the simulations at Busch Gardens and Walt Disney World, simply have no souls. Let's not be too pious about this — I enjoy Disney World and clockwork mallards — but there is danger in them. And that is that they'll finally crowd out the real thing.

September 1986

MASK OF MEDUSA*

When Kim Shkapich returned from Japan where she'd been supervising the production of John Hejduk's book *Mask of Medusa*, she was naturally full of stories. She seemed particularly struck by the wizened gent who'd directed the printing of the book, a man officially designated a "Living National Treasure." Our system of honorifics somehow doesn't embrace this kind of reverent national sentimentality, but if it did, Hejduk would top my list for enshrinement.

John Hejduk is an architect about whom it's only possible to write an homage or a diatribe. His work is situated with such precision and produced with such commitment that its ambiguities can only be seen philosophically, as didact's gaps, designed to query and to lead. Seeing his beautiful oeuvre of over 30 years assembled in *Mask of Medusa*, one cannot resist its power of instruction. It exposes its issues in the best way, not through harangue or seduction, but by example. More than any other architect producing today, Hejduk is engaged in exemplary research. He teaches by inviting witnesses.

For the past 10 years, Hejduk has been the dean of the school of architecture at Cooper Union and has fashioned the place into what is easily the most singular and visionary architectural school in the world. At a time when most schools are heavily invested in the evasions of pluralism or in selling out to the spurious practicalities of "development," Cooper remains dedicated to architecture's prosody. It's all Hejduk's doing. The school doesn't exactly institutionalize his sensibility as much as it depends on it for inspiration and protection. Hejduk — the eternal investigator, the "paper"

*Review of John Hejduk, ed. Kim Shkapich, introduction by Daniel Liebeskind, New York, 1985.

SECURITY
(*Oslo*) John Hejduk

architect – is a larger-than-life vision of what a student should be, in every way attenuated. He's literally large, a gigantic six foot eight, and filled with the congenial madness of the romantic, framing delicate metaphors in his almost impossible Bronx accent.

Hejduk began his own architectural studies at Cooper, went on to Harvard in the early 1950s, had a Fulbright in Rome, worked in various offices – a broad, if not immediately exceptional route. His early work is very much of its time, the sort of organicized modernism that sought to enrich pared forms with a more fecund sense of shape and material, modestly sensualizing received models with fieldstone and curves. In 1954, however, he was offered a job at the University of Texas, where Harwell Hamilton Harris had just been installed as dean. Hired with Hejduk were Colin Rowe (a theorists of great influence in American architectural education) and the painter Robert Slutzky, educated under Albers and devoted to the investigation of De Stijlian rigors. The three annointed themselves "The Texas Rangers."

The time in Austin proved incredibly fertile for Hejduk. He immediately set himself a project which was clearly informed by what must have been a most happy symbiosis among the Rangers. It was to be a suite of 10 houses, each an investigation of the nine-square plan of the canonical Palladian villa (the subject of Rowe's later essay "The Mathematics of the Ideal Villa"). As a compositional discipline, the Mondrianesque paradigm – the enrichment of an abstract minimum – was paramount. As a more strictly architectural investigation, the Miesian mode, with its fascination for the details of pure intersection and its distilled strategy of elements, suffused.

Hejduk completed seven of these Texas studies, and they are a remarkable corpus, austerely drawn with the hardest leads, toying persistently with the edge of the envelope beyond which architectural abstraction becomes mere composition. Unbuilt, perhaps unbuildable, the drawings nevertheless motivate production, presaging the derived investigations of influenced architects like Peter Eisenman and establishing the parameters of the nine-square problem, one of the classics of architectural pedagogy. They also lead directly to Hejduk's next series of studies.

In *Mask of Medusa* the Texas houses are presented in plan, elevation and axonometric, the preferred modernist mode of representing three dimensions. Axonometric projection is privileged for its "objectivity," for the fact that, unlike perspective, its every dimension is true to scale, yielding a favored flat, anti-illusionistic space. In making his projections of the Texas Houses, Hejduk used generating angles of 30 and 60 degrees. What this yielded on the page were (given the square basis for the underlying plans) a series of shapes that approached the diamond, unbalanced in a kind of latent aspiration to a 45 degree relationship to plan. I impute this latency not simply because of what came next for Hejduk, the Diamond House series, but also because of historical precedent in the work of Mondrian and van Doesburg.

In any event, the subsequent Diamond projects represent a striking development. The act of rotating the plan to yield the diamond, while still indebted to cubistic concerns, proved to be a tremendously stimulating move. First, it generated a system in which the third dimension seems intrinsic rather than derived, in which space is subsumed by plan rather than simply its by-product. Its visible rotatedness also implies the fourth dimension in its irruption of the stasis of the square. The diamond thus becomes more strictly architectural even as it becomes more purified in its abstraction. And, as Hejduk himself has noted, the diamond is also a kind of ideogram for perspective, diagramming station point, cone of vision, vanishing point, and — along its hypotenuse — picture plane.

The discovery of this hypotenuse marks a crucial divide in the evolution of Hejduk's work. For Hejduk, the hypotenuse became architecturalized as a wall, the moment of "entry-exit," a plane of transformation as well as designation. This retrieval of the wall marks the point at which Hejduk's architecture becomes truly temporal and spatial, resulting in a number of consequences. Most immediately, it liberated subsequent work from the hemming frame of the Texas and Diamond series, that circumscribing residue of painterly inspiration. Thus untrammeled, the work became newly free, and Hejduk's forms emerged as autonomous objects, rather than operations within a system. A series of projects in the late '60s and early '70s celebrates this literal pulling apart of elements, the freeing of shapes from rationalist compaction. An increased use of models is another pleasure of this conquest of air.

But most dramatic of all was Hejduk's invention of the wall house, the creation of what to me are his first really great works. The wall is architecture's most intrinsic datum. By discovering the wall through the long compositional research of the Texas and Diamond projects, Hejduk was able to use it in a new way. His enormously influential 1973 scheme for the Bye House, designed for a site in Ridgefield, Conn., is seminal. Floating in front of a wall compounding both backdrop and frame are three sinuous room/elements, foregrounded like scenographic clouds in a theatric sky. Behind the wall is an apparatus of support comprising stair, plumbing, another chamber, and a long perpendicular hallway which elongates the composition and adds ritual duration to the physical movement among the elements.

The wall projects represent both a turning point and a point of great maturity in Hejduk's research. They stand at the peak of a trajectory of investigation that, for all its originality, was centrally engaged with issues at the formal core of "classical" modernism. As the Texas Houses were in many ways enlargements of preoccupations that had stirred Mies and Mondrian, so the wall projects were partially the product of an awakened interest in Le Corbusier – in his plasticity, color, sense of space and motion, and his certain way of deploying multiplicity. This interest in Corb coincided with a larger absorption in things French: a fascination with Parisian surrealism, a new attention to the novel, to Flaubert and Stendahl, to Robbe-Grillet, to an idea of risk and the fascinating tenuousness of narrative.

Hejduk sometimes describes the subsequent transformation of his work as a movement from an architecture of optimism to one of pessimism, a description that both occludes and reveals. Certainly, he has exceeded the minute certainties of geometric investigation and become absorbed in the resonance of dissonance. His recent work has also left behind the centering certitudes of the received architectural program. This "pessimism" is one which no longer finds sufficiency in "the house" as a research armature and which is no longer able to treat any aspect of architecture as, in effect, a given. Much of the more recent work has been produced under the rubric of "Masque." The intent, it seems, behind this invention is to extend the lyricism of his architectonic concerns to the structures of life.

The Masque abets architectural narrative-making by allowing a retrieval of the mimetic. Hejduk is interested in the line between masque and mask, in architecture as both the guise and the concealment of social life. The creation of these architectural dramas entails much risk. The poet's search for penetrating realignments of the familiar can lead – as is the case with so much architecture nowadays – to depressing recapitulations of the banal, to a pseudo-mystic poetics of kitsch. Hejduk's work, though, is so achingly genuine, so affecting both formally and dramatically, that there is never any doubt of the profundity beneath the simplicity. It may be pessimistic work in its persistent disengagement from conventionalism, but it's sheer optimism in its longing for an architecturally angelic, for strategies for reuniting space with an idea of the sacred.

The project for The 13 Watchtowers of Cannaregio, designed in 1979 for a campo in Venice, is structured around a narrative program which proposes that the city designate a lifetime inhabitant for each of the identical towers, to pass life in monumental, watchful solitude. The program also includes a sort of on-deck house in the campo, where another citizen awaits a vacancy on the death of one of the 13. Elsewhere in the city is a "House for the Inhabitant Who Refused to Participate." Working from this outline, Hejduk crafts a lapidary exploration of the dimensions of the distance between this regulated content and a form which artistically redeems its essence. Central to the success of the project is an acute interpretation of the typology of the tower and of the historically mesmerizing character of Venetian space, a hoary artistic objective and an object of persistent fascination for Hejduk. The more recent "Berlin Masque" fixates another terrain. If the Venice project was preoccupied with rituals of solitude, Berlin is concerned with forms of propinquity. A funfair-like spray of objects is arrayed on a hedge-hemmed site. Each piece is designed independently but enjoys a clear familial relation to the others. The forms are compounded of simple, materially straightforward elements that create a landscape of both repose and rebuke. The whole comprises a carnival of conciliation aimed at inventing an ambiance of contemplation and humility. Sitting, as it does, near the wall and the former headquarters of the Gestapo, it counterposes its own frailty and lightness to the oppressive banality of the adjacent evils, like grass growing on the tracks to Auschwitz.

Let's hope for another 30 years of such work, collected in as handsome a volume. This beautiful book is a tribute to the craft of both living national treasures involved with it.

November 1986

THE NAME GAME

What would status be without its symbols? Shopping at Tiffany's the other day for a baby's birth bibelot, I came across a swell example of the self-reflexive sublime: a ceramic morsel wrought in the image of a Tiffany-blue gift box. Clearly, this is the perfect "gift from Tiffany's," but not exactly a suitable offering from a godparent. I couldn't be sure that a one-year-old would get it. So he didn't.

Consider, then, the copy from a recurrent real estate ad in the *Times*, promoting a subdivision on Wickapecko Drive in West Allenhurst, New Jersey:

Through all your years of achievement, you've known that some day a residence as uncompromising as your standards would be envisioned. And so it has at Milwin Farm. Milwin Farm exemplifies that which you seek in quality and tradition. A setting that rivals the Normandy coast of France. Patrician dwellings designed by master architect Robert A.M. Stern. Milwin Farm is a reflection of your accomplishments. An eloquent expression of your position in life.

Bob Stern. Bo Bern. Banana Fana. Fo Fern. Fee Fi. Mo Mern. What is it about a name? In this ad, "Stern" represents an islet of specificity in a maelstrom of hype. It's meant to assure that these million-dollar tract houses, er, dwellings, are patrician as all get-out. To compensate for the troubling Our Crowd character of the "Stern," there's the impressive inscription of the "A.M." It's a familiar architectural strategy: the occlusive formula, vowel + *M*. Think of I.M. Pei, "A.M." also adds an implicitly Latinate, classicizing tone ("ante meridiem"), even as it invokes the morning and a man ready to confront it — the Protestant work ethic spelled out. And in its literal elongation of Stern's presence on the page, who knows what satisfactions this pair of letters may offer to an architect who, as PBS viewers know, is smallish.

But these attenuations do not suffice. It isn't simply Stern we confront in the ad, but "master architect" (M.A., the invert of A.M.) Stern. This serves to distinguish the mini-château sketched at the top of the ad from the otherwise indistinguishable parvenu palazzi elsewhere on the page. It also sets off the little master from lesser lights. From, for example, the thrice-named James Stewart Polshek, who is described in promotional copy for his Delafield Estates (prices "as low as $595,000" — but, then again, these are merely "homes") as a "celebrated architect ... Dean of Architecture at Columbia University." How this must gall Stern: sure, *mastery* should beat out *celebrity*, but then there's that deanship, signifying Polshek's mastery over Stern, who is merely Professor at Columbia, though his covetous eye has long rested on Polshek's chair.

Even more frustrating to Stern must be his almost total absence from ads for another of his rustic productions, St. Andrew's. Here, a photograph of one of the gabled "town-homes" appears with an inset photograph of ... Jack Nicklaus. The juxtaposition is rich with the imputation of authorship, and, indeed, "Jack" has redesigned the historic golf course nearby. The point, though, is that the Golden Bear is present as an aura, not an author. Clearly his image (not to mention his person) looms far larger than Stern's in the public imagination: we're a culture that esteems the manly control of small balls above almost all else. But smiling Jack offers an additional imprimatur. I'm reminded of a joke about the man who's made a fortune on Seventh Avenue and decides to move from West End Avenue to Fairfield. It's time, he tells his wife, to trade in the Rubens for a Goya, if you get my drift.

Celebrated Dean Polshek has also suffered in the compromised-luster department lately. I couldn't help noticing that the sign advertising the building he designed on Sixth Avenue in the Village gave him equal biling with Andrée Putnam, the dreadful Parisian decorator who did the model apartments — and, indeed, who seems to have done the model apartment in every new luxury building in town. Putnam, of course, doesn't really need to *produce* anything, being herself glamorous: Lillian Hellmanesque wrinkles, voice from the throat (or the crypt), slathered in Kenzo, visible through a toxic Gitanes fog, New York's most superannuated disco chicken. Her actual decorating palette is as minuscule as it is photogenic. A black-and-white checked floor, an Eileen Gray settee (Putnam made her killing buying up the rights and reproducing the furniture of deceased modernists), a stainless knick-knack or two and just a soupçon of Zolatone. Her only design innovation to date was the placement of little glass shelves at nose level in the guest bathrooms at Morgan's. Then again, perhaps this was the inspiration of the ex-con owner.

Putnam is the Tiffany box incarnate, the perfect package, never mind that it's empty. Even better, since she decorates with the sort of modern materials that architects haven't quite relinquished, she appears, by inference, actually to be designing. Having dotted the *i*, she's treated as if she's written the whole book. The science of shopping triumphs again. While developers scramble to put Putnam in their places, we await the man or woman who will put Putnam in hers.

December 1986

DWELLING MACHINES

One of Le Corbusier's most enduring turns of phrase was his description of the house as a *machine à habiter*, a dwelling machine. There's something vaguely shocking still about this formulation which seems, in its skeletal logic, to oppose all we hold dear about "home." In a world increasingly beset by a technology run amok, the domestic environment is a last refuge of our private humanity, unparsable aggregation of the qualities that sum us up. We trust home to be aid and comfort to individuality, not the point of entry into the alienating, mechanized uniformity of modern times.

Of course, there's another view. I recently inventoried all the appliances resident in my tenement bedroom, a population that includes television, humidifier, air conditioner, halogen lamp, telephone, answering machine, electronic clock, IBM typewriter, and indispensable boom box. Indeed, I harbor ambitions to add VCR, CD player, and dehumidifier, to name only a few of the self-evident candidates for enshrinment in the electronic pleasure dome that increasingly describes the common environment of Americans. In this consuming view of matters, technology's a benison, convenient and fun, accessory to possibility, not just a link in the chain of our enslavement to a life of horrid mediation, homogenization, reification. Home is where the state of art is, doorway to a bright future.

The "problem" of technology, the designated cultural Janus of our age, thus finds special resonance at home. Home is not simply our present residence, it's the domicile of an entire ancestry of myth, seat of deep-rooted ideas about how we want to live. Burdened with this heavy baggage, the problem of the swelling as an architectural issue likewise takes on special weight. After all, the house is not simply the primary totem of how we individuate within the culture, it's also a principal means of how we

now, but then...?

seriality

187

aggregate. While houses may not exactly invent our social relations, they certainly make them visible. Homes may be our castles but they're our cathedrals as well.

All of which is to say, we're deeply schizoid over whether our homes should be a point of entry for technology or a point of resistance. We fetishize the discrepancy, crazily dealing with it. Not long ago, I read that Steven Jobs, avatar of technology, was in the process of building himself a new and very expensive house. Jobs can certainly build any sort of house he wishes, presiding as he does over millions made from the Apple computer. His choice? A scrupulously reproduced Victorian. But it's a Victorian with a twist. It's wired to the hilt, stuffed with the latest consumer tech, fiber optics glowing behind the hand-carved wainscoting.

What I'd like to discuss here are some of the ways in which the forms of home have diversified since the time the world became rational, sometime during the 18th century when the Enlightenment pulled the cord that turned on modernism's incandescent bulb. The consequence of this irruption of tradition's dogma has been the emergence of a culture in which forms and myths have become increasingly plural. Instead of the stable hegemony of practices that characterized life in "traditional" societies, we live at a time in which stability is the by-product of diversity. To some, this is threatening – witness the longings of post-modernism and its dream of the certainties of a uniform "classical" past. But this position only adds to the bouillabaisse. Clearly, to speak of the architectural components of "home" nowadays is to summon a range of choices, many of them in nominal competition. To design is inevitably to choose.

Let's begin with Le Corbusier, a pivotal figure, self-situated between the idealistic naiveté of the 19th century and the rationalisms of the 20th century. Corb's first office job was chez Auguste Perret in Paris. Perret, whose offices were housed in his masterpiece, the apartment block at 25 bis rue Franklin, was the great apostle of the structural clarities of the re-inforced concrete frame, a predilection not lost on Corb. When Perret handed him his first paycheck in 1908, Corb used part of it to buy a copy of Viollet le Duc's *Dictionnaire raisonné de l'architecture française*, a key text in the invention of the idea of modern architecture as a logical discipline. In the book, next to an illustration of the gothic flying buttress, Corb wrote; "Art lives by its skeleton. As Auguste Perret was telling me, grasp the skeleton and you can grasp the art."

Legend has it that the aging Corb kept two pictures on the wall of his

DYMAXION HOUSE
Buckminster Fuller

room: the Parthenon and the Maison Dom-ino. The image of the skeleton of the Maison Dom-ino (1914) is one of modern architecture's great totems, a hymn to its rational possibilities, the building stripped bare by its builders, even. Corb conceived this mass-produced house skeleton as a partial answer to the need to reconstruct after the war the damage then being inflicted on Flanders. It took on the Dom-ino moniker because the plan view — rectangular slab punctuated by perimeter columns — looks like a domino, elegant directional increment in that game of infinitely extendable modularity.

Looking at the image — columns, slabs, and stairs raised on a blocky proto-pilotis — one is not exactly suffused with that moist array of inchoate longings signifying home. There's no evidence of the hearth here, never mind the front door. This is because the Dom-ino project — like many other exemplars of heroic modernism — sought to house not simply the huddled masses but architecture itself, to find cultural accommodations for the activities of designing. In his 1922 book, *Vers une architecture*, Corb juxtaposed the image of the Parthenon with that of steamships and motorcars. His point was not that we'd come a long way, rather that the Parthenon and the steamship sat in similar relationship to the zeitgeist, expressions of the physical character of the culture at its most succinct, relevant, and perfectly elaborated.

From the skeleton of the Maison Dom-ino, Corb fleshed out the form of his machines for living. In the house and studio he designed for Amédée Ozenfant in 1923, the project for the Maison Citrohan of 1921 (its name a play on the Citroen automobile), a version of which was executed as part of the great Weissenhofsiedlung organized by Mies at Stuttgart in 1927, and in the housing project at Pessac of 1924–26, he established the essential parameters of the Corbusian pod. They do meet the test of economical manufacture that Corb elevates to the status of "natural law," and, these projects do accord with the modern architectural mood of the time, the flat-roofed, white-walled, strip-windowed style that was the complicit manner of the European avant-garde in the 1920s.

However, they're simply not mechanical. One often sees photos of Corb's villas foregrounded by Corb's car. That car's some sinuous, flow-lined gizmo with flared fenders, wire wheels, and bug-eye headlamps. Next to it, even Garches looks puritanical, all about Mediterranean repose and volumetric stability rather than the fast paced kinesis of the motor and jazz age. Its most literal link to the visual culture of machinery is the metal railing,

190

endlessly described as being like a ship's. Of course, the machine metaphor is available in the accessible image of simple efficiency and directness of expression. But, at the level of function, this functionalistic architecture doesn't accomplish anything particularly new. There simply isn't much you can do — never mind for the moment those things which you might imagine, feel, or be — that you couldn't do in the immediate predecessor of these houses.

The reason for this, I think, is that the work to be accomplished by these dwelling machines was primarily social: the Corbusian house was more lubricant than motor, meant to grease the skids of the great social apparatus that Corbusier envisioned, an instrument that architecture would underlie like a skeleton, deploying its organs along rational, mechanistic lines. Concurrent with these house designs, Le Corbusier was also designing his demonically rational model cities, the Ville Contemporaine and the Voisin plan for the decimation of Paris. These schemes for "industrial" cities were true *machines à habiter.* An apt depiction of the likely character of mechanical social relations, the quality of inhabitation in these schematically stratified environments, is offered by Fritz Lang in his concurrent screen gem *Metropolis,* as graphic a presentation of a citizenry mechanized as art has offered.

This vision of the city of efficient aggregation is crucial in thinking about the question of "home" today because one of the crucial divides in our consciousness of the domestic is visible along the fault line that distinguishes house from housing. These are the poles of our dilemma over how we're to live. For those still harboring aspirations to the traditional American dream, resurgent in the forms of comfort-fascinated yuppification, the house has resumed its status as beau-ideal. A recent issue of *New York* magazine featured a cover story on the waxing "return to the suburbs," where, it seems, cadres of fresh-minted yuppies are fleeing the taxing and insalubrious communalities of the city in search of the idylls of privatization that propelled their parents to like climes. Architectural collaborators in this "drang" also abound, from the egregious Stern and his kitschy suburbanism to the Florida halcyon of the much published fantasyland at Seaside. Clearly, such fetishistic longings after nostalgic individuation are, among other things, an assault on the sort of values embodied in the dwelling machines pushed by Corb in the '20s and their vast lineage.

This isn't exactly fresh territory. In the revisionism of the past decade or two, modern architecture has taken heavy heat for its role in the impoverishment of modern life, whipping tendency for the undercurrent dep-redations of rampant bureacracy and militarism. Early Corb — theorist Corb — has been useful to this assault precisely because of the enthusiasms of his dogmatic linking of the expressively spare with the socially impoverished. His vision of the orderly green and hygienic city, a happy dream of 19th century social engineering (spring though it did from a confrontation with the dark satanic cities of the industrial age, their inhabitants crushed and asphyxiated), was easily appropriated for more sinister regulatory purposes by the social engineers of the 20th. Still, our architecture forms itself in relation to these images, even as their underlying ideological basis is torqued. Yet there's that lag, that dissonance between form and content. The preferred manner of social discipline in the Reagan era, after all, is not the penal geometry of Soweto or urban renewal, it's Disneyland, the mysti-fying pluralism of the universally ersatz. We live in an era when the most powerful instrument of consciousness is television. We turn the channel and another image appears but the message is always the same, our relationship to it is always the same. Like it or not, this is architecture's context.

All of which is to say that a lack of clarity about the conditions of house and home should hardly be unexpected. The values of our (post-) techno-logical culture are distinguished for having overcome that old modernist conceit of "honesty" and "integrity," the idea that there was a necessary isomorphism between society's rational unfolding, scientifically under-stood, and the outward forms of its physical self-construction. "Home" reveals itself not in any single form but in a skein, a system of images whose content comprises both great nominal variety and an unmistakable narrowing. In the real estate section of the *New York Times*, thousands of available domiciles are reduced to the standardized pith of haiku: two rms, riv vu, all util incl, no fee. A reading of this yields certain conclusions. Saliently, one observes that the apartments available in Manhattan are both small and hugely expensive. Interpreting simply at the level of vulgar soci-ology, this pattern implies an urban precinct either dominated by a popu-lation of highly paid single persons or else of Soviet-style crowding: get out of the goddam bathroom Natasha, I've got to be at Smith Barney by nine.

One might say that these are want ads for the Ville Radieuse. The new vision, however, rescues that dour geometry via a number of improvements. First, each unit contains a television set, simultaneously sealing and global-izing it. Second, given the locational imperatives of phones, PCs, and other electronic links — which is to say, no imperatives at all — we no longer actually require any particular visual system of spatial ordering: any site will do. And, finally, we've given each building a name. Grim visions are thus forestalled by nomenclature: name it and disclaim it. In Manhattan nowadays every apartment block has a moniker, preferably one shared with a plains state, Montana, Dakota, Idaho, whatever. It's no different than TV or advertising, the relentless differentiation of an ever narrowing formula.

Let me invent a little history. There are three principal streams of architectural development in this discussion that successively collide and reconfigure themselves to form the history of the modern home and I'd like to look briefly at each. They're all related to my underlying theme here, the deformations of domesticity under the pressure of a culture increasingly rationalized according to the possibilities offered by the growth of technology. The first of the threads is the idea of the home as the manufactory of model citizens, the zone of some kind of social therapy. The second is the idea of the home as an appliance, a literal tool as much as a venue, a *machine à habiter* in the way we most generally understand the phrase. And, finally, there's the idea of the home as the preserve of the personal, the terrain of our individuation. This last category isn't precisely like the other two, having a hoarier presence. What's of interest is the way in which ideas about the private are manipulated to serve in light of the other two streams.

The notion of the architecturally therapeutic is a product of the secular revolution of rationalism, the first great human potential movement. The favored model image here is Jeremy Bentham's 18th-century Panopticon. This all-seeing supervisory construction was only the most synoptic representative of a time when Western culture was suddenly alive to the possibility that its deviant citizens, its criminals, its mentally disturbed, its poor, might not simply be disciplined, punished, maintained, or concealed, but actually reformed via the ministrations of science. Architecture, mother art, had a special place in this scheme. The idea that a certain spatial order would translate itself into a comparable order of mind and imagination became an early and sweepingly believed item of faith that, if implicit in earlier times, was now provided with a sound ideological basis.

Central to all of this was an animating biological metaphor in which a vision of society as organism was imposed. In various visions of the body politic, health was considered a product of the relationship between individual constituent cells and the whole. The most salubrious alignment was debated with verve. In the early 19th century, for example, a great argument raged between the prison building societies in Boston and Philadelphia over the way in which the configuration of jail cells was to support differing theories of the therapeutic aggregation of the incarcerated community. The issue devolved to the precise degree of isolation appropriate, the extent to which privatization of the criminal individual would result in the reform of his or her malformed soul.

morality & design ... seriality again.

Clearly, in any social construction, the relationship of the individual to communality is seminal. This is how we distinguish the emergence of society from the State of Nature. The history of modern architecture's social agenda is a study in the attempt to concretize, one way or another, some version of this relationship. Characteristically, the activity of housing has been overcome by the hubris of shaping. Victor Considerant, social philosopher Charles Fourier's otherwise forgettable architect, declared of his enterprise, "architecture writes history" and proceeded to design a utopian commune modeled after Versailles, appropriating the forms of monarchic hierarchy to egalitarianism's job. And why not? If everyone's a king, why not live in a palace?

This point's not exactly about style. Who's finally to say whether the Doric or the Shingle is conduit to democracy. We know that meanings attach to signifiers, after all. But it's one of architecture's favored fallacies that form invents function. At some level, this is a happy, congenial error, utopianism's delusion. Utopia, though, lapses into dystopia with ease as forms conceived as liberation are appropriated by oppressors. The line that passes from the Fourierite phalanstery to the Radiant City to the ordered Alphavilles of Ludwig Hilberseimer to Pruitt-Igoe and the disciplinary excesses of urban renewal is a direct one. Each of these examples is predicated on the imposition of the routines of architectural order on other kinds of relationships. *... reworking Jeneks !!*

or usurpers ... Jamaican drugs barons — S. London c. 1987

In Western architecture's mainstream, the touchstone of a deep logic has long been geometry: Euclid has been and remains the great arbiter of architectural sense. The unspoken premise behind projects like the Radiant City and its kin is precisely the idea that life itself becomes rational to the degree that living it becomes geometrical, a kind of architectural analogue to the square meal. Like life in the cloister, there's a vision of order here that's imposed according to the strictures of some putatively higher authority. The potency of this particular set of relationships continues to amaze.

Whitgift Almshouses !!

One of the most publicized series of nominally domestic projects of recent years has been Peter Eisenman's suite of numbered houses, a couple of which have actually been built. As you may know, their main design shtick is the idea of a kind of unstoppable geometric rigor. Taking a certain array of spare architectonic elements (or phonemes in the enervated linguistic analogy that prompted the work) — columns, planes, openings, etc. — he makes them dance through the application of several simple rules of transformation. What Eisenman has produced, in effect, is a crude, low mathematical machine for the production of dwellings. Although the end product of this apparatus is a fairly straightforward modernist composition, what has been supplied by the Eisenman initiative is a strategy for the mechanization of intuition, a little mental factory for cranking out totems of rigor. In the best known of these products — House Six — there's an incident that strikes me as symbolizing an important risk in the mechanical rationalization of dwelling. I refer, of course, to the chasm placed between the twin marital beds of the inhabitants. Of course, one might observe that this condition is endemic. But the chasm is literal: there's a hole in the floor between the beds, the result of some precious inevitability in the system that simultaneously designs and explains the house. Is this crazy or what? The point, of course, is that, judged sui generis, the house is perfect, doing exactly what it sets out to do. Here's utilitarianism perverted — mannerist functionalism, if you'll tolerate the concept. Eisenman is functionalism's Fawn Hall: incredibly efficient within a designated range of activity, oblivious to all consequences at the periphery.

To me, the riskiest legacy of modernism's two centuries or so of history is its mood of orthodoxy, a mood which the now standard critique over-identifies with its forms, as if the right angle were a recent discovery. Now, orthodoxy is hardly a fresh threat; just ask Socrates or Galileo. What makes the critique particular — and to my mind risky — is the way in which it inevitably links the sins of the modern with the sins of culture gone tech. In some ways, modernism brought this on itself by proclaiming its love of linkage. However, what I'm trying to argue here is that there's been a species of baby-with-the-bathwaterism resulting from the fact that modernism was never really up to its self-proclaimed vanguard role in embodying technology. Rather, the sins of Taylorized industrialism (Corb was just nuts about Frederick Taylor's *Principles of Scientific Management* (1911)), the higher slaveries of militarism, industrial capitalism, and reborn totalitarianism were allowed to tar the happy possibilities of science.

I think there's another history of modern architecture that privileges a

[handwritten margin note: Hellman ... it looks technical functional etc.]

different kind of machine for living, one consecrated to convenience and liberation rather than to the mechanization of the human subject or the schematic representation of dim theory. We have, over time, had two characteristic responses to technology and its possible places in our daily lives. One is the optimism bred of a vision of rendering the world and its secrets and pleasures both more accessible and more malleable. The other, as emblematized most searingly in the vision of Frankenstein's monster, is of technology become autonomous, taking over, running us instead of us running it. So much of our architectural production nowadays does seem to be premised on a spasm of self-primitivization, as if by aping some bygone decorative strategy, we'd somehow escape the risk of impending holocaust.

Earlier attempts at self-primitivization, in the halcyon days of the 1960s, produced a number of retrievals of the Rousseauian State of Nature. The counterculture resided in an amazing variety of self-built shelters: tepees and domes, yurts and cabins, a profusion of dwellings constructed according to autonomous ideals. Poignant, sure, and vaguely ridiculous, but this was as beautiful a vision of utopia as we've lately had.

Such counterculture housing types constitute a double critique of social technology. These dwellings — and their communal clusterings — were powerful optings out of the regimenting culture of the Protestant ethic, an act of rebellion against the uniform drear of countless recalled suburban childhoods. What continues to impress about these arrangements is not simply the utopian optimism of their sought-after social relations but their linking — via an implicit theory of ecology — of social purpose with the act and scene of dwelling via a critique and reinterpretation of technology. If the counterculture and its subsequent extensions have a vital message to convey about the technological, it's that the forms of technology are not autonomous, that they can be distinguished. The phrase "appropriate technology" describes an extremely powerful concept that allows resistance to the dominating idea of a relentless Darwinian advance of scientific knowledge and its replacement by a more useful and appropriate notion of agency and responsibility.

Given the character of the times that spawned it, it's not surprising that the attitude of the counterculture toward technology was essentially adaptive and cooptational. One thinks of various images of domestication, of houses made of shingled school buses or, most seminally, of Steve Baer's Zomes, those funky geodesics fabricated from retrieved automobile shells. This strategy of appropriating "the man's technology," as Huey Newton

(Protestant prescription)

called it, was effectively a way of turning a generation born to privilege into a homegrown version of the Third World. Those were the days, after all, when large numbers of us thought of ourselves as a bridge, tried to identify our links as stronger than the economic rationales that were the only visible affinity among the presumptive citizens of the Ville Radieuse or the suburbs.

This tribal consciousness, the backwoods equivalent to a more traditional sense of class, did not simply cement a feeling of solidarity and resistance, but helped to kindle the search for a more genuine, indigenous, human house form, unpolluted by the taint of consumerism or other coercions. Unlike Adam's pre-social house, the primitive hut of the counterculture was like the purposefully simple architecture of the Shakers or the ritual succinctness of a Dogon village. It was a domestic architecture suited to straightforward, unmediated social relations. Places like Drop City were comparable to the early projects of the Soviet Constructivists — our most bracingly modernist architectural prototype for communal living. In both instances, the vision of a harmonious egalitarian life-style was the most potent generator of organizational ideas. And, for both, the major formal address was to the problematic of the technological, the question of living in light of the machine. That the attitudes ultimately embodied were apparently opposite was simply a sign of the difference in times and setting.

In early revolutionary glory days in Russia, as that brief enthusiastic sun shone on a society emerging from centuries of superstition and despotism, the message of the machine and of manufacture was one of liberation and promise, the apt and consonant iconography of the triumph of a scientific world view. By the time of the even briefer countercultural efflorescence of the '60s, technology seems to be everywhere in the hands of the oppressor. Geopolitically speaking, the dominating struggle of the times, a struggle that absorbed us all — thanks to the insistent presence of TV — was the Viet-Nam War. Night after night we were shown scenes of the struggle of a people against the arrogance of the culture that epitomized technology. The Vietnamese, living in the virtuous squalor of "primitive" huts and caves, those hooches torched and napalmed on a thousand broadcasts, were able, by dint of principles and will, to resist and ultimately conquer the Budweiser-swilling aggressors and their air-conditioned nightmare. Clearly, the primitive was here identified with humanity and life.

But this isn't exactly my point. The activists of the counterculture in the '60s and the Constructivists in the '20s were after very similar things: the creation of a space in which people could grow equal. The instruments of the search were also comparable: the collectivization of domestic work, communal cooking, shared child care, the autonomy of an intimate community. These are the mighty social goals of an age. The great problem of the moment, the one I'm trying to speculate about here, is that we find ourselves in a time when technology is largely disengaged from the prospect of a liberatory role. For the community of architects, surely, the agenda of the '60s still constitutes the last useful social agenda we've had. The reasons are scarcely obscure. After all, the country is led (over TV) by an *idiot méchant*, whose view of the world is bound by the technological hydra of holocaust and TV.

Earlier I proposed to discuss the contraction of the domestic environment as one of the abiding tropes of the housing question nowadays. As the countercultural examples just alluded to should suggest, this is a possibility that cuts both ways. On the one hand, we have the condition of coziness and malleability, the reassuring democracy of the small dwelling, the private ideal that has provided such a resonant symbol of individual freedom from young Abe Lincoln's log cabin down to Frank Lloyd Wright's Usonian proposals to its apotheosis in Levittown, where this symbol of individualism was cut according to the exigencies of the assembly line. A distinct domicile is, indeed, something worth fighting for, no matter how close to home the struggle must be waged.

But the more sinister, narrower, dimensions of this contraction seem to dominate nowadays. The New York market with $1,500 a month, 350-square-foot studio apartments harbingers something even more frightening. In a passage from David Lodge's novel *Small World*, the author describes the apartment of one of his characters, a translator from Tokyo who

lives alone in a tall modern apartment block. He is able to afford this accommodation because, though well appointed, it is extremely restricted in space. In fact, he cannot actually stand up in it, and on unlocking the door, and having taken off his shoes, is obliged to crawl, rather than step inside.... The window cannot be opened. The room is air-conditioned, temperature controlled and soundproof. Four hundred identical cells are stacked and interlocked in this building, like a tower of eggboxes. It is a new development, an upmarket version of the "capsule" hotels situated near the main railway termini that proved so popular with Japanese workers in recent years.

Lodge's description goes amusingly on, prompting the reader's knowing incredulity. In fact, though, a marginally less goofy version of this building actually exists, designed by Kisho Kurokawa and built in Tokyo in 1972. In many ways the building is not exceptional. Its lineage can be traced from Moshe Safdie's Habitat in 1967 back to the famous experiments in industrialization and prefabrication undertaken by early modernists such as Walter Gropius and Konrad Wachsmann. It was also constructed in the light of considerable interest in the American mobile home industry that, during the '60s, was discovered by official architectural culture. The mobile home was, in effect, the naive realization of many of the most cherished hopes of modernism. Factory built, standardized within its envelope yet malleable to a degree, mobile (and thus potentially global), cheap and (best of all in many ways) tacky, which simultaneously signified that it was "popular," oscillating with good social vibes, it simple needed to be gussied up and rationalized according to the atrophying precepts of *hoch* modernity.

The expression of enabling technical means is an ancient architectural bugbear. In general, as received today, it has been largely limited to the celebration of structural technologies. Even now, given the constraints of gravity and tradition, these essentially primitive expressive possibilities tend to be classicizing and limited, Mies van der Rohe being the salient example. At the Farnsworth House, there's great clarity of skeleton and enclosure, crisp steel joints and seamless glass, but the electrical conduits and plumbing remain invisible. In Richard Meier's houses, the effective Omega point of the research initiated by Corb with the Maison Dom-ino, the technical presence is largely totemic, wafting from a palette of standard, if artfully employed signifiers: dimensional refinement, minimalist detail, an overall smoothness of finish squeaky with precision milling, and pipe railing.

This is scarcely a fresh observation. Buckminster Fuller — that great forgotten genius of American architecture — made it visibly articulate in the late '20s (concurrent with the European research into the so-called International Style) when he designed his mighty Dymaxion houses (and, recognizing the inevitable American symbiosis, Dymaxion cars). Bucky's great vision was in recognizing that a house in the 20th century bundled an array of systems which far exceeded the requirement for any exigencies of shelter. I quote his famous lyric (to the tune of "Home on the Range"):

> Roam home to a dome
> Where Georgian and Gothic once stood
> Now chemical bonds alone guard our blondes
> And even the plumbing looks good.

The Dymaxion houses are distinguished for the conceptual parity they offered to the full range of building systems, redeeming plumbing, lighting, electrical service, and ventilation as legitimately architectural investigations. Clearly, the Dymaxion houses were the real machines for living. Their coincident mechanical appearance was the result not of a hunt for an apt and up-to-the-minute metaphor, but of a direct fertilization of the process of design by information from the disciplines that were grappling with the same issues extra-architecturally, aeronautical design most prominently.

Despite the coprolitic sexism of Bucky's hymn to the dome, his most important precursors in a new envisioning of the house as a socially supportive complex of systems were feminists like Charlotte Perkins Gilman and, more directly, Catherine Beecher, whose 1869 project for an "American Woman's Home" virtually invented the idea of a service core. As a social polemic, Beecher's linking of technical innovation with an advance in the condition of women far outstrips the loony, positivist mysticism of Fuller's enterprise or, for that matter, the blank, Taylorized dystopianism of Le Corbusier's. To me, this vision of the technical seen as at once expressive and liberating is most bracing, the way it ought to be. Unfortunately, Fuller's legacy is most immediately visible in radomes and Airstream trailers. And a feminist architecture, supportive of egalitarian ways of living, awaits further movement toward extinction by the American social dinosaur. Architecture, after all, doesn't make history, merely awaits its impress.

As fresh technology comes faster and faster knocking on our doors, the question of absorption becomes more and more vital. Speaking of knocking on the door, I was in Miami for the first time last year and visited a big condo development called "Williams Island." All big condo developments in Miami name themselves thus, entire of the main, a nomenclatural strategy meant simultaneously to evoke tropicality, exclusivity, and security. The latter is especially crucial in a town whose aura is so wrapped in violence, Don Johnson City. The most striking thing about Williams Island was — perhaps predictably — not the curvy condos, the ersatz Mediterranean village, or the perfect golf course, but the security system. In lieu of a key, citizens of the island are given little cards that, en route from entry to apartment, must be stuffed into a variety of orifices which control passage through a sequence of checkpoints. This, in itself, was not so remarkable. What was remarkable to me was the fact that each insertion was communicated to a central station, where a computer logged and printed out a record of each penetration. Security, in effect, was purchased at the cost of submission to draconian, Soviétique, surveillance. Wealth chose to live in the electronic Panopticon, surrendering privacy to feel secure.

One of the historic sets of poles in the discussion of housing is the opposition between community and privacy. A more presently arresting opposition, though, is between privacy and surveillance. To my eye, there's no act that more directly clarifies the character of today's social compact than that extended moment at the airport where one — like the Williams Island resident — is obliged to present identification, certify credit worthiness, and jump through the metal detecting hoop as one's baggage undergoes adjacent radiation. At the airport, the Panopticon of domestic tranquility is extended to encompass the globe. As the possibility of private movement is ever more vitiated, the concept of "home" is continually diminished.

Prospects for the domestic are severely hemmed, in large part by the imperatives of the culture of mass consumption, by the geography of television. TV is the ultimate machine for living, an implement for investing any set of fragments with the logic of parity. *Gong Show, Dating Game,* Biafra, Linda Evans, Nixon, Holocaust, anything with an image particular enough to be distinguished feeds the system. So too with architecture. Consider this photo caption:

Blake meets with members of the household staff, in the library. The mansion contains many fine examples of decorative arts, including antique oriental rugs and silver, handcarved mahogany lecterns, paintings of the late 1800s, a Ming Dynasty vase and a pair of Empire satinwood side tables valued at $14,000 each.

Architectural Digest? No, the quote is from a Dynasty fanzine, which features precise descriptions of the Carrington mansion: a fiction. The breakthrough here is the specificity with which the ersatz is described and represented. Similarly, in the current architectural climate, appliqué — the arts of Erewhon — attains the status of a science. The new living machine imprints a pre-digested memory, stripped of the resonance of the personal particular, on the pod. Where this consumer architecture and the Panopticon of social discipline meet is on the common ground of an exalted certainty. In Disneyland, the Ville Radieuse, Attica, TV, nothing can go seriously wrong. History's Nielson rating.

Let me end with a little coda, a tithe to some new domestic architecture for which I feel some enthusiasm. The lecture series in which this diatribe figured was concurrent with a retrospective of Frank Gehry's work, surely the most stimulating architecture being built in the States today. Gehry's houses in particular confront a number of the issues I've breezed by here. Certainly, they have technology as one of their primary agendas. The physical elements in the Gehry palette have often been described as cheap, off the shelf, tacky. This misses something. These pieces — studs, ply, galvanized metal — represent precisely the technical means indigenous to most of our domestic architecture. Gehry has simply been frank. In this sense, Gehry's the Bucky Fuller of available technology, confronting the task of making the plumbing look good but doing it out of *Sweet's*.

In his own justly celebrated house, Gehry also takes on the problem of individuation in a culture bent on the exaltation of the replicable. To a piece of received architecture, he adds his own, idiosyncratic skin. Instead of finding history by excavating, via the act of simulating recall, Gehry chooses to add another stratum. He auto-historicizes, piling on his own layer, not artificially subtracting the present to fake a past that can never be more than an absence. Finally, Gehry pursues a meaningful fragmentation. Houses decompose as their elements — individual rooms and spaces — assert their own independence and separate identities. This is a powerful critique of the pod. Opposing the dumb totalitarian logic of separate but equal, Gehry substitutes a world of variation. Privileging the eccentricity of individuals, Gehry's work avoids the cozy domineering gestalt of pre-packaged certainty. Replacing the predictable uniformity of high-mod or post-mod's pastiche, Gehry offers us the truer comforts of uncertainty. I think this is inspirational. Art, after all, is our great hedge against the oppressions of a universal sure thing. And it's the addition of our private arts that makes a house a home.

1987

CANTICLES FOR MIKE*

What we observe is not nature itself, but nature exposed
to our methods of questioning.

WERNER HEISENBERG

1. A VERY BRIGHT LIGHT

Webb's penetrating ray illumines the classical, architecture and mechanics.
Its heat "cooks" the dimensions of the little temple to a boil of perfection,
to a grill of order, to a degree of rationality adequate to more recently available maths. The light is mechanically pellucid, outlining an architecture
that's flawless, mutable only under the gaze of a shifting observer. That
temple is Architecture's. Webb designs the processional of its worship down
the nave of the Thames, his river of time.

2. THERE'LL ALWAYS BE AN ENGLAND

The little sub cruises past a full deployment of English social arrangements.
Henley — like Ascot, Wimbledon, or the other annual dissipative perks of
Anglo-*noblesse* — is a spectacle of advantage. Webb's dad was accountant to
the regatta, entitling his son to a choice view from the official Steward's
Enclosure, a Pepperland scene of brass bands, tea, sandwiches, and old boys
in straw boaters flanking the finishing-line. Clearly, regatta is simply

*Introduction to "Mega V": Temple Island: A Study By Mike Webb, Exhibition Catalogue.

eponym to event, the larger festival of social calibration informed by the satisfactions of a photo-finish, distinction registered only in a flash.

3. CHILDHOOD'S ENDS

"Heaven lies about us in our infancy", wrote Wordsworth, one of Webb's predecessor romantics. Archigram's struggle was – in part – to retain the imaginative privileges of English boyhood, to erase continually the barriers between research and play, between architecture and toys. Henley is Webb's primal scene, remembered through the constantly shifting perspective of time's motion, presented through the mystifying succession of differences demanded by movement through space. Memory play is mnemonic, conservative, but analytic as well. Webb the Atomist is looking for architecture's tiniest increment, the moment at which the whole complex field is contained in a single, primary dot.

4. SCHEHERAZADE

There was a lot of anxiety in London as Webb prepared for this exhibition. Would he finish, prepare a satisfactorily full suite of drawings, cover the walls? Wrong anxiety. Can one expect the dilator, the visionary, to be other than dilatory? The telling of the tale, after all, forestalls as well as reveals: if the end arrives too early, the tale is eclipsed. The recollected heaven of Henley is Webb's state of nature, his proper time, misty 18th-century conceit, the childhood of the modern, antedating crisis. The act of drawing vitalizes.

5. THE SIN PALACE AND THE TUBE

A story is told about Webb carrying a model of the Sin Palace through the London Underground. Rushing to enter a train, he was not quite quick enough and the model was caught in the closing doors, crushed. It had to be rebuilt from scratch. T.E. Lawrence left the completed manuscript of *Revolt in the Desert* in a London railway station. It had to be rewritten from scratch. What do these stories have in common? The perils of the rails? The fragility

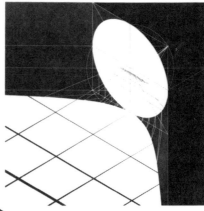

ABSTRACTION ON HENLEY REGATTA
Mike Webb

Isometric projection of the "setting up" of a so-called one-point perspective projection, comprising the image, contained within what appears to us to be an ellipse, and to the observer a circle ... and the plan (a horizontal gridded plane) from which the image is generated. Note also the cone of vision, and the parabola formed when it intersects the gridded plane.

The image is executed as a line drawing, each component line being of equal weight. If the image is the projection of the gridded plane on a surface perpendicular to the observer's center of vision (the definition of a picture plane), then the thickness of the grid lines will be a function of their distance from the observer. At, or near the horizon, the lines would be infinitely thick.

When drawing the plan, it is customary to construct only that part of it that is of interest; to draw the whole plan would require a sheet of paper the size of the universe, and perhaps the shape of the universe. So, since an undifferentiated grid is without a significant zone of "interest", an arbitrary choice was made to depict only what you see in the drawing. But the choice too has impacted on the image, so what the observer sees is an image ... modified by the presence of another observer — us.

of creation? The tenuousness of record? The wages of sin? No, just two representations of the necessity of a caesura, a cadence to wandering. For his part, Webb denies the incident in the Tube, having moved on to cones.

6. A CLASSIC EXPERIMENT

The question of whether light propagates as wave or particle has been a centerpiece in the invention of modern physics. In 1803 Thomas Young conducted a classic experiment. In front of a source of light (sunlight coming through a pinhole in a screen), Young placed another screen, in which he had cut two vertical slits which could be individually covered: When light shone through either of the slits singly, it spread out – diffracted – on the wall. However, when the light shone simultaneously through both slits, something radically different took place: the light struck the wall in a pattern of bands of alternating light and darkness. Explaining this as interference, a commonplace of wave mechanics, decided the issue, it seemed: light was a wave. Einstein had other ideas. For him, light was made up of particles or photons, an idea for which there was also convincing experimental proof. This evidence, however, did not disprove the conclusions of Young's theory. Quantum mechanics was obliged to rethink the universe in order to attempt to account for this apparently contradictory duality, seeking new patterns that transcended the classic requirements of causality. Webb, too, is searching for a fresh and unifying pattern by running Young's experiment anew. His regulating periscope, with its binocular aperture, reconstructs the 1803 device but adds an Einsteinian modification. The dot screen superimposed anterior is a filter for photons. While the experiment is ongoing and results not yet conclusive, there is no question that Webb is playing with the full deck. Quantum mechanics has changed the space of architecture and Webb is a pioneer of its exploration.

7. ST PAUL'S AND THE SPITFIRE

Certain persistent originating images emerge over and over. St Paul's (not St Peter's), the Spitfire (not the Hurricane), the London Bus (the old Routemaster, not its boxy successor). To be sure, these are objects united in their

Englishness, but that's not so central. More crucial is the studied perfection of their compound curvature. Webb recalls a very early fascination with Wren's resolution of the intersection of vaults, the way in which the almost weird reconciling shapes deform attempts at penetration. Webb's incision in the Henley temple dome is a related act, a simple auguring which sets an incredible sequence of events in motion, which opens up transformations of matter, space, and light. Those fascinating British machines address paradigms of perfection as well as the idea of motion and the delights of a cowled mechanism. But clearly it's the curves which attract. Webb restores to architecture a difficulty of surface, producing an ineffability of light.

8. ALICE AFORETHOUGHT

Webb's trip alludes to another Thames journey, taken by Lewis Carroll and the Reverend Robinson Duckworth in the company of the three Liddell sisters on July 4, 1862: "as memorable a day in the history of literature as it is in American history," by the lights of W.H. Auden. While the recollective lines "All in a golden afternoon/Full leisurely we glide" preface the ensuing book, Alice's own journey begins with her fall down the rabbit-hole. Descending, she snatches a jar of orange marmalade from a passing shelf but hesitates to drop it "for fear of killing someone underneath." Martin Gardner points out that Carroll certainly knew that in free fall Alice wouldn't have been able to "drop" the jar, which would have remained suspended in front of her. He further notes Carroll's kindred description, in the novel *Sylvie and Bruno*, of the difficulty of taking tea inside a falling house. These problematic descents evoke Einstein's famous "thought experiment," in which an imaginary falling elevator is used to explain part of the Theory of Relativity. The moving bodies in Webb's wonderland are likewise constituents of a thought experiment. With them Webb invents a motile landscape, at first unfathomable, but finally minutely responsive to the demands of his gaze. A memorable voyage through mind's architecture.

9. LORENTZ

Webb has spoken of his fascination with a curved plot of the Lorentz Transformations, a parabola which he detects to be similar to a curve he himself achieved by plotting measured subdivisions in perspective against "true" dimensions in the picture plane, the space of representation on one axis, that of the represented on another. Hendrik Lorentz produced one of the steps immediately preceding the Special Theory of Relativity. His mathematics — taken up virtually whole by Einstein — describes a way in which what an observer in one frame of reference sees can be translated into what an observer in another frame sees. These equations are called the Lorentz Transformations and they provided Einstein with a means of explaining the paradox presented to classical mechanics by the idea that the speed of light remains constant for all observers, regardless of their own motion. The solution is the nub of modernism in physics: the idea that a single phenomenon differs under different observation, that, in effect, an observer cannot observe without changing what is seen. That sub drifting downstream is Webb's monument to relativity's presence in architecture.

10. RESURGAM

What else should a submersible do but "rise again"? Tithe to the first sub, sure, historical gesture, origin. But, derived conoid shape notwithstanding, the sub's a shark, cruising under the regatta, threatening — but what? The complacent regulation of upper-crust sport? The tidy and accurate recollection of childhood's afternoons? Or, perhaps, the race's complacent homage to Newtonian motion, the easy Galilean mechanics of another infancy. The danger, clearly, is real. The repressed inevitably returns.

11. DISC TO ELLIPSE

The Special Theory of Relativity proposes that a moving object appears to contract in the direction of motion as its velocity increases. This is a phenomenon suggested by the famous Michelson—Morley experiment and elucidated in the Lorentz Transformations. A physicist called James Terrell has proposed an optical explanation of these relativistic contractions. Imagine an observer looking at a sphere from a very great distance. The lines connecting the observer's eyes to a sphere in a plan view will find two points on the sphere that approximate its diameter. Now imagine an elevational view of the sphere from the observer's vantage point and imagine that the two observed points on the perimeter of the sphere are connected by two vertical lines to a screen beneath it. Suppose that the sphere is moving very fast, relative to the speed of light, from right to left. If it is moving fast enough, the light from the point on the far left edge is blocked by the movement of the sphere in front of it. At the same time, the sphere moves out from in front of signals that used to be on the back side of the ball, leaving them visible to the observer. An illusion of rotation is created. At the same time, the two points projected on the screen beneath the sphere have moved closer together. This is a representation of the contraction due to motion described in the Lorenz Transformations. What has happened is that the moving sphere, by getting in the way of some of its own signals and out of the way of others, appears to rotate. This, in turn, causes the projected distance between any two points on the sphere which are aligned with the direction of motion to decrease. The faster the motion of the sphere, the greater the apparent rotation and the closer together the two points projected on the screen. The components and mechanics of this example are not dissimilar to those Webb deploys in his experiment. In both instances, there's a change in the character of a projected image governed by a shift in the relationship of object and observer. And, in both instances, the relevant geometry is spherical. The elongation of a sphere is an ellipsoid. Mutatis mutandis.

12. PYTHAGORAS

Pressed on the question of early influences, Webb brings up his schoolboy introduction to Pythagoras. The theorem was an opening for Webb into a world of order and logic, into the careful argumentation of mathematics. The relationship between space and time propounded by Einstein is similar to the relationship between the sides of a right-angled triangle in the Pythagorean theorem. By substituting "space" for one of the legs, "time" for the other, and "space–time interval" for the hypotenuse, a relationship is produced which is conceptually similar to the relationships described in the Special Theory of Relativity. Relativity makes physics geometrical. Webb's research explores the same territory but in reverse. His representations seek to make geometry physical, to give it time, to unearth its latent relativity, and to pull architecture through every transformation that his experiment entails.

13. WHITE SHADOWS

How to explain the white shadows which streak Webb's idyllic landscape? Are Webb's trees spectral quasars assembling light? If white light is shone through hydrogen gas and then through a prism, the familiar deployment of colors from red to violet results, but with a crucial addition: over one hundred black lines corresponding to the specific energy amounts required to cause hydrogen electrons to jump from one energy shell to another. The shadows aren't merely graphic, they're emissions.

14. JOHN HENRY

In popular American legend, John Henry was the railway man who challenged the new steam hammer to a spike-driving competition and bested it. Webb has executed these drawings over the space of many years, laboriously, by hand. There's a poignancy to his exquisite work that springs from the tenacity with which it refuses to give up its craft. That Webb's curves are constructed not by computer programs and high-speed plotters but by means of the traditional instruments of drawing both redeems them as art and — by asserting art's willingness to know science — gives architecture new life. As the Theory of Relativity restores the centrality of the human observer, so Webb's profound journey brings architecture home.

1987

MACHINE DREAMS

Machines invented architecture as we know it. As buildings became mechanical and their means of production industrial, literal differences between architecture and machinery became increasingly indeterminate. Around the beginning of the 19th century, machinery surpassed building in complexity, precision, and innovation; architecture ceased its life on the frontiers of technology — the ocean liner, not the cathedral, was the leading edge. This was clearly a compromised position and architects were confronted with two choices: reappropriate someone else's technology or resist the whole thing. The history of architecture over the past 200 years has been dominated by the long wave of this cycle.

Not that this has been the only relevant issue, in the history of modern architecture, but this discussion has dominated the question of expression. Today, as architecture emerges from its Reaganoid snooze, its relationship to science and technology — one of architectural modernism's deepest amours — has returned to the foreground. To be sure, every building begs the question of its means. Glorious modernism, though, argued for the continuity of means and forms. The rationale was evanescently moral, clumping an idea of expressive "honesty," a vision of the times, and a "scientific" (if often vulgar) politics. While this routine has dimmed, the questions it sought to engage have burgeoned.

Symptomatic of the resilience of the mechanical trope is the architectural media's generous coverage of two buildings completed during the past year. Richard Rogers's Lloyd's building in London and Norman Foster's Hong Kong and Shanghai Bank in Hong Kong take the task of literalizing architectural technology as their primary expressive agendas. These beautiful buildings do make perfect sense, and make it in a climate hungry for workable logics. If architecture is to have a prosody (never mind a syntax), it needs a language. And what more logical place to look than architecture's material condition, to statics and joinery, materials and servicing, issues that architecture shares with machinery in general.

Several design shows this season have dealt — in varying degrees — with the problem of inscribing an architectural poetics within the field of its technology. At P.S. 1, this fall's "Building: Machines" (organized by Glenn Weiss) exhibited the work of three practices involved in addressing the building/machine conundrum. Peter Pfau and Wes Jones contributed four projects that gyre and gimbel nicely along this particular edge. The first is partially parodic in mood, a series of "primitive huts" got up in nominally sophisticated means. To shelter a given rectangular volume, the architects produced a set of solutions — represented in beautiful models — in which the task of enclosure is accomplished with a set of archetypal architectural shapes compounded of the familiar elements of steel construction. The irony here is that the steel is used in a way that's analogous to a more original primitive, say timber. In both classes of origin, there's an idea about a "natural" minimum set of rules and combinations. The point, though, is that despite a common gravitational ancestry, each technology has its own zero points, its private myths.

Pfau and Jones aren't inventing machinery, they're reinventing it, and their viewing glass is not a little dark. The halcyon days of the kinetic being clearly past, much of their grafted mechanical imagery is so much detritus. This is polemically so in a project for homeless housing, compounded of literal scrap and inserted into scrap space in the city, development's residue between buildings. It's also a governor of the mood of their major project, a Californianized Unité, proposed for a site in LA's Manhattan Beach hemmed by an oil refinery and a suburb, as succinct a spatial summary of modernism's dilemma imaginable. The collision of Le Corbusier's rationalized hyperscale megasuburb with the mesmerizing "natural" machine architecture of the refinery, all surrealized by SoCal atmospherics, promises more than the project finally delivers. But it's a really nice try.

My favorite work was the talented Neil Denari's *Solar Clock*, proposed for the ramparts of the Tower of London. This enormous object, shunting around the walls of the Tower, is meant, in Denari's words, to be "so intrusive and reflective that, as a confrontational device, it cannot be avoided." As both polemic and object, the work is successful, poised as it is between its nominal rationale and the more combative logic of an infernal machine.

The specifics of its form are adequately enigmatic to keep questions of the union of architecture and machine open and provocative. Clearly, the clock's an alien, a robotic juggernaut slouching toward a change of day. Still, in purpose and presence, it ticks with continuity, of time, and of place.

Over at the Brooklyn Museum, the big "Machine Age in America" documents a time when designers related to the machine without ambivalence or irony. It's an alright show, simply documentary, zealously predictable in its choices. It memorializes a period — between the wars — when machinery was viewed as the new nature, as logical a source of motif to Walter Dorwin Teague or Raymond Loewy as an acanthus leaf was to a Greek. It was also the time when designing and styling definitively diverged, when the modern sensibility of imposing a malleable and occlusive image on an object received from other hands became dominant. There are plenty of beautiful things to be seen in Brooklyn, but the most resonant message is of paradise lost. The efforts of the designers of this period — both the streamliners and stylists on the one hand and the more indigenous investigators (like Bucky Fuller) on the other — set the inescapable context for all later investigations.

The roughly contemporaneous developments documented at the Cooper-Hewitt's "Berlin 1900–1933: Architecture and Design" present certain additional possibilities for architecture's relationship to the characteristic objects of modern times. For me, the most stunning things in the exhibition were drawings of a sinuous and fantastical architecture produced by Hermann Finsterlin, Karl Krayl, Erich Mendelsohn and the great Hans Scharoun. What's amazing about these trippy, alternatively crystalline and curvaceous drawings are their correspondences with the visual art of the counterculture of the '60s. Then, too, art tried to reconcile a spirit of liberation and an enthusiasm for the prospects of the technical with a deep distrust about the uses to which capital was putting science. By contrast, the depredations of the regimented modernism displayed in an adjacent room seem positively repressive in their shortsighted vision of a social organization that seemed to propose the democracy of universal alienation.

One last image to end. At the IBM Gallery (apt locus!), there's been a show called "Tokyo: Form and Spirit". The underlying rubric, a contrast between the material culture of the Edo period and the city of the present day, seems suggestive but the final result is fuzzy and disappointing, clarifying little about either form or spirit. The strategy has been to juxtapose old artifacts with a group of installations designed by a group of leading

Japanese designers. I was pretty much unimpressed with these, perhaps because of my high expectations. However, among them is an amazingly beautiful work, the design of Hiroshi Hara, one of the most interesting architects in Japan.

Hara's work is a rumination on the way in which the electronic technology of the computer, modeled on human mental processes, is supplanting the more biomorphic character of the physical machine. Perhaps I overstate the analytic qualities of Hara's work. The issue of biomorphic versus electronic, "mentalistic," space, is really no more than a point of departure. Hara's a poet: he sensualizes the territory rather than establishes it. The work itself consists of a series of parallel planes of plexiglass into which human, mechanical, and electronic forms have been etched. In addition, embedded in the plex panels are a multitude of tiny lights. Over a 15-minute cycle, an amazing, mesmerizing light show is performed by this apparatus, firmly uniting vivid space-making with a succinct elaboration of the electronic presence in human events. A perfect spot for a stoned afternoon.

Checked my box recently and found in it a letter from Leon Krier reacting to my recent assault. You may recall that I bashed the young master for his continuing activities in support of the late Albert Speer, whose achievements in the field of mass murder, Krier feels, should not be allowed to distract us from his purported attainments as an architect. "Should the German language be banned because the Nazis happened to speak it?" Krier queries. To answer this question I urge Leon to reconsult his Saussure, paying particular attention to the distinction between *langue* and *parole*.

February 1987

SILICON IMPLANTS

IN BROOKLYN

Urban renewal lapsed from writ to epithet for a reason. Intoxicated by its vision of a tabula rasa, urban renewal was blind to what it destroyed. As poverty was transformed into "blight," destruction became salvation. In the end, the massive urban renewal of the '50s and '60s was defeated by both the rebellion of its victims and the sterility of its vision. Nobody believed in it any more.

The proposed MetroTech complex in downtown Brooklyn is a classic revival of urban renewal's old time religion. If all goes as intended, 10 square blocks will be razed (or renovated) and replaced by a complex of "high-tech" office buildings and extensions to Polytechnic University. To this end, between two and three hundred residents and 60 some businesses will be sacrificed. In place of a zone of scruffy diversity will rise clean and mono-lithic regularity. Price tag: three quarters of a billion dollars.

MetroTech is being promoted by a collaboration of Polytechnic University, the New York City Public Development Corporation, and a private development combine, principally Forest City Enterprises from Cleveland, which was brought in on a noncompetitive basis. The developer's motives are, of course, clear. For its part, the university gains space, a vague semblance of a campus, and a "better" environment. One imagines, too, an inspirational vision of the kind of entrepreneurial frenzy that takes place in the storied free enterprise zone behind MIT, professors lolling in a warm bath of venture capital as they shuttle from classroom to consultancy.

The city's projected role — which includes a heavy array of subsidies, dramatic upzoning, de-mapping of streets, and the seizure of necessary properties — is argued via a familiar mantra of benefits. The first, job creation, depends on a market more hyped than proven. At the moment,

215

the 14,000 new jobs promised at MetroTech represent only an extrapolation of the numbers of people who might legally fit into the new buildings if they were all built and fully occupied. And the second big argument, job retention, while worthy, does seem to sap some of the strength of the first. Here, the terrorizing specter is New Jersey, sucking jobs across the Hudson. In fact, the two committed charter tenants for the project — Brooklyn Union Gas and the Securities Industry Automation Corporation — are both relocating rather than creating jobs, jobs which are presently, and likely to remain, in the city.

The argument, then, is largely spatial, that these jobs should exist in this place as opposed to some other in New York. Several rationales are offered. The most impressive, comprehending claim is for the revitalization of downtown Brooklyn. From that perspective, a large infusion of jobs at that place is vital. The trouble is, while employment may be the animating economic force behind this development, it's hardly the only key to planning cities. The frenzy to feed at the high-tech trough — putative salvation of every municipality from here to Bombola — has elbowed out a more complex understanding.

Two very different categories of employment are, in fact, being hyped under the "high-tech" rubric. The first is the vision of Route 128, Silicon Valley, and Kendall Square, zones for the research, invention, and manufacture of advanced technologies. Employment in such places tends to come in two distinct classes, split between well-paid engineering types and low-paid manufacturing workers. Whatever the social arrangements, though, locales like Silicon Valley are stamped with the imprimatur of the future (despite the bashing presently being administered by chips from the East), outposts of hope for an economy in which traditional manufacture has grown stagnant.

While this is clearly the image MetroTech seeks to cash in on, the facts suggest a second vision of "high-tech" employment. A large part of the offshore movement of Manhattan's office force is prompted by the need to find quantities of cheap, second-tier, "back-office" space. This is required to house the vast number of computer operators necessary to sustain the electronicization of capital, to enter the system's billions of transactions into the cybernetic web. Driven from physical proximity by stratospheric rents and the noninteractive character of its activity, back-office space has been loosed from most traditional urban constraints. Power and some mode of commuting are all that's required for these high-tech sweatshops. It's just this kind of space that MetroTech will provide.

MetroTech's problems of planning and design are precisely the problems of architecture minus the informing content of a relationship to the form and activities of the city. The predispositions and methods of urban renewal dovetail neatly here with those of the "urbanism" of Route 128 or Silicon Valley: both prefer the convenience of the clean slate, where they can simply do one thing at a time. One of the reasons Silicon Valley is such a signal failure as environment is its total ignorance of the interrelation of things. As a result, housing is in desperately short supply — especially for those at the low end of the ladder who are, as a result, obliged to endure horrendous commuting on clotted highways, where they do, at least, enjoy the momentary democracy of idling abreast the equally immobilized Porsches of their employers. Imagine Flatbush Avenue.

Like Silicon Valley, MetroTech is blind to housing, and current community opposition to the project turns on the issue of displacement. Threatened, the developer now advertises his sensitivity to the difficulties of relocation by offering an inventory of possibilities for homes elsewhere. Now, whatever one thinks of the quality of the developer's intentions (and my prejudice would be not to think a great deal of them), the fact remains that the residents and businesses presently on site are to be moved away. For a small business, this is a likely death knell: the rate of failure of relocated enterprises is overwhelmingly large. For the cadre of artists who've worked for years to restore buildings and vitality in downtown Brooklyn, the trauma's as real. Indeed, for anyone, especially the resourceless poor and elderly, forced removal from a place chosen and known is a terrible crime.

If there's a bottom line about the future of MetroTech, it's that it should not proceed without providing housing on or adjacent to the site for any resident who wants it. Given the small absolute numbers involved, there's simply no excuse not to. By the same token, existing businesses should be given the option of remaining within the project or nearby. The sterility of Silicon Valley can be avoided only by planning for an urban ecology that privileges continuity and preservation over such one-dimensional block-busting schemes as MetroTech. The sun has set on this kind of urban renewal.

As design, MetroTech is both mediocre (work of the firm Haines Lundberg Waehler, of whom one expects no better) yet perfectly of a piece with its social agenda. Like any typical suburban complex, the scheme is conceived as a campus, organized around a central open space. In order to obtain this configuration, the designers propose to close most of the streets internal to the project, including four blocks of Myrtle Avenue, an unusually dumb move from the point of view of traffic. Around this square will be placed eight office buildings (the largest of which, the gas head-quarters, bears a near-genetic resemblance to one of Pelli's Battery Park City towers) and one building for Poly U. As an aggregate, these would drastically increase the scale of the area and alter its character, recasting the finer grain of Brooklyn at the magnitude of Manhattan.

Despite its nominally sylvan representation, the street-closing strategy is central in this densification. By closing and "de-mapping" the streets, the developers add their area to that of the buildable site, thereby increasing permissible area under the FAR (Floor Area Ratio) formula. In addition, the developers are seeking relief from height and setback restrictions in order to construct buildings of far greater bulk than presently exist anywhere nearby. The largest building adjacent, the beautiful and subtle phone company offices put up in 1931 by the great firm Voorhees Gmelin and Walker, might have offered an excellent precedent for the scale of new construction. Instead, it will be dwarfed by the insensitive abutment of these gross neighbors, whose siting will guarantee a pall over the main open space during much of the year. But the point of the plaza looks to be more ease of supervision than the provision of amenity. There's no real urbanistic or functional reason for these buildings to be clustered other than self-defense. Circle the wagons, it's still Brooklyn out there.

Finally, there remains the question of MetroTech's relationship to the larger pattern of redevelopment in the area. If architects have learned anything over the past 20 years about the design of cities, it's simply that the logic of the parcel must inevitably defer to the more complicated and diffi-cult logic of the whole. Like all "urban renewal," MetroTech is a generic solution, an increment of expansion in the life of the generic city, a way station on the road to Erewhon. However virtuous its purpose, however helpful it eventually (after its 22-year holiday) proves to the tax base, it could sit on any convenient and yielding territory. As architecture, it invents nothing, adds nothing but bulk to substitute for the time-borne skein of social and architectural complexity it subtracts. The point isn't that these offices shouldn't happen in Brooklyn. The point is that they shouldn't happen this way. Too much of value is lost for no reason, too many people made homeless for profit.

March 1987

ALAN BUCHSBAUM 1935-87

Alan Buchsbaum died on April 10, a casualty of Aids. His third hospitaliz-
ation lasted less than a week. Although many friends had allowed themselves to be lulled by the frail straws of new antibiotics and evanescent
improvements in his condition, Alan knew it was the end and faced death
with sad equanimity.

While his hospital room was better than most, Alan's presence was a
constant rebuke to its shortcomings. Gravely ill, though, he surrendered to
the therapeutic oppressions of its hygienic modernism. I don't know how
much strength the clinical austerity of the place sapped from Alan, but
being there must have been a special trial. Alan read environments immediately and with nuance, deeply understood their mentalities, and responded
directly. He loved artful, comfortable places and designed them better than
anyone I know. How terrible his last days were in an environment of little
art and less comfort. He'd wanted to die in his beautiful loft but ebbed too
fast.

In many ways, Alan Buchsbaum's architectural career was dedicated to
redressing the deprivations of places like modern hospitals. Educated at
Georgia Tech and MIT in the late '50s and early '60s — at the height of
modernism's bloodless self-confidence — he came to New York and began
work conventionally, spending five years as a designer in a succession of
offices. Ending his apprenticeship, he embarked on a Wanderjahr, mostly in
Italy and Japan. The impact was indelible. It's not so much that the journey
was transformative, overwhelming in its revelations; rather, it was a passage
of corroboration, a visit to places where the settings of conviviality and daily
life had reached states of architectural perfection, where the arts and rituals
of comfort were set out with fascinating grace and exquisite detail. Raised

in Savannah, Georgia, Alan had come early to such scenes of civility and had them always in mind.

Other influence. The ocean liner is one of modern architecture's great metaphors, functionalism par excellence. The appeal is of beauty at once innocent and elaborate, an overwhelming aesthetic derived mechanistically from the pure exigencies of use. This is vulgar functionalism. Its discourse justifies motif-lifting at best and an architecture of constraint – the efficient drear of that hospital room, – at worst. But Alan, a modern to his toes, was also a child of that irresistible liner. His lineage, however, descended from a somewhat different set of images and possibilities. Alan wouldn't have been mesmerized by ships' power and vastness or even by their particular vocabulary of shapes, the gross heroics of modernity; rather, he'd have been enthralled by the careful craft of their fittings, by their ingenious solutions to tight problems of space and materials. He'd have adored their glamor. Alan was crazy about atmosphere.

In 1967, Alan set up a practice with two friends, calling it the Design Coalition, a classic '60s moniker. The early work was much of its time, graphic, whimsical, exuberant. A hairdresser and men's clothing shop in Great Neck, constructed in 1969 on a bare-bones budget, iconographizes supergraphic profiles – a real head shop. The publication history of the project is revealing and typical: German, Japanese, and English architectural magazines; a New York newspaper; and, Alan's favorite, *Ameruka*, a USIA effort directed at propagandizing the Poles. The point's the broadness. Alan was always well published, snapped up with equal relish by specialist journals, shelter mags, and daily papers – not for any flacking or self-promotions, but because of the work: from the first sophisticated yet accessible, artistic, and comfortable. Indeed, Alan, in time, developed into an apostle of comfort, famously accommodating. It wasn't simply that his residential work was so livable, so unconstraining. Alan's spaces are always inviting, the kinds of spaces that virtually invite flopping on the couch or taking a long, luxurious bath. Alan designed places to be in, not to stare at. The kind of comfort I'm trying to describe, though, is more about attitude than artifact. Alan was an architect who genuinely believed in program, in architecture's creative location in the terrain of desire. He had a seismographic sense of his clients' needs, quirks, and aspirations, and a willingness to go to considerable lengths to satisfy them. In a loft for Ellen Barkin, for example, this extended to hundreds of yards of voile, festooned with theatric abandon in lieu of rigid walls: an actress's dream.

Alan's early reputation as a real originator centered on the invention of the so-called "high-tech" style. One thinks, for instance, of a loft done in 1976 in which Alan composed a bedroom wall of an undulating plane of glass blocks and lit it with a row of blue runway lights. It's an incredibly memorable image, resonant and influential, very much of its moment. The point about high tech, however, is that it really isn't, particularly. What's being described is more of an off-the-shelf attitude, a willingness frankly to engage the lexicon of ready-made materials and the inevitable late-20th-century landscape of appliances. And, without question, this possibility began to be most mightily engaged with the rise of loft living in Manhattan. A better name for the high tech Alan pioneered might simply be Canal Street (its literal source) or, better still, Downtown.

Alan Buchsbaum was a leader in interpreting and organizing the collective epiphany that resulted from the great move to lower Manhattan. It was as if a sensibility and a moment were destined for each other. Not that Alan was just a post-modern *bricoleur*, craftily accumulating: he was a designer, a real creator. The elements of the broader Downtown style were quickly established. Building on the cheap and on one's own familiarized a generation with the demands and possibilities of studs and sheetrock and with an aesthetic of incompletion and rearrangement. The use of lofts as both living and work spaces also interrupted standard notions of the deployment of the elements of home. Instead of the cellular model, the loft generated an architecture of archipelago, a spray of islands of symbol and use. For architects, working in loft spaces retrieved one of modernism's most cherished possibilities, the free plan, excluded from the repetitive requirements of traditional urban dwellings. People would live differently here.

This possibility was enabled not simply by the spaces available but also by their new inhabitants. The idea of "alternative lifestyles" is surely overworked but it's just as surely the historic purview of artists, the population that first liberated lofts for living. And, the message of the crucible '60s — so important to Alan and his client generation — was certainly that the possibility of living with artistic latitude was a necessity and not a privilege. Alan's work was a continuous explication of this opening, an account of the joyous merger of the personal and the physical, a way of creating satisfying yet malleable wholes from impossibly disparate materials. In all of his designs, things sit comfortably together, like guests at a perfect dinner party. And Alan (who once wrote restaurant reviews in the *Village Voice* under the pseudonym "FAT") loved dinner parties. He liked being spectator and participant at that happy symbiosis of pleasure and necessity, always watching for the moment when food, conversation, furnishings, lighting, melded into what was for him, the supremely architectural moment.

In an interview once, Alan remarked that he liked things that were "a little bit off." It's a fine description of an important aspect of his work, the idea of difference short of dissonance. And it catches the kind of laid-back, modest, self-description that Alan — who had no patience for the posturing and polemic of the architectural salon — was inclined to. "A little bit off" is the natural condition of the spaces where Alan worked. Intervening in the city's old buildings means never confronting anything plumb, dealing always with spaces askew. Never mind the nice portrait of culture, the phrase surely locates the architect's task of reconciliation, both of the order of things, the harmonizing of stereos, Cuisinarts, family portraits, and Barbara Krugers, and the order of personalities, the inhabitants and the designers. Alan was a genius in the exploration of this territory between certainties, whether in his amazingly fresh color choices, his beautiful juxtapositions of unexpected shapes and textures, or his creation of utter felicity from improbable diversity.

In an early project, Alan (always a wizard at cabinetwork) designed a storage system supported on springs, in order to compensate for the unevenness of a floor. This was a real "high-tech" approach, the imposition of an ideal solution on a resistant reality. He soon grew beyond this sort of response, inventing a style both considered and relaxed that was all his own. Alan freed objects — high tech, historic, funky — from the trammels of received wisdom about their ethics and use, reemploying them with marvelous originality. In his drawings, furniture, rugs, and in his architecture, there was always richness without excess and precision without parsimony. Alan created a body of work that will endure not only as a pre-eminent emblem of our moment but as an abiding inspiration to the world of design. Alan Buchsbaum was an extraordinary ornament to downtown, to New York, to architecture, a presence of rare vitality. How we will miss him. But how he'll live on.

April 1987

eather Alston, who spoke at the event, told *BD*: "There may be ability for architects resulting rom terrorist attacks. We are not aying they would always be able, but there could be a case to nswer. What you have designed an come back and affect you. We all it the 'oops factor'."

Her warning was reiterated by the head of construction law at versheds, Richard Ward. He

DOM in London, was one of the architects calling for clear guidelines on what architects are expected to do. "It is very important that new standards are implemented to raise the bar and to educate people about these issues," he said.

Regulations could cover building materials, escape routes, security access, prevention against collapse, signage,

Designing Out Crime Association and who also spoke at the conference, added: "A designer might be designing a factory that has no connection with terrorism. But if that factory site is next to a laboratory for live animal experiments, for example, then that could make the designer responsible."

Knight also said that architects should alert planners to the need for anti-terrorist measures.

oms: £1bn MoD barracks revamp

ars in the first instance, but uld last for a decade – delivering each firm a guaranteed £o million worth of work a year ntil 2013.

It is the biggest construction ntract from the Ministry of efence in recent memory. In e first five years alone, it is nning to upgrade accommotion for 16,000 servicemen d women up and down the untry. This means that it will andon dormitory-style bar-

racks in favour of single rooms for each person.

The project involves newbuild and refurbishment and the consortium, Debut Services, expects to sign formal appointment documents as prime contractor in October for the first five years.

Aedas TCN has drawn up a generic plan which will employ a mix of standard and modular construction.

But the project will not guar-

antee the same level of fees throughout, according to Aedas TCN director Peter Chappell.

"The more we do, the more efficient we become and the lower the design cost will be," he said. "That is written into the agreement.

The Single Living Accommodation Modernisation programme is part of the MoD's push to help retain servicemen and women for longer, according to ministers.

Architects pay low-ke

BD 1547   13-9-

As the eyes of the world focused on the gaping void in the Lower Manhattan landscape on Wednesday, a clutch of international architects looked to the future after launching yet more ambitious schemes to rebuild on the site of the World Trade Centre.

Among those on the list were New York-based architects Raphael Viñoly, Michael Sorkin and Peter Eisenman, and an international contingent featuring OMA, Foreign Office Architects and Zaha Hadid. Their plans were launched in the *New York Times*.

Meanwhile, UK architects observed a minute's silence on

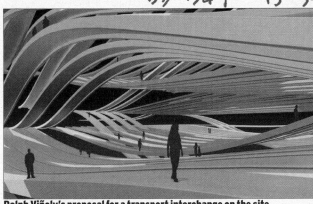

Ralph Viñoly's proposal for a transport interchange on the site.

September 11, eschewing more ostentatious events. Even London branches of US firms such as SOM and KPF were low key in

marking the anniversary, and American Institute of Archite London chapter decided agai organising an event for memb on the anniversary day, inst arranging a tour of London's (Hall for about 70 architects a friends on the evening September 10.

In New York, architect firms were also reserved in th commemorations. Mane Duffy, the firm that previou occupied an office in the so tower of the World Trade Cen closed its office on Wednes allowing staff to commemo the day as they saw fit, rat than arranging a formal c mony for the firm.

The anniversary has spar events and publications exam ing the implications of attacks for design and constr

RECONSTRUCTING

THE HOLOCAUST

Recently, an architect called Allan Greenberg sent me a set of plans for a once-proposed Holocaust memorial he'd designed for a site in Battery Park. Greenberg's a dogmatic classicist, wrapped up in quixotic and inexplicable pursuits. And, at first glance, his memorial seemed merely more of the same kitsch. A quadrifrons arch in stone, segmented portals, pilasters, mouldings, the whole dreary apparatus of antiquity, surmounted by a hollow 60-foot shaft. It reminded me of those First World War cenotaphs by Lutyens or of the Albert Memorial, that ugliest of such mnemonic piles.

Greenberg's drawings were accompanied by a trot. Part of its agenda was to rationalize the forms, present their ostensibly biblical origins, explicate the basis of their architectonic iconography. Again, I found the explanation initially unconvincing, irrelevant. But, the more I looked at this little text, the more I felt the tug of another reading. There were elements of the memorial by which I was genuinely moved. A 365-page book — a page turned every day — in which the names (or the phrase "A Child of Israel") of the six million Jewish dead were to be written. Nearby, the words of the Kaddish were to be carved. The memorial was to lie astride the route of arriving immigrants, framing a view of the Statue of Liberty, Ellis Island, and the Atlantic beyond, a reminder of a road untaken by the Holocaust's victims. And that shaft on top was described as a chimney, framing a tele-scopelike view skyward, inevitably recalling to someone standing under-neath the destiny of flesh at the camps.

There was no gainsaying that Greenberg's act of commemoration and grief was heartfelt, that it was capable of affecting people. The power of the words alone could transcend almost any setting. More, this was clearly Greenberg's own testament, expressed via his formal vocabulary. Nevertheless, the architecture was so tendentious and specific that its appropriateness as collective expression must immediately be called into question. Whatever else it undertakes, public art acts as surrogate, custodian of collective memories and values. Thus, it's hemmed between the struggle for invention and the need for experiences that speak plainly to values of consensus. This task seems especially fraught in commemorating the Holocaust. How to make metonyms for a thing so horrendous? Is anything beyond iteration even appropriate? Clearly, the space between that event and its representation is a place of risk and ambiguity.

The same week Greenberg's scheme came my way, I was given a copy of John Hejduk's work "Victims," also a passionate labor of years, another very personal act of coming to grips with Nazi evil's radical enormity. Designed for a site in Berlin once occupied by the torture chambers of the Gestapo, Hejduk's work is an essay in the poetics of singular abstraction. The site is to be occupied by 67 elements, each accompanied by a brief text, serving as a sort of pre-emptive mythmaking. The individual pieces include a workshop for a paper restorer, a catfish pond, and a "Room for those who looked the other way." A typical text accompanying a beautiful drawing of a little Hejdukian bridge explains the "Drawbridge Man": "After seeing Carpaccio's *Venetian Bridge* he was inspired to reproduce the bridge shown in the painting (with modifications) for his drawbridge. He and the Carpenter made measured drawings for the construction of the drawbridge. He left unanswered the question of the sense of it all."

Hejduk and Greenberg take opposite approaches to transcendence. Hejduk looks for the sense of it all to grow out of the accumulated weight of mystery to be found in and around his enigmatic architecture. The plight of these victims is generalized, plunged into the stream of victimization's larger history, yet simultaneously attached to Hejduk's creative autobiography. Greenberg prefers a direct, if often idiosyncratic, address; complicit, conventional symbolism, never mind the frailty of the compact as to what such symbolism should be. While the two works are worlds apart in architectural quality, they do make clear something of the range of expressive correlatives available to architects. It's a question that's increasingly relevant as the number of physical responses to the Holocaust is suddenly on the increase. I'm not sure of the reasons for this. Perhaps the aging of the generation of survivors adds impetus to the physicalization of memory. Or perhaps distance has increased dispassion's possibility, making these crimes more speakable, allowing more ready institutionalization.

New York is to have a Holocaust Museum and Memorial at the southern end of Battery Park City, currently being designed by James Polshek. While the scheme is still in development, its main outlines are clear. There are three components: a museum, a memorial, and a condominium. The profits from this latter are being used — à la MOMA — to pay for the construction of the museum. I find something profoundly disquieting about this arrangement. The question is not exactly about the financial stratagem (although one would think that direct fund-raising for such a project would be possible in New York, if anywhere) but about the museum's aura, about profanation. Clearly, some mixes are incompatible. One wouldn't add a condo at a cemetary, at the Lincoln Memorial, at Treblinka itself. We recognize certain recombinant forms as croppers. This is no place for those Live at Five transitions from happy talk to horror. The idea of a Holocaust museum undergoes permanent deformation via this kind of elision. I don't think the Holocaust is ready for this kind of compatibility.

Polshek's design — in outline — seems a sound enough armature for the addition of exhibitions (being done by a different designer) upon which the real impact of the place will depend. The experience is to be a historical one, with a special emphasis on the European Jewish culture of the 19th and 20th centuries that was obliterated by the Nazis. Separate from the museum, culminating the route through its exhibitions, is the memorial. The form selected for this space is a cube, to be built of glass, perhaps with a partial outer casing of stone. Polshek describes this space as at once awesome and peaceful, a place of isolation offering the opportunity for self-communion. His intention is to create an environment that moves not through "symbolism" but by means of its "quality."

This notion of a compelling architectonic abstraction would seem to establish a third strategy of commemoration, differing from Greenberg's programmatically specific and Hejduk's programmatically diffuse iconography. However, the glass cube — which recalls Louis Kahn's proposed memorial, also intended for Battery Park — is not an iconographically neutral statement but bears with it the history of modernism's now institutionalized symbol system. That was one of modernism's points, the asymptotic inclination to the minimal. But, the "religion" of simplicity, Euclidianism, transparency, even "space," is nonetheless specific. It's the iconography of no iconography. It is, however, susceptible to drift, to the inevitable imprecision of cosmic ambitions. There's some irony, for example, in the fact that a building generally considered among the greatest in creating a spiritual atmosphere with minimum modernist means is a crematorium, built in Stockholm by Gunnar Asplund, all simplicity and landscape, though including a large orienting cross.

James Freed's design for a national Holocaust museum in Washington, DC, is marginally more engaged with the overtly representational issues addressed by Greenberg and Hejduk. His project — which sits near the Mall — shares in broadest outline the same *parti* as Polshek's, a museum with a contemplative memorial appended, also a somber six-sided figure of the ineffable. And, as at Polshek's, the visit is structured as a journey, a linear route through the history of catastrophe. But Freed ventures more, attempting to assimilate aspects of the tectonics of annihilation. Before executing his design, Freed — himself a refugee — toured the camps. And, in his Washington building, he has incorporated unmistakable allusions to architectural incidents recorded there. His scheme is organized around a courtyard that is lined by towerlike constructions in brick. While these materially allude to a building next door, their detail recalls the architecture at places like Auschwitz. The blind fenestration, the metal bracing, the brick arches, all traffic in an unmistakable symbolism of the sinister.

The line this strategy skirts is kitsch, modernism's flip side. While Freed's rendition is somber and considered, it's an idea that proceeds by increments in the direction of the theme park, the ultimate denial by the erection of simulacra, Anus Mundiland. And, like the sorcerer's apprentice, once engaged, where can it stop? At the entrance to Freed's building, children proceed to the right and adults to the left. Should this recall the hideous divergence at the gates of the camps? The circuit of the museum begins with a ride up in an elevator. When this is crowded, will people think of gas chambers? Freed's building has a portico that defers to a large and dreary neo-classical building next door. Should this inspire recollections of Speer and Troost, of Hitler's fascination with architecture?

At the scheme's presentation to the Fine Arts Commission, State Senator Roy Goodman took exception to the project, declaring that the memorial looked like a "gun turret." While I find this reading willful and difficult to justify, it still points up the kind of incitement to interpretation a work like this provides. Not that this shouldn't be so. But the task of finding symbols adequate to the enormity of the Holocaust that retain their resonance in a culture habituated to the manufacture of disposable iconography is monumentally difficult. Simplicity, idiosyncrasy, genius, and convention are ways around this, yet they are only outlines. The mnemo-technics of the Holocaust has only begun to be defined.

In thinking about these collected responses, though, my main feeling was satisfaction in their numerousness. Naturally, I preferred those works that were the expression — as with John Hejduk's "Victims" — of long investigation coupled with singular vision. But with some events, genius is less paramount than familiarity, than absolute presence. If "never again" is the Holocaust's distillate lesson, then "never forgotten" must be its consequence. Reverence must take many, many forms: the weight of this crime is so great and so unredressed only profusion can do.

June 1987

ZAHA HADID

Zaha Hadid burst onto the architectural scene four years ago after winning a competition to design "The Peak," a deluxe private club on a mountainy crest overlooking Hong Kong. Although the insolvency of the sponsors prevented construction, this may have been just as well for Hadid. The riveting dynamism of her images could only have suffered deceleration by being materialized in the full three dimensions.

Motility is the main hit of Hadid's graphic, and her images pursue it along two distinct axes. First is her use of Suprematist-style distortion, perspectival acceleration away from the picture plane. Like the one-point conceit of a 3-D movie, forms rush forward, gathering speed along attenuating curves. It's the same convention that thrusts the viewer into hyperspace in sci-fi films, stars turning into streaks, every body a vanishing point.

Cinema-struck, Hadid purveys seriality as well as simultaneity. Many of her images incorporate the idea of the frame: motion à la Muybridge, architecture as sequence. It's a powerful idea, attractive to many. Architecture's inherent space-time is animated by the motion of the viewer, by passage. Hadid, hemmed in by a single enframing canvas, is confronted by a stationary observer, requiring the architecture to get a move-on. Obligingly, buildings explode or flicker.

While this may not be exactly a fresh apprehension, Hadid pursues it with special lustiness. Ingesting her high-speed images gives pleasure unmediated by the anxieties of theorizing. Her escape from the turgid terrestrializing of explanation may be accounted for by her generational position. Hadid was nurtured in the '70s at the Architectural Association in London and later at the Office of Metropolitan Architecture, the firm of Rem Koolhaas and Elia Zenghelis, two of the AA's mainstays. Their research —

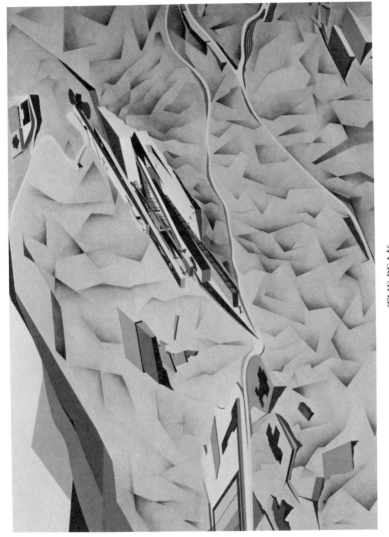

THE PEAK
Zaha Hadid

along with that of, among others, Bernard Tschumi — set out the territory Hadid was to make her own.

As mentioned earlier, this group's well-spring, image-wise, was Soviet architecture of the '20s — that great unfinished symphony — and especially the gripping unconstructed fantasies of Tchernikov and the animate dancerly compositions of Malevich. Added to this heritage, though, were certain rational methods of maneuver, particularly in the rhetorical realm. Our team's penchant for analysis resulted in quantities of rectitudinous gridding, palimpsestuous layering, overliteral frame-by-framing, and, ultimately — as new rubrics were sought for old enthusiasms — in clear spoiling of the fun.

But there were also the seeds for a comeback. Koolhaas, in particular, had a tooth for Lapidoid kidneys and Hockney blues, for the high-minded goofiness of the surrealism that was contemporaneous with the more chest-thumping style of the pride of the Proun. In Koolhaas's own work, this is mostly experienced as a tension. For Hadid, it's far more a liberation: the defiance of gravity shapes both tectonic and attitude. These fly-apart drawings fragment happily, unfettered by too-rigorized theory or history. Hadid seems perfectly cool with the extension of the Style Soviétique to the netherlands of Niemeyer and Googie, Lautner, and Lapidus.

The major project in her current exhibition at Max Protetch Gallery is a scheme for a small office building in West Berlin. It's a very promising work, indebted to Corb and Rem, speaking through Suprematist phonemics, but visibly her own. To some degree, understanding the building obliges one to read through the paintings and drawings got up to pre-present it. For Hadid, drawings are at once a strategy of investigation and a strategy of control. Her vivid images stake out a territory through invention, cooptation, and exclusion: what's left unsaid has been as crucial as what's spoken in her progress.

The primary address of this work is to the invention of a specified class of formal ideas. These strategies are substantiated by graphic wizardry, setting out a whole territory for inference. What's left undeclared is that whole set of architectural particulars that culminate in construction. Hadid is at a moment where her image-making obligates a choice, a decision as to what it stands for. Certainly, the work's entitled simply to exist sui generis, to be judged as painting. But here's a one-way ticket to the architectural margins. First, such product always begs the question of attribution when produced by an office; and, it risks the charge of Zandra Rhodesism, stylist, imitable. Already, graphic Zahaisms ooze from the neophyte drafting boards at the schools of architecture, trivializing her vision by reducing it to a compendium of mannerisms.

Another possibility is the cloisterish role of the theorist, the apostolic shtick, sanctified by abstinence. But this ain't Hadid, not the situation of her mind. She is, in fact, far more interested in the problem than the principle and this has led her, inevitably, correctly, to the builder's stance: the Berlin projects are for real. There's a touch of poignancy here. Skeptics have bashed her for the unreality of her tableaux, but this was also part of their integrity, the visionary's freedom of action. Some of this will likely now be lost in the usual exigencies.

Certain deformations of her graphic also become inevitable. Everyone's been pointing at a painting in the Protetch show that depicts a glazing detail in the Berlin building's curtain wall. Whatever the joint's merits as art, this is clearly a signal of a shift in intent. The issue its "artistic" character raises is of adjacent universes, the idea that this construction detail enjoys a parallel life in a set of (unseen) construction drawings. In a way, this possibility mocks the paintings, reduces them to advertisement. Like binary stars, the two systems are locked in each other's gravity, tugging at each other's meanings. The moment will eventually come when the question "Why paint this?" will be raised. My hunch is that by then Hadid will be exploiting other systems of architectural eloquence that will render the matter moot.

Mario Bellini — subject of a fine little retrospective at MOMA — bridges a key epistemological break in industrial design. His work — which now spans close to 30 years — coincides with the great displacement of mechanical by microelectronic technologies. This represented both a spiritual and a practical problem for designers. On the one hand, the character of the mechanisms they were consigned to make useful and beautiful had been radically transformed. Consider, for instance, the difference in the workings of manual and electronic typewriters. On the other hand, though, the moment of interface remained essentially stable: fingers were still doing the walking. The design of typewriters, tape decks, computers, and like appliances remained an exploration of the boundary between the kinesthetic and the mechanic. While there may have been drama in the transformation beneath the shell, human users persisted in having two hands, two eyes, and limited amounts of sitzfleisch.

Bellini's investigation commences at this conceptual and literal seam.

The idea of a protective yet interrogating enclosure is at the heart of his work. His invention moves both in and out from this joint. For his wonderful Persona office chair, the regulation of the body-receiving skin required the careful elaboration of the internal mechanism. For his pioneering P 101 desktop computer (for Olivetti, with whom Bellini has longed designed), the shape of the keys became a crucial investigation. Bellini has reformulated the idea of a cowling. This investigation's been a kind of recapitulation of evolution. Early machines housed their mechanism in rigid, if sculptural, shells, dinosaurian protection against shocks. This line of inquiry culminated in a series of wedged-shaped objects, lectern-like in their reception to human touch, conceptual turtles, if contoured to an implicit aerodynamism.

From this emerged two other directions. The first was a more aggre-gating sensibility, the sort that produces satellites and space stations, un-hindered by atmosphere: the look that informs Bellini's latest typewriter designs. These designs are especially "architectural," privileging elevational views. The other was the idea of membrane, a more literal skin, reliant and impermeable, warding off blows and dust — the electronic analogue of the germ. The Divisumma calculator's the breakthrough, with its taut, nipple-like keys, a beautiful bar of yellow tactility.

This kind of vivid anthropomorphism is especially legible in the furni-ture, this language of skin, skeleton, and guts. The wonderful "Cab" side-chair zips a leather skin over a metal skeleton with brilliant economy, yielding an austere yet sinuous result. The "Figura" office chair is literally belted, dressed in its upholstery, fuzzing engagingly the differences between dress and stuffed dermis, well wrought and well turned out. And, as with all of Bellini's work, the chair's beautifully modernist in its passion for con-sideration: it's not just the eye or the mind that takes pleasure, but the lumbar and the tush as well.

I read in the papers that the Soviets have invited Comrade Trump to Moscow with an eye to having him build them an eyesore. If there's a line at which glasnost lapses into counterrevolution, this is it. Centralized econ-omic planning may have been a drag, but is Atlantic City the alternative? Then again, as long as he's over there, perhaps the hero of the Wollman Rink might offer to reconstruct our poor buggered embassy.

July 1987

TRUE WEST

Several months ago I made my first pilgrimage to Vegas. I certainly had the right traveling companions for such a Po-Mo voyage: Nevin the lapsed academic screenwriter and Wolf the Viennese architect, also making his first hajj. The trip promised to be nonstop male bonding and ironic landscape deconstruction, a classic.

Las Vegas has been a high architectural *Heiligenstadt* since Robert Venturi and Denise Scott-Brown published their *Learning From Las Vegas*. The work was an effort to redeem the town from a reading of unreconstructed kitsch by obliging its monuments to dance to the art-historical minuet. Caesar's Palace (the slide on the left) was compared to Bernini (the slide on the right), thereby aiming to eviscerate certain distinctions that might otherwise crop up in such a comparison. Thus was glitz to be transmogrified into an advert for the eternal verities.

The key to this calculated misreading (pace Bloom) is in the values it elects to subvert. Now, I'm as amused as the next ironist with the juxtaposition of the Golden Nugget and Saint Peter's. The problem with the Venturi effect is its politics. Let's not forget that the activities conducted in those casinos are both opiate and rip-off, that their calculation is exquisite.

The arty view displaces this manipulation, obscuring it in a schlag of decor. There's a choice being made here: one elects to see the glitter and reflection and to ignore the hundreds of surveillance cameras. My mind inevitably wanders to Reagan: the First Totem, the great dissembler, Vegas incarnate in DC. The point is, he lies. It lies too.

All of which is to say that despite our three sweet tooths for kitsch, despite the allure of the gaming tables, despite the pleasure of acting the rat pack with a college degree, despite the Jacuzzi-complete junior suite at

Caesar's, despite the mesmerizations of the tawny, sun-struck landscape, we didn't have such a great time. Vegas was a downer. Low point was the Jerry Lewis, Sammy Davis Jr. show at Bally's. I was the only one who stayed to the end of the performance, a satyagraha of self-congratulation. I told Wolf and Nev that I wasn't leaving until I heard Sammy sing "Mr. Bojangles," which turned out to be the last number of the show. Frankly, I could care less about "Candy Man" or "What Kind of Food Am I?" And isn't that the worst of it: total victim of the culture. I couldn't even get up and leave.

Well, eventually we left, Nev and I parting company with the returning Wolfie at the airport. And it's a good one, looking like Caesar's Palace as designed by Walter Gropius. Slot machines on the deplaning level. McCarran Airport is a key seam by which the visual culture of Las Vegas enters the wider picture, so it's a place that's easy to have mixed feelings about. I'll admit mine were partly positive: *machines à risquer* seemed a reasonable pass for modernist activity.

The big problem with Las Vegas, though, is that, despite the hype, it really does lack art direction. Las Vegas the reality isn't as good as Las Vegas the hyperreality, the one you see on, say, *Crime Story* or *One From the Heart*. The city is just too visually discontinuous for the naked eye. Las Vegas is a stage set for television.

As we drove across the desert, looking at maps of it, military matters came to mind. The landscape is carved into reservations, some for Indians, most for the military tribes. Names like "Chocolate Mountain Aerial Gunnery Reservation," a Reaganism if ever there were one. The birds, the bees, the cigarette trees, the big plutonium mountain.

In Utah, we were strafed by B—52s. I've always been moved by the poetic mendacity of warplanes with their undersides painted sky-blue, off to drop A-bombs from heaven. It was small wonder that Nevin and I spoke at length about fission. We also spent a fair amount of time calling out sightings of the stealth bomber as we neared its test base. Over there!

A longing for Los Alamos rose in us as the bombing ranges flicked by. Our goal became to view Little Boy and Fat Man (or was it Fat Boy and Little Man?), the original bombs. Forsaking pueblos and additional weird geology, we finally approached the town, quivering with mingled fascination, irony, and dread. Here, after all, was, if not the heart, at least the pituitary, of darkness. It was raining when we screeched to a halt in front of the Los Alamos museum and dashed for the door.

Unfortunately, we got there five minutes before closing time. We

FAT MAN AND LITTLE BOY

pleaded for admission, promised we'd stay only till five, but the silver-haired docent shook her head and barred the way. "Once you're in here, you won't want to leave," she warned. So we left, driving slowly around the town, past Dunkin' Donuts and Burger King, trying to peer through the veneer of horror-movie normalcy, looking for clues, for some specifying artifact or incident that would reveal the place for what we knew it was. Oppenheimer Drive notwithstanding, we didn't find it.

The next day, though, we did. Back in Albuquerque we discovered that there was a National Atomic Museum at a big air base at the edge of town, next door to the sinister Sandia Labs. We went at once and knew right away we were on the right track. At the entrance to the base, guards obliged us to get out of the car, show ID, endure suspicious gazes, fill out forms, sweat a little. After we were vetted, though, the armed sentry gave us directions spiced with promising phrases like, "turn right at the B–52." Jets flew over-head. This was for real: no 7–Eleven here. Eventually we arrived at an unprepossessing, if capacious, former hangar, its surrounding tarmac littered with profuse deconsecrated bombers and missiles. Closing time was hours away. We entered.

Inside were the bombs. Bombs by the dozens, deployed with dogmatic museological positivism. In the beginning were, indeed, Fat Man and Little Boy, the Ur-bombs, parents of the end of time. The hall was arranged chronologically and display after display expounded – with affectless prose – on the Darwinian descent of America's nukes from relatively primitive beginnings, on to the macho 25-ton H-bombs of the '50s, down to the incredible profusion of today's designer nukes, styled for the job.

Now, a museum of the bomb is a fairly iffy enterprise: it's tough to package genocide as a tourist attraction. Not that the nation is without a grand tradition of zany academies. Leaving Vegas we'd paused for gas in a shopping center that also housed the Liberace museum. Cadres of Japanese tourists were filing in. Such is the fallout from freedom of religion. Once you buy the idea of valorizing anything, certain routines immediately follow. All museums need some form of test ("anything Lee owned," for example) that will satisfy the need to sort through what is to be included or denied. As the distinctions become finer, we're confronted with connois-seurship.

At the atomic museum, the pre-eminent principle of organization was, it appeared, design. According to this version of history, the main line of evolution was from the crude and cumbersome to the slick and compact.

This is an essentially aesthetic understanding, proposing an ideal relationship of form and content, a precisely realized synthesis of bang and buck. As with most modern architecture, bombs enter the artistic realm down the avenue of functionalism, the idea that the status of art can be justified by the detection of the activity of doing something, anything.

At both Vegas and Albuquerque, sustaining such an aesthetic requires prodigies of exclusion, rigorous insulation from any concern for consequences. When the bomb designer murmurs "beautiful" at the glint of sunlight off freshly milled titanium, at the MIRV's sinuous curves, one hopes that this is not a deliberate reverie of genocide. On the other hand, it's clearly a pornographic appreciation, a valuing of something that's unquestionably harmful to someone. Bomb designers can ogle their nukes, generalissimos at the Pentagon can stir over velvet paintings of contrail-streaked sunsets, just as Bob Guccione presumably stiffens at the beaver shot of Miss October. They believe in this stuff. For the rest of us, such appreciation is more problematic, filtered through irony, complicity, or fear.

Writing this column gets harder and harder for me. The reason, I think, is that so much architecture — especially in the city — has become like so much bomb design. Appreciating it formally demands that the terms of the discussion be totally hemmed, that the question of effects be trivialized. I don't want to be Letterman, leering month after month at Stupid Architecture Tricks. Writing about the quiddity, the stuffness, of architecture increasingly seems a sellout, an act of self-repression, when substance is lacking. Loving building, I prefer to engage it optimistically, don't want to write constantly about Vegas. While my dismay at the current course of events is undimmed, my passion to denounce is ebbing; I'm enervated by irony.

Is the phrase "visionary dreariness" Wordsworth's? It does seem to capture the quality of the diminished architecture that's become vernacular in New York. Not to mention the style of this column. You'll forgive, I hope, this bleat of fatigue and resentment. I'm writing this on my birthday, it's too damn hot in this room, and I'm dreaming of those wide open spaces. I'm sure spleen will return in the fall.

August 1987

THE GARDEN IN THE MACHINE

Beautiful Ford sits in the history of the captivating void, straddling a tradition of interiority whose shifting metaphors have long served to situate architecture in the world. Ford is the union of greenhouse and panopticon, a synthetic regulatory paradise, the concatenation of Mies and the Crystal Palace, an eleemosynary hothouse, a frame for the cultivation of charity's bureaucracy. Ford's garden stands for the foundation's product and Ford's building represents its idea. What qualities, then, are Job One?

Just as the greenhouse embodies the dream of nature under regulation, Ford's program is no less ambitious. Its mandate lists among its enterprises "the establishment of peace; the strengthening of democracy; the strengthening of the economy; education in democratic society; and improved scientific knowledge of individual behavior and human relations." This is a virtual recipe of the State of Nature: the garden is its microcosmic recapitulation. At Ford, paradise is always foregrounded. Sitting in an office, preparing to unlimber sums in service of some civilizing enterprise, a Ford staffer gazes out not simply at verdure in captivity but through the glass curtain to 42nd Street and the city beyond. The sight, then, is a superposition, the city placed, from this vantage, in Eden. Ford's garden is Central Park in miniature, redemptive greenery, sylvan viewing armature.

In the garden sits a small pool, just about the only thing able to sit there given the calculated lack of benches. Instinctively, passers-by have chucked miscellaneous coins into the water. A sign reassures that the paltry collection is destined for Unicef and not local coffers. Nevertheless, this act culminates a tripartite charitableness that the place represents, configuring a circle. To begin, Ford's megacharity, dispensing gigabucks ad majoram gloriam …? Then there's the building, which "gives" a city ravenous for

FORD FOUNDATION
(New York) Kevin Roche

amenity this charitable boon. And, finally, those nickels and coppers — if paltry and dulled next to the shining brass behind — stand in for the source of this largesse, the willingness of generations to shell out for a Ford, the democracy of consumption's desire, the waters of the source.

If Ford has had an effect in New York, it's as a contribution to the specification of amenity. Ford's a key initiatory event in the benighted rewriting of the zoning laws into the bonus system, the "let's make a deal" operation whereby bulk is exchanged for benefit; that zero-sum game in which clear deleteriousness is swapped for some allegedly mitigating contribution to the commonweal. The zoning law — like tax deductibility — is a legislated incitement to charity, a recognition that good works are seldom selfless, especially when big bucks figure. Ford makes a fine conceptual initiator because their garden is a charitable act *without* a quantifiable consequence. The open space is pure benefit, entailing no sacrifice of urbanist good behavior: we're talking twelve stories and street lines held, fine materials and genuine design. Quality Is Job One.

But if the motives for Ford's garden appear beyond reproach, its effects have further significance. Concurrent with Ford was its commercial doppelgänger, the Hyatt-Regency in Atlanta, Portman's first great atriumized hotel. The agenda for both places was not simply the valorization of the void, the reassertion of vastness as a totem of architectural worth, it was the invention of a new mode of colonizing space. During the late '60s, America was having a certain amount of difficulty with the containment of the Other. In Viet-Nam, the defense of Ford's five points had driven official America to the point of genocide. It is scant coincidence that the first Ford president to occupy the new building was McGeorge Bundy, one of the "architects" of that policy in his role as our first National Security Advisor. The policy was not without an urbanism. One of its centerpieces was the so-called "strategic hamlet" plan. Across the countryside, a set of defensible walled villages was created, little model cities functioning with Foucauldian rationality, safe from the darkening influences of the surrounding Otherness, their order offering both security and influence, gardens for the cultivation of "our" Vietnamese.

This is certainly recapitulated in the Portman oeuvre, the global inscription of the homogenizing void. While Portman's scope is vast, however, his ambition is circumscribed. Those hotels directly colonize little more than their own territory, uniform environments in differing contexts, the certainty of finding the identical Martini anywhere. Ford's ambition is a little grander. Its missionary motive is affirmed not merely by secure interiority, but by the visibility of the city beyond. Here's the departure from Central Park. The landscape there, if disciplined, is nonetheless indigenous, hemmed by the exigencies of the local climate. Chez Ford, the planting is not. The Ford atrium simulates the climatology of another, more temperate latitude, a place where magnolias, japonicas, bougainvillea, and jacarandas flourish, lush, if just short of the jungle. Like the paradises housed under 19th century glass, this is a thoroughly dependent landscape, a forest in captivity, a zoo; and its two backdrops — the hierarchic bureaucratic rationality of Ford's and the intemperate order of Manhattan — affirm the centrality and potency of this landscape. Like the Ford Foundation's ideological agenda, the garden is a representation of exemplary change. The deformation of the natural landscape, its artificial shift in latitude, complements the putatively superior social relations of the bureaucratic paradise that surrounds it, also the product of a slight shift. Nominally, unalienated citizens performing nominally good works in clear sight stand in contrast to the greedfueled and compartmentalized activities native to the town (never mind that the building deploys the full bureaucratic apparatus, from the president's big room on top to separate dining areas for large and lesser cheeses).

The Ford Foundation, as both social and architectural enterprise, is neatly isomorphic with its world view. Happy colonizers overlook literal fruits, symbolizing their labors. Unseen, a labyrinth of pipes and ducts, fans and fertilizer pipes sustains the enterprise, pumping transformative stimulus like money from Ford. In this symbolic array, the workers finally represent the product of the garden, standing themselves for charity's harvest, for a world of capitalist orderliness in which citizens will toil in contented uniformity and in which all will know their place. The payback will be a view of that garden — the great Rousseauian suburb of the mind — and a raft of luxus durables, those shining brass typewriter podiums and Kleenex covers standing in for the T-Birds and Lincolns that will surely sit in every driveway when this terrestrial nirvana is finally effected. It's an almost irresistible vision of happy order, a containment vessel for the invention of a very particular paradise, a model of what America can make of the world.

1987

MINIMUMS

I set out for my daily *dérive* and waft downtown. First stop: Washington
Square. It's a beautiful day and the park looks lovely, at least from the
perimeter. The axis up Washington Place is bowered and calm and, for
once, the fountain is on, its plume feathering perfectly in a light breeze. I
skirt the edge of the park, not wanting to risk the visit to what, mostly, is the
Disney World of Despair.

Walking the edge, though, obliges me to enter the jogger stream. Here,
I come face to face with a succession of prostheticized model citizens of the
New Age, bristling with mechanical extensions, like Futurist shock troops.
Starting at the bottom, the hundred-dollar Japanese sneakers, totems of
mobility, little Hondas for the feet. Moving up, the gossamer shorts,
emblazoned with the logo of some multinational sporting goods company.
The T-shirt allows a freer range of signification. Mickey Mouse or politics,
what's the difference, it's only images. The most important element is
uppermost, the walkman. As the joggers stride counterclockwise around
the park, who knows what signals impel them forward?

Forgive my inclination to make these persons into Alphavillians; I don't
want to get into robotomy, rather, to inquire where the degree just above
zero of architecture lies. The question of minima is crucial: in the age of the
simulacrum, the possibility of architecture's disappearance looms. If — as in
the aerospace industry or the movies — environmental simulations rival (or
surpass) built reality, architecture's terms are ineluctably altered. It's the old
promise of shamans and hippies: better in your head. Architecture really
can become obsolete.

Design reacts to this question in various ways, whether it's Ludd signal
manipulation or some more fervid embrace of things to come. The

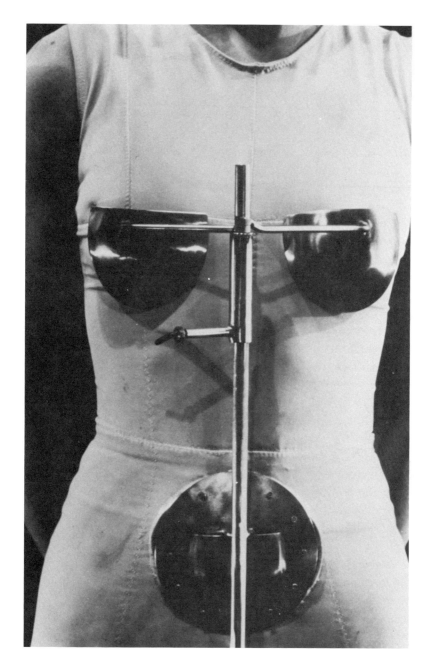

ARMOUR FOR THE BRIDE
(*Duchamp Project*) Liz Diller & Ric Scofidio

contraction of the life-support pod has been a very stable enterprise among architects for many years (we were all drawing bubbles in the '60s) and its current end product is not-a-million-miles-off joggerismo, if with a more Vernean styling job. Less is more is not simply the credo of Miesians; it embraces the sensibility of engineers — to whom architects must look — and their quest for the elegances of minimum solutions to complex problems.

The dark face, of course, is custom-Taylorized technologies. The fashion for the capsule, that joined the dreams of industrialized building to the possibilities for getting really wired up, is today carried to the max by the Japanese with their famous bachelor-pod hotels, actual buildings! This sort of work is simultaneously affecting and appalling, interesting research into basics yet horrifying for its conclusions, its rationalized squeeze on the space of habitation. This is the danger zone where social and mechanical problems grow indistinguishable.

The low-tech companion to such high-gloss minimalism is raw packaging. I was in Brazil this summer and visited favelas in Rio and São Paulo. These awful places describe another self-sufficient minimum, about as bad as it gets. The official policy of redress is a still minimum vision. At the farthest fringes of the city, the government builds rows of tiny, bare-bones houses. To be sure, they're more solid and sanitary than the bric-a-brac shacks of the favelas, but they're hours from employment, obliging endless and expensive hours of commuting. The swap's minimum convenience for minimum hygiene. Some deal.

And yet, it should be possible to discuss the minimum in architectural terms, in terms that don't presume either some form of physical deprivation or cruddy philosophic primitivism, the search for the built analogues of Borkian original intent. Two sites, versions of favela and jogger, seem available. The first is at the locus of construction, the idea of a purely technical minimum, the phonemics of building. This exults in trabeation and joinery, in the outlines of statics. Here's architecture at its most reflexive, tail-bitingly concerned with self-representation, necessary to good work but finally a dead end.

The second possibility originates with the body. Familiarly, here's architecture as the measure of persons, an insight that devolves mainly into mere proportioning. To begin with the body, though, is to valorize architecture's social dimension, to insist that it proceed from necessity. To be sure, its minima can be as scary as any others: a Walkman's one thing, but a spacesuit? And yet, these are surely primitive huts for the times.

Perhaps I overstate the case against the spacesuit. Over the summer I visited NASA's Ames Labs in California and saw the latest in rigid, extra-vehicular outfits, the AX5, designed by Vic Vykukal, one of America's great hidden-design geniuses. Not only is the AX5 one of the most beautiful designed objects I've ever seen, at once sublimely functionalist and wackily Schlemmeresque, it is also an apparatus of liberation, of extension, of genuine prosthesis, the body simultaneously augmented and housed. Exciting.

I've a couple of architect friends called Liz Diller and Ric Scofidio. At a recent show at the Storefront for Art and Architecture, they presented a series of projects under the rubric "Bodybuildings." Their work — long involved with such boundary conditions — may be familiar from projects such as the fantastic structure under the vaults of the Brooklyn Bridge Anchorage used in the performance of Matthew Maguire's *Memory Theater of Giulio Camillo* in 1986, the sets for last year's La Mama production of *The Rotary Notary and His Hot Plate*, or the gate piece from 1985's Art on the Beach at the Battery Park City landfill. The two also completed a particu-larly beautiful installation in San Francisco this summer (another stop on the trip that took in the space suit) called "the withDrawing Room."

All of this work is concerned with an experimental alliance of tectonic and social realms. At the formal level, Diller and Scofidio are leading expo-nents of the Cooperschule, of the sort of scrupulous mechanic exploration that has flourished at Cooper Union (where both Diller and Scofidio studied and now teach) under the leadership of John Hejduk. It's a primary modernist tenet they observe, the irrevocable transformation of architec-ture by the machine, a practice that traces its primary lineage to Leonardo, the first great genius of the prosthetic.

Their beautiful mechanics are never abstractions but always situated. The relevance of the theater for them is in its provision of a narrative ready-made, a preconceived object of desire. I intend this Duchampian allusion. It isn't simply that the *Rotary Notary* sets are a musings on the *Large Glass* or that the plays they've designed for are deeply invested in fresh metaphor. Diller and Scofidio are part of something larger.

There's an architecture nowadays that responds to the main under-takings of surrealism, at least shares its deadpan relationship to culture and its distorted or recontextualized object fixation. The work includes the floating chairs of Diller and Scofidio's "withDrawing Room" (architecture's primary source of irony is gravity) and abounds in mirrors and slightly infernal machines like those in their theater pieces. Other important figures include Hejduk, whose work imparts a Blakean innocence to dry minimalism, juicing it up. Also, Coop Himmelblau, greats from Vienna, full of integrity, keeping a kind of countercultural courage from the good old days, using the surreal to keep them trippy, generating their buildings from "automatic drawings."

But such a surrealist sensibility is a troubled hybrid. Architecture's inherent reductiveness tends to take the edge off the struggle to be wild, as does surrealism's predilection for minimalism and gesture. Look at Duchamp after all. Quit painting at 40 (the perfect Madison Avenue mid-life crisis) and turned himself into an idea. Is this the corner people like Sherrie Levine — the Joe Bidens of the art world — have painted themselves into? Is this the problem of an architecture that's too direct?

Still, there is a difference between devouring science and resisting it. The strategy for many architects has been to turn surrealism into technique. This problem dates at least from Duchamp. The difficulty is keeping the madness in the method, keeping it from getting classicized. The new surrealists — fed from various sources — face big risks here. But the test is joined! There's a group of architects just on the point of building their first big-scale projects. Hejduk and Himmelblau, most notably, who will prove if an architecture of such carefully magical origins has the real power to exceed style. The question is — in the age of TV — whether surrealism can still unbalance reality. I've got high hopes.

Please. The Landmarks Commission is currently considering designation for the two banks on the west side of the intersection of Eighth Avenue and 14th Street. As you may recall, the domed bank on the north was in the process of being trashed by the infamous Eddie Garofalo, the same contractor who illegally demolished four buildings on West 44th Street in the middle of the night two years ago on Harry Macklowe's behalf. The bank was rescued only by the quick action of Joan McCoullough, a Chelsea resident who spotted the brewing crime and forcefully intervened with the Landmarks Commission and the Buildings Department to foil the deed. A local hero.

These are beautiful buildings, both separately and together. My correspondent, Ted Grunewald, has sent a most moving communiqué on their behalf, winningly comparing them to the twin churches on the Piazza del

Populo in Rome. And they are an amazing pair, at once a gateway and two little neo-classical locomotives, pulling their blocks along: a miracle of accidental urbanity. Protection is badly needed: development schemes are burning up the boards at Beyer, Blinder, Belle — and the sledgehammering thugs lurk in the wings. There's no possible reason to deny the banks Landmark status, every argument to offer it.

October 1987

CORB IN NEW YORK

I grew up in the suburbs of Washington, DC, in a subdivision that was the first in the area composed entirely of "modern" houses. And they were. Although some (including ours) had conventionally pitched roofs, others were more canonically flat or "butterfly": there was no mistaking these crisply composed, largely glass houses for the indigenous brick colonialoids and sidinged rancheros that surrounded. My bedroom had a floor-to-ceiling wall of glass, opening onto greenery. Fortunately, much of the greenery was the next-door neighbor's, a landscape architect who'd worked for the Olmsted brothers. From an early age, this was my vision of modernism, the Corbusian trinity: space, sunshine, greenery.

This year marks the 100th anniversary of Le Corbusier's birth. In the view current, Corb is venerated as a form-giver, deprecated as an urbanist. There are those who prefer early, phonemic Corb (the fashion) and those who favor the plasticity of his later years, but there are virtually none who find his views as an urbanist defensible. The man's widely held as the fount of Cartesianist urban renewal, the sinister geometrizer of the city, the villain of every manipulative bestiality from Pruitt-Igoe to Sixth Avenue. To be sure, he's holdable to some account here. The polemical propositions of his exuberant youth, the Ville Radieuse and its superposition on Paris in the Voisin plan, are ripe totems of regulatory anomie. That oh-so-replicable vision of towers in the landscape has by now rationalized the production of several generations of social engineers and architectural hacks. It's easy, at some level, to see the relationship between Coop City or the penitential projects of the South Bronx and Corb's endless spreads of cruciform high-rises.

But to insist on the ignobility of this conception is to miss its grandeur.

UNITED NATIONS HEADQUARTERS
(*New York*) Associated Architects

Corb's directed imaginings were backdropped by two indelible vistas. The first was the grim industrial city and its hideous slums. The second was the history of reformist polemic descending from Fourier and the utopians through the more succinctly physicalized propositions of the garden city and modern movements in architecture. Corb — and those who shared and expanded his view — must be credited with a dignity of intent that, for me at any rate, retains its luster. Whatever else it's come to represent, the Radiant City was a stirring answer to the tubercular drear of the industrial town.

An obvious problem was the grafting of this ex-novo organization onto existing cities. Argument's sake brooked no compromise, wanting old to give way to new. And so the Ville Radieuse was received and interpreted, alas. The formal reaction has been predictable. Writ now has it that design in cities is to be Borkian, a distillate of some sort of urbanistic original intent. Of course, as with Bork, the reading has a hidden agenda. This formalizing of urban relations strips the social from consideration. The presence of a real civil compact is reduced to a question of street walls and cornice lines. Well, okay, as far as it goes. But throttling the visionary is going too far.

There are several sites around Manhattan that offer an uplifting (if under-realized) rendition of the Corbusian dream, places that have always spoken to me about what was stirring about that well-glazed childhood room. On the master's centennial, I think it's important not just to intone the ossifying chant of his irreplaceable genius but to celebrate lesser works that have truly profited by his example, profited beyond quirk or style, works that broaden our urbanism.

Architect George Ranalli and I paid a visit to the United Nations the other day. That complex is perhaps as close as New York comes to having a genuine work by Le Corbusier in its midst. Its lineage is direct. Shortly after plans for the project were first discussed, Corb sailed for New York and began work on a scheme, before a site had been chosen. After the Rockefellers tithed the East River acreage to the organization, he rapidly developed what came to be known as "Project 23-A" and awaited the commission.

It never came. Instead, a committee — headed by Wally K. Harrison — was appointed to carry out the scheme. That group's achievement and its compromise make a nice parallel to the work of the body it worked to house. The results were very close to Corb's proposed massing but everywhere lacked his touch — never mind the *brise-soleil* meant to cover the walls of the Secretariat. Clearly, Corb (who claimed that the sketchbook containing his studies for the building had been stolen from him by persons unknown) had been ripped off. What stands today — while indisputably under the influence — wants the subtlety and finesse it might have.

And yet it's wonderful. The thin blue-green slab with its marble ends is like no other tower in the city, a different kind of tall building. The Assembly building, for all its ungerminated detailing and expressive timidity, still manages to soar, to distinguish itself from any other space in town. There's an atmosphere in these buildings, a connection to one of the great modernist lineages that simply can't be found elsewhere in New York. The ensemble — the very idea of ensemble — has a sweep and an excitement that never fails to strike me, day or not, fair weather or foul. Unmistakeably, this is the site of important work.

The architecture is sustained by its beautiful setting. Corb meant the UN complex to stand as a kind of mini-Radiant City, the slab in the garden. The relieving spaciousness of the environment is a tribute to the force of his idea. The manicured lawn, the energetic (if bowdlerized) statuary, the riverside promenade, and the handsome foliage conspire to make a rare and pleasurable place, dignified, bracing, even serene. It's an exception to the remorseless grid and a fabulous relief. More, it's a genuine vindication of another idea about the fabric of cities. The day after our visit, George called me up to recall having been taken to the UN as a child by his mother, to say what an impression it had made, how it played on his imagination. Rare the building that projects so bright an optimism.

Corb realized a fragment of the Radiant City in the famous Unité d'habitation in Marseilles. This gorgeous apartment building in the countryside on the outskirts of town summarizes Corb's strategies for knitting together of town and country. Raised above the lanscape on pilotis; arraying deeply textured balconied façades; vigorously colored; ingenious interlocking, doubly exposed apartment plans; internal social "streets"; and a sculpted roofscape intended as an elevated piazza, replacing the land lost underneath the building.

Deracinated versions of the Unité appear around the world. New York's most succinct is Washington Square Village, a project that, in its way, alludes to virtually the whole field of Corb's enterprise. Designed by S.J. Kessler and Paul Lester Weiner in the mid-'50s, the two blocks are near contemporaries of the Marseilles Unité, itself completed in 1953. Clearly, the American architects were moved by the same image of modernism in nature, never mind that the verdure had to be imposed on the site. The buildings themselves likewise follow Corb. The primary coloration on the façades, the curvilinear roof forms, the raising up to allow the underpassage of Greene and Wooster Streets, all clearly show the stamp of influence.

These are not buildings that many presently choose to defend but I've always been fond of them. After the fumes, filth, and decay of the surrounding environment, I like to walk underneath the buildings into their calm central park. I like the superscale square they invent with the buildings on Mercer and La Guardia. I like walking their adequately bowered perimeter. I like emerging from the Wooster Street under, to sight along the eastern edge of Washington Square to the rising spires of midtown or pursuing the wonderful sequence of spaces downtown through Pei's project and into Soho. What a pity that Philip Johnson's dreadful Tisch Hall terminates the view up Greene with a blank wall, a typically thuggish piece of urbanism. Likewise a pity brutal Bobst doesn't open to the east towards Shimkin Hall's monumental entry to make something more of that single pedestrianized block.

For me, the meaning of these buildings doesn't simply lie in their embodiment of a holy architectural heritage. They're the legatees of an attitude that's sadly departed from architecture's discourse. Another image sums it up. Looking east on many streets in the Lower East Side, one's view frames two architectures. In the foreground, a field of tenements — crumbling, minimal, dark. Rising in the distance, set among lawns and trees, bristling with balconies, commanding super views, are the coops built by the ILGWU (designed by Herman Jessor, the architect of Coop City) just a little earlier than Washington Square Village. It's not great architecture, but it's architecture that grows out of a great idea. And that's simply that sun, greenery, and space are worthy of struggle, that architecture's politics is centered on the fight for decent habitation.

Is this getting maudlin? On Corb's 100th birthday, though, it's important to recall that his architecture was undergirded not just by art but by fervent ideology. Le Corbusier's imagined city may have been dogmatic, over-simple, and naive, but it was rare and beautiful, too. We could do worse than living in a garden. ... if properly tended...

Leonard Stern, owner of the *Village Voice* and thereby my oppressor, the man who ultimately profits from my willingness to write for peanuts (er, birdseed) has gotten good press for donating some of his jillions to help the homeless. Consider, on the other hand, the droll ad his real estate operation is currently printing. The headline: "'Prime office space in Manhattan doesn't cost as much as you think' — New York City." The subhead: "And a bear doesn't sit [sic] in the woods!" The copy exhorts big business to flee Manhattan, emulating the example of predecessors like ... Rupert Murdoch! Ah, the interlockingness of it all! Wealth does tend to make so many contradictions invisible.

October 1987

CANON FODDER

Sometime in 1984, two young architects from Chicago, Paul Florian and Stephen Wierzbowski, were approached by the Dean of the School of Architecture at the University of Illinois at Chicago to take charge of the exhibition program there. Agreeing, they quickly conceived an ambitious idea for a show. Surveying the field of recent architecture, they — like other observers — were struck by a prevalent tendency, shared with the culture in general. An architecture obsessed with fragmentation and instability, "torn between history and technology," was emerging, its product visible in a wide variety of work both theorized and built.

In its first incarnation, their idea was to show between 40 and 50 examples that fit into this vision, aiming at a comprehensive depiction of what they felt to be a crucial development. An application was dispatched to the National Endowment for the Arts for funds, and letters were sent to a who's who of contemporary architecture soliciting the "sponsorship" of prestige. Alas, Florian and Wierzbowski had far greater success with this list than with the grant. While most of the architects contacted wrote back to allow their names to be placed on the list, the NEA sent them back a no.

Undaunted, they reapplied. Unimpressed, the NEA re-rejected. But the two architects were still unwilling to give up. They prepared a proposal for a scaled-down version of the exhibition, to feature the work of a smaller group of architects (Coop Himmelblau, Peter Eisenman, SITE, Krueck and Olsen, Eric Moss, Hiromi Fujii, and Zaha Hadid) who they thought might outline the territory under investigation. Another grant application was prepared for a show that they were now calling "Violated Perfection: The Meaning of the Architectural Fragment." Unfortunately, the results were the same: nothing doing. Florian and Wierzbowski gave up.

Not long after the final rejection, though, Wierzbowski was lunching in Chicago with Aaron Betsky, a young architect then working in Frank Gehry's office in Lost Angeles. On hearing Wierzbowski's tale of trouble, Betsky became intrigued with the project and offered to collaborate with the two Chicagoans by trying to find a West Coast venue for the show. At the end of their tether, Wierzbowski and Florian agreed and awaited word of the enterprising Betsky's efforts on their (now) mutual behalf.

When word came not long after, it was not of a show but a publication. Betsky, as it turned out, had gone to Rizzoli in New York and sold them on the idea of a book called *Violated Perfection*, about the cadre that had formed the core of the original exhibition idea. Florian and Wierzbowski agreed to collaborate with what had become Betsky's project by compiling a dossier of works that would illustrate a Betsky text. All three were satisfied by this new arrangement: the original idea would emerge in a print version.

However, the same day that Betsky cut his deal at Rizzoli, he had lunch with Philip Johnson. At this point it's important to introduce a vital subplot. One of the most sought-after plums in architectural culture lately is the directorship of the Department of Architecture and Design at the Museum of Modern Art — whose founding director was, of course, Philip Johnson. Since the death of Arthur Drexler, Stuart Wrede, the museum's curator of design, has been acting in the post. Interest has been intense for months on the cocktail circuit as to who would get the job. Wrede was widely considered to be without Johnson's support, and it was clear that Drexler's successor (like Drexler himself) was to be anointed by Johnson. Indeed, a number of hopefuls had already been summoned for their luncheons with Philip, the glittering prize dangled in front of them for their delectation. Among those thus entertained were young Betsky and Joseph Giovannini, a writer at the *New York Times* and my own former architecture school classmate.

At any rate, back at the Four Seasons (it's by now July of this year), Betsky told Johnson about the book (imagining, no doubt, that its museological possibilities would not go unnoticed). Nor did they: glomming on, Philip became enthusiastic and told Betsky that "Violated Perfection" would be a great show to have at ... the Museum of Modern Art! Johnson, sliding seamlessly in, called Wrede at MOMA ("very enthusiastic" according to Wrede) and proposed a show about what Wrede calls certain "new neo-Constructivist" work. "It struck me," says Wrede, "that this was a very new tendency for him.... I said, 'Yes, we can do it on condition that you be the guest curator.' "

Poor Wrede. If ever a man were trapped between a rock and a hard place, it was he. Here's the guy who holds the key to his future, "all enthusiastic" to do a show as soon as possible, demanding a favor. Wrede's already scheduled a fall show for his predecessor in the design curatorship, the well-connected Emilio Ambasz, and adding Philip's baby to the schedule would clearly put two heavy hitters in his debt. And Philip's show could — if properly managed — serve a fine prelude for the glasnost-enabled Constructivist show Wrede's contemplating for a slot a couple of years hence. (On the other hand, the show can't be too big, lest Wrede wind up pre-empting himself.) Finally, though, this is the portrait of a man with only one choice, and he made it: the show's being hustled into a slot in June, absolute record time as these things go.

But indulge another parenthesis. Back in June, Joe Giovannini told Philip about his own plans for a book (tentative title: *The Deconstructivists*) on much the same subject as Betsky's, admittedly one much in the air. Even as he related them, Giovannini felt his ideas and enthusiasm being sucked up. "Johnson's receptive to ideas because he hasn't got any," Giovannini says. "He's a curator, he needs material, he doesn't generate any material of his own. But he's a mimetic genius."

When Giovannini next heard from Johnson it was October. Philip called to tell him about *his* show and to pick Giovannini's brain about potential participants. One thing's clear: by the time Johnson (who'd also been sent two letters by Florian and Wierzbowski soliciting sponsorship) heard from Betsky, the appropriation of the subject might well be said to be over-determined.

Now, of course, Philip was obliged to perform power-brokering's primary act: deciding who's in and who's out. Absent a primary idea about the subject matter, Johnson shops around — much the same way he approaches design. The initial cut had been done by Florian, Wierzbowski, Giovannini, Betsky, et al., but things needed to be finalized, and so the scene was set for a ritual of consensus and complicity, a transfer of rights from the originators to the appropriator. And, as with so many of the ceremonies of the Johnson cult, this one was enacted at a boys-only dinner at — where else? — the Century Club.

On October 28, the following gathered in a private room: Philip, John Burgee, Peter Eisenman, Frank Gehry, Aaron Betsky, Joe Giovannini, and Peter Zweig and Mark Wigley, two young academics recently elevated to the Johnson retinue. Airfares for some were picked up by Philip. Not present were Florian and Wierzbowski, completely cut out, never having received, as Wierzbowski recently wrote me, a single "letter or phone call regarding 'Violated Perfection,' our opinions about it, or a request for permission to use the title."

As the group mills over cocktails, Johnson circulates, pad in hand, refining his list (rather, the original Florian–Wierzbowski list). Tschumi in or out? Someone says he's decorative. Giovannini urges him in; he doesn't make the cut. Danny Libeskind is argued: the consensus is pro. He's in. Finally, it's time to sit down. "We're gathered here for the education of Philip Johnson," Philip Johnson begins.

The conversation is lively, Johnson suctioning it up, dangling participation in the show in front of the architects present, essays in the catalogue in front of the academics and critics. When matters take a theoretical turn, Johnson seems uninterested. "There are too many ideas at this table," he announces at one point. There's another announcement as well. Wrede is to have the directorship.

Word of the show gets out quickly, Eisenman going so far as to announce it during a lecture at Columbia as the most important such event since Johnson's "International Style" show of 1934, his debut splash at the Modern. And indeed, "Violated Perfection" (although the title may not be used, the rapist overtones are nicely apt) should provide an end bracket, a hasty, tasty swansong. The show's a quickie *envoi* aimed at coopting the future. Like "The International Style," the June show will be about the reduction of an architecture of polemic, contention, and vitality to the necrophiliac realm of motif, the transmutation of research to fashion, the liberation of form from content so as to make it useful for appropriation by hacks.

And there's no surprise as to who the leader is. I bumped into Peter Eisenman the other day. He pulled a couple of Xeroxed drawings — an elevation and a plan — out of his pocket and asked me if I could guess who'd designed them. The work was weakly modernist — a dimly done elevation and an incredibly klutzy collagist plan — of a sort unlikely to gain a student promotion to the second year of architecture school. I couldn't guess why I was being shown this work. Of course, it turned out to be Johnson's, and Eisenman — longtime loyalist — carried on about how impressive it was that the great man was able to change his stripes so late in his career, as if Johnson had ever done anything but. Naturally, the building will get a little better when the kids in his office get to work on it. And, come June,

Johnson will be able to take them over to the museum and tell them to try to get it a little more like Zaha or Peter.

A last word. The issue is not who's in the show; everyone on the current list (shrunk to a "nucleus" of five by latest count: Eisenman, Gehry, Himmelblau, Hadid, and Libeskind) has produced innovative and beautiful work. Indeed, some of the people proposed for the show are particular pals of mine, and I — along with a variety of mutual friends — have been wondering about what position to advise them to take, what position we'd take were we in their place. Last week wonderful Wolfgang Prix of Coop Himmelblau was in town for his rendezvous with Philip (who had floored him with flattery and perfect German), and a bunch of us took jet-lagged Wolf to a long, boozy dinner dedicated to this question.

H.H. Richardson declared architecture's first commandment to be "get the job." Johnson goes this credo one better, having declared publicly, "I'm a whore." It's a bad attitude: a project is simply not worth any cost. However, an architect who wants to build is surely hard-pressed to turn down a job (or route to a job) that he or she thinks can be carried out in such a way that the work itself is uncompromised.

Here's the dilemma. How great's the taint? What does it mean to have one's work on the wall of a brothel? What's the relationship to the madame's values? MOMA's not *Das Haus der Deutschen Kunst.* A show at MOMA is powerful certification and it can help a career enormously. Philip knows this uncannily well, and this is exactly his power. Realistically, how is it possible not to participate?

My conclusion? Just another little compromise. I wish only success to the architects who'll be part of this show, but I do feel so sad about the system.

I've just spoken to Philip, who called full of disarming Judy-and-Mickey, *Babes in Arms,* energy: let's put on a show! When I asked him where the idea had come from, what it was, he allowed as how Betsky and Giovannini had been the initial inspiration and that he'd "thought it was a good idea." I pressed him about what the show was, what it stood for, and he responded that "it represents a direction that interests us." But what's it *about,* I wondered?

"That's what we're trying to work out. That's why I've got [Mark] Wigley."

"And where'd you get Wigley?"

"From Peter."

I wasn't quite ready to give up. I asked him again to try to specify what the participants had in common. "The work looks similar," he answered. "It recalls Constructivism. And it's antipostmodern, antimodern, and all that. It's no big deal, really, this is not a new International Style show."

I said that Peter'd been saying it was.

"Maybe for Peter it is," Philip flashed.

December 1987

DRAWING PLEASURE

Chris Mcdonald and Peter Salter are two youngish London architects who have, in a collaboration of five years, produced a set of projects of great subtlety and distinction. Virtually their complete work is currently on display at the Storefront for Art and Architecture, and it's really good.

Their complete work is, in fact, a series of drawings, done to a uniform set of graphic conventions. In ink, in line, unrendered, uncolored: plans, sections, and elevations. While these may be architectural representation's bread and butter, to draw this chastely is to take a pretty strong position in the discourse wars. Here, the way of a drawing is as crucial (if not more) than the what. Mcdonald and Salter make their particular claim via a conceit of the technical, by indentifying with a very specific moment in the chain of elaborations that designers use to materialize building.

By privileging — for instance — the sketch or the working drawing, attention is focused on certain kinds of architectural ideas. Sketch celebrates image just as a working detail exults in joinery and fit. Salter and Mcdonald's special moment is the advanced schematic, just shy of a construction drawing but virtually ready to be sent to the shop. This obligates them not simply to a high level of formal clarity and a fairly exacting degree of resolution in matters of measure and material but also commits them to a rigorousness in solving questions of program, in specifying patterns of use.

The idealist turn in architectural thinking from which we're now emerging was especially interested in — surprise, surprise — the most reductive styles of representation, imagery that was sufficiently sketchy, schematic, or abstracted to hold corrupting quiddity at bay. This association of immateriality and essence has corroborated lots of mannerisms between

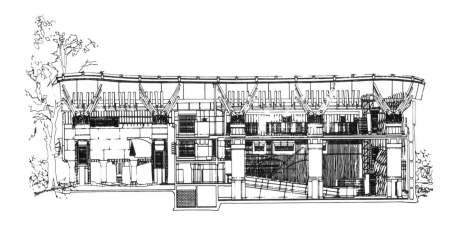

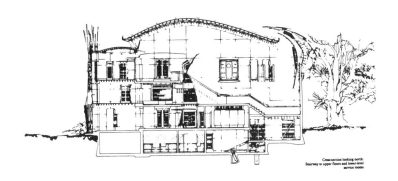

Cross-section looking north:
Stairway to upper floors and lower-level
service rooms

SECTIONS OF ICI PAVILION
John Salter and Chris Mcdonald

the poles of Eisenmanian acrostics and Gravesian doodles; at both extremes space is seen as far more conceptual than physical. In an attempt to change architecture — to reinfuse its meanings — its representation, the very techniques of its invention, were burdened with an ideographic system that was often hermetic to the real concerns of building.

Salter and Mcdonald are ready to go. Although their work is yet to be built, alas, Salter and Mcdonald are emerging as key players in re-establishing real complexity, in resisting the autonomy of the drawing, the idea of its complete equivalence. That isn't to imply that their drawings are less than beautiful on the page; rather that they participate in a strategy that reflects good old Otto (of whom more later) Wagner's self-righteous bromide: "The impractical cannot be beautiful." I'm only trying to make a narrow point here: these are drawings that must be understood and judged not only technically but as a *kind* of drawing, not only in terms of the values of composition in two dimensions but as direct incitements to building. Here is not architecture by analogy; metaphor, however rich, that's afraid of any real action.

That said, the two have been canny about what they've chosen to design. The projects are all sited, scaled, and programmed to bring out their best. Corb wrote "the plan is the generator." Salter and Mcdonald understand this, do really superb plans: rhythmic, graceful, and thoroughly elaborated. A big country house by an ever-so-English trout stream and a religious retreat on a windy Scottish fell are both studies in the long, spinal, *parti*, elements strung out to take advantage of topography and orientation. S & M've got an Aalto-esque feel for the curve and a truly deft command of the twisting and cranking moves that allow mainly orthogonal forms both to aggregate and undulate. Their spinal tapping tour-de-force, though, is a competition project for the Accademia Bridge in Venice, a brilliant intertwining of parallel tubes, perfection.

These are plans that bear real study, the pleasures not just of getting stoned on their graphic invention but of wandering through them *as if they were buildings*. The sections certainly help. A beautiful sectional drawing (never mind a really beautiful idea) is very difficult to do. Because it depends on clarity of construction and modulations of light and space far more than it does on visible organization and spacious composition, a sectional idea is especially exacting. Salter and Mcdonald are unusual in the growing complexity of their sectional research, an especially impressive accomplishment given the often limited means at their disposal.

The long plan projects show particular finesse in achieving not only spatial variety but in responding to site, climate, and season. At the retreat center, for example, the architects take advantage of a shift in topography to bring the sod of the site across an upper level of the building, inviting sheep to graze on the roof. Some version of pastoral! The big country house has a long winding glazed gallery along one site, a greenhouse with its roof members pitched against the side of the main structure lean-to style. At first glance, the section seems too funky and informal, given the really sinewy elegance of the plan, but a closer look (this work always merits a closer look) impresses with the architect's discipline, the tightening up of the space away from the light, the ways it opens in wonderful variety to its heliotrope exposures.

Salter and Mcdonald's most exposed work is probably a scheme they did for a trade pavilion at the British national agriculture fairground, scene of an annual livestock show. The project's long, independent, transparent roof is supported by five giant, treelike fan-trusses atop trunky columns, apparently inspired by a hoary oak, which stands at a corner of the site. Along a side are a row of intricate, bundled timber columns, which support a series of elaborately latticed decks and screens. Within there are intricate timber enclosures that house various services. The building's an essay on the descent of furniture, starting from the living tree, through the massive requirements of architectural structure both of and in the image of the tree, through a variety of more delicate bindings and combinations, down to the literal furnishings.

The plan is also very beautifully worked out, as adept at organizing use as it is in composing volumes and surfaces. Its family of shapes is lively with mild curvature and rounded corners and — because of this — Salter and Mcdonald have already been situated in the midst of a mild debate about "romanticism" and "organicism." These don't strike me as particularly useful terms, given that their ideological content is presently near nil. Looking at Salter and Mcdonald's morphologies, though, it's clear that they're part legatees of one branch of modernism's research.

There was a moment around the turn of the century when the double fascinations of craft and nature resulted in the flowering of an architecture that was the product of the modern eye turned on the wild world. This may be the very definition of Romanticism, modernity's own special filter for nature. Never mind. Louis Sullivan and his prairie legatees, Greene and Greene and Maybeck on the West Coast, Charles MacIntosh and the

Glasgow school, Victor Horta and Art Nouveau, the Viennese Secession of Wagner, Olbrich, and Hoffman all worked to reconcile the nominally conflicting demands of mechanical rectitude and "natural" sinuousness.

If Mcdonald and Salter have a period of origin, this is it. Their predecessors have suffered some eclipse in recent years with the hegemony of straighter branches of modernism, but the tradition's been kept alive by a wide variety of expressionists, Wrightians, Goffoids, ecologists, hippies, Japanese, and other sensitive souls, unafraid of the metaphor of the body or the unruly tendrils of a morning glory. I can't say whether Mcdonald and Salter willingly own up to this heritage but it's there. Long may it flourish.

Speaking of Otto Wagner, there's a show of his drawings at The Drawing Center; rather, a show of drawings from his office, since his hand is not likely to have figured physically in many of them. No matter — his genius fairly gushes from every sheet, his brain guiding each stroke of his delineators. And what delineators they were. Standing in front of a favorite image, I could hear other visitors walking around the room, gasping audibly as some particularly staggering rendering came into view. These drawings are the products not simply of an imagination on wings but of a tradition of technique that's unlikely to be seen again. Talk about anal retention, the microscopy of this work beggars description.

Don't let me overstate this, though. The interest of these drawings far exceeds the fascinations of manual discipline: there's amazing art here. Particular winners among the works on display include the well-known blue and white partial elevation of the Postal Savings Bank that many of us used to have on our walls in poster form; some swell, lightly washed sketches of one of the stations on the Vienna City Railway; a sublimely concise little elevation of an exhibition building from 1903, and a tiny, wonderfully composed perspective of a church from 1916 in which the building — seen obliquely — seems to be angling out of frame, chugging away like a Pullman car.

Before we leave Vienna, let me mention one other show: a didactic exhibition of the work of Adolf Loos in the gallery at Cooper Union. Loos, of course, belongs to the generation after Wagner and has been, for the last 5 or 10 years, an object of considerable veneration among architects of a more intellectual turn. There are several reasons for this: Loos produced buildings of philosophical austerity ("he built them a thought," Karl Kraus exclaimed of one of his houses); he hung out with everybody's favorites from the contemporary avant from Wittgenstein and Kraus to Schoenberg and Tristan Tzara; he produced a famously zany entry in the Chicago Tribune Competition of 1922 and, finally, he left behind a small but biting body of polemic, the most famous instance of which was his essay "Ornament and Crime." Indeed, although Loos built several near masterpieces, his greatest contribution was a fearless assault on the smug verities of fin-de-siècle culture and, if for nothing else than this, his seat in the Right On Pantheon is forever assured.

January 1988

BRAVE NEW WORLDS

When I look at the work of Lebbeus Woods, certain comparisons inevitably come to mind: the fantastic interiors of Piranesi; the soaring vistas of Hugh Ferriss. The latter seems especially resonant. To be sure, for raw delineating power, Woods is our greatest, our Ferriss. And, like Ferriss, Woods has long supported himself making other architects' work look good: it's the guilty secret of many offices that a rendering by Woods often accomplishes more by way of design than was there to begin with.

But it's the visionary side of Lebbeus Woods that is of concern here. For Woods is, as his portfolio attests, a creator of worlds. Like Hugh Ferriss, his territory of invention is the city. Over the past 10 years, Woods has produced an array of striking urban visions, the latest of which — "Centricity" — is presented in *Architectural Record* (February 1988). But, despite a certain kinship of chiaroscuro, the comparison to Hugh Ferriss is a limited one. Ferriss was the great extrapolator, setting out his astonishing views of what American cities (and especially New York) might be on the basis of ideas — whether of enormous buildings, traffic separation, or zoning — that had currency but lacked expression. Indeed, the power of his images was precisely in the way they concretized expectation. There was never any doubt that these things might be.

In this, Ferriss participated in a tradition of graphic polemic that was central to the modern movement. Sant'Elia, Tony Garnier, Le Corbusier, and Frank Lloyd Wright a little later were all suppliers of imagined urban futures, corroborations of the larger workability of their architectural projects. Of this particular set, perhaps Sant'Elia is a better model for understanding Woods. Unlike the city of Corb, Garnier, Wright, or Ferriss, Sant'Elia's was less a reproduction of feeble social theorizing than a deliber-

i.e. purely visual ?!!

GEOMECHANICAL TOWER
Lebbeus Woods

ate attempt to break out into an unknown, a tool of research rather than propaganda. Here is Sant'Elia's own description, full of the peppy cadences of Futurism:

The problem of modern architecture is ... to raise the new built structure on a sane plan, gleaning every benefit of science and technique, settling nobly every requirement of our habits and spirits.... Such an architecture cannot be subject to any law of historic continuity. It must be as new as our state of mind is new and the contingencies of our moment in history.... In modern life, the process of consequential stylistic development comes to a halt. Architecture, tired of tradition, begins again, forcibly, from the beginning.

In the mesmerizing, astonishingly wrought vision of Lebbeus Woods, we never have the sense of confrontation with a perfected vision of the present, the architectural rationalization of suburban or skyscraper theory. We are plunged into unfamiliar territory, a world of architecture beginning again. Not that an aura of familiarity is wanting. The viewer grapples for some certifying comparison, riffing through oil refineries, the middle ages, 19th-century technical construction, to try to gain a visual handle. What we see, though, is none of this. We're not even sure that the scenes are terrestrial. Woods's structures betray no familiar routines of use or of inhabitation. Yet clearly there are activities accommodated here. The whole is suffused with the support of a mysterious technics, evident in the presence of strange alchemical apparatus and alluded to by Woods in his enigmatic texts.

This is an important clue. In many of Woods's drawings there is writing, sometimes legible, as often not. Like his architecture, the writing's about longing, about a straining after language. Woods has written: "We should build our buildings and then discover how to live and work in them." The drawings are his avenue of inquiry, his process for this discovery. And Woods continuously leaps ahead of himself: the utter clarity of his images defies any presently possible account of them. While the written accounts may be mired in an aching unreadability, the drawings deliver an account — precise, measurable — of phenomena which, for now, exceed explanation. Woods's breathtaking images force fictions upon us, innumerable strategies of coherence, different assimilations of the raw data, fresh personalized hypotheses, lodes of unverifiable elegances.

The suffusing technical aura is also crucial. Woods's polemic is about science, about an architecture conceived in the light of the Einsteinian revo-

lution. Among their other agendas, Woods's cities are graphic models —
metaphors — for the new physics. The connections are diffuse and undog-
matic, to be sure. Nevertheless, they assert Woods's implicit belief that
architecture, if it is to retain vitality, must be a part of this inquiry. While
architecture may have long ago abandoned its position at the leading edge,
he asserts that it must, at the very least, be conscious of science's findings.

This architecture is — not to resist a phrase — science fiction, a supple
rhetoric of things to come. It abounds in sites for events, rituals, and techniques now only dimly imaginable but pregnant with expanded hopes. One
with the greatest of imaginative expectations, it invents the vernacular of a
culture that's yet to be. At a time when the proprietorship of anticipation
has been almost completely ceded by architecture, when visionary roles
have been either coopted or renounced, Woods shows nothing but bravery
in pursuing his new worlds. And in Woods's sure hands, architecture begins
to get one back from George Lucas and Ridley Scott.

I recently received a questionnaire that wondered whether the US
government should spend more on a search of the universe for extraterres-
trial forms of life. I ticked the "no" box. Not that I'm uninterested in finding
neighbors out there, just that the mode of inquiry — massive radiotelescopy
— seems to narrow rather than expand the field of speculation, imprisoning
the future within the confines of a narrow wavelength, demanding that the
unknown accommodate itself to the limits of our technology. Woods's
search seems to offer far richer prospects, a genuine utopia, unequivocal
about its *a*-geography, the mentalism of its mapping.

Yet Woods's work is engaged and critical, not just acquiescent babble.
Some lines from Brecht's poem "1940" evoke the problematic: "The
designers sit/Hunched in the drawing offices./One wrong figure, and the
enemies' cities/Will remain undestroyed." Brecht thought of bombers, but
our architectural technique shares the calculus. Woods clearly enfolds the
Janus of technology and terror in his vision, seeking to redeem science for
the arts of the marvelous. He struggles to restore the very idea of the city to
a humanizing terrain, implicitly criticizing its decay into a receptacle for the
irrational. The epicyclical undergirding, the inevitability of return, offers
the hope of life/cycle; the craft and casual decay of his urban fabric retain
everywhere the evidence of the hand, not his alone but the unseen
imagined hands of a citizenship; and tech's sting is averted by architecture's
privileging. Woods's vision assails the placelessness of mediated culture by
mesmerizing us with location.

Late in the sequence of drawings for the Centricity, forms slowly metamorphose, sloughing off Euclid for more biomorphic shapes. Architecture is evolving here as Woods struggles to bring it to life. One sees the fervid inventor in his lab, commanding matter into a new order, making not just those cycling atoms and molecules but the orbits of the universe dance to an irresistible tune. Here's a glimpse of the grand Woodsian synthesis, the ultimate harmonizing of the spheres, the fresh totality. Mechanics, excited by light and genius, becomes biology. The final images of the Centricity — the "free-gravity" and "free-light" machines — loose architecture from its most primary constraints, barely materialized wisps of longing for an eventuality we know must come. Lebbeus Woods prepares architecture to soar from becoming to the incredible lightness of being itself.

It is a striking feature of contemporary architecture that the visionary style, once so prominent, so central, is now so lacking. Our avant-garde, such as it is, pursues inquiries that seem ultimately solipsistic — private investigations which, however poetic, long for no comprehending grandeurs. Part of this reticence is reactive, a retreat from the regulatory oppressions of a checkered history of great plans. Lebbeus Woods's bold imaginings are vital and restorative. His imaginary cities walk the visionary's inevitable fine line between coercion and fantasy with the elegance and grace of Philippe Petit. Centricity argues not for the superiority of some specific practical arrangement but for the liberatory prospect of imagining broadly, fervently. His ever-expanding discourse of the almost possible is an inspiration not just to build, but to think.

February 1988

SKYSCRAPERS FROM A TO Z

AMERICA

Where else but the United States could the skyscraper happen? Where else concatenate avarice, ambition, bureaucracy, speculation, underdevelopment, technology, and the waiting grid? While not exclusively American, the tower's thoroughgoing here, ubiquitous. No city of substance lacks a skyline, a clump of spires — however few — that signify the threshold of arriviste urbanity. Skyscrapers are part of the minimum apparatus of American urbanism, joining expressways, domed stadia, air-conditioned shopping malls, and gentrified dereliction. As once the bank was signified by the gold leaf on its dome, now it requires marble mullions and a reach exceeding the grasp of the Phone Company Building across the street. The town's leading law firm cannot be suitably housed elsewhere. The tower speaks by conferring address.

HARDY AMIES

I was once asked, "For whom do you design? What are you thinking of?" It is an ideal man that we are working for. He is a decent citizen, pays his taxes. He is well aware of all that goes on around him. He reads the *Wall Street Journal* but he also knows his way around the Museum of Modern Art. He is 39 long. He can be any age; he looks forty-five but his bank balance is that of a man of seventy.

Hart, Schaffner, and Marx. Kohn, Pederson, and Fox. Amies' man is the Modular of the Multinational Style. In the design of the American skyscraper, the architect has almost always been coextensive with the client, a room full of 39 longs, a Mont Blanc in every breast pocket. The well-dressed executive has not only been the paradigm for occupancy, he's been the model for the building itself.

ATRIUM

Distended into misnomer by acromegaly, the attenuation of the interior courtyard has soared to unprecedented heights. John Portman, little acknowledged as a skyscraper lion, has, in effect, turned the skyscraper outside in. His hotel courts rise so high, buildings can easily fit inside them; they're packing cases for skyscrapers. In the case of his Marriot Marquis Hotel in New York City this is literally so. Set within the central space is a cylindrical elevator shaft rising 53 stories, constrained like a pig in a poke.

Portman's places reclaim as void the cancelled space consumed by ordinary towers and offer regulated vistas which, if outer-directed, would encompass the unregulated, uncontrollable, uncertain city. These gargantuan atria seek to compensate for the inclemencies of cities befouled by industrial and cultural effluent by appropriating nature. Portman's places — which at their most luscious extremes look like Bernini on an acid trip — are inevitably swaddled in enough dangling greenery to refoliate the Amazon Basin. Their most refined precedent, however, is Kevin Roche's Ford Foundation Building, a seminal inversion of modernism's classic vision: the park's now in the tower. The city — so un-natured, stripped so bare by its buildings, even — retains a little indoors, just a reminder.

BABEL

Ruskin antedated all towers by this first. In his initial Edinburgh lecture of 1853 he declared:

" 'Let us build a tower whose top may reach unto heaven.' " From that day to this, whenever men have become skilful architects at all, there has been a tendency in them to build high; not in any religious feeling, but in mere exuberance of spirit and power — as they dance or sing — with a certain mingling of vanity — like a child builds a tower of cards."

BARTLESVILLE

This little town in Oklahoma is home to Frank Lloyd Wright's Price Tower, the greatest of them all. Designed in the '20s for a Manhattan site but unrealized until the '50s, it's Wright Agonistes, a bristling, angular, bundle of energy. Relegated to the plains, Bartlesville is Broadacre City's revenge on its maker, "the tree that escaped the crowded forest." Brilliantly expressive at every level of resolve, it's also a social condenser, mixing living and work places. More Wright:

The elevator building — tall, taller, tallest. The skyscraper is a fireproof American natural. Once upon a time confined to the congested areas of monstrous cities a landlord's ruse to have, to hold, exploiting excess concentration an expedient snare — adding picturesqueness to the urban sky the American skyscraper has now escaped. Here you will see it starting out upon adventure now relying upon its own virtues for its very life.

As a free-standing quadruple in its park, casting its shadow upon its own ground, it may be not only beautiful and economical but truly advantageous concentration — in our crowded areas of cities its concentration was disadvantageous. But the skyscraper did hasten the coming era of decentralization. Hitherto a doubtful human asset adding to traffic problems of undesirable congestion instead of relieving them the skyscraper here becomes a free agent for a desirable concentration.... So on the rolling plains of Oklahoma comes a fresh realization of the modern advantages of architecture yet unknown to the big city. As trees in the forest have no chance to develop their own individuality to full expression of their own character as would be seen if they were isolated, so the quadruple skyscraper now has a chance to be itself, free standing in the countryside. The upended street here bears natural advantage for a natural use of the technical advantages of our own time.... Witness the release of the skyscraper from slavery (commercial bondage) to human freedom.

BESSEMER

Sir Henry, of course, invented a steel making process which, by forcing a blast of air through molten iron, removes impurities in the metal and adds enormously to its strength and ductility. The useful possibilities were quickly recognized.

BRECHT

How would Brecht have spoken to Wright? Here's what he wrote in a stanza of the "Late Lamented Fame of the Giant City of New York." First stanza's before the Crash:

> Those skyscrapers —
> The men who piled their stones so high
> That they towered over all, anxiously watched from their summits
>   the new buildings
> Springing from the ground, soon to overtower
> Their own mammoth size.
> (Some were beginning to fear that the growth of such cities
> Could no longer be stopped, that they would have to finish their days
> With twenty stories of other cities above them
> And would be stacked in coffins which would be buried
> One on top of the other.)

Second stanza's after:

> What of skyscrapers?
> We observe them more coolly.
> What contemptible hovels skyscrapers are when they no longer
>   yield rents!
> Rising so high, full of poverty? Touching the clouds, full of debt?

The architect and the poet might have seen eye to eye.

CATHEDRAL OF COMMERCE

On April 24, 1913, Cass Gilbert's masterpiece, the Woolworth Building, was illuminated when President Woodrow Wilson pressed a button in Washington. Two years later, the Panama—Pacific Exposition cited it as the "most beautiful building in all the world erected to commerce." The name itself was the coinage of a well-known New York clergyman of the day, Dr. S. Parkes Cadman, who thus baptized the latest bifurcation of form and function:

When seen at nightfall bathed in electric light or in the lucid air or summer morning, piercing space like a battlement of the paradise of God, which St. John beheld, it inspires feelings even for tears. The writer looked upon it and at once cried out "the Cathedral of Commerce" — the chosen habitation of that spirit in man which, through means of change and barter, binds alien people into unity and peace.

The idea to build a new tallest building in the world (it remained the newest until 1930) in the gothic style had come from Frank Woolworth himself, the king of the five and ten cent store, who'd been greatly taken, while visiting London, with the Houses of Parliament. Woolworth had amassed his huge fortune on the basis of three retailing principles: (1) all merchandise must be fixed at the price of 5 cents; (2) everything must be paid for in cash; (3) merchandise must be displayed on counters so that customers might see and choose each item themselves. True to his principles, Woolworth paid cash for his building. Marcel Duchamp, with perfect recognition, included the building in the category of ready-mades.

It should be noted that Woolworth was only the first in a line of secular cathedrals. The Paramount Building in Times Square, designed by C.W. and George L. Rapp of Chicago in 1929, was called "The Cathedral of Motion Pictures." At the same time Charles Z. Klauder was building the "Cathedral of Learning" to house the University of Pittsburgh. Gilbert himself had a somewhat more sanguine description of the skyscraper: "The machine that makes the land pay."

CHICAGO TRIBUNE

Two years after winning the Chicago Tribune competition of 1922, Raymond Hood wrote:

My experience, which in reality consists of designing only two skyscrapers, does not justify my expressing an opinion as to whether a building should be treated vertically, horizontally or in cubist fashion. On the contrary, it has convinced me that on these matters I should not have a definite opinion. To use these two buildings as examples, they are both in the "vertical" style or what is called "Gothic" simply because I happened to make them so. If at the time of designing them I had been under the spell of Italian campaniles or Chinese pagodas, I suppose the resulting composition would have been horizontal.... Nothing but harm could result if at this stage in our development the free exercise of study and imagination should stop, and the standardizing and formulating of our meager knowledge and experience should now take its place. It might be proper to say something precise about the different styles but I am as much in the air about style as I am about everything else.

The Chicago Tribune competition is easily the most commented upon event in the history of the skyscraper. In general, it's read as having a double poignancy. First, as a moment at which dizzy eclectics confronted the moderns: on the right-hand screen Raymond Hood, on the left Gropius. The lecturer offers a knowing wink: *après ça, le déluge.* The second observation is traditional to architectural competitions and is focused on the runner-up. As Corb was to the League of Nations or the Palace of the Soviets, so Eliel Saarinen is to the Chicago Tribune, not first, but best.

It's an analysis that hangs on a pretty slim reed. Tafuri admires Saarinen's tower as the prolegomenon to a range of "enchanted mountains," telescoping, set-back towers that proliferated through the '20s. More, the "organicism" of the building/mountain is seen as vindicating both the theory and practice of Louis Sullivan, who was, by then, plunged into miserable obscurity, scant two years away from his death. Writing in bitterness after the competition, Sullivan fulsomely praised Saarinen and derided Hood:

Confronted by the limpid eye of analysis, the first prize trembles and falls, self-confessed, crumbling to the ground. Visibly, it is not architecture in the sense herein expounded. Its formula is literary: words, words, words. It is an imaginary structure, not imaginative. Starting with a false premise, it was doomed to a false conclusion, and it is clear enough, moreover, that the conclusion was the real premise, the mental process in reverse of appearance.

But if the range of submissions to the Tribune competition was broad, it was even more remarkably thin. The amazing welter of images — a now indisputable totem for plurality — was also an exemplar of the way, in changing, things remain exactly the same. This great moment was an announcement that the character of the urban office tower was utterly fixed, that the only alterations to which it would be subsequently susceptible were sartorial. In terms of the organization of the lives of its inhabitants, the social and physical character of their workplace, the proposal of Hilbesheimer, the most degree-zeroid submission, differs not one whit from that of the klutzily eclectic Holabird and Roche, winners of the third prize. By 1922, the typological development of skyscraper was more or less at an end.

LE CORBUSIER

In 1935, a reporter from the *New York Times* accompanied Corb to the Rainbow Room atop the RCA Building to admire the view. "But," according to the story which later appeared in the paper,

the modern architect was not particularly impressed. He was looking for architecture, not theater, and shy, besides, of succumbing to drama so melodramatic. Moreover, he was looking for architecture in his own sense of the word — in this case, the city that is a machine for living in — not merely frightfully expensive scenery built to knock the beholder's eye out. "They are too small," he said, looking straight at the Empire State Building, tallest in all the world of filing cases for men and standing on one of the biggest pieces of ground devoted to that purpose in the city.

NOËL COWARD

From *Law and Order*: "I don't know what London's coming to — the higher the buildings, the lower the morals."

DANGER

Acrophobia becomes an urban privilege with the rise of the skyscraper, further elaborating the lexicon of fears modern life makes available. Fear first translates to danger for those who actually construct the towers. Dolores Hayden cites an English reporter's account of one byproduct of the construction of the Woolworth Building:

Anybody in America will tell you without tremor (but with pride) that each story of a skyscraper means a life sacrificed. Twenty stories — twenty men snuffed out; thirty stories — thirty men. A building of some sixty stories is now going up — sixty corpses, sixty funerals, sixty domestic hearths to be slowly rearranged.

This neat calculus has now diminished and the human cost of high-rises must be figured with more inexact standards, with greater concealment. An unpublicized secret of the Portman hotels is the prodigious inducement to suicide their vast atria seem to provide. The folklore of every city in which such spaces sit is flush with stories of hapless revelers crushed to death in mid-Martini by the misery-ending plunge of some stranger.

The real danger in a skyscraper, though, is not free-fall but fire. Survivors plucked from the roof of some towering inferno by intrepid helicopter pilots is one of the stable tropes of the nightly news. Ditto, the charred remains the morning after. A skyscraper fire can begin for numerous reasons — from bad wiring to smoking in bed — and its spread can fly in an unimpeded rush through ductwork or plenum, elevator shaft or electrical chase. But the skyscraper fire transforms the history of building fires in that they cannot, by definition, be escaped or fought from without. Just as the skyscraper's enormity defeats conventional hose and ladder technology, the latest strategies for protecting tenants envisage points of refuge within the burning building rather than total evacuation. The fate of the occupant is tied too intimately to that of the building: like a space ship, life can only be led within.

DECO

The United States went unrepresented at the 1925 Exposition des Arts Décoratifs, the "showcase of modern design" meant, in part, as a long-delayed response (global warfare had intervened) to the Cologne German Arts Exhibit of 1914. America was absent because then Secretary of the Interior Herbert Hoover when approached about official participation replied that America possessed no modern design. (The Germans did not participate for other reasons.) Never mind, the influence entered America nonetheless on the backs of a thousand decorators.

For the first time, a modern decorative system swept the country, establishing unity, if not parity, among objects of every class, from ashtrays to skyscrapers. As the redoubtable Emily Genauer wrote on the fashion page of the *New York World Telegram* one December in the '20s: "The affinity between art and decoration is so close this season that presently the two words will belong with other twin terms like Bread and Butter and Scotch and Soda." Paris wasn't the only retail source. Early as 1919, a shop dealing in goods produced out of Josef Hoffman's Wiener Werkstatte was being operated by the architect Joseph Urban, an Austrian émigré, at the corner of

Fifth Avenue and Forty-Seventh Street. Urban later contributed several major ziggy-zaggy monuments himself, including the International Magazine Building of 1927, the Ziegfeld Theater of 1926, and the New School of 1930, which features a pip of a Poelzigesque auditorium, still in use.

HARLEY EARL

Harley Earl was, for decades, the head of the "Art and Color" section at General Motors: the man who defined automobile styling as we know it, the man who invented the tail-fin, the man who codified the apparatus of the annual automotive image change. Earl's prominence as successor to designers like Bel Geddes, Loewy, and Teague, marks not only the displacement of style by styling in industrial design but the capture of the high ground from architecture by consumer durables. Indeed, with the Earl epoch, American architecture in general and the skyscraper in particular saw their own transformation into no more than a particularly large and slightly more durable variety of consumer object.

EIFFEL TOWER

Barthes says the Eiffel Tower is a "pure – virtually empty – sign" and "ineluctible, because it means everything." Well, sure. But to the skyscraper its message is quite specific. With the construction of the Eiffel Tower, the skyscraper's main routines of meaning were fixed, its expressive dimensions secured. Standing free, iconically exact, technologically rooted in the 19th century, judgeable by a relentless rhythm of extent, this was pure skyscraper. The virtually empty sign only reflects the virtual emptiness of the signified. The iconography of the skyscraper embraces little more than that of this tower: the elevator lobbies and landings, the view-point, the panoramic restaurant. The skyscraper's utility lies exactly in its emptiness, the refusal of its spaces to specify their occupancy, waiting the textureless inhabitation of bureaucracy.

HUGH FERRISS

The Virgil of the skyscraper, the singer of its song. Ferriss, the architect who chose simply to draw, gave the skyscraper a context in representation that it was never fully to assume in life. As America's pre-eminent renderer for decades, he kissed vitality into myriad unmaterialized schemes. His drawings for countless colleagues imputed a brooding boldness, a sense of mass, a sinuous darkness, to the skyscraper. He established the tower's time of day: midnight.

Under Ferriss's hand, skyscraper building was transformed from technique to cause, from object to urbanism. Ferriss both spiritualized and naturalized the tower. Without doubt, his greatest work is the series of drawings made to dramatize the zoning envelope studies done with Harvey Wiley Corbett in 1922. Here we see the skyscraper successively materialized from a crystalline matrix of pure architectonic matter. At a stroke, Ferriss recast the character of the skyscraper from technology to geology, from assemblage to carving. No coincidence that Ferriss's disappearance from the scene precisely reflects the skyscraper's glassification, its lunge to insubstantiality.

FOSHAY TOWER

America's most charismatic national monument is Washington's, the monster obelisk on the Mall. Wilbur Foshay, a Minneapolis manufacturer of kitchen utensils straight out of William Dean Howells (who had himself called skyscrapers "the necessity of commerce and the despair of art"), bankrupted himself building an office building of identical shape in the difficult year of 1929. He nevertheless succeeded — thanks to the enormous chiseling of his name on all four sides of the summit — in adequately animating the thrusting signifier to assure, if not immortality, at least a certain blessedness of memory. Thomas van Leeuwen has unearthed a stanza from a local wag, penned at the tower's dedication:

> A symbol of that other shaft
> Revered the nation through
> The vision of a dreaming lad
> In stone and steel come true.

FOUNTAINHEAD

Well-known reactionary novel by Ayn Rand, better known 1949 film starring Gary Cooper and Patricia Neal. The hero — Howard Roark — is an architect, who dynamites his own work — a housing project which interestingly pre-capitulates the equally celebrated blasting of Pruitt-Igoe — rather than see it altered and sullied. Ironies abound: Roark is the defender of modernism against the academicism of the critical establishment.

At any rate, the dénouement takes place at the summit of a skyscraper, built under the sponsorship of a finally found, "individualist" client, a newspaper baron called Gail Wynand. He describes his apocalyptic ambitions for the tower, claiming:

The age of the skyscraper is gone. This is the age of the housing project. Which is always a prelude to the age of the cave. This will be the last skyscraper built in New York.... The last achievement of man on earth before mankind destroys itself.

In the filmed version, Neal enacts the ascent of a re-sexed spermatozoan up an exterior construction elevator, buffeted by Reifenstahlian winds, until she reaches the Zarathustrian Cooper waiting at the summit of the huge shaft. Standing in the position of potency, they overlook the city, a tiny pool of human ejaculate, a glistening fantasy of male puissance.

FLATIRON

Amiens at 23rd Street, photographed at all hours by Edward Steichen, a Monet for moderns. The architect, Burnham; the year, 1903. Its incredible lightness of being is part serendipity, the triangular plan a product of pure extrusion from an anomaly in the grid created by the cross-slash of Broadway. The Flatiron is the most elegant justification yet for the skyscraper's characteristic mode of created value: simple multiplication.

GOD IS IN THE DETAILS

In a sartorial morality, codes lie in stitching. The skyscraper, in its present incarnation, functions in the fashion system. By the 1970s, production of skyscrapers in America had been completely brought in line expressively with the strictures of men's clothing: the tailoring of comparable goods to the needs of a limited range of envelopes and the creation of a system of marginal distinction by which both signature and status could be discerned. On the production side, firms were organized between bespoke and off-the-peg designers. Down-scale offices like Kahn and Jacobs and Emery Roth produced ready to wear goods while the likes of Cesar Pelli, Skidmore, Owings, and Merrill, Philip Johnson, and, a little later, Kohn, Pederson, Fox, were sewing custom.

The typical corporate client, of course, was an upper-middle-class male whose primary acquaintance with elaborate visual systems was his daily dress. This had undergone a number of important transformations since the war. In 1950, *Esquire*, still in its heyday, introduced the so-called "Mr. T." look, and, for perhaps the first time in history, men and buildings came to dress identically. "Mr. T." (like Mr. T-Square) was "a trim look characterized by natural shoulder, narrow lapels, and straight hanging lines." Fabrics and colors were drawn from an extremely limited range. Despite such vagaries as the small checks of 1952, the "Continental" look of '56, Ivy League details, Madras jackets, and a certain waxing of lapels, this look (the fabled Brooks Brothers # 1 Sack Suit being the central paradigm) dominated men's dress until the "Peacock Revolution" of 1966–67 when *Gentleman's Quarterly* declared, "men's fashions will never be dull again."

HANCOCK BUILDING

The giant insurance company has long been a patron of high profile towers. SOM's 1969 Chicago effort suborns mixed use to a single reading. Dramatically trussed, "Big John" strains to become a pyramid but the batter's too mild to form a point within its hundred stories. The slope does, however, nicely force perspective from below. Another happy piece of symbolism is Hancock's similarity to an oil derrick, brother instrument of extraction. It's easily the best minimalist tower of the period. The only problem is the wimpy travertine plinth.

More or less concurrent is Harry Cobb's Hancock in Boston, the double-notched, reflective-glass rhomboid. This is no time to go into the long history of the speculum. Still, it's clear the fashion for mirror panen-demic among designers is more than mere invert narcissism. Mirror does "solve" a couple of thorny problems. First, it's thought to accommodate to the skyscraper's two most difficult contexts: the historic city center and the context of no context of surrounding skyscraper kin.

Hancock addresses the first issue, "reflecting" Richardson's Trinity Church, consuming it, an inoculation against dominance. There's a conceptual parity established among church, tower, and sky, all mentalized and made immaterial. The same process crops up in uniformly glassy milieu, where the images of opposing towers bang back and forth in a barber shop game of infinite regress. Of course, the real reason architects love mirror is that it's at once transparent and volumetric, giving guiltless rein to the play of shapes.

INTELLIGENT BUILDING

What a concept! Colloquially, it refers to a nirvana of regulation afforded big buildings by the advent of the computer. Linked by fiber optics, central control is imposed on heating, ventilation, elevators, lighting, security, fire protection, as well as telecommunications and electronic office services. The aim, according to one avatar of such technologism, is "to make buildings behave much like living things, continually gathering information through different senses and adjusting their behavior in response." Definitively, the walls will have ears and work will take place in the belly of the beast.

The rise of the intelligent building augurs a transformation. As the skyscraper itself becomes an organism, the living things forced to inhabit it turn subsidiary, to parasites, microorganisms. Instead of controlling their environments, they'll be controlled by them, by the highly sensitive pantactic apparatus, by the pre-programmed statistical conceits of homeostasis. Unfit, anomalous subjects, trapped in the office when the computer lowers the temperature for the expected departure of the section for lunch, will simply have to bring sweaters.

HENRY JAMES

From *The American Scene*:

One story is good until another is told, and skyscrapers are the last work of economic ingenuity only till another word be written. This shall be possibly a work of uglier meaning, but the vocabulary of thrift at any price shows boundless resources, and the consciousness of the finite, the menaced, the essentially *invented* state, twinkles ever, to my perception, in the thousand glassy eyes of these giants of the mere market.

KING KONG

We all know the last line of the film, spoken over the great gorilla's lifeless form: "It wasn't airplanes. It was beauty killed the beast." But which beauty? Instinctively one guesses the blonde, the pheromonal Fay Wray. But mightn't it have been the architecture, the Empire State's spire, chosen from a large number of possibilities in 1933? Had the ape's aesthetic sensibilities run to the Daily News or McGraw-Hill buildings, his fall might have been only to the flat top of the slab.

The undergraduate wisdom on the symbolism of Kong counterposes nature in all its blind instincts against civilization and its insuperable mechanization. But this mistakes Kong's monstrosity. He fell because he was too big to take the stairs, because he simply couldn't or wouldn't ride the elevator, because he made a mess of the city. In 1945, the Empire State Building killed a plane, which struck it at the 76th Floor. In the scissor, stone, paper calculus of these things, then, it was airplanes that killed the beast, airplanes and their master, the tallest building in the world.

At the time of the film's 1976 remake, the world's tallest building had become two: the twin towers of the World Trade Center. Kong's scale — insufficient to embrace both towers — obliged him to choose. Alas, the choice was Hobson's: both towers were exactly the same and offered exactly the same consequences. Is it a wonder the ape died depressed? It wasn't helicopters that killed him, or even buildings. It was ambivalence.

KING KONG
1933 & 1976

NIKITA KHRUSHCHEV

From *Khrushchev Remembers*, his memoir: "If you've seen one skyscraper, you've seen them all."

LARKIN BUILDING

Wright's Larkin Building — created for a giant Buffalo soap manufacturing and mail-order business — is a paradigm for virtually every aspect of the skyscraper save height. His brief was to create an archetypical headquarters for 1,800 office workers charged with processing an avalanche of more than five thousand pieces of mail-order correspondence per day. Tucked among the enormous factories of the corporation, the building produced by Wright is a veritable factory of bureaucracy, its desks serried into a paper-work production line of visible efficiency, illuminated by its great central light-court.

As a type, Larkin mediates between the factory and the office tower, softening the oppressions of both by offering an architecture of character, amenity, and mild polemic. Part of this comes from the paternalistic decorative agenda promulgated by the "enlightened" corporation and its architect. Larkin is ornamented with slogans, half Horatio Alger, half Mao Tse-tung. "Honest labor needs no master. Simple justice needs no slaves," reads one. Part of this comes from the architecture itself. The visiting Erich Mendelssohn noted that "The directors are only separated from the employees by a railing. This has a double aspect — an incentive and democracy." This reading was extended by the visitor to a vision of a kind of functionalist colonialism: "The building conveys a spontaneous *élan* out of an early felt logic of development — too early for this intransigently rough colonial country, but early enough to arouse a whole generation, to instruct them and to drive them on further."

Wright himself pandered, declaring:

Finally — it seems to me — that the American flag is the only flag that would look well on or in this building; the only flag with its simple stars and bars that wouldn't look incongruous and out of place with the simple rectangular masses of the exterior and the straightforward rectilinear treatment of the interior. I think our building is wholly American in its directness and freshness of treatment. It wears no badge of servitude to foreign "styles" yet it avails itself gratefully of the treasures and the wisdom bequeathed to it by its ancestors.

LARKIN TOWER

The other Larkin building. Proposed by the architect John Larkin in 1926 for a site now occupied by Hood's McGraw-Hill, this 110-story tower could have been the first building to exceed the height of the Eiffel Tower.

LIBERTY

The Statue of Liberty of 1886 fills a small lacuna left in the conceptual framework of the skyscraper by its great establishing genius, Gustave Eiffel. The asymptotic signification of the tower is redressed here by the act of cladding. Questions of quiddity are satisfied by ultimate reification: the thing's a woman. Here, in the only instance of a skyscraper definitively female in its iconography, Eiffel is midwife at the birth of the second great skyscraper tradition, haberdashery. In the yin—yang relations between architecture and its engineering, Eiffel occupies both sides. In his tower, the primacy of construction gives form to a masterpiece. At the statue, the engineer repairs undercover, allowing the fascinations of structure to be subverted by the exigencies of dress.

MARINA CITY

The history of the doubled skyscraper can be traced to Bertram Goldberg's executed 1959 design for the twin towers of Marina City in Chicago. Of course, the pre-history of such soaring doppelgängers is hoarier, dating at least back to the binary spires of ecclesiastical westworks. The tendency is first incarnate in Manhattan in the great doubled apartment towers on Central Park, the San Remo and Majestic of 1930, the Century and Eldorado of 1931, or the Waldorf of 1936. As with Chartres or Notre Dame, though, the twinness rests on a unitary base, attached. Marina City elevates the concept to a scale previously unheard: identical towers, identically oriented, right next to each other.

MILE-HIGH SKYSCRAPER

If the measure of the skyscraper is measure, Wright's 1956 proposal is the definitive essay in the "metaphysics of extent." It was also the master's ultimate embrace of the morphologically contradictory impulses of phallus and suburb. While Wright could argue, on the one hand, that the city and its skyscraping densities were pestilential and anti-democratic, he could likewise realize — as in the programmatic rationale for Bartlesville — that the skyscraper could function as liberator, that the vertical concentration would free up territory below for the happy labors of fresh-air breathing yeopersons: instead of ravaging the city, this skyscraper was to be the city, containing its every aspect. And it is surely satisfying that our greatest architect produced the scheme for what would have been our tallest building. More, Wright definitively one-ups Corb, supplanting his vision of a replicant forest of towers-on-a-grid with one big one.

MOVIES

When the Crash killed construction after 1929, the skyscraper was reincarnated in Hollywood. It's a key shift, this displacement of construction by representation. The depression only accelerated the national appetite for escape and many unemployed architects migrated west to accommodate. Indeed, the studios were organized along the lines of the big architectural offices and developed distinctive architectural styles. Paramount's Art Deco, Universal's Gothic and — most famous of all — MGM's B.W.S., or Big White Set, were pre-eminent. Leading architect defectors include Cedric Gibbons of MGM and Van Nest Polglase of RKO, the two best known, as well as such titans as Hans Poelzig and the redoubtable Joseph Urban. These and their collaborators are the heroes of the skyscraper's continuity, keeping its lust alive on a million flickering frames of celluloid until the real thing could rise again.

MULLION

The warp in the skyscraper's skin.

NEW YORK

Home of the skyscraper, if only demographically, and, without a doubt, the site of the emergence of the first skyscrapers to fit the Sullivanian query as to "the chief characteristic of the tall office building." He outlines his response to this question in his celebrated article of 1896 "The Tall Office Building Artistically Considered":

At once we answer, it is lofty. This loftiness is to the artist-nature its thrilling aspect. It is the very open organ-tone of its appeal. It must be in turn the dominant chord in his expression of it, the true excitant of his imagination. It must be tall. The force and power of altitude must be in it, the glory and pride of exaltation must be in it. It must be every inch a proud and soaring thing, rising in sheer exultation that from bottom to top it is a unit without a single dissenting line.

But this is written by a Chicagoan and, if heart-felt and bracing, hardly embraces Manhattan's genius loci. The New York skyscraper occurs at the intersection of greed and grid. Regulated by the patterns of property, it finds its identity eking out singularity within the constraints of a uniform matrix. And yet, the genius of New York as a skyscraper city is not in any of its monuments but in their aggregation: New York is skyscraper city because it has produced the New York skyline. Property relations have been the guarantor. In a speculative market where value is virtually measured by inches, prime buildable sites are, by definition, either on or adjacent to other prime buildable sites. While legislation, geology, and art have played their roles in the invention of the skyline, the most forceful hand has been the old invisible one.

The result has been an architecture of densification, tending always to maximum concentration and scale. Its aesthetic melds replication and excess in a sort of hyper-pituitary San Gimignano effect. The parameters of superiority are judged very narrowly, the rules of the system are altogether complicit and yet the aggregate results can go out of control. Stability is always accorded to what presently passes for convention; history is just bunk. This is the way in which the city renews itself, by a continuous destruction of predecessor insufficiencies. Like a forest, the city tends to climax. Unlike the forest, the dominant forms continually mutate, a superior growth is always possible, relegating currently hegemonic species to the shade.

BEVERLY NICHOLS

From *The Star-Spangled Manner* of 1926: "a skyscraper is the most exquisite setting for a passionate love-affair which has yet been devised by man."

ISAMU NOGUCHI

In front of the 1967 tower for the Marine Midland Bank, a flush façade SOM slab of matte black spandrels and black glass, stands a large red cube, poised on one corner. The cube's the work of Isamu Noguchi, designated sculptural presence of the era. Skyscrapers have long embraced adjacent scultural programs as certifications of their own artistry and as evidence that their visual systems are extensible across the broad range. In the age of their greatest self-confidence, the typical icon was a reduced version of the skyscraper itself, sculpted or muralized at portal or lobby. By the '60s, as corporate modernism devolved towards signification degree zero, the universal anonymity of total control, the necessity of the marker continued unabated but its content had virtually evaporated. The art world accommo-dated. Sol Lewitt and Don Judd were in the galleries, commanding both attention and high prices. Their kin stood in front of a hundred tall build-ings, wanly certifying the affectless pretensions of the larger packages behind them.

ORIGIN TALE

According to the mechanically determinist theories preferred in the usual texts, the modern office building was invented in Chicago towards the end of the 19th century by a remarkable collection of architects including Daniel Burnham, Elihu Root, William LeBaron Jenny, and Louis Sullivan. This theory proposes that the rise of the skyscraper was — mainly — the consequence of the twin technological advances of the newly available rigid steel frame and the development of a safe and efficient elevator mechanism. The expressive side of the tale is similarly functionalist. The Chicago school is adduced as great for its prescience, its proto-modernism, for initiating the long march that was to culminate half a century or so later in the Seagram Building. Thus, for example, Sullivan's Schlesinger and Meyer store (later Carson, Pirie, Scott) is remarked upon primarily for the long, simple, undecorated bays of the upper stories, while the freaked out decoration below is found paradoxical, in the words of one standard historian, "like the work of another man." Take this tale as you will.

PHALLUS

The skyscraper is the instrument for the reproduction of the land on which it sits. Thrusting erection, glistening shaft, mighty tool, sky-penetrating giant, it cannot resist its own metaphor. As Sullivan described one of H.H. Richardson's buildings: "here is a man for you to look at ... a real man, a manly man; a virile force ... an entire male ... a monument to trade, to the organized commercial spirit, to the power and progress of the age ... a male ... it sings the song of procreant power ..."

Or, as Benjamin de Casseres has it in *Mirrors of New York*:

> We in New York celebrate the black mass of Materialism
> We are concrete
> We have a body
> We have sex
> We are male to the core
> We divinize matter, energy, motion, change.

QUINTESSENCE

Can it be other than the Chrysler Building? Certainly it offers the compleat mythos: strainingly tall spire, named for a big industrialist, a brief hour as tallest in the world, *strong* image. The building — constructed in the years 1928–30 — was the work of William Van Alen, an architect of orthodox American beaux-arts background who somehow exceeded himself and then disappeared. His innovations, of course, include that stainless steel crown, the greatest top of them all; enormously well proportioned setbacks; the famous basket-weave pattern in brick (recalling perhaps Semper's vision of the skin of the primitive hut but certainly clarifying the implicit haberdashery of the cladding of tall buildings); a lobby of surpassing flamboyance and luxus; the frieze of hub-caps and automobile tires; and an acute correction of the perspectival distortions that plague horizontally banded tall buildings when viewed from the ground.

ROCKEFELLER CENTER

Rem Koolhaas has called it "a masterpiece without a genius." To be sure, a committee labored long on the project, dragging it through a succession of incarnations. Never mind the presence of Hood, and Ferriss lurking in the background, it is hard to assess who did what. But what is the achievement of the masterpiece?

Here's the summary of the public relations poets retained by the developer:

The Taj Mahal lies in solitary grandeur on the shimmering bank of the Jumna River. Rockefeller Center will stand in the midstream rush of New York. The Taj is like an oasis in the jungle, its whiteness tense against the gloomy greenness of the forest. Rockefeller Center will be a beautiful entity in the swirling life of a great metropolis — its cool heights standing out against an agitated man-made skyline. And yet the two, far apart in site and surroundings, are akin in the spirit. The Taj, in tribute to pure beauty, was designed as a temple, a shrine. Rockefeller Center, conceived in the same spirit of aesthetic devotion, is designed to satisfy, in pattern and in service, the many-sided spirit of our civilization. By solving its own varied problems, by bringing beauty and business into closer companionship, it promises a significant contribution to the city planning of an unfolding future.

The spirit of this description is not so far off. Like the Taj, Rockefeller Center's a totem, an endlessly researched icon of urbanist success, the pre-eminent integration of the skyscraper into a satisfying vision of the city. Setting aside for the moment the ample satisfactions of its architectural expression, the moving masses of chiseled limestone, the astute decoration, the composition of the ensemble, one element stands out in its historic situation: the plaza. As Tafuri observes, Rockefeller Center presents the first ostentatious presentation of a commercial development as civic attraction for an entire neighborhood. And its small but powerful intercession in the grid has become the absolute model for subsequent urban amenity: in the luster of Rockefeller Center a thousand plazas are reflected.

What's striking about the reception of this relatively paltry piece of open space is its self-imposed contradiction. As *Fortune* magazine described it in 1936, Rockefeller Center was to "combine the maximum of congestion with the maximum of open space." The plaza is one strategy of reconciliation, an intensely charged compensatory signifier, meant less to alleviate than to justify congestion. And, second, it is the only partially realized scheme to place gardens on the building roof tops, like plots of land thrust upward, caught by the act of extrusion. The plan view of the complex thus becomes like an aerial photograph of a rural factory in wartime camouflage, the little fake towns and fields spread across its vast roof arguing for its very non-existence. So too are skyscrapers civilized.

MONTGOMERY SCHUYLER

America's first great critic of architecture rapidly understood the skyscraper not simply as a type but as a "problem." As corrective he was a strong advocate of regulation. And he had strong feelings about the kind of skyscrapers he wanted to see. "The most successful of sky-scrapers," he wrote in 1899, "are those in which the shaft is made nothing of, in which the necessary openings occur at the necessary places, are justified by their necessity but draw no attention to themselves."

This proto-functionalism is also reflected in Schuyler's affection for Paul Bourget, a writer whom he quoted repeatedly, especially the following passage about Chicago skyscrapers:

The simple force of need is such a principle of beauty, and these buildings so conspicuously manifest that need, that in contemplating them you experience a singular emotion. The sketch appears here of a new kind of art, an art of democracy, made by the crowd and for the crowd, an art of science in which the certainty of natural laws gives to audacities in appearance the most unbridled the tranquility of geometrical figures.

Thus early were the standard saws of skyscraping set firmly and irresist-ibly in place.

SEAGRAM BUILDING

The holy of holies, the omega point of the plaza and slab, Rockefeller Center reduced — Seagram is the initiatory artifact of the great age of the multinational skyscraper style. By the time he designed Seagram's, Mies van der Rohe had come along way from the ghostly immaterial glass of his seminal skyscraper studies of the 1920s. Seagram is stunning for its quiddity, an essay in substance. The building swells with dignity, the windows very dark, bronzed to match the genuine bronze of the mullions and spandrels. *Luxe* materials are used unstintingly: deep green marble, travertine. With Seagram, the definitive displacement of craft by material and mechanical precision had arrived. The skyscraper sememe was pared to the bones and ready for replication. Seagramoid slabs grew like post-shower champignons around the globe. Soon, too, bronze the color had displaced bronze the material as the absolute signifier of civic dignity, visible in street lamps and shop fronts, bus shelters and waste receptacles. Seagram's had been flattered to death.

SINGER BUILDING

While Ernest Flagg's Singer Building held the world's tallest title only briefly, it retains the distinction of being the tallest building ever demolished, torn down in 1967–68 for an SOM black box. Easily the most phallomorphic tower ever erected, the penile bulge at its top was of Mansardic inspiration, Flagg being one of America's great advocates of the "French School". But it was also inspired by Flagg's conscientious reformism, his prescient fear of a city cast into a permanent pall by overbuilding and into permanent chaos by excessive density. Singer covered but a fraction of its site, a 612-foot tower a scant 65 feet square. It's also a building of which it was boasted — with legitimate pride — that no worker was killed during construction.

SOLOW BUILDING

Built in imitation of the First National Bank of Chicago Building of 1965–69, designed by C.F. Murphy and Perkins and Will, Solow (along with its doppelgänger, the Grace Building) was designed by Gordon Bunshaft of SOM and put up in the mid '70s. The down and outward swooping curve of these buildings precisely replicates the contemporaneous fashion for bell-bottom trousers. The New York versions are to be distinguished from the Chicago by the presence of cuffs, highly unfashionable.

SPANDREL

Woof to mullion's warp. Louis Sullivan is the acknowledged master.

SUPERMAN

Able to leap tall buildings at a single bound.

TAYLORISM

Frederick Taylor published his *Principles of Scientific Management* in 1911. The date marks the birth of social engineering in its modern guise. Taylor was the leading apostle of the "scientific" management of labor productivity and corporate administration, of so-called "functional" management. This sort of goal-oriented operation was easily extended into the social realm. For architecture there were various consequences. Taylor was much admired by those seeking to rationalize the form of the city (Corbusier among the foremost), especially through the expected efficiencies of zoning and the logic of concentration. Naturally, the Taylorite organization of the factory shop-floor for efficient production found its mirror in the bureaucratic manufactories found in skyscrapers. Time and motion melded seamlessly with time and space in the deployment of architectural energies. The skyscraper is Taylorism verticalized.

TRANSAMERICA BUILDING

Pereira's prick, as it was once called by San Franciscans after its erection there in 1972. It's one of the greats, the first and only true realization of the skyscraper's longing to pyramidalize itself. The effect is mitigated only by the appearance of two rectilinear ears in the building's upper stories: unfortunate, if inevitable, consequence of the fact that an elevator shaft cannot itself diminish as it climbs skyward.

TRIPARTISM

Accompanying his submission to the Chicago Tribune competition, Adolph Loos included the following: "The great Greek Doric column will be built. If not in Chicago, then in another city. If not for the Chicago Tribune, then for someone else. If not by me, then by another architect."

Master ironist Loos was both wrong and right. If just that column has yet to be perpetrated, its equivalent already had been and continues to be. Virtually from the time it had begun to be talked about, the skyscraper had conceptually thrived on the ease of analogy with classical architecture, with the column in particular. There it was, after all, a tall object with a base, a shaft, and a top, just like a column. And thus treble, it accorded easily with other trinities, most especially with the most memorable subdividing in Aristotle's *Poetics*, the larger artistic beginning, middle, and end. Or, to use another analogy, shoes, suit, and hat.

As Diana Agrest has pointed out, though, the history of the building/ column dates back at least as far as Enlightenment times and she cites, as one example, the wacky column house of the Desert de Retz near Marly, designed by de Monville. This is certainly a prime example of memory serving as a primary means to meaning. And, surely, in the hey-day of the eclectic skyscraper (now returned to us once again) images of antiquity were primary guarantors of content. But the triplet has by now been more broadly functionalized, merely designating locations, not prescribing solutions. Having been presented with pure extrusion as, at least, a possibility, there's a certain collective incitement among architects to consider articulation at, minimally, these three locations. As symbol devolves into logo, it's imperative that something be pressed on.

The top naturally emerged as primary. Skyscrapers reconceptualized the city into two planes, the plane of use and the plane of meaning. The tops of buildings constituted a heavenly city divorced from the realities of production. Small wonder early expression turned on a broad variety of sacred architecture: gothic spires, pyramids and mastabas, the tomb of Mausoleus, tempietti of various descriptions. Put another way, if the shaft comprised the skyscrapers use value, the top was surplus value: here, indeed, was the symbolic paradise of capital. Perhaps the most succinct top of this era is that which surmounts the great building designed for Irving Trust at the head of Wall Street by Vorhess, Gmelin, and Walker in 1932. At Irving, capitalism's priesthood is literally housed. The top contains a magnificent chamber for convening the ritual meetings of the bank's board of directors.

UNITED NATIONS

There's some irony in the fact that Le Corbusier's only executed skyscraper was neither designed nor built by him. Here's the history. Shortly after plans for the project were first discussed, Corb sailed for New York and began to work on a scheme. What emerged was the famous "Project 23-A", a *brise-soleil*ed slab in a garden, a mini Ville Radieuse, Rockefeller Center's slab simplified and rotated 90 degrees, its greenery restored to grade. Corb awaited the commission.

It never came. Instead, a committee — headed up by Wally K. Harrison — was appointed to carry out the scheme. What they (re-)produced was clearly the Corbusian *parti* and Corb's vehemence at the appropriation (he even claimed his sketchbooks had been stolen) is perfectly understandable. And yet, the UN's beautiful: the force of the idea overwhelming the mediocrity of the detailing, the dissipation of its intended particulars. Here's a skyscraper like none other, the slab grazing in its perfect garden, its frail harmony with nature goading the faint songs of cooperation attempted within.

VERTICAL ASSEMBLY BUILDING

The VAB at the Cape Canaveral Space Center is, without a doubt, the emptiest signifier in the free world. Designed by Urbahn, Roberts, Seeley and Moran, the vast VAB is a maximum atrium minimally designed, the largest "empty" space ever captured. The building skyscrapes both by virtue of its own immensity and because of its functioning as a containment vessel for the skyscraper in its most literalized form, space rockets. These not simply reach directly into the heavens, their proportioning and set-backs directly recall classic forms. More, their tripartite organization into "stages" shares a common vocabulary of proportion and gestalt. The VAB, like the atrium, is a microcosmos, a benign environment, pared of risk, but also, of course, of the full measure of thrills.

WAR

Colonel W.A. Starrett, the most public of the great New York construction dynasty, wrote in 1928 that "building skyscrapers is the nearest peace-time equivalent to war."

WORK

In Fritz Lang's *Metropolis*, status and hierarchy are questions of up and down, workers toiling in subsurface drear while privilege sports in sun and air. In the skyscraper, the matter devolves on the old in and out. Despite basic verticality, status is adjudicated in relationship to the perimeter. An "economic" floor plate for an office tower demands that a large part of the work-force be seated away from windows. In practice, this relegates the low-paid, mainly female, clerical population to viewless, artificially lit zones at the building's center or else to privacy-minimal office landscapes separated from executive areas by distance and finish quality.

The role of the skyscraper as a bureaucratic population concentrator is being modified by the transformations wrought by the burgeoning electronic office. There are two principal effects. First is the heightened rationalization and discipline imposed on clerical work, the increasing creation of the "electronic sweatshop." The computerized office affords vast new possibilities for both speed-up and surveillance, the monitoring of a worker's every keystroke. Second is a more geographical effect, new possibilities for anomie, mediation, and dispersal.

The need for literal propinquity vanishes before the computer's ageographia. In one possible near-term future, physical contact becomes the privilege of the managerial élite. The vast clerical work-force is obliged to find its own space, harnessed to the CRT at home, piece-working. The corporation frees itself of the need to provide health-care, day-care, or any physical facility at all. In this calculus of dispersal, the non-producing component is simply turned off, excised from the network. Thus is the skyscraper even more potently symbolized. Turned from the literal panopticism of the viewing platform, it becomes pan-electronic, the center of a nexus of surveillance whose extent is now illimitable.

WORLD TRADE CENTER

The significance of this duo lies both in its twoness, the fact that two completely indistinguishable world's tallest buildings could have been constructed at once, and in its barely affected stainless steel walls. With definitive exactitude, the World Trade Center extracts the skyscraper from the realms of architecture and places it squarely in the territory of consumer durables. Styled to approximately the same degree (and with comparable finesse) as a toaster or microwave oven, the skyscraper's traditional strategy for infinity-extrusion is supplanted by a freshly imposed vision: infinite replicability.

X-BRACING

Just one way we build 'em high.

X-CITY

An unbuilt 1946 scheme by Wally K. Harrison for what was to become the site for the United Nations building, a vision that finally played itself out at the Albany Mall. As Rem Koolhaas has noted, X-City was a modernistic revision of the urbanist ideology of Rockefeller Center, an attempt to update the idea of renewalist ensemble along more Radiant City lines. The "X" offers a double nominalist strategy, alluding first to a designated object of experimentation, as in aircraft nomenclature, and second, to the plan configuration of the principal, skyscraping building. The curves of its not quite touching double slabs have strong biomorph overtones, chromosomal in shape, unfulfilled harbingers bearing a dim unrealized pattern.

MINORU YAMASAKI

For want of a "Y", I break policy, the exclusion of architects from this lexicon. I justify this by having omitted to mention the architect as author of the World Trade Center. Nonetheless, there's a larger point: history differs from biography. The skyscraper, in the immensity of its economic and technical address, does tend to marginalize its agents even as it reduces its inhabitants to the status of ants.

ZONING

New York's 1916 Zoning Law is often attributed to the Equitable Building, completed in 1915 to the designs of Graham, Anderson, Probst, and White, the successor firm to D.H. Burnham. The tower was built to a floor area ratio of 30 and, according to many, the 1916 Law was the direct result of Equitable's virtually meteorological effect on its surroundings. The alternative reading is simply that architects – glimpsing the alternative – entered into a pact of the phallus, to save the thin tower from the risk of premature economic obselescence.

Either way, the Zoning Law – which codified the character of set-backs and the skinniness of towers – was, as Koolhaas has so succinctly put it, "a back-dated birth certificate" for the skyscraper.

1988

DECON JOB

Asked to participate in the 1976 "Idea as Model" show at the old Institute for Architecture and Urban Studies, Gordon Matta-Clark arrived with a set of photographs of housing projects in which all the windows had been broken. He also brought a rifle and shot out every pane in the exhibition room. His behavior was judged scandalous, the glaziers were hastily summoned for amends, and Matta-Clark's contribution was suppressed by the Institute's director, Peter Eisenman.

It's now ten years since Matta-Clark died, at age 35. There's some irony in the fact that the fine retrospective of his brilliant work — mounted first at the Museum of Contemporary Art in Chicago, organized by Mary Jane Jacob, now at the Brooklyn Museum — has arrived just in time to coincide with the "Deconstructivism" show at MOMA. I can't help wondering how Matta-Clark would have responded to an invitation to participate in that spurious enterprise. Imagine Matta-Clark — a founder and carpenter of the restaurant Food, a man who kept soup boiling in his kitchen for wayward friends — at the Four Seasons or the Century Club being interviewed for inclusion. Would he have come with his chain saw or his BB gun? Actually, he'd probably not have been invited. Eisenman, once burned, would have told Philip Johnson "no" and that would have been that. Such speculations aside, though, Matta-Clark's memory looms over MOMA, making Brooklyn a magnificent refusenik salon. What a difference. His was a genuinely radical critique of architecture, not simply an effort to invent or appropriate a formal language merely connotative of instability. Matta-Clark had a keen eye for the tension between architectural art and its mode of production, and it's exactly that insight that so lifts his work.

I've written about most of the architects who appear in the MOMA show, in several cases with great enthusiasm: the formal content of the exhibition holds no surprises, though many great beauties. What must be questioned, however, is the rationale for assembling this heterogeneous set of practices into a canon. This task of compaction has fallen to Mark Wigley — Johnson's current gauleiter for the intellect — who has attempted to impart a gloss of theoretical consequence to a collection originally united by no more than motif. He's additionally burdened by the ponderous bifurcate neologism of the show's title, which, sort of, imputes connections with both Russian Constructivism (the motif) and deconstruction (the presumed content). But the connections are fuzzy. Wigley argues that the work under analysis, while not actually resulting from "an application of deconstructive theory," happens "to exhibit some deconstructive qualities." The essay he offers amplifies this ambivalence. Blind to any real historical insight, Wigley's repetitive text is instead decorated with deconstructionist clichés: denying ultimately the relevance of deconstruction to the architecture, it reclaims the former for the discourse of the latter's defense.

In fact, Matta-Clark has crept in to haunt the show. A picture of his great 1974 *Splitting* project appears at the beginning of the catalogue essay as one of several illustrations of what "deconstructivism" allegedly is not. For Wigley, what Matta-Clark's project is about is no more than "breaking" buildings. The deconstructivist architect, on the other hand, supposedly acts as psychoanalyst, locating the "inherent dilemmas" within building. For Wigley, though, the architectural unconscious thus liberated is freed from but a single preoccupation: the Euclid Complex. When the repressed is finally induced to return through deconstructivism's newly "reopened wound" (allegedly sutured up since the originating Constructivist gash), it turns out to be no more than a crooked version of Greek geometry.

Wigley digs himself a very deep hole at the beginning of his essay with a series of truly breathtaking assertions in which he offers a Platonized version of architecture as a straw first term for his dubious essentialist dialectic. "Architecture has always been a central cultural institution valued above all for its provision of stability and order," he begins, reducing all architectural history to a phrase. Once it is so simplistically summed up it can them be simplistically dismissed:

These qualities are seen to arise from the geometric purity of its formal composition. The architect has always dreamed of pure form, of producing objects from which all instability and disorder have been excluded. Buildings are constructed by taking simple geometric forms … and combining them into stable ensembles following compositional rules which prevent any form from conflicting with another.

And, perhaps the most sweeping banality of all: "Architecture is a conservative discipline that produces pure form and protects it from contamination."

Such forthright formalism belongs not to architecture itself but to the definition of it given here. Surely no real deconstructionist practice could describe architecture as "pure form," but rather as a *performative* practice that has specific social effects. Whatever formal autonomy the practice might enjoy is surely relative rather than absolute. Wigley's idealism renders him myopic, blind to the fact that architecture literally constructs social spaces, routes of circulation, capitals of commerce, palaces and ghettos, arenas of family life. What his account represses — from the beginning, through its very definition of architecture — is any account of its effects.

This certainly follows Philip Johnson's take on things. His own preface polarizes architecture into simplistic, binary oppositions: the purity of the International Style versus the disorder of deconstructivism. Wigley has apparently bought this vision of architectural history without question, meekly carrying out Johnson's curatorial commands. So much for deconstruction's insubordinate style. However, anticipating a likely criticism of his master's discourse, Wigley defends several of the works' direct appropriations of obvious Constructivist precedents (partially enumerated by Johnson, whose depth of insight is suggested by his request to a MOMA curator for any Constructivist materials "with diagonals in them") against the charge of historicism, of "deftly extract[ing] the avant-garde works from their ideologically charged social milieu by treating them as just aesthetic objects." Never mind the ideologically charged social milieu into which the projects are presently injected; this extraction is exactly what Wigley's essay works to accomplish. Indeed, it's the essay's relentless splitting of architecture from the social that betrays deconstruction's best possibilities for architecture.

Wigley glosses the formal character of the work in the show as a marriage of a high modernist aesthetics of surface with the "radical" geometry of Constructivism. He does argue that this becomes a social enterprise by being "structural" (by which he apparently means posts and beams and not Lévi-Strauss). The new work thus breaks and "infects" the orthogonal box and it is this that constitutes its "subversion of architectural tradition." Now, Gordon Matta-Clark was one of the great revelatory box breakers of all time. But his purported failure was to have broken the box from the "outside," yielding no more than the "picturesque representation of peril" as opposed to the real threat Wigley claims the work in the show represents because it: "like some form of parasite" (this incessant Derridean metaphor is the main instance of deconstruction in the essay or the show) has "infected the form and distorted it from the inside."

This pseudodeconstructionist theory of the inside job is, however, able to distinguish objects only on the basis of an imposed intentionality (they were using — consciously or not — Constructivist geometry to warp modernism). Assuming Wigley excludes projects like Matta-Clark's brilliant "Conical Intersect" of 1975 or "Caribbean Orange" of 1978, which have a profound infecting effect on stable architectural relations precisely by confronting the datum of use, not just construction, there has to be some higher destabilization, some test of the actual threat. Here, though, the argument becomes infected by its own most gaping contradiction. Of course, the institutionalization of this architecture (is deconstructivist dinnerware far behind?) would seem to beg the question of just how threatening it can really be: even psychic structures get etched into the material world. Wigley attempts to get around this by, in effect, claiming that the deconstructivist structural parasite turns every column into a fifth. Drawing on the historically ignorant idealism that animates his argument, that is, on the idea that structural stability and functional utility inhere uniquely (in the allegedly hegemonic paradigm to which the work in the show supposedly responds) in the forms of modernism, Wigley then argues that deconstructivism is able to make architecture that is just as "rigor-ously" structural and functional as any modernist building! This gripping circularity argues the return of the status quo rather than a challenge to it.

Needless to say, to be swayed by any of this, you have to buy the flimsy first premise, that Wigley's mock version of modernism (an illusory compound of Platonic cubes and spheres that simply represses Aalto, Expressionism, Goff, Kiesler, Scharoun, Webb, and the innumerable other apostles of complexity and contradiction who stand behind the work in the show) is architecture's central problematic — which it is not. Even if it were, Wigley's recourse to an infecting new geometry scarcely puts modernism at risk. The appearance (for it's just appearances that we're speaking of, appar-ently) of a structural threat (that is to say, of the building actually falling down) was, of course, also one of the tasty hors d'oeuvres on (earlier) modern architecture's plate. The long cantilever hardly sprang full-blown from Danny Liebeskind's head, nor the column that just didn't *seem* to have the beef from Wolf Prix's. By the test of structure "pushed to where it becomes unsettling," the Wright of Fallingwater or of Johnson's Wax (that cantilever will fail ... those columns will fail ... but no!) more than passes.

But this is trivial. Finally, function must figure formidably in the critique of Functionalism. Wigley claims that this new architecture is dangerous *because* it works exactly like it's supposed to, exactly like the previous version. The house is still a house, the gentleman's club is still a gentleman's club, the apartment is still an apartment, the biological research lab is still a biological research lab, etc. There's no questioning of these social arrangements, the division into these categories in the first place. Which brings us back to Constructivism. Although Johnson and Wigley prefer to read its content as no more than geometry and "structure," its particular threat merely to composition, there's more, just the way there's more to Matta-Clark. Ignoring the radical social agenda of so much of that architecture (communal living arrangements, workers' clubs, propaganda trains, and other "social condensors") Wigley depicts the history of Constructivism as one of surrender, a chronicle of the evisceration of the vigorous prerevolutionary geometries of Tatlin and (especially) Malevich by the practical realities of building.

But one of Wigley's fulcrums of preference for decon over Con is that unlike the good, unrealized Russian work, his new crop "inhabits the realm of building." However, it seems this realm has fairly elastic boundaries, mapped once again by intentions, not facts. Now, I'm sure that any interrogated Constructivist would hardly have denied the intention to build. Likewise, the protagonists in the show. But there's a certain amount of Emperor's New Clothesism here. Most of the projects in the show simply aren't built and appear only in projective representation – just like Constructivism. Indeed, the most prominent recently built examples – Bernard Tschumi's *Follies* at the Parc de La Villette – are not only uniformly cubic (that box I thought we'd infected) they look just like constructed Constructivism. I guess this fits into Wigley's argument, though. If it looks like a duck, and sounds like a duck, and smells like a duck, it must be a horse.

Philip Johnson and Mark Wigley are great trivializers. By locating the affinity of these architects in "the diagonal overlapping of rectangular or trapezoidal bars" they relegate to the lame routines of art-historical analysis work that is both very diverse and richly sourced. Wigley reiterates — again and again — Derrida's notion of "difference within." But where in the best of Derrida this notion is used to acknowledge the fact that no practice can be hermetically sealed against a social "outside," in this apologist essay difference is limited to — contained within — mere formalism. Difference within becomes indifference to the real social stakes of architectural practice.

Deconstruction is a discourse very much under siege at the moment. One of the most serious charges brought against it is that its insights have been secured through a blindness to historical and political analysis. One need not condemn all of deconstruction (as some have) to condemn the MOMA show's dumb use of it: dumb because it tells us nothing about what might be valuable or important in the best of the works collected. And dumb because rather than performing any of the brilliant analyses of which deconstruction is capable, here it merely denudes the work of any real complexity. Wigley — by repressing virtually all of architectural history — contributes to the ideological operation of homogenizing it, disinfecting it so that no scent of politics remains. Gordon Matta-Clark's clarity would clearly constitute a threat to that operation.

I never met Gordon Matta-Clark — really wish I had. His work sets so many relevant formal and polemical agendas it seems almost unbelievable that he produced it in such a short span of years. His deconstructions, his pointed dysfunctionalism, were all about edge, about revealing it, honing it. Unlike Wigley's Yuppie Constructivism, all about no more than image, Matta-Clark's work was accompanied by a vigorous politics. He wasn't interested in just tickling the system with a teetering tease, he went too far, an x-ray exposing the property at the heart of architectural propriety. His work was always about excavation, never repression. One imagines that it would be tough to eat foie gras from a Matta-Clark plate. We sure could use him now.

July 1988

WHERE WAS PHILIP?

> You cannot not know history.
> PHILIP JOHNSON

> I do not believe in principles, in case you haven't noticed.
> PHILIP JOHNSON

It seems that *everyone*'s an ex-Fascist nowadays. There's Kurt Waldheim, the well-known Austrian ex-Nazi, and Herbert von Karajan, the well-known German ex-Nazi. Then there's Paul de Man, the renowned Yale professor, recently deceased, who, it turns out, wrote pro-Fascist articles for Belgian newspapers during the war. And of course there's always Martin Heidegger, the late philosopher, Nazi Party member, and prominent ex-friend of the *Führerprinzip*.

These creeps have been getting a lot of print lately, and the question everyone seems to be asking is, what difference does it make? Do we have to reconsider *Blindness and Insight* (de Man) or *Being and Time* (Heidegger) or the UN resolution on Afghanistan (Waldheim) just because their authors might also have abetted the mass extermination of certain unfit persons? And should we expect some kind of apology?

The *Times* gave ample space last summer to the revelations about de Man, but nobody ever seems to ask these questions about that raffish old ex-Fascist Philip Johnson — arts patron, museum trustee, friend of the mighty, dean of American architecture, and designer most recently of William Paley's new building to house the Museum of Broadcasting. Of course, it's not exactly as if his work could seem any *more* opportunistic. And, it's true, nobody has produced any pictures of the elegant tastemaker sporting in the Balkans in SS drag. Still, to coin a phrase, *where was Philip?* Let's return to the 1930s, when the young Museum of Modern Art curator had more on his mind than promoting a new architectural style and himself.

In 1934 the beginning of Johnson's political career was heralded by the following four-line headline in the *Times*:

TWO FORSAKE ART TO FOUND A PARTY/MUSEUM MODERNISTS PREPARE TO GO TO LOUISIANA AT ONCE TO STUDY HUEY LONG'S WAYS/GRAY SHIRT THEIR SYMBOL/YOUNG HARVARD GRADUATES THINK POLITICS NEEDS MORE "EMOTION" AND LESS "INTELLECTUALISM."

What a lark for the self-styled disciples of self-styled American Fascist Lawrence Dennis. "We shall try to develop ourselves," declared Johnson's friend and MOMA colleague Alan Blackburn, "by doing the sort of things that everybody in New York would like to do but never finds the time for. We may learn to shoot, fly airplanes and take contemplative walks in the woods."

There was, to be sure, some vagueness about the program of and membership in the new party. "We have no definite political program to offer," declared Blackburn, the party mouthpiece. The two also declined to reveal membership data (an estimated high-water mark was fewer than 150). The one thing that was certain was the choice of shirting. Imagine the conversation when this was decided. *Brown is too ... seasonal. Black? Like those Italians? Silver? Déclassé! Gray?* Gray! *Wire Turnbull & Asser!*

Tiring rapidly of Louisiana and the Kingfish (whose embrace of the two-man volunteer brain trust from New York City was apparently less than effusive), the pair switched crypto-Fascist demagogues, now sucking up to the revolting anti-Semites and right-wingers William Lemke and Father Charles Coughlin, donating at least $5,000 to their activities. In his book *Demagogues in the Depression*, David Bennett describes the two fellow travelers in 1936:

Johnson and Blackburn ... appeared at the Coughlin convention, ostensibly representing the "Youth Division of the NUSJ [National Union for Social Justice — Coughlin's organization]." Although inactive in Union affairs, they were fascinated by radical politics and their financial aid gave them access to party organizers. Later they were to form the quasi-fascistic National Party.

Indeed, Johnson, who grew up in Cleveland, even attempted a run at the Ohio state legislature in the mid-1930s. Such an irony: just as the world might have been spared years of carnage if Hitler had only been admitted to architecture school, imagine the architecture that might have been avoided if the electorate had had the prescience to make young Philip a legislator.

As the 1930s progressed Johnson began to sign his name to a variety of articles for the publications of the lunatic fringe, quickening the pace of his pro-German maunderings as world war approached. For instance, in a 1939 issue of *Today's Challenge*, an article titled "Are We a Dying People?" offered the latent master builder's views on the master race. "The United States of America is committing race suicide," he warned. Deploying statistical evidence of the precipitous decline of the "white" race, he rebuked the "philosophy of Individualism and Materialism" as "eugenically bad" for failing to fulfill "the imperatives of racial maintenance."

Then, in a mighty peroration subtitled "The Will to Live," Johnson offered a truly chilling metaphor to describe the way in which this will is to be exercised. "Human will is a part of the biological process," he declared. "Our will ... interferes constantly in the world of the lower animals. When English sparrows threaten to drive out our songbirds, we shoot the sparrows, rather than letting nature and Darwin take their course. Thus the songbirds, thanks to our will, become the 'fittest' and survive."

This was written in *1939*.

As it turns out, the national origin of those sparrows was not meant entirely metaphorically. Credentialed as European correspondent for Father Coughlin's scurrilous, Jew-baiting paper *Social Justice*, Johnson filed, as war accelerated, a stream of tacitly pro-Nazi dispatches mocking the English. (And his fine aesthete's eye and celebrated wit were fully operational even in the midst of war. "It is said, with how much truth I am unable to say," he wired in a dispatch from the summer of 1939, "that a large London hospital had had to add to its staff because of the increased accidents caused by the 'volunteer' nurses. I can only vouch for the fact that most of these volunteers look very bad indeed in their baggy uniforms; I have heard Paris audiences laugh out loud at them.")

Likewise, his anti-Semitism is filtered through his refined sense of what really matters. Back in Paris, he wrote:

Another serious split in French opinion is that caused by the Jewish question, a problem much aggravated just at present by the multitude of émigrés in Paris. Even

I, as a stranger in the city, could not help noticing how much German was being spoken, especially in the better restaurants. Such an influx naturally makes the French wonder, not only about these incoming Jews, but also about their co-religionists who live and work here and call themselves French. The facts that [Léon] Blum and the men around him are Jews, that there are two Jews in the present cabinet, Messrs Zay and Mandel, and that the Jewish bankers Mannheimer, de Rothschild and Lazard Frères are known to stand behind the present government all complicate the situation.

Philip made the danger in this complication clear in another *Social Justice* article, published in July 1939: "Lack of leadership and direction in the [French] State has let the one group get control who always gain power in a nation's time of weakness — the Jews."

The undoubted high point of Philip's career as a journalist came as he accompanied the Nazi blitzkrieg to Poland in September. Arriving in Berlin shortly before the invasion, Johnson crossed into Poland to get the story. In a dispatch in the September 11 edition of *Social Justice*, he found the Poles "so excited and so worried about the crisis which they feel is at hand, that they arrested me at the border merely for taking pictures." Later he ridiculed the defensive efforts being undertaken by that hapless nation, puny measures that, he related, caused his German pals to roar with laughter when he reported them.

The Polish police weren't the only ones suspicious of Philip's activities at the border. Near Danzig he encountered William Shirer, who describes their meeting in *Berlin Diary*:

Dr. Boehmer, press chief of the Propaganda Ministry in charge of this trip, insisted that I share a double room in the hotel here with Philip Johnson, an American fascist who says he represents Father Coughlin's *Social Justice*. None of us can stand the fellow and suspect he is spying on us for the Nazis. For the last hour in our room here he has been posing as an anti-Nazi and trying to pump me for my attitude. I have given him no more than a few bored grunts.

(Johnson responded to this in a 1973 interview in a British architectural journal, saying about Shirer, "[He is] a very irresponsible journalist ... very third rate writer.")

Meanwhile, back on the Polish beat during the Nazi invasion, Philip proclaimed his "shock" at his first visit to the country of "Chopin, Paderewski and Copernicus." Under the subhead JEWS DOMINATE POLISH SCENE he wrote:

The boundaries of Europe seem to the traveller to [sic] the most part arbitrary lines. But here was a real boundary. Once on the Polish side I thought at first that I must be in the region of some awful plague.... In the towns there were no shops, no automobiles, no pavements and again no trees. There were not even any Poles to be seen in the streets, only Jews!

Later Philip visited Lodz, "a slum without a city attached to it." It didn't take long to find out who was to blame; it was the 35 per cent of the population who happened to be Jewish and who, "dressed in their black robes and black skull-caps and with their long beards ... seem more like 85 per cent." Philip retained his fine sartorial eye. No gray shirts here.

At the end of 1939 Philip returned to the US where he lectured to the American Fellowship Forum, the Nazi-front group behind *Today's Challenge*. Then, late in 1940, he went back to Harvard to study architecture. In 1943 he was drafted, and he served two years. At the end of the war he resumed his curatorship at MOMA and shortly thereafter began his architectural practice, going on to become the most celebrated designer in America.

And what about some sort of apology? Some version of the Waldheim grovel? There never has been one from Johnson — not publicly, at any rate. However, apology or no, he has been forgiven. When Philip was up for election to MOMA's board of trustees in 1957, someone had the bad taste to mention that the man had spent years as, er ... a Jew-bashing Fascist. John D. Rockefeller's wife, Blanchette, already a museum trustee, rose to the occasion with suitable noblesse oblige. "Every young man," she said, "should be allowed to make one large mistake."

October 1988

ET IN ARCADIA EGO: EMILIO
AMBASZ'S STATES OF NATURE

Fancy spreads Edens whereso'er they be;
The world breaks on them like an opening flower,
Green joys and cloudless skys are all they see;
The hour of childhood is a rose's hour ...
JOHN CLARE, *Joys of Childhood*

"The Aleph?" I repeated.
"Yes, the only place on earth where all places are — seen
from every angle, each standing clear, without any confusion or
blending."
JORGE LUIS BORGES, *The Aleph*

My chief problem in writing the story lay in what Walt Whitman
had very successfully achieved — the setting down of a limited
catalogue of endless things.
BORGES, commenting on *The Aleph*

Emilio Ambasz also compiles catalogues of the ineffable. Patiently, repeatedly, he works to materialize a recurrent idyll of place. In project after
project he has mapped and remapped his private order of signs, patiently
bringing into view this halcyon world elsewhere. "Emilio's Folly" is a likely
Aleph, a summary offered with the full imprimatur of the unconscious.
Writing about it, Ambasz offers a canny origin tale: "I never thought about it
by means of words. It came to me as an image: full-fledged, clear and
irreducible." Full-fledged, certainly for housing the recurring repertoire of
Ambasz's imagery, a lexical dream.

First, the landscape, pampas or prairie, literal or conceptual setting for

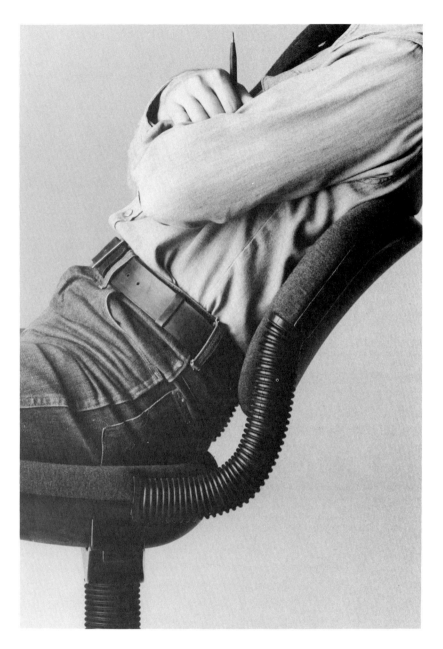

VERTEBRA CHAIR
Emilio Ambasz

virtually all of Ambasz's architectural work, his mental elysium. Swarded green, pastures of plenty rolling to infinity, there's a parity among all that grows in this fertility. Metaphor translates inexactly to morphology. If his inserted architectural particulars are not exactly biomorph, they're nevertheless naturalized as growths, geological, ordered rifts and crystals thrusting up out of a subterranean lode.

Then, the sky. Ambasz once confided to me that the key to successful architectural presentation lies in beautifully photographed models. Leaning close, he explained that such representation could be obtained only from the photographer with "the best sky." I liked the idea that the priesthood of simulation held a wizard-proprietor of the sky, Phaeton with a Nikon. As Ambasz's green plains merge along a faint horizon with Louis Checkman's perfect blue heaven, a universe is born, like the Aleph, under an all-encompassing dome.

Not to enervate the metaphor, Ambasz's architecture is preoccupied with the procreative cycle. Habitation inevitably occupies a cave-like space under ground. In the "Folly," these caves are the repositories of the totems of childhood: kids are mnemosyne, and herd. Fertility symbols abound. That lone lemon, flung up on its baldachin to signal the folly's entry, invites bent-kneed druids at sun-up. The mountain pushing from the square terrestrial orifice is unmistakable. And the architect, poling himself across the amniotic expanse, re-enters the primal scene, to peer up the mountain's shaft at clouds scudding over its "zenithal opening." Departure is via "a man height tunnel leading to an open pit filled with a fresh mist." Ambasz's architecture privileges a retrieval of simplicity, a paring down, the integrity of innocence. His geometry is of abiding directness, favoring squares, triangles, circles, used with little complication. Fervently minimalist, his interventions in the landscape investigate the signification of the least, the smallest sign suitable to materialize architecture. At the house at Cordoba, two vertical planes intersect. At the Schlumberger project in Texas, the landscape is animated by squiggly lines and a spray of tiny tempietti. This is architecture aiming at a kind of divinity, a vision of paradise, Emilio in Wonderland. In this technicolor dream of the afterworld, architecture merely annotates, inscribes godly doodles on a near perfect terrain, punctuating with tiny classicisms, like beauty marks on a Regency belle.

This vision is not distant from another origin-absorbed architect's. "May I take you to the shores of a mountain lake," he wrote:

The sky is blue, the water is green, and everything is at peace. The mountains and clouds are reflected in the lake, as are the houses, farms and chapels. They stand there as if they had never been built by human hands. They look as if they have come from God's own workshop, just like the mountains and the trees, the clouds and the blue sky. And everything radiates beauty and quiet.

The writer, of course, was Adolf Loos, an earlier avatar of the architecture of the indigenous spirit. It was a sensibility he conceded to both the farmer (like Ambasz, the unmediated dreamer) who builds directly from the unconscious and the engineer (Ambasz's alterity, of which more later) whose constructions he held to be similarly naturalized. Loos, fixated with tomb and monument (which he thought architecture's only pure artistic subjects), longing for a return to origins, enamored of America, mesmerized by technology and nature both, derogator of ornament, is one of Ambasz's unmistakable ancestors. The passage of half a century permits the continuation of his ideas but the sting's gone now. Ambasz — the gentle Argentine — is a fabulist, not a polemicist, but there's a vision which persists, a common idea seen from another side.

Ambasz aphorizes: "Europe's eternal quest remains Utopia, the myth of the end. America's returning myth is Arcadia, the eternal beginning." Arcadia's the social version of childhood, the innocent interlude before the fall. While Arcadia is certainly the central myth in Ambasz's doxology of cultural renewal, it isn't precisely the muzzy standard Arcadian dream. Formed, though he was, in the '60s, he's no hippie. Ambasz continues, "the traditional vision of Arcadia is that of a humanistic garden. America's arcadia has turned into a man made nature, a forest of artificial trees and mental shadows."

Here's the opening through which the machine is invited to enter the garden. An abiding American type — intact from Jefferson to Horatio Greenough and down to Silicon Valley tinkers casting their mental shadows on electronic workbenches out back, in the garage — is the democratic mechanic. This heroic person differs both from Loos's instinctual farmer and his engineer, collapsing aspects of both. Ambasz once arrogated the then-fashionable conceit of the *bricoleur* to describe his work and self. It's close to the truth, the tribal handyman, collector of odds and ends. But the notion stands, in its anthropological origins, at a myth-maker's remove from the facts. This exultation of instinct is strategy, of course. Ambasz is an artist of great deliberation. He prefers, however, the rhetoric of accident and innocence. Like Thoreau, Wordsworth, Rousseau, or Lewis Carroll, he knows very well that childhood has a politics.

Ambasz has always been one of architecture's most astute auto-mythologizers. Even now, he arouses cocktail circuit speculation about questions of his own childhood and upbringing. I think, however, of two publicity photographs. They are photos of Ambasz wearing, as it were, different hats. In the first, it's a Greek fisherman's cap, a briefly popular variation on the generic worker's headgear that projects Ambasz as humble craftsman, not unlike Whitman's famous portrait for *Leaves of Grass*. The second photo has him in slouched felt. The conceit now is of the private eye, the mental investigator, the preferred metaphor of inquiry for a skeptic age. The union seems emblematic of his apparently oscillating modes. His talent is reconciliation; he's the Handyman of the Continental Op, polyglot poet, speaking two tongues of modernity.

Ambasz has had the usual young architect's frustration getting his schemes built, although this hasn't sapped their influence. He has, however, enjoyed nothing but success as an "industrial" designer, more often than not in collaboration with his silent partner, Giancarlo Piretti. A series of projects — most notably the "Vertebra" office chairs — have placed him in the first rank of that disciplined discourse of design that grew in Italy in the '60s and '70s. His own production grows from what was undoubtedly a seminal experience for Ambasz the designer: his curatorship of the Design Department at the Museum of Modern Art during the early and mid-'70s. As is well known, his most important show was "The New Domestic Landscape," a massive celebration of Italian modern design. For Ambasz, the *bricoleur*, collection is research, acclimatization to a sensibility. He emerged from the show with his compulsions intact, ready to join a phenomenon he had himself ordered and codified.

The beautiful Vertebra chair (which one notes has become one of Hollywood's preferred signifiers of modernity and post, swiveling in dozens of establishing shots) has by now become Ambasz's own Modular. Of course, it appears, as scale and advertisement, in many a magazine spread of Ambasz's interior design work, those classic unpopulated photographs in which occupation is not permitted to gainsay elegance. The Vertebra is the Modular's mental shadow. Le Corbusier exhausted Mr. Modular with the Venice Hospital project when he turned the totem on its side, put it to bed. But Modular was never able to sit down, place itself in an attitude of anything but exuberance or repose. It's not insignificant that Ambasz is perhaps best known to the world as the architect of a marvelous machine for sitting, at last a comfortable place for the Modular to get to work, a chair of infinite accommodation, expanding and contracting not as seat of a Golden Mean but to support everyone in his or her slightly different requirements.

Ambasz loves mechanism both as the obvious outcome of the mechanic's arts, and as a sort of surrogate citizenry. As his offices are populated with Vertebrae, a metonymy that renders the furniture at least partially human, so his larger landscapes share this animating impulse. At Mexico, New Orleans, and Seville, components of program float on artificial ponds, nominal boats, rationalized via the faded ethic of flexibility, but really so many mechanical ducks, going through the changes of a continuous picturesque reordering. The Mercedes Benz showroom is a perhaps even more sublime naturalizing of the machine's happy habitat in the steel garden. Grazing like sheep on a terrain of pure, glowing artifice, Ambasz has produced some version of pastoral indeed, a nirvana for the 1980s.

There's another way in which Ambasz's investigation of architecture and landscape is continuous with his mechanical design. Both investigations are strongly minimalist in character. Unquestionably, Ambasz's formation is broadly influenced by the heroic earth-movers and outdoor minimizers of his approximate generation, the Michael Heizers, Don Judds, Carl Andres, Richard Serras, from whom he has absorbed the twin impulses of boldness and simplicity in the creation of "site specific" works of art. To this list must also be added Isamu Nogouchi from whom Ambasz has learned, it seems, many of his configurational niceties and a certain delicacy.

But this litany of spare gesturalists hardly accounts for the machine work. Of course, the ghost in every machine, functionalism, rears its antecedent head. But functionalism, as it's been received in architecture, has seldom been about the machine's real issues, simply about its image. Ambasz's machines are better than this, about what the engineers like to call "elegance." Art world minimalism has always been studied in its abiding ignorance of complexity. Indeed, the compulsive repetition and relentless paring down were hostile to both technology and its demon elaborations. To the engineer — the object of Loos's reverie, Emilio in the cap — functionalist minimalism is not about being simple, it's about being concise.

It's a quality Ambasz and Piretti's industrial design is especially rich in, not simply mechanically but expressively as well. The Vertebra chairs, for example, are distinguished from their innumerable kith by the way in which they efficiently identify and solve one of the few abiding issues of ergonomic chair design: the structural integration of seat, back, and arms. Alone among such products, Vertebra uses the arms as the structural linkage between seat and back, eliminating the most generically irritating redundancy in office chair design. The success of the product is not simply in solving the issues of sitting but in a shrewd vision of just the relevant question of elegance.

Ambasz further tempers his minimalisms with that mild Argentine sense of surreality. Bricolage, of course, is the very manufactory of surrealism, with its random juxtaposing of objects found who knows where. But Ambasz the *bricoleur* has always been more conceit than reality in his work. The real affinity is with a specific class of surrealistic landscape, especially as rendered by the classicists of the genre, Delvaux, Magritte, Dali. Under that contemplating blue sky, or within the strictures of mystified architecture (everybody's favored physical representation of mind: those, rooms, those nooks, those crannies), strange things live, inapt machines lounge, long shadows grow over a generic mental landscape. Ambasz, too, makes such landscapes, both on his incessant plane and in his rehabilitations. At the Banque Lambert, perspective is forced on a wooden model of the exterior of the housing building which glows mysteriously at the edge of the banking floor, poised, to all appearances, to burst into flame.

Surrealism, of course, is vision not substance. The Hudson River school painted railroad trains puffing through Sylvania with an altogether different view. They may have felt perplexity but they lacked surrealism's animating irony, our century's own favored mode of coping. Ambasz is likewise no ironist: there's no suspicion mingled with his love of the elements of his work. Indeed, as Aldo Rossi might be said to clarify De Chirico, so Ambasz absorbs the surreal landscape by purging it of its dark clouds. Equally, he pares his minimalism of the masculinist aggressiveness that was its own dirty dark side. The architecture which results has the sweetness of a man unembittered. Not a bad vision of the world, this innocent, nurturing posture.

Ambasz aims at an architecture without threat. About the work is an abiding sense of the ecological, nature's own system of decorum. The sort of reticence about grade that the work persistently displays is part of this, a deference to Mother Nature. In refusing to accept the elevational datum of the everyday, Ambasz clearly suggests that his places are to be the sites of special rituals, a condition emphasized by his particular concern for the act of entry, almost inevitably attenuated and processionalized. The attitude persists even in his city projects. At the Salamanca Plaza project, for example, the new square is suppressed, leaving treetops at grade, impelling visitors into the sheltering terrain.

Ambasz's agricultural fixation strikes clear affinities with rosy 19th-century romanticism and with its architectural translation via Morris. The agricultural settlement in Georgia, the Chicano coop, the gardens at Ludenhausen, are all invested with the ritual ethic of growth and renewal. For Ambasz, ritual is program, architecture's armature of meaning. Clearly, the culture for which he would design is one that has its festivals at solstices and equinoxes, on the day of planting and the afternoon of the harvest. Ah, wilderness!

Alfred Kazin has written of Thoreau that he made "nature his beloved, the perfect Other." And Whitman agrees — with his usual self-serving expansiveness — that "the universe has only one complete lover and that is the poet." Ambasz's preoccupations with Americanness are, in a direct sense, a tactic for the capture of nature in a specifying embrace, a form of courtship. Like any lover, he manfully avoids giving offense. Ambasz is Thoreau without *Civil Disobedience*: his work is a meditation on cooperation. The world he describes is one in which the social contract is modeled on the family, a series of ordered enclaves of voluntary cooperating, like-minded individuals for whom myths retain the power to inspire the rhythms of days. The order of things reflects the order of society. As with the Shakers, those functionalists of the spirit, elegance is the only excess.

It seems most appropriate that Ambasz's first built work, just completed as this is written, should be an enclosed botanical garden, a series of greenhouses in San Antonio. The great greenhouse is one of the most mesmerizing architectural achievements of the 19th century, coincidence of technological advance and the arrival of the modern view of nature. Those architects were, like Ambasz, hypnotized by the possibilities of paradise. Paradise, however, had received a politics from the Enlightenment: it was now utopia. Nature, newly taxonomized, had become rational. The great tropical islands under glass constructed during the period were theaters of nature, polemics of possibility counterposed to the drear of urbanization and industry. Of course, these zoos for nature also had a dark side, hymns to regulation, the first great modern theme parks.

San Antonio is Ambasz's first realized ideogram for the world. These beautiful gardens contain virtually all the elements present in his earlier

"Folly" and developed in projects over the years. Punctuated landscape, entry through the earth, colonnaded courtyard, captive water, artificial mountains — here the glass shapes bursting out of the ground — attenuated processional, mists, symbolic trees, "hieratic secular temples sitting serenely in the landscape"; all are found in this palpable paradise. The garden is truly Emilio's Aleph, the biosphere of his "infinite greatness of place."

John Updike has called Borges a "cosmogonist without a theology" and the description also fits Ambasz well. His continual grasping after benign totality is filled with the inspirational poignancy and valor of the poet. Looking freshly for sources, his is the struggle to make architecture innocent. What happier preoccupation for an architect than to domesticate science, to make gardens, to "dream perfect dreams for us." Let *Tintern Abbey* sum this romance up:

> Therefore am I still
> A lover of the meadows and the woods,
> And mountains; and of all that we behold
> From this green earth; of all the mighty world
> Of eye and ear, both what they half create
> And what perceive; well pleased to recognize
> In nature and the language of the sense,
> The anchor of my purest thoughts, the nurse,
> The guide, the guardian of my heart, and soul
> Of all my moral being.

Dream on, Emilio.

1988

RICHARD ROGERS, LLOYD'S,

AND AFTER

Two apparently dissonant facts. Richard Rogers's building for Lloyd's is a masterpiece. After less than a year in use, the client set about having it redesigned.

The source of this conflict is architecture. Rogers's work is controversial (remember the Gae Aulenticized Beaubourg!) not because it's made in error — outside Rogers's control — but because of its position. Rogers produces a thorough, very specific, modernism. Virtually alone among building practitioners, he's inscribed in his work a fully elaborated vision of both construction and use, a vision sustained by prodigious technique.

Modern is — inter alia — a movement of great stylists. Boullée, Eiffel, Mies, the Protean Wright, Kahn, Foster — and Rogers. Clearly his is now a language with breadth enough to admit him to this discourse. But what distinguishes modernity as an historic position, of course, is the elevation of its speech, the fact that its styles were explicitly to meet the tests of use. Functionalism is only the most obvious example of an architecture that had as its project the investigation of the expressive possibilities of purpose.

Mainly this inquiry has found its purposiveness in construction. "Form follows function" is read with useful narrowness, elaborating the way in which literal building elements — pipes, beams, joists — serve in the life of the physical building. Although there's an argument for the responsiveness of such thinking to the actual conditions of human habitation, this has never been functionalism's long suit. Mere clarity becomes the touchstone of rationality. Nevertheless, functionalism in its various streams has offered a number of clear visions of social relations in space, ranging from the celebration of the pod to the equipotential dream, clearly one of Rogers's own.

Rogers is a sublime functionalist. With Piano and Foster, Maki, a few others, he's a leader in the most fully satisfying conversation in current architecture. At Lloyd's, the inquiry has penetrated throughout, control is almost absolute. As with all styles which seek to overlook nothing, which offer considered answers for everything from windowframes to workspace, there's no moment in the work where other systems sit unaccountably (well, except maybe those teak work-stations). Lloyd's is a building that has truly interesting, often beautiful, solutions to a wider array of designed elements than any other in years, a huge achievement. Here is detail to rank with Scarpa, Mies, and de Klerk!

But there is something out of phase. Looked at structurally, it seems reasonable that Rogers's functionalist social idiom — well-serviced open space ready for mobile occupation — would very neatly accommodate the needs of "the room" within its ideology of the changeable. Rogers could hardly be expected, though, to account for the promiscuous migration of image. This was, it seems, a client with a blinding investment in a particular sartorial identity for which Rogers's tailoring was clearly too Mod. Every time the young broker catches a glimpse of his bowler in the CRT screen, there has to be a twinge of discrepancy. Lloyd's begs the rising entre-preneur's most vexing social question: is he or she appropriately dressed? The new environment certainly gives a mixed signal. Here's the nub, then. Functionalism — reformist in its ideological underpinnings — draws the line at the idea of the style for the job. Not that it demands mylar suits, neces-sarily, but Rogers's response turns on his own vision of process abstracted, not the bathetic comforts of decor. It can be no other way. This is what it means to be an artist.

That said, it's also true that the building hardly comes from left field. Typologically, it's more than familiar. Lloyd's great functional predecessor is Wright's Larkin Building, dedicated in 1906. The two works share a *parti*: the luminous court surrounded by decks of open office. Both are hortatory idealizations of the workplace, visions of a particular bureaucratic harmony. At Larkin and Lloyd's there's a displacement of the energies of private endeavor onto a nominally extravagant collectivity, an economy that balances the spirituality of the atrium or nave against the Taylorized allot-ment of the desk or work-station. Larkin is even festooned with slogans commanding the religious docility of the workforce. Lloyd's offers, in lieu of chiseled aphorisms, the flickering incitement of prices flashed on robot television screens, not to mention the sonorous tollings of the Lutine Bell every time an Exocet hits pay-dirt in the Gulf.

LLOYD'S BUILDING
(*London*) Richard Rogers

Both Larkin and Lloyd's are inspired by specific, strong, deterministic-style programs. Larkin, after all, was a mail-order house, dedicated to the processing of vast amounts of paper via the repetitive organization of the assembly line. Indeed, Larkin is the first fully realized monument dedicated to the industrialization of office work. Likewise, Lloyd's accommodates a highly ritualized early capitalist enterprise, an underwriting Souk comprised of semi-autonomous operatives whose strong tribal identity is, in part, conferred by propinquity. If Rogers has erred at Lloyd's, it isn't in failing to grasp the mechanics of the ritual, or in failing to translate its every verse in fresh prosody; rather, it's in paring away the touchstones of memory literalized, the exact dimensions of prior experience. The occasional dong of the Pavlovian bell is apparently not quite enough to set flowing the spittle of shared tradition.

This is an historic confrontation for Rogers. He was, of course, thrust center-stage by Beaubourg — one of the greatest constructions of the age — a project which was specifically about re-ritualizing an ossified cultural practice. The problem of the museum was its hemming in by the one-dimensional compartmentalizations of *Kunstwissenschaft*. The new agenda was to accommodate the anti-strictures of the '60s (as filtered through that premature hippie, André Malraux). Of course, there was an abiding contradiction: the new spirit of participation and diversity was to be accommodated in an enormous, centralized, altogether French institution. In a way, this parallels the primary modernist operation, the exultation of circulation as a means of accommodating the idea of collectivity. Unfortunately, escalators speak merely to aggregation.

This conflict was also summary for the architectural tradition for which the Piano and Rogers scheme provides such a brilliant summation. The issue about the mechanic megastructures which had so proliferated in the magazines over the previous decade or so was exactly the question of building one. As an ideological riposte to the enervated atmosphere of contemporary production, an Archigram fantasy was a potent, liberatory fiction. At their most attractive, such projects proposed completely to recomprehend daily life as architectural, to offer the services of the designer as relevant to every thing. More: as style, these projects were beautiful incitements to system building, to a near-medieval inquiry into ramifications. And, finally, they were another chapter in the peculiarly British romance with technical construction, a vision of engineering as virtually analogous to natural systems.

In Archigram's trajectory, for example, the line is traced from gigantism and statical heroics to invisibility, to the telephone jack in the trunk of the tree. It's a courageous argument, this lunge to invisibility; one which recognizes the real spatial consequence of networking technologies, their actual ageographia, far more succinctly than any recapitulation of high Victorian tech. But it's also suicidal. If Rogers has resisted the leap into the abyss, it's certainly in large measure because he sees himself as an architect in the grips of the near-term dilemmas of construction and because he sits squarely within tradition, a willing collaborator in the functionalist project.

There is, we know, a branch of that history which threads its way from Paxton and Brunel, through Sopwith and Spitfire, to the Meccano-strewn nursery of The Architect. It's an anglophile version as beloved as it is self-centered, a local chapter in the global saga of men and their machines. But this history of fervid embrace ignores both the telling modifications of purpose — the sixtiesness of it all — as well as the pleasures of architecture, the idea of form-making that exceeds the engineers' idea of terse minimalism. This, then, is the territory of Rogers's excellence, the honing of the raw data of (mainly) metal construction into a lilting song of assembly. As a form-maker, Rogers has a thousand ways of exceeding necessity while retaining the tension of its appearance.

Rogers arrives at this linguistic turn through years of immersion and influence. Early projects — the house for his parents, the lovely PA Labs in Hertfordshire — were slightly funked Mies, loosened by Southern California and the Smithsons, franker about structure than systems. Nevertheless, the main lines of the inquiry emerged fast: the lightweight exoskeleton, the spine, the free plan, the evanescent wall, the expressive ducting. There's a fascinating sub-text as Rogers and his various collaborators examine the line between clarity and coding; try to decide just how far the expressive possibilities of exposure might go.

Of course, what this debate is really about is decoration. "Form follows function" is, after all, simply another way of locating architecture's expressive purview, recentering its terms. As an aesthetic strategy, functionalism proceeds by punching up some privileged figure, just as any other strategy does. However, an idea about clarity is inevitably retained. The problem is *how* to make things clear. For example, there's a period in Rogers's work — the highwater marks of which are the microchip factory in Gwent and the labs in Princeton — in which all ducts, pipes, conduits are painted to distinguish both the character and separateness of individual systems: air handling one color, sprinkler water another, electrical a third.

What this symbolism suggests is that the idea of organization is expressively sufficient. The order of things, thus absorbed, become meta-stylistic, equivalent manipulation. This leads to a difficult disequilibrium. The incredible technical refinement of a Rogers building begs the question of the refinement of its use. Rogers tends to solve problems of use via the ethic of flexibility, the pre-eminent '60s, take on the democratization of program. In this view, specification is oppression, the imposition of a pattern that risks rigidity. The down-side, of course, is that the citizen-inhabitants of these zones of ready transmogrification might prefer the more familiar certitudes of a more specified way of doing things. Clearly, this is what happened at Beaubourg — an artifact that exceeded the culture's ability to consume it — and this is what seems to have happened at Lloyd's.

Ironically, the welter of arbitrary signifiers in Rogers's work, the brightly painted polymorphic rhapsody of the mechanical, has obscured the wonderful way in which his buildings sit in their physical environments, their succinct external object relations. Lloyd's is smashing in its realm, ingeniously accommodating the medieval street pattern, allowing it to help invent very subtle symmetries; elaborating on its prototypical cousin, the Victorian Leadenhall Market; and elegantly gracing the long skyline view. The Rue de Renard elevation of the Beaubourg is one of the finest inser-tions of the age. And how great it is to come upon Patscenter, cruising the fields of Princeton. Whatever problems there may be in fit between these buildings and the cultures they house, there's no mistaking how finely they're cut in response to the visual cultures which house them.

With Lloyd's, Rogers's art has become fully mature, ripe. This is really a brilliant piece of work; a real arrival, full of tremendous new richness and elaboration. It's a building that has immediately come to occupy pride of place above ten thousand architecture students' desks, an emblem of what can be done with enough discipline and vision. Shame on any architect who tampers with its greatness.

1988

AUTO DA FE

The poet Andrei Voznesensky originally intended to become an architect. His plans were interrupted. In 1957, shortly before graduation, the Moscow Architectural Institute burned. He recalls the event in this poem, "Fire in the Architectural Institute":

> Fire in the Architectural Institute!
> through all the rooms and over the blueprints
> like an amnesty through the jails ...
> Fire! Fire!
>
> High on the sleepy façade
> shamelessly, mischievously
> like a red-assed baboon
> a window skitters.
>
> We'd already written our theses,
> the time had come for us to defend them
> They're crackling away in a sealed cupboard:
> all those bad reports on me!
>
> The drafting paper is wounded,
> it's a red fall of leaves;
> my drawing boards are burning,
> whole cities are burning.
>
> Five summers and five winters shoot up in flames
> like a jar of kerosene.
> Karen, my pet,
> Oi! we're on fire.

Farewell architecture:
it's down to a cinder
for all those cowsheds decorated with cupids
and those rec halls in rococo!

O youth, phoenix, ninny,
your dissertation is hot stuff,
flirting its little red skirt now,
flaunting its little red tongue.

Farewell life in the sticks!
Life is a series of burned-out sites,
Nobody escapes the bonfire:
if you live — you burn.

But tomorrow, out of these ashes,
more poisonous than a bee
your compass point will dart
to sting you in the finger.

Everything's gone up in smoke,
and there's no end of people sighing.
It's the end?
                    It's only the beginning.
Let's go to the movies!

It's not recorded who first saw the red-assed baboon mooning through the windows of the Art and Architecture Building in the early morning hours of June 14, 1969. That conflagration, though, which consumed theses of its own in its roaring updraft was not the first of the trials by fire the building faced.

First was the ordeal of the code, its victim the Larkin-*parti*, Paul Rudolph's early conception of a voided core, rising full height, pin-wheeling trays of space all round. Without the Fire Marshall's intervention, the events of 1969 would have been the more horrendous. Without it, too, the supple final outcome would have been forestalled. The last incarnation of the A&A to come off Rudolph's boards was the best. Instead of the showy single shaft, it was an interpenetration sequence, spaces calculated for both variety and use instead of mere, however thunderous, drama.

Light my fire, fire my light. Rudolph has spoken of a vision of the building's end as "a magnificent ruin." This gorgeous, romantic, 19th-century vision may have found premature, unintended consummation but it points to the A&A's paramount impossibility. How do we imagine ruins, after all. Shadowed and mysterious in moonlight? A&A excels here, hunkered however improbably in New Haven, as it rises, craggy as a castle, to reach the troubled night sky.

Such romance virtually cries for a conflagration, for the glow over the hill that turns out to be the blazing manor in Du Maurier's (but more especially Hitchcock's) *Rebecca*. Let's go to the movies! A troubled past is eradicated by the smoldering heat of an unbanked passion. The romantic — and Rudolph takes full marks for romance — can never be satisfied by the creeping decay of wind and rain and moss. His castle wants to be lashed by the storms, impaled by lightning, set afire to stir howls of lament over what was or might have been.

But remember too how the manor may have been lit in its recalled use. Not brightly, not with the regularity of the electrician's vision, but with a multitude of flames, flickering controllably. A place of deep shadows and dark recesses, dancing tapers and crackling swags. Such light begets complication and Rudolph's building is a marvel of complexity.

The original lighting scheme is almost candlelight, the hundreds of seventy-five-watt bulbs sconced down on unadorned conduit. Perhaps too bright in their feint at adequacy, they nonetheless hold a line for mystery. A great fire is hardly unexpected here. The one thing missing was always a proper hearth. Unfulfilled by the now eradicated jury pit (site of so many skewerings and roastings), its proper place was in the studio, where its warming glow might have inspired and bathed the drafting tribe in its heat. Without a home, the banished fire made one of its own, thus irresponsibly causing a ruin too soon. Too soon, but not too late for the Phoenix. The ruin waits to blaze again.

1988

GEORGE RANALLI:

THE DOMESTIC APPARATUS

From time to time, I meet George Ranalli at Rafetto's pasta shop on Houston Street. The shop's a survivor, vestige of an old style of commerce, saved by the tenacity of the Village Italian community and by a certain retrospective fashion. It's a landmark in the discontinuous geography, the relic texture, of an urban culture that obliges — in its growing tenuousness — the nostalgic dispassion of the anthropologist or the tourist — for me, at any rate. George seems more naturally its heir.

The fresh pasta is sliced with a long unguarded blade from sheets placed into a clattering old machine, inevitably raising anxiety for the fingers of the operator. Each order is then carefully wrapped in paper. One day, after George had paid for his little pile of fettucine, ravioli, and tortellini, the shop assistant pulled a plastic bag from under the counter, and made to put the purchases into it. The bags were new, emblazoned with the name of the shop, and immediately seemed out of place, the impositions of an ensuing era. George declined the bag, asked the woman to tie his parcels together with string as before. She happily did this, producing an elegant assemblage, to be carried with three fingers, just so.

George Ranalli is both a creator and preserver of worlds, a precisionist. A man of great culture, he knows the intimacy of ritual and physique. For George, a place like Rafetto's is summary because it frames and structures both social relations and the production of artifact, because its pleasures grow from a social compact that reproduces itself with weightless delicacy in the environment. Ranalli's compassionate view of architecture is like his vision of community, full of courtesy and tradition, respectful of craft. It's a vision that suffuses, this effort to find succinct, economic, and beautiful unities between the acts of living and the acts of building.

RANALLI STUDIO
(*New York*) George Ranalli

Calling Ranalli's architecture domestic no more diminishes it than describing it as civic inflates it. For Ranalli, architecture is a poetics of living. His prosody embraces both the specifics of a refined, rigorously investigated tectonics and profoundly realized strategies of inhabitation. His is not an architecture of uninhibited gesture but of deep consideration: a deductive architecture. Ranalli doesn't aim at universal space-making but at privileged moments, created in the light of cultural choices.

Not to mention the light of New York, Ranalli's lifetime home and passion. His domestic projects investigate a fundamentally fresh condition for residential architecture born of new economic and spatial particulars. The conversion of industrial loft space to residential use has demanded (and liberated) the inscription of new architecture within existing spaces. The interior thus becomes freshly analogue both to the site and to modernism's own dilemma of participation. One with the modernist dream of tabula rasa, the absence of any history of residential inhabitation turns the issue to one of colonization, rather than simply extension.

In his own first apartment, Ranalli confronts a fairly distilled version of this condition. Within a "converted" building, his is a "studio" apartment: kitchen, bath, and a bed-sitting room, inhabitation degree zero. More, it's a rental, not the zone to lavish the indulgences of permanence. The single advantage is a high ceiling. Into this difficult, if typical, environment, Ranalli has inserted an apparatus for living, a crisp and elegant sheetrock armature to invigorate the cramped quotidian. This is no reductive *machine à habiter*, no social or physical complexity-ignorant minimalism. Ranalli's aim is inclusive, maximizing, supportive: architecture.

Most loft design evokes the spirit of the supermarket, responding to spaciousness with little more than array. Ranalli, though rising to the opportunity for formal experimentation, refuses to forsake the accumulated distinction that attaches to the rites of life. He designs with the graciousness and method with which he shops. Dining is equipped with a virtual room, a step-up booth that isolates and celebrates this central event in social life, a temple and an oasis. The "loft bed" is nothing of the kind. Clearly, for Ranalli, going "up to bed" is an important caesura from the activities of the day. The ascending stair has a grandeur that at once expands and exceeds the small dimensions it occupies.

The same ritual means are deployed in his second apartment, elsewhere in the same building. However, the apparatus has been considerably expanded. Together, the two lofts make a fine instrument for calibrating

Ranalli's progress, the growing subtlety of his research. At the level of *parti*, affinities are strong: the elevation of the sleeping area to secure both privacy and grandeur as well as to gain space and reserve the most accessible zone for greatest activity; the fixed, honorific, space for dining with its celebration of the table; the entry cycle of compression and release.

The crucial differences are in an expansion of expressive range. The new apartment is a small summary of Ranalli's own situation as an architect, a fairly remarkable testament to the inexorable deepening of his means and his confidence. Loft one, if conceptually rich, was materially poor, an essay in the aesthetics of limit. The second incorporates a broader palette. Consider only the table. A beautiful slab of green marble rests on a projection from the sheetrock interior façade that carries the sleeping area. Between marble and ledge is a bar of brass, a mediatory gravity connection. At its outboard end the marble is supported by a single leg of raw steel, welded from sheet into a complex shape beautifully expressive of bearing. The thinness of the slab, the massiveness of its steel support, and the precise but minimal engagement with the wall cooperate to form an immensely subtle piece of design, profoundly architectural in its engagement with fundamental issues: materiality, stability, spanning, bearing, and joinery. For Ranalli fabrication is revelation, its transparency a signal pleasure.

In his new loft, Ranalli also tithes the indigenous, baring a single wall of brick, texturally backdropping in nubbly abrasive red the sleek marble green and also identifying by contrast the intersection between the powdery, near immaterial (but rawly volumetric) sheetrock aedicule and its harboring condition. The act of uncovering is historic, a recognition of the pattern of successive habitation. There's also a kind of economy in the exposure, a balancing of layering on with a sloughing-off. This kind of attention (recurring in other projects via other forms of retrieval) differs from the fallacy of the palimpsest that is coming to beleaguer architecture lately. Architectural memory resides only in the lingering physicality of the past, not in its reproduction. For Ranalli the source of authenticity is both memory and invention. He never simulates, always situates.

The Twenty-Second Street loft extends the vocabulary. Somewhat more spacious than either of Ranalli's own residences, the size enables the internal aedicule to stand free. Harboring boudoir and bedroom, reached by an intimate, privatizing back stair, the relative autonomy of the structure allows a more direct reading of its form. If a person's home is his or her castle, this is clearly the keep, the zone of ultimate interiority and security.

Battered, slit, and crenellated, it needs no Freudian to decode its protective encapsulation of domestic intimacy.

In this loft, too, Ranalli's brilliance as a metalworker is dramatically corroborated. First, in the astounding brass canopy which glows golden over the marital bed. This is an elaborate machine consecrated to stasis, an essay in fragile stability. Supported both resting and suspended, the very excess of its elaboration — the literal hundreds of artfully patterned screws used to fix the sheet brass to its rigidizing wooden frame and the multiple means of support — certifies the character of its aesthetic utility. Ranalli pushes an element with a familiar history (be it in the history of canopied beds or mirror-ceilinged bachelor pads) into the airy realms of art.

Similarly, the planar steel furniture used in the living/dining area of the loft appears in full maturity. The chairs and table participate in the same vocabulary of configuration that informs Ranalli's larger-scale keep-making, with the full array of incisions, slots, and angles. It's furniture that's enormously architectural, not just in the sense of the fullness of its formal inquiry but in its engagement with the expression of the architecture's key physical issues, with the primal pleasures of statics. Indeed, the continuousness of sensibility across materials, scales, and uses is one of the most empowering and mature aspects of Ranalli's work. This is an artist who proceeds with the full confidence of vision, expanding by increment to an ever fuller, ever richer consistency, completely in command of both means and ends.

The recent project for the Milan Triennale — "Living in a Loft" — carries the argument advanced in these three residences to a kind of conclusion. Here, means that are in many measures familiar — the marble table, the metal fittings, the white sheetrock house, the stair, and a magnificent new chair created for the occasion — are abstracted by un-use, by the absence of inhabitation by either persons or property. The condition of "loftness" is likewise extended to embrace the exhibition space which is colonized by the apparatus of domestication. Reflexively, living is identified in its precise specificity — eating, sleeping, sitting, etc. — with artistic activity. It's a nice synthesis and conceit, the "museum" project almost ready to move in.

Ranalli's largest completed project to date is the conversion of the Callender School building in Newport, Rhode Island, into a group of apartments. Each unit is organized around a façade, about Ranalli's abiding conceit of house within the house. Liberated by the magnitude of the rooms which house them, these interior buildings attain a magnificence of scale — three stories — impossible under the constraints of Ranalli's earlier work. Each is a brilliant piece of scenography, at once accommodating the peculiarities of the housing enclosure — the pitch of a roof, the fly-by of a truss, the axis of an entry — and suavely elaborating a common compositional core. And, for the first time in Ranalli's residential suite, there's applied color, at once rich and moderate, skilfully used to abet a sense of layer.

In the oblique studies for the internal arrangements of this project, the sense of the whole as a kind of interiorized village comes through strongly. It's a moving vision of urban life: the façades strain to aggregate, blocked by the intervention of the cellularizing walls of the individual units. The hallowing of the individual units is also a credo of entitlement, an urbane proposition for a kind of ideal city. And there's no mistaking that the city in question participates in the sort of elaborate village life Ranalli invents for himself in Manhattan and sojourns in frequently on his visits to Italy, the clear spiritual home for this social sensibility.

The urban is enfolded into the domestic. The façade which presents itself to the living space converts it to a domestic piazza. For Ranalli, then, the social space of the family is a recapitulation of the social space of the city, participating in a successively elaborate chain of cementing volumes that give unity to the lives of both individuals and collectivities. It isn't that Ranalli exactly sees the domicile "in the image" of the city; rather, he sees design as continuous, inventing at all scales — from chair to plaza — the idea of a physicalized, affirmative setting for social life.

To date, Ranalli has completed a single project which directly confronts the space of the city, the shop renovation "First of August" on Lexington Avenue in Manhattan. Here, the familiar pattern of crenellations and intervening slopes reappears as a literal façade. However, instead of the punched solidity of his interior elevations, this is a steel grid, filled with glass, its seven part horizontal rhythm nicely syncopated with the brownstone façade which rises above it. Ranalli has described the lattice frame as a "voidal solid," a fine turn of phrase. And it points to one of the project's great successes, the shifting character of the piece under different lighting conditions as it transforms itself from reflective solidity to back-lit transparency.

Entering, one walks down, passing through the thickness of the original brownstone façade into the unrenovated ground floor shop. To get to the new area above, it's necessary to pass back through the thickness of the wall into the space of the gridded addition, up a spiral stair, through the wall again, arriving at a compressed lateral space paralleling the street and mirrored at both ends to emulate its infinity. One then confronts another façade — painted green — which forms not simply entry to the space behind but holds a reception desk and acts as an end wall for the enfilade of rooms. These — variously show and dressing rooms and a beauty salon — are arrayed along an interior street which cranks winningly at midsection, reinforcing a reading of length.

This richly animate and processional space brings to mind the best known of Ranalli's unbuilt projects, the Frehley House of 1980. Frehley, one of the most beautifully represented works of recent American architecture, is the work that definitively assures the entry of Ranalli into the pantheon of prismacolor heroes. But beyond the seductions of Ranalli's fine hand, his disciplined, revelatory, and supple drawings, the project has extraordinary character. Helmut Jahn, member of the jury that gave the project a PA Award, offered in his published remarks that it reminded him of a Rhine *Schloss*. It's an apposite comparison. The erstwhile client was rocker Ace Frehley, of the group Kiss, as near as one gets nowadays to the likes of loony King Ludwig.

The Frehley House unites Ranalli's domestic preoccupations with the strong processional sense of the First of August, placing them in an idealized (though fully intended) landscape. Set at the right-angled nexus of a canal and an underground entry passage, the house is organized around an interior courtyard which anticipates the domestic piazze of later work. The plan is taut and ordered and the sections are strongly sensitive to a vertical layering of light, the movement from funereal underground to the brightly sky-lit upper chambers. Abetting this graded wash from dark to light, the house modulates from gridded masonry to glazing during its ascent. Sitting mid-canal, its two prows directed along the axis of flow, Frehley harbors a combination of solitude and defense, refuge and resistance.

The geometric preoccupations of the Frehley House — especially the primacy of the cube and a symmetrical attitude towards its erosion — recur not only in Ranalli's interior architecture but in the competition projects for the Peak in Hong Kong and the Opera House in Paris. Both of these are aggregations of this primary form. The massive, brilliantly organized Paris project is knit into the texture of the city both by the down-scaling effects of the build-up of its village of cubes and by the idea of the seriality of its family of forms, paralleling the party-wall complicity of the 19th-century

Parisian apartment blocks. As collaged into an aerial photo of the existing context, the Opera House almost disappears. This is not evidence of self-effacement on the architect's part, but of unusual canniness and respect. Ranalli doesn't respond to Paris with a stylist's glib drag, with veneered camouflage, but with an analyst's acumen, with an understanding of the origins of things.

As a builder, Ranalli has a keen vision of increment, a musicianly comprehension that architecture is necessarily additive, governed by a set of relationships that are revealed everywhere throughout its structure. At the Peak, the serial increment — succinctly embracing program and proclivity — has both a scaling and a rhythmic effect. While the precipitous site and castellated character of the building clearly extend themes that are familiar from Ranalli's earlier work, there's an intensity that's revealed by magnitude. In an earlier incarnation Ranalli was a jazz drummer and he's never forgotten either the importance or the limits of rhythm to ensemble. The Peak has a palpable beat, a discipline reflecting a confident vision of the whole. As at Paris, the demands of scale have expanded Ranalli's scope without any compromise of his vision.

The same is true of Ranalli's two skyscraper studies, the Chicago Tribune and the Times Tower, both for exhibitions. The projects pursue familiar tectonic concerns — the combination of simple geometries, the relation of solid and void and "voidal solid" — in vertical attenuation. As with all his work, they're propositions grounded in the reality of the city and the logical extension of carefully developed formal concerns. The Chicago project investigates a stepping shift in energy from the horizontal to vertical with a deft 90 degree rotation to establish a clear frontality. Particularly elegant is the skyward dissipation of the glass core in a series of glass half-vaults. The Times Square building continues the dialogue between opaque shell and perforating glassiness with greater finesse, and its prow-like elevation — a small version of which forms a quasi-bay window at Chicago — is some kind of ultimate in directionality.

The powerful Viet-Nam memorial project, the great steel blade slicing across the relief of corpses, intensifies but not does alter fundamentals visible throughout Ranalli's work. In one sense, the blade cutting through the rectilinear mass suggests the fundamental act of carving volumes, the origins of architecture. But such a benign reading is, of course, belied by the visible risk and horror that underlies its symbolism. The memorial's architecture speaks of the tactility of intersecting steel and concrete, boldly symbolizing the distortions that arise from the "double edged" character of materials in a moral universe. Ranalli's rage against this "war of assassins" is the precise reflection of the passion for tranquility and life that suffuses his work.

More, perhaps, than any architect of his generation, Ranalli appreciates his roots. As he cleaves to a social tradition — compounded of a tenacious vision of home, neighborhood, urbanity, and justice — so he participates in the elaboration of an architectural tradition. Corb is clearly at the head-waters and Ranalli's careful studies of his houses are manifest; from Kahn's elaboration comes a simplicity and refinement of means; and from Scarpa a vision of detail, of setting, of craft, and of mood. It's no over-inflation to suggest that Ranalli is the natural legatee of this investigation, that this most substantial modernist tradition continues its growth in his hands.

The publication of a monograph mingles hubris and courage, begging the question of its moment. For Ranalli the time is visibly ripe: this is a mature artist. The number and scale of the projects is not large but this is signal of both Ranalli's strength and his dilemma: it is simply very difficult in the context of American practice to pursue the kind of meticulous, substantial, and craft-intensive practice that Ranalli devotes himself to. The condition's rife with frustrations but Ranalli's persistent dedication to the painstaking elaboration of his course is exemplary . He simply refuses to accept either the theorist's reticence or the degraded modes of production that account for most of our building nowadays. Along with a small number of others, Ranalli is engaged in a struggle for the space of architecture, for its very possibility.

1988

POST ROCK PROPTER ROCK:

A SHORT HISTORY OF

THE HIMMELBLAU

The year 1968: annus mirabilis. Kids in the streets, Paris shut down, Yellow Submarine, moon-landing, the *White Album* — and Coop Himmelblau. The pedigree is political, countercultural, Rudi Dutschkes and Tim Learys of architecture, ready to change everything in defense of the marvelous. Coop Himmelblau makes architecture in the light of rock and roll. One year earlier, "Strawberry Fields Forever" was released by the Beatles and "Light My Fire" by the Doors, outlining the terms of the new practice: rebellion, otherness, and flaming desire. "Architecture is not accommodating," they chant in one of their pithier manifestos. "Architecture is not a means to an end. Architecture does not have to function. Architecture is not palliative." To paraphrase another source: architecture will be convulsive or not at all.

John Lennon offered the following in an interview: "The blues is a chair, not a design for a chair or a better chair ... it is the first chair. It is a chair for sitting on, not a chair for looking at or being appreciated. You sit on that music." Himmelblau rose from the blues of Kiesler, Pichler, Abraham, Archigram, and more. Part of an uncanny generation (why the '60s blooming of rock in Britain, why the concurrent architectural Merseybeat of Vienna?), their early work was square with the prosthetic mood of the times, with the idea that alienation's antidote began with the body: tune in, turn on, drop out. The late '60s and early '70s saw them suitalooned up in thrall of the pneumatic, exalting the personal, putting people at the center of Leonardoan spheres of the thinnest polystyrene, preferring sensation to sensibility, tension to compression, biologizing everything.

At one with their peers (and with countless anonymous Hegels of the counterculture), this attitude of extending the organism led to a preoccupation with looping and feedback, to a recasting of the notion of "organic" architecture away from the appropriation of "natural" forms (the Nirvana of the Kiesler generation) and toward a more liberated version of extension. Wolf and Helmut are McLuhan babies (Marshall himself forgotten now for the crime of premature Baudrillardianism and for being Canadian). If architecture is an extension of the body, let's wrap ourselves in it and waltz around the Ring. Let's see us in it.

If projects like the walk around Basel or the giant football game were Himmelblau playing riffs from the Beatles, there was also the flip side of that dialectic: the Stones, Mick and Keith, the Scylla and Charybdis of every parent's nightmare — Lord save my kids from Rock and Roll. The Stones were, after all, the original art band, a category which gave them an edge in endurance over the arcadian Beatletude in relation to which they stood for negation. The Beatles were, if anything, a pre-modern formation, rife with intimations but somehow other-Victorian, Edwardian even. Archigrammatical, their enthusiasms reduplicated those of the 19th century: they were Coledridgian druggies, Burtonian orientalists, Morrisanian arcadians. The Stones were always more modernist: angry and ironical, self-conscious primitivizers, blues-lovers, impatient with the indigestible sacher Torte of the Baroque. The Beatles' Erewhon is Pepperland. For the Stones it's Altamont. Let it bleed.

Early Himmelblau investigated both sides of the cycle. The soft projects, space-suits and suds city, were complemented by the likes of the "Hard Space" of 1970. Three people are wired up to strings of twenty explosive charges, strung out in a long field. Each beat of the heart set off a blast: lub-dub, KABOOM. It's a project that unleashes from latency the tension in every balloon, introduces the thunderhead into the Pepperland blue sky. The Hard Space project culminates a line set out in one of Himmelblau's earliest propositions: "Walls no longer exist. Our spaces are pulsating balloons. Our heartbeat becomes room. Our face is the building façade."

This dedication to a purely psychic architecture, a monument to the solipsist side of the '60s, must necessarily end in explosion or implosion, the doppelgänging impossibilities of too much or too little action. Or so one might think. The genius of Himmelblau has been actually to carry on the research, transmogrifying a passion-born impulse, the radical lust for innocence, the sometimes violent rush to untrouble the world by the hot victories of imaginations on fire. For them the struggle wasn't simply to make architecture but to be it.

There's a pivotal project from around 1973, a "house with wings." It's a

ROOFTOP REMODELLING
(*Vienna*) Coop Himmelblau

sketch of a little vertical villa with a couple of DC-9 wings projecting from the roof, landing gear extended. A fissure extends around the top of the house which, more or less, suggests the possibility that the roof might disengage and soar or — at the very least — that the act of consolidating house and plane has led to the nicely cosmetic rupture. It's the rapture of the rupture that's the key. There've been other winged houses but none so fissured with unease. Like nervous birds and unearthly silences, it's the harbinger of quakes to come.

About the same time as the "house with wings" came a project in London called "The House with the Flying Roof," carried out in an abandoned row house on the serendipitously named Polygon (the figure that's almost a record label) Road. The ideogram for the project was a sketch of the house's roof (wrenched along a fault line like the house with wings) soaring off, pulled by a balloon, exposing the interior to the elements, mossy rain-induced growths and the happy random havoc of architects and students. The cycle completes itself: violence antecedes regeneration. The Rainy Taxi learns to fly.

The balloon's the thing, the sphere that runs through project after early project not just of Himmelblau but of so many co-generationalists. Redolent of Bucky, literalization of the biosphere, surface maximizer, hierarchy frustrater, planetary analogue, mini-cosmos, the reasons multiply. But the sphere's stronger as metaphor than form; perhaps too much of an easiness and too promiscuously succinct. The balloon signifies a mobility that's lighter than air but it's also a trap. In 1971, the boys prowled through Basel in their "Restless Sphere," barefoot inside the logoed, four meter, plastic appliance. It's an alien, sure, a threat to the smug bürgerlich streetscape; but it's also a trap, our side stuck inside, like kids without immune systems, protected from death-dealing nature by a membrane so frail.

The miracle is that the work has simply grown sharper, slicing and burning through the amniotic sac of its early nurturing. The implications of the rent roof on Polygon Road were ripened at the first "building" project, the Reiss Bar in Vienna. Observing (or corroborating) that "Reiss" was embedded in "reissen," the verb to split, the project postulates a 48-centimeter-wide crack, zigging and zagging up opposite walls. The conceit of the crack's a small stretching of the room, a pulling apart, the split sustained by parallel vent tubes got up to look like great bolts — their washered ends (as if) punching through the street façade — and by two benign spikes over the bar.

The project (as idea) breaks through too, materializing (as image, as pre-tectonic) the kinds of seismic activities that would come to shake, rattle, and roll Himmelblau down the road. The project also breaks through as place, a first sky-blue beachhead in Vienna's central first district, the world's pre-eminent architectural hot-house, hallowed ground, where legends rise out of candle shops, and all that's Austrian conspires to make the difficulties or privilege. More, Reiss is just down the way from that Bar None, Loos's immortal Kartner American, a shop's width of pure rebellion, a shrine to jazz to come, blowing Biedermeier down as surely as rock and roll was affront to the smug myopic prosperity of the memoryless Austrian post-war.

And then there were shoe stores, no breakthroughs but much elaboration: rays of fluorescent tubes as façade-piercing vectors; barriers (between in and out; this function and that) dissipated; structure and bearing toyed with. But something is happening. The soft side is ebbing, the hard predominant. These are the years of the Sex Pistols, The Ramones, and Patti Smith, the stomping of disco by thick-soled shoes. In 1978, a project puts it all together. The benign illuminated spike that hovered above the Reiss bar returns in flames in the Hot Flat project. Proposed for the Hoher Markt Square in central Vienna, Hot Flat is Himmelblau's Michelerplatz, an affront of searing visibility. Its agenda is at once a proposition about housing — large, cheap, well-wired, loft-like spaces at the center of town — and a critique of the destiny-wielding speculators and municipal bureaucrats who are its main mode of production. The project is a conflagration of rage. There's a big billboard on the roof, which, in one collage, flashes the image of a Japanese Coca-Cola bottle: at once analogue to the American Flag marquee of the Loos Bar and an auto-critique of the real limits of the media to liberate. Plug in, yes, but to what?

Dominating the project, though, is not the soft remnant of the TV suits and omni-possible bubbles of earlier days; rather, it's the great spike driven laterally through the building, holding communal rooms and supporting a "flame-shaped glass roof" which rises to the upper stories of the building. The spike signals a shift in metaphor. The site of embodying architecture, making it corporeal, has shifted away from the direct inscription of the creator or user's body to an act of directly animating architecture itself. Himmelblau has become Frankenstein and the building their monster. Architecture stands impaled and in agony. It's a brilliant image, but still not quite there, still undercuts its own self-mutilating aggression with the cryogenic deep-freeze of the symbolic. Wanting to set the world on fire, they're caught between burning and building, toying with whether to strike the match.

At the "Tough Corner," an exhibition system for the Vienna biennale, the decorative stuff is all gone, the materials have gotten raw, the direction is sure. There's no longer any question of illustration: the elements are not prosthetic but real, the game of equivalence is over. In 1979 come more vector projects, more spikes. One proposes to plunge from roof to parlor of a house in Düsseldorf. This other's a real declaration of independence, a 54-meter aluminum stake driven through the heart of Olbrich's Secession building. The death drive transfigures the work. "If there is a poetry of desolation then it is the aesthetic of the architecture of death in white sheets," they poeticize. Whatever the reasons, they're clearly in a fury, plunging angry daggers into monstrous architecture. "And that is how the buildings have to be. Unpleasant, rough, pierced. Blazing. Like an erected angel of death."

The dialectic of wing and flame, the successive materializations and dematerializations of some compelling gestalt continues to drive the projects to the end of the (ambivalent) '70s and into the early '80s. In a study for a transformed Karlsplatz, a new datum is establish 15 meters above the old and dominated by a 120-meter-high steel "wing," the wing now indistinguishable — as ideogram — from the drawn and modeled image of a flame. For Munich, they propose a 40-meter wing which rises and falls — flaps or flickers — with changes in temperature. At Essen, they suggest burying the university under heaps of slag and topping it off with a blazing wing. Finally, on December 12, 1980, at 8:35 in the evening, a real, one-and-a-half ton, 15-meter-high wing is suspended from a crane in the courtyard of the technical University in Graz and set ablaze. Goodness gracious, great balls of fire.

And then, the Red Angel bar. The (self-) exterminating angel has (roll over Beethoven …) become the angel of sound. While the wing has not exactly become domesticated, interiorizing the angel both constrains and frees it. The wing has ceased to beat and batter, attaching itself instead, becoming part of the organism. This angelic turn becomes general. An angel, after all, is a mediatory being, a messenger from the ineffable, the analogue of dreams. Gregory of Nazianus, sixteen centuries before Himmelblau, wrote: "The angel is called spirit and fire: spirit as being a creature of the intellectual sphere; fire, as being of a purifying nature."

Exactly. These are the messages of the angels ballooning in the Blue Sky: architecture must be seared fresh to rise anew.

It all comes together at the Red Angel. Housed in an historic building in the first district, a venue for beer drinking and rock and roll, place and program were sufficiently saturated to power up the new intervention. The angel's incorporeality, materialized as noise, is metonym for architecture's elusive body. The wings stretch off along opposing axes, deferring in size to the disparate energies of the two spaces. They're made of clay (a pun on "ton" — which in German means both clay and tone — is available), intended to "concretize" sound but also, presumably, to encapsulate architecture's inevitable feet, from up above. The wings are unreticent about piercing their hemming walls but only feint at their powers of disruption. A "tone-line," a shining stainless steel vector, pops out and in, tapering to a needle to inoculate the thick historic walls with incredible penetrating thinness.

The hits begin to arrive in a flurry, with the confident liberation of a mind-expanding palette. Himmelblau has become more than an idea, it's got a lexicon now. The intoxicating tension between elements and figures expressed and expressed again only deepens and extends the magical mystery tour. Haus Elek has a triangulated, wing-shape *parti* but the bits leap out and recede like a rebus. Elements are invented and reappear. Elek and the unbuilt shoe store number 12 have noses, folded culminating triangles which signal entry and apex. At the Merz Boarding School, designed for Stuttgart, an existing house becomes a Merzbau. The bar which impaled the hot flat is now not the element of disruption but of joinery, like the suturing ducts at the Reiss Bar. Nicknamed "How a Fledgling Learns to Fly," there are plenty of literal references to bird-forms and flight but the real aviator is Himmelblau.

Here, for the first time too, is a sure complexity of plan that the smaller compass of earlier projects has been able only to hint at. The impulses of formal commingling and autonomy are made to seem familial; fraternal twins rather than annihilating opposites. Ideas of movement penetrate to the project's core: the implicit, rhythmical cadence of forms dislodging them-selves from the Euclidian orthodoxies of the original building; the move-ment of pieces displaced by apparent fracture, the movement of space in a not quite determinate spiral; the movement of kids via a welter of encour-aging stairs, hallways, and routes. A wonderful, trailblazing project, full of tension and integrity.

The discourse is continued and refined with the Berlin Youth Center of

1983 in which "the open system" is put into words for the first time. In this "architecture without objectives," politics, polemic, and form are tightly aligned. The project seeks to differentiate without enforcing separation, leaving the final degree of distinction with the user, abrogating the historic complicity of the architect with conforming clarity and insuperable individuation. This is architecture much mis-read by those who see only the fracture and miss the joinery, who want the Stones without the Beatles. As idea, there's parallel with Kiesler's endlessness, "the search for everything behind the merely functional needs of everyday living." Himmelblau might have written this Kiesler credo themselves: "We don't want cellophane between two pairs of lips; we want the naked touch."

The concurrent apartment complex "Vienna 2" vigorously reasserts the liberatory pragmatics of the hot flat: housing is to be large, housing is to be malleable, housing is to be architecture. The project impresses not simply for its suave section and sexy assemblage but for its development in plan of a pervasive triangular figure, off-spring of the wing. The triangle has become a pair of long legs, another motile, bodily, image but more grounded. The V-shape — victory, peace, the European bird — is also the icon for the pointed joining of two, symbol of a coop practice. The angel of architecture is increasingly embodied — legs, wings, nose — yet remains phantasmatic, elusive.

Now a house — perhaps a lure — for the angel's residence awaits construction on a nearly airborne coastal site near Los Angeles, commissioned, aptly enough, by a psychoanalyst. The "Open House" is the first (free) standing incarnation of open architecture. This is the house that began with the famous "eyes closed" sketch for many Himmelblau's oversold signature. But what about it? Sure, there's the hoary surrealist aim of the "dictation of thought without control of the mind," an abiding youth culture trope, an angelic pursuit, the beginning of innocence. But the privileging of the sketch is more than just a strategy for clearing the decks: it's a brave signal of intent, a vow of no compromise, a pledge of truth and consequences. Breton (the ur-rocker) analogizes automatism to a melody, a structure imposer, "the only structure that responds to the non-distinction ... between sentient and formal qualities, and to the non-distinction ... between sentient and intellectual functions." Like an angel, like the ecstasy of rock and roll, automatism offers a royal road to the unfathomable. Architecture begins with a melody.

The true consequence of this journey can be chaos. Chaos may be a little overfamiliar nowadays, especially in its studied inscription in architecture. However, the idea behind this latest upheaval in physics does have real implications for us. Chaos calls into question the idea of linearity, Newtonian classicism, the reductive notion that physical problems can be solved definitively, that simple rules or equations ultimately rule or equate simply. This radical deterministic optimism is summed up by that Pangloss of Newtonianism, Pierre Simon Laplace, who postulated a celestial intelligence which could "embrace in the same formula the movements of the greatest bodies in the universe and those of the lightest atom; for it, nothing would be uncertain and the future, as the past, would be present to its eyes."

This is exactly the line of Himmelblau's resistance, the insistence on retaining complexity. A commonplace of the study of chaos is the so-called "Butterfly Effect" or, more properly, the idea of "sensitive dependence on initial conditions." The image comes from meteorology, a science which has long labored after the Newtonian grail of predictability. In the pre-chaotic model, faith had it that small events were without real consequences, that the system would simply slough them off. The post-chaotic view celebrates these slight contributions: the fluttering of the butterfly's wings over the Ringstrasse redounds above Bedford Square. Systems tend to complexity, not simplicity, or, in Benoit Mandelbrot's phrase, "clouds are not spheres." And this, this voyage from sphere to cloud, is precisely Himmelblau's. You don't need a weatherman to know which way the wind blows.

The Open House is a shrine to the sensitive dependence on initial conditions. The impetus to retain — with utter fidelity — the character of the first sketch is exactly this. Instead of trying to smooth things out, rationalize an impulse without ready quantification, Himmelblau trusts the evidence of their sensibility, and then struggles to retain it — whatever the consequences. "All the lines in the drawing have been built" they write in guarantee of a project. Clearly, this is the terrain of their art. Instead of retreating into the tactic of the impossibility of building, they attempt to build the impossible.

At the little Bauman (sic) Studio, resistance to the "impossible" has both a structural and an acutely social Viennese meaning. Like all of Himmelblau's construction, Bauman is tense, elegant, succinct, and determinate, in the structural sense, "like an airplane." Both Bauman and the Open House devolve structurally on single improbably thin-seeming columns, odes to the compressive strength of steel. This is the expression of risk flaunted. The risk, of course, is not structural — there's no danger of anything falling down – but conventional. It proposes a beautiful efficiency incomprehensible to the lock-step of column grids and safe indeterminacy more normal to building. The single column is a fluttering butterfly: the decision to rest the whole on a single support has consequences throughout the structure. Himmelblau is full of such butterflies.

This piquing of conventional arrangements also extends to the smug complicit certitudes of the building codes. Bauman's witting pricking is the flip side of Hot Flat's raging slash and burn. Bauman's jokes are epistemological, based on the realization that the code can be confounded if something can simply be redescribed. An illegal room, labeled storage, ceases – from the point of view of bureaucracy – to be a room when a folding stair is added which (with the opening of a door and the working of a mechanism) leads outside. The structure is a "practical" joke, the bifurcating paraphraxis which creates new, and newly useful, meanings. The extravagance is both loving and ridiculous. Himmelblau is also able to induce others – even the highest municipal authorities – wittingly to play the game. A nominally illegal roof-top project is sanctioned when the mayor of Vienna decides that it's not architectural construction but a work of art and hence immune to sanction.

Himmelblau, naturally, is seen to advantage on the roof-tops. Like a spidery Fantomas, a black cat (they prefer the favored '60s feline, the panther), they prowl the Vienna skyline, seizing what they will, hunkering on the historic domicile of the fantastic. Two amazing roof projects are in varying degrees of construction. A ravishing set of offices nears completion not far from Wagner's retrospectively stolid-looking postal savings bank. Like the earlier Iso-Holding offices, these new quarters reveal that Himmelblau are not simply ideologues or fantasts but builders, capable of stunning subtlety of detail and celestial modulations of both incoming and outgoing light. They're spacemen too, delicately layering, framing, freeing. Arrestingly, they never furnish their work, rather make inhabitation both possibility and responsibility, and a pleasure. Open architecture.

The pop of the tops, though, is Ronacher – embroiled now in the delicate and deadly ritual of Viennese architectural politics – a triumph straining to happen. Now the idea of "a multi-media theater in every form of performance" has resonances far beyond Ronacher. The reform of theatrical space, for architecture, has long borne the imputation of the reform of the world stage. As Teatro Olimpico definitively lines up the newly liberated vanishing space of the Renaissance. Garnier provides the relentless manufactory of pre-cinematic illusionism, Gropius proposes the expression of narrow totalizing modernism, Ronacher goes it all one better, appropriating the city as its scene.

But there's also a more specifically Viennese lineage for this mighty flexible opened-up theater. The Kiesler-gene again has its effects. Following the Meyerholdian explosion in theatric possibility and flowering of Constructivist theatrics, Vienna, the world's most self-conscious theater city, was caught up in debate and innovation. Jacob Moreno's "Theater of Spontaneity" was surely Himmelblauian in impulse. Kiesler followed (there was litigation over who influenced whom, so Viennese) with his own spiraling *Raumbühne*, the "Space Stage." The rhetoric with which he announced his innovation has a comforting, familiar, sound:

> The Theater is Dead.
> We are not working for new decoration.
> We are not working for new literature.
> We are not working for new lighting systems.
> We are not working for new masks.
> We are not working for new stages.
> We are not working for new costumes.
> We are not working for new theaters.
> We are working for the theater that has survived the theater.
> We are working for the sound body of a new society.
> And we have confidence in the strength of newer generations
> that are aware of their problems.
> The theater is Dead.
> We want to give it a splendid burial.

Which brings us to the problem of the city, the "meat" on architecture's bone. For Himmelblau, the city's the ultimate terrain of proof for the sensitive dependence on initial conditions. The history of city planning has been all insensitive dependence: not on the distant transformations engendered by fluttering wings but on the enormous magnification of tiny insight. From Haussman's Paris to Costa's Brasilia, enlargement has substituted for elaboration. At Melun-Senart, a plan for a segment of the vapid Parisian fringe, innovation lies in the degree to which Himmelblau is able to resist replicable certitude, the vigor of the clash between "little L.A." and "little Manhattan." The difficulty lies in retaining a cogent enough weirdness as scale multiplies particulars into irrelevance.

The hope's in the conjunction of materiality, method, and metaphor. "The Skin of the City" (1982) shows again that a tight allegiance to metaphor animates, that the butterfly (if etherized, spiked and mounted) is always kept in mind. From a gridded layer of reinforcing nerves, the layers of urban skin, the planes of indigenous technologized materiality are peeled back to become an "intervention," like a surgeon's. "The Dissolution of Ourselves Into the City" (1988) returns the body work to its point of origin even as its universe enlarges. Via successive degrees of irresolution, portraits of Helmut and Wolf dissolve into the city plan to be recuperated as fragments, as elements. Like a mega-Situationist meta-*dérive*, they float through the town, materializing according to impression and accident, snow-angels imprinted in the crust of the city.

In Coop Himmelblau's architecture of dreams, the returning repressed is us. They're a pair of transplant surgeons, farming the body, harvesting bones, skin, veins, the very idea of physiognomy to make architecture. Animating clay, they're dybbuks of desire. Under their sure, mesmerizing gaze, beams become panthers and crouch in art galleries and on the rooftops, ready to spring. The complex organism of the city is biologized, rescued from the Foucauldian nightmare of mechanical regulation that afflicts it. Architecture, beating like a heart, pumps life's blood into the everyday. Technology becomes the plaything of imagination, peeling off the foolish economism of the system. Architecture is now. Or never.

1988

FOOTNOTES TO PESCE

1. The reference is, of course, to Mike Nichols's film *The Graduate*. In a key scene, Dustin Hoffman — sheepish, bemused, and undecided — is fêted by his parents on taking his degree. Advice is proffered from all sides, most memorably by an obnoxious relation who counsels, epigrammatically, "plastics." We read the advice as a joke, a road decidedly not to be taken, a visibly degraded option. Devalued by ubiquity, plastic was the emblem of the culture the young man would then have been at pains to avoid, the very substratum of consumption.

In later years we've also learned that one of the principal depredations of petrochemical compounds is their non-degradation, that to their ubiquity must be joined their eternity. Pesce, though, reads through this content to rearrive at form, precisely to plasticity. Here he inscribes his ontogeny. The "Pratt" chairs, serially stiffening from limp to supportively firm, rising up as cro magnon to homo sapiens, ecco la sedia! This evolution is also a reversal. As petroleum formed from dinosaurean decay, the limbs which strain to emerge from the "Dalila" and other anthropomorphic furnishings reconvert this hydrocarbon materiality to the stuff of life.

2. This deathly physiognomy recalls Artaud: "Le visage humain est une force vide, un champ de mort."

3. This is by no means the first time that the suggestion has been offered that the name "Pesce" is pure nominalism, a fiction. Born in La Spezia, son of a sailor, educated at Venice, canal house there, canal house in Paris, loft near Canal Street in Manhattan, the reading seems almost over-determined. Still, there's something fishy here: the supporting motif simply doesn't occur. Indeed, unlike Frank Gehry, with whom he has recently been in competition, such figuration never figures. Pesce, to repeat, has an

ontogeny, not a phylogeny: human form is his obsession, nothing lower. On the other hand, Pesce's inquiry is unmistakably Jonah-like. Formed from an acute view of the belly of the beast, industrialization's maw, Pesce navigates the shoals of modern culture with sure direction.

4. Frottage is also the emblematic perversion of the city and its culture of crowds.

5. For his 1988 show of furniture in New York City, Pesce chose the name "Modern Times Again." The reference to Charlie Chaplin's film was signalled by Pesce via his deployment of the pieces on display around an enormous papier mâché cane — the indelible symbol of the "Little Tramp" made monstrous. As always with Pesce, many strategies are at work. The gigantism of the cane recalls the like acromegaly of the "Moloch" lamp, the Luxo with the pituitary disorder, grown — like Amedee's foot — troublingly large, and recalling the precursor Moloch of Fritz Lang's *Metropolis*, that more anxiety-ridden European version of Chaplin's *Modern Times*. The two jumbos reside in Pesce's bestiary of the inanimate, his private Bomarzo of forms amok. Pesce's gigantism is the analogue of the tramp's hapless sentimentality. Both are strategies of attenuation, rendering the subject under scrutiny larger than life.

For Pesce, as for the factory-slave Tramp, mass production looms enormous. Their tactics of resistance seek to recuperate the civility submerged in the dogmatic Taylorized impetus to regularize. Here's the nub of Pesce's physiognomics: a guide to an irregular multiplicity. While humans number in the billions, no two are alike. Why shouldn't the same be true of chairs, tables, bricks, or bottles? Thus do objects accrete their politics.

6. Precisely the point. (Hu)man is the essential measure of (hu)man. Conflating the approach with Le Corbusier is fundamentally in error. Mr. Modular was generic, after all, classicizing, universalizing, Greek. Pesce's drive is to make anomaly unexceptional, thus to let the exceptional prove the rule.

7. The author is not the first to observe this double valent quality in Pesce's work. The priestly figure of the architect dissolves into a newly conflated doppelgänger as Homo Faber and Homo Ludens are playfully relinked. This aspect of play in the work of Pesce cannot be overstressed. Here, too, the meaning is double, embracing both a principle of pleasure and a liberated play of signification, a bracing and spontaneous juggling of meanings. Signs of the times.

8. There seems to be no question that Pesce has paid a certain price for

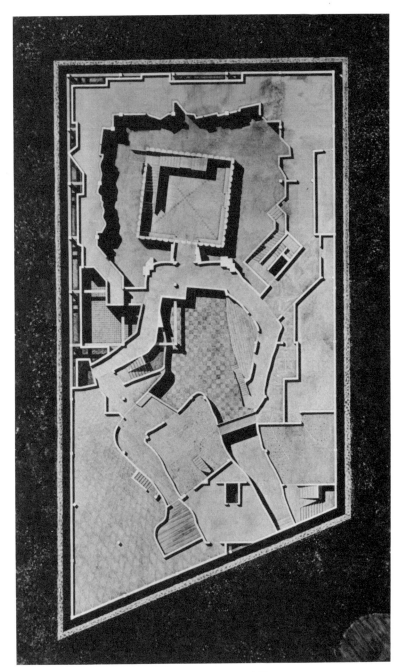

MAISON DES ENFANTS
(*Parc de la Villette, Paris*) Gaetano Pesce

the deeply, enjoyably, subversive aspect of much of his work. Not surprisingly, the penalty is marginalization. The Pahlavi Library, Les Halles, La Villette, the Highrise in Manhattan, were all in signal violation of the supine protocols pre-advertised by the hosts for these several competitions. It's no small measure of Pesce's character that resistance to such insidious politics was high on his agenda. But, as always, other strands are present. Pesce has always seen his architecture instrumentally, as the fulcrum with which he would unhinge existing relations, both social and formal. Thus, he invites the status of outsider, a sort of constructive marginalization. To unseat the comfortable conventions of architecture, Pesce must self-celebrate this aspect of otherness, an architecture from over the border, a practice of going too far in the face of a design culture which is incapable of going far enough.

9. Breton described the Exquisite Corpse as "a game of folded paper played by several people who compose a sentence or drawing without anyone seeing the preceeding collaboration or collaborations." The now classic example, which gave the game its name, was drawn from the first sentence obtained this way: "The exquisite corpse will drink new wine." The game was held in considerable esteem. "Finally," wrote Breton, "we had at our command an infallible way of holding the critical intellect in abeyance and of fully liberating the mind's metaphorical activity."

10. Pesce's feats are transubstantiative. While Robert Morris created well-publicized works of art from thick felt, he did no more than accept the material, barely recontextualizing it as "fine art." Pesce's intelligence is far more alchemical. The resin-impregnated felt is made to perform "contrary to nature." The magical stiffening is a persistent motif in Pesce's investigations. In his universe things are fundamentally soft, hardening to necessity, that old procreative (af)firming.

11. The lines are from *Paradise Lost*.

> Did I request thee, Maker, from my clay
> To mold me Man, did I solicit thee
> From darkness to promote me?

Their presumed significance is in their use by Mary Shelley as the opening epigram in her novel *Frankenstein*. Pesce, constantly recasting the human form — at La Villette, M. Hubin's house, the "Dalila" chair, etc. — strives also to animate clay. Surely, he is our most Promethean architect, cracking master, heating and cooling forms from becoming to being. Irish and Peruvians notwithstanding, the implication is that all construction is self-portraiture, every architect a golem-maker.

12. Another double valence. The sitter, manipulating the seat, parallels the activity of the maker. Seat, thus, site of another politics: participation.

13. The plan form of the running child further distinguishes the project from the "run of the mill" architecture, all nostalgic industrial forms and backward glances, which surrounds it. Pesce's work is uncannily, famously, candid and direct. Wonderfully unmannered, it stands as a rebuke to the appropriate behaviors of most current practice.

14. This affinity for holes is part and parcel of Pesce's holism. For him, the womb is the originating space — a cave, not a primitive hut. His rhapsody is thus not trabeated, constructed space; it is space which is carved and shaped, stretching into the earth, into the surrogate earths of Pesce's imaginations and technique. The Museum at Basel, the holes at Les Halles and la Villette, the Church of Solitude, the Cappodochean skyscraper on the Seagram's site, are all interred in this medium of visceral privilege.

15. Naturally, Pesce has a special affinity for landscape. Uniquely, he apprehends it as the continuation of architecture by other means. He treats the earth's surface as a graded wash in which construction simply subsides into topography. This is not camouflage but consistency, a recognition of the imprint of origins, the seat of memory.

16. Self-inflation only in the pneumatic sense.

17. To be sure, there's a rich sexual implication. And what a welcome relief after the voguish puritanisms characteristic of currently fashionable modes of abstraction. Parity dispels the hint of chauvinism, fecundity any whiff of prurience.

18. The polymorphism of the polymath!

19. Undoubtedly, there's something biblical about all of this, related to the persistent Old Testament metaphor of "clothing." As God is described as "clothing" the earth during creation — an obvious armature for the layering of meaning — so Pesce builds up the density of his sensibility by working out from the body. At this level, all his projects unite along an axis of sequestration. Restoring the centrality of the human subject, he does not — as in typically modernist practice — "clad" the "skeleton" of his buildings with a "skin" of expression. Rather, he clothes their inhabitants with a raiment of construction, displacing solipsist autoerotics with a far more meaningful principle of pleasure and content.

20. Pesce is no Aristotelean. In *De Partibus animalium*, Aristotle claims "that which is superior and most noble, considering high and low, tends to be up high; considering front and back, front; considering right and left, right." Pesce's claim on genius comes, in major measure, from his refusal of this sort of distinction, from his insistence on the equality of every part. Never straying from the insight of these beautiful politics, Pesce imparts a nobility of use and a utility of magnificence to all his creatures, large and small.

1989

CIAO MANHATTAN*

When I was a boy, my father and I used to go clamming. Standing ankle deep in the seaside mud, we'd scrape for cherrystones, filling a pail. Because my father was the sole eater, we'd only take a few dozen each trip. Our catch was nonetheless regulated by game wardens who patrolled the beach, empowered to command the rejection of young clams, to preserve the population. The medium of inspection was a brass ring: any clam small enough to pass through had to be thrown back.

The idea of a "New York Architecture" also invites a brass ring. As with those Cape Cod clams, something's needed to define the consumable population, some principle of exclusion and inclusion. What principle yields this bucketful? Here's what I gather: this is a collection comprised mainly of work done in or near New York City, mainly by architects from the more or less respectable category (the higher hacks are admitted but not the unselfconscious toilers who make most of the cityscape) who mainly practice in or near New York City. This ring has a dimension, but it's elastic, happy to let pass quite a few mussels and oysters (not to mention sharks).

But the elastic ring may be a necessity, given the organizing trope. "New York Architecture" is a classification without an obvious basis just at the moment. Sure, there are possibilities — region, type, history, metaphysic — but none's really the throat-grabbing, noose-tight category that invents the subject. Of course, this might be a very canny position. If there's a consciousness that typifies current New Yorkism, it lies in the commingling of anxiety and hype. "If you can make it there, you can make it anywhere" is the mantra of empty struggle elevated to credo.

*Introductory essay to *New York Architektur 1970–1990*, Munich 1989.

New York, capital of capital, exults proprietorship *über alles*. Forms have always followed. At its origin, Manhattan parsed itself with bold irrevocability by self-imposing America's premier grid, a primal mapping of property relations. Special conditions sprang, eventually, from the confront-ation with anomaly, the grid's dissipation at the island's heroic edges: Central Park, the rectilinear eye of the storm; the rivers — Hudson, East, and the concrete flow of Broadway, those great skewers of the orthogonal; and the twisted by-ways of Dutch downtown, the ever tugging seat of the irrational, lying wait.

Up through this skein pushed the bar graph of value, extruding archi-tecture. And, within it, flourished the roiling ecology of the neighborhoods, New York's greatest accomplishment, the manufactories of both assimi-lation and diversity. Our architectural inventions were narrower: the scaling up of the party-walled domicile as it marched towards the cliffs of densifi-cation, from rowhouse to tenement to block-sharing and then block-filling apartment houses. Then we made the skyscraper, never mind other claims at origin. This was omega, a form which rapidly rose and exhausted itself, cycling in less than one hundred years into auto-parasitism.

There are also further, urbanist, claims on the genius loci, a little less indigenous: that the municipality housed millions in its projects, however Voisinoid; that Olmstead and Moses, their ancestors and heirs, built mighty roads and bridges, covered acres with parkland, provided sites of recreation for millions; that the town generated complicit climax forms, hard-edged avenues, zoning-fired set-back profiles, and the whole lexicon of unex-pected juxtapositions that resulted from uneven development, continuous immigration, and anything goes.

But now, it's pretty much over. Exhausted by this activity, riven irrevo-cably into two cultures, the town's become historic and indifferent, done with fresh ideas. Sure, sure, we're an old city, densely built and filled with compacts about what's supposed to be. And, sure, points transpacific seem destined to become capitals of the twenty-first century (never mind the it's not many years off that cities will be not simply indistinguishable but continuous). But the central fact remains: whatever individual activity is stimulated by mad synapsing Manhattan, whatever flights this pituitary city goads, the renunciation of the New has become the central fact of construc-tion even as the excluding cycle of publicly assisted greed squeezes our well of variety dry.

Consider Battery Park City, The Third Manhattan, the current urbanist

BATTERY PARK CITY
(*New York*)

paradigm of our municipal Mussolinis. Initiated during the Rockefeller regency, the site's an invention, a real estate speculator's wet dream, land created out of nothing. It's landfill in the Hudson River, adjacent to Wall Street, where a commercial risorgimento in the 1960s is officially credited to Nelson's brother David, lion of the Chase Manhattan, whose new bank building was the first big "prestige" project the area had seen in years. Following on, Battery Park City was the administrative creature of a Moses-like public authority, able to raise its own funds and create its own agenda, freed from the niggling restrictions of the normal public bureaucracy.

The first schemes were thundering, heroic, pyrotechnical, megastructure: vast waterside plazas, edged by gigantic architecture. But the fashion for such excess was waning and a new idea came to take its place. Battery Park City would be a careful recapitulation of the spirit of New York, a perfected version of its native forms. The basis, naturally, would be the street grid and the site was duly platted and subdivided into developable parcels. Public spaces — most prominently a waterside promenade — were laid out. Finally, an aesthetic code was imposed which sought to distill the essentials of the "classical" New York Apartment House: brick construction, articulation of the base, a bit of decoration, etc. Whatever one thinks of the results (and there are highs and lows), the point is that the mode's now characteristic. Retrieval has become both the consequential initiatory and corroborating act.

Due East of Battery Park City, just on the other side of the island, is the so-called South Street Seapost. Occupying old buildings from the former Fulton Fish Market, newly constructed pavilions in the manner of the old, and a series of recycled smaller structures from the last century, and arrogating the aura provided by an adjacent maritime museum, the South Street Seaport is the Rouse Corporation's New York outpost. Like its kin in Boston and Baltimore, it's a retail zone, a miasma of boutiques meant to suck in yuppies and tourists, in the guise of offering a slice of history. It's also a machine for differentiating a consumer population.

One of the more striking sights of a pleasant summery afternoon in New York City is that of the citizenry of Battery Park City sunning themselves on the riverside promenade and in the several tiny parks and plazas located among the apartment buildings. It's halcyon, an urban idyll, an activity that should be the minimum right of every city dweller. What strikes, though, is the utter homogeneity of the tanning population. Like South Street Seaport. Battery Park City is, effectively, a demographic instrument, an urban magnet for young, visibly fit, largely childless, almost entirely white professionals.

It isn't simply the fact of the enclave, or the proximity to Wall Street that sustains this, it's the architecture. The appliqué of gentility (here expanded to include a minimum urbanism) is the designated domain of this population, whether in their post-modernized office buildings, their genially cloned downtown restaurants, or their marginally enlived domiciles. Make no mistake: this isn't the heart of darkness exactly, it's just that it displaces something, that it's yet another factory of hyperreality.

Significantly, uptown, a nearly identical drama is being enacted. There, on the West Side, also along the river, Donald Trump — rapacity incarnate — has acquired the largest hunk of undeveloped land remaining in Manhattan, a former railroad yard. Trump proposes to erect a condominium Xanadu, originally called Television City (after a major tenant he was hoping to seduce) and now more frankly Trump City. The original plans were drawn up by Helmut Jahn and featured a gross phalanx of towers (including one meant to be the world's tallest) sitting on a massive podium. A deafening public outcry forced a re-do and Trump turned to the same architects who had produced the (much lauded) Battery Park City scheme.

The expectation, of course, was that they would manufacture a plan sufficiently rich in the signifiers of "historic" urbanism (of which the Jahn scheme was so aggressively bereft) to allay the fears of the public, especially those in the immediate neighborhood, forced to share already dysfunctional transportation and other strained services with a huge new population. The scheme is presently in doubt, in some measure, it seems, because of the impossibility of packaging the densities desired in a semblance of "traditional" scale. But it's the operation that's the key. And, indeed, it's recently been repeated once again, a few short blocks from the Trump site at Columbus Circle where an aggressively large (if perfectly legal according to existing zoning) scheme by the hapless Moshe Safdie for an office and apartment complex was thrown out by an approval-desperate developer in favor of a marginally smaller version from Skidmore, Owings, and Merrill, done up in the current version of good taste, camouflage offered in lieu of meaningful urbanism.

The city, then, is afflicted by a plague of semiosis, a St. Vitus's dance of occlusive signification. Architecture has been devalued by its real proprietors to the level of Madison Avenue: a certain cleverness will do for the endless repackagings that drive the architectural economy. The real issues are territorial: by what means and by what time can the homegenizing upscaling be pressed into every corner of Manhattan? This is the developer version of Manifest Destiny, the assertion that it's the natural right of white folks to occupy all of the island. Localizations of development, surges within discernible boundaries, are merely the medium for the run-up in real estate values. Like the policy of "Strategic Hamlets" that guided the failed latifundianization of the Vietnamese countryside during our late imperial adventure there, the mentality of carve and conquer is relentless in Manhattan.

Another conquest. Times Square is our historic epicenter, commingling our essences — dynamism, variety, vulgarity, art, pleasure, sleaze, corruption, publicity, anonymity, promise, and change without end. Immemorially, this free-fire zone of self-expression has been simultaneously constituted as liberation and threat, a place at once exalted and loathed. Times Square has, in every sense of the word, been irregular. A theater of behavior beyond bounds, it has also been a setting for architecture outside of conventional discipline. As the premier slashing of the grid by irregularizing Broadway, it liberates an archipelago of sites and conditions for the jostling colonization of stressed-out activity.

The self-sustaining ecology of Times Square — the mash of costumers, pimps, actors, theatrical agents, three card Monte players, hoteliers, pin-ball artists, ticket scalpers, costumers, porno exhibitors, barkeeps, pizza vendors, tourists — is the place where the grid of rationality that seeks to structure the city according to the routines of consolidated profit simply breaks down, a compendium of everything and everyone the system doesn't desire. Scarcely a surprise, then, that the greatest barrage of municipal and developer firepower laid down in the past ten years has fallen on Times Square, an enormous and successful effort to expunge Anathema.

There are major prongs to the attack. First, a quasi-public development authority — like that at Battery Park City — was consecrated to "do in" 42nd Street with a suite of enormous new buildings and the conversion of a block's worth of "historic" low-priced movie houses (magnets for the undesired poor) into "legitimate" theaters. The centerpiece of the scheme is an overbearing clutch of kitschy Mansardic towers from the office of the arch-hack himself, Philip Johnson. Although this awful project attracted enormous amounts of flak from the public, it turned out to be simply drawing fire from an even larger initiative.

While debate over 42nd Street raged, a change in zoning regulations provided a windfall for developers not simply there but all over the area. To stimulate the transformation, the city offered builders the opportunity to construct towers within a so-called "special district" which were substantially larger than those permitted under normal limits. This inducement proved, of course, irresistible: the area is now a forest of girders and formwork as one gigantic tower after another is brought on-line.

As with the much vaunted Battery Park City design guidelines, the authorities have tried to take the sting out of this enormous transformation by promulgating a set of obligatory decorative standards for the new buildings on the old square. It's the forest for the trees syndrome again, as if the "messy vitality" of the original could be reduced to a question of signage. Nevertheless, this is exactly what has been done, another menu for another banquet of empty signifiers. Each of the new buildings is obliged to tattoo its bulk with advertising and other supergraphic media, reducing a complex ecology to a matter of decor. Within a few years, the square will be converted to an office canyon, endlessly flashing its neon incitements back and forth across the maw.

The proper name for all of this is "gentrification." Now, gentrification amasses a number of qualities. First, it inevitably displaces — it's about expropriation, one class making a move on another. But it's also about re-occupation. Space must be recast, reacculturated. What distinguishes gentrification from the old model "urban renewal" is that while the latter loves effacement the former thrives on the digestion of the old aura, a parasite. Its claim, though, is to restore, to reinscribe eradicated ingredients. In Manhattan, the gentrifier's beau-ideal is the loft and Soho (always a new name) its ancestral home.

Contemplate the archetypal loft. It's a void, as undifferentiated as possible and the bigger the better, the magnitude of the capture signalling its raw consequence. The primal loft always asserts that it has been emptied, stripped bare of the particulars of its previous occupation. Its floors have been sanded smooth and sealed with urethane. Its walls have been sprayed a spotless uniform white. Its ghosts have been exorcized.

What's left, the certifying relic texture, is architecture, those cast iron columns, tin ceilings and grandly scaled windows and rooms. There's an adequate certification of historic detail and the sure knowledge that such extensive space is itself historic, unrealizable afresh under current conditions. And the walls hold art. Like the geometric baubles in the plazas in front of our old International Style skyscrapers or the flashing signs of brave new Times Square, the art validates the space. On the Lower East Side of Manhattan, the Thermoplyae of gentrification, the shock troops for the erasure of the poor were the art galleries. The irony lies in the fact that these lofts, galleries, and boutiques are by and large the only commissions available to talent in town these days.

Official architectural culture knows the city according to a narrowing set of standards, the contractions of consumer pluralism and its dedication to producing endless things which are merely distinguishable. This architecture has as its only agenda the production of strategies for telling it apart. The city is, at once, both shopping mall and museum, a distinction which is itself continually effaced in American culture as museums become appendages to their gift shops and stingless art has no ambition beyond ornament: the Museum of Modern Art rebuilds itself in the image of a shopping mall; Battery Park City is peppered with easy-access art; and so it goes.

In the climate of today, architecture's only substantial claim in New York is as a "Landmark." Indeed, the absence of sanction for any other constructive value has transformed the municipal Landmarks agency into a virtual rump planning department, the planners having relinquished authority to the developers. But landmarking is a very frail bulwark, finally answerable only to staid historical routines: unfortunately you can't landmark people's lives. Nor, it seems, are we even able adequately to revere our best buildings. The narcissistic trashing of the Guggenheim and Whitney Museums registers the low ebb.

The simple fact of the matter is this: New York is no longer a center for the building of serious architecture. Sure, talents burn bright in this irresistible city, small projects by under-utilized talents abound, the airports and fax lines are jammed by would-be consumers of what we make. But, casting memory back, it's hard to discern just what our last really distinguished building was. My own candidate for the door-closer is Roche's Ford Foundation. It's certainly a rich example of the culture of the end of the line: the philanthropic arm of the nation's premier industry, arguably the one which has brought our cities to their knees by its hammerlock on the convenience of mobility. The foundation occupies a beautifully crafted, sumptuous cathedral from which funds are disbursed to further American charity's favorite aims: education, the arts, small ameliorations of the lots of various colonized peoples, at home, and — especially — abroad: gentrification with global reach.

The *parti* is also apt to an ecology that's run its course. A fragment of nature is sustained like an art object in its climate controlled museum. From the offices flanking Ford's court the city, viewed through the foliage, is softened, converted to modernism's great vision of greening compatibility. But it's false, of course. On the other side of the glass lies unbreathable air and a population obliged to spend its nights sleeping over grates in the sidewalk, huddling for warmth.

1989